THESAURUS OF AMERICAN SLANG

Thesaurus
of
American
Slang

Edited by

Robert L. Chapman, Ph.D.

1817
HARPER & ROW, PUBLISHERS, New York
Grand Rapids, Philadelphia, St. Louis, San Francisco
London, Singapore, Sydney, Tokyo, Toronto

FIRST EDITION

Designed by Karen Savary

Library of Congress Cataloging-in-Publication Data

Chapman, Robert L.
    Thesaurus of American slang / edited by Robert L. Chapman.
       p.   cm.
    Includes index.
    ISBN 0-06-016140-X
    1. English language—United States—Slang—Dictionaries. 2. English language—United States—Synonyms and antonyms. 3. Americanisms—Dictionaries. I. Title.
PE2846.C465   1989
427'.973'03—dc20   89-45029

---

89 90 91 92 93 CC/RRD 10 9 8 7 6 5 4 3 2 1

THESAURUS OF AMERICAN SLANG

A

AC-DC
adj Erotically attracted to both sexes

ambidextrous, bi, double-gaited, swinging both ways

ace
1 *n An expert, as in "She's a computer ace"*

[chiefly Brit] boffin, crack hand, [chiefly Brit] dab hand, flash, heavyweight, hotshot, hot stuff, mavin, mean bean, no slouch, the one that wrote the book, piss-cutter, pisser, pistol, powerhouse, pundit, star, whiz, whiz-kid, wiz, wizard

2 *n A one-year prison sentence*

boffo, book, boppo, one-spot

3 *v To execute perfectly; do a superior job, as in "He aced the entrance exam"*

ace it, cream, cream up, do a grand, go great guns, hit it, max, max out, take care of business, TCB, whale

4 SEE **JOINT**
5 SEE **PAL**

acid

n LSD (lysergic acid diethylamide), a hallucinogen

A, ad, animal, beast, big D, black tabs, blotter, blue acid, blue chair, blue cheer, blue dot, blue flag, blue heaven, blue mist, blue Owsley, blue splash, brown dots, California sunshine, candy, cherry top, chief, clear light, coffee, cracker, cubes, cupcakes, D, deeda, delysid, domes, dot, electric Kool Aid, flake acid, flash, flat blues, flats, four-way hit, gelatin, ghost, grape parfait, green dragon, green swirls, green wedge, Hawaiian sunshine, hawk, haze, instant Zen, L, LBJ, Love Saves, Lucy in the sky with diamonds, Mary Owsley, microdots, mighty Quinn, mind detergent, one-way hit, orange cubes, orange micro, orange mushroom, orange Owsley, orange sunshine, orange wedges, outer, Owsley, Owsley's acid, Owsley's blue dot, peace, peace tablets, pink Owsley, pink swirl, pink wedge, pure love, purple barrels, purple flats, purple haze, purple microdots, purple ozoline, Raggedy Ann, royal blues, Sandoz, squirrel, strawberries, strawberry fields, sugar, sugar cube, sugar lumps, sunshine, Swiss purple, tabs, travel agent, trips, twenty-five, two-way hit, vials, wedding bells, wedding bells acid, wedges, white lightning, white Owsley's, white Sandoz, yellow dimples, yellow fever, yellows, yellow sunshine, Zen

☞ *The great number of slang terms for narcotics probably reflects both a need for coded reference to an illegal substance and a desire to be chic and up-to-date, in addition to the need to distinguish varieties.*

act

n A dramatic mimicking, as in "He did his Clint Eastwood act"

bit, number, riff, routine, shtick, takeoff

Afro
n A frizzy hairstyle worn by blacks

fro, 'fro

ages
n A long time

an age, a blue moon, a coon's age, a dog's age, [esp Brit] donkey's years, a month of Sundays, since God knows when, since Hector was a pup, a smart spell

angel
1 n A financial supporter of any enterprise; a patron; a backer
2 SEE GAY

bankroll, butter-and-egg man, cash cow, grub-staker, meal ticket, staker, sugar daddy

angel dust
n phr PCP (phencyclidine) inhaled or smoked as a narcotic

ace, ad, amoeba, angel hair, angel mist, angel puke, animal, Aurora Borealis, black whack, busy bee, Cadillac, cigarrode, CJ, Columbo, cozmos, cristal, crystal, cyclones, Detroit pink, devil dust, dime of buzz, dipper, D O A, dummy dust, dust, earth, elephant, embalming fluid, flake, fuel, goon, goon dust, gorilla tab, green, green tea, heaven and hell, herms, heroin buzz, hog, the hog, jet fuel, juice, K, Kaps, K-blast, killerweed, Kools, lovely magic, magic, magic dust, mean green, mintweed, mist, monkey dust, new magic, orange cryst, peace, peace pill, peaceweed, Peter Pan, pig killer, puffy, rocket fuel, scaffle, sheets, star dust, super grass, super Kools, surfer, whack wack, wobble, wobble weed, wolf, worm, zombie buzz, zoom
☞ *The great number of slang terms for narcotics probably reflects both a need for coded reference to an illegal substance and a desire to be chic and up-to-date, in addition to the need to distinguish varieties.*

Annie Oakley
n phr A complimentary ticket

Chinee, Chinee ducket, Chinese ducket, comp, freebie, Oakley, paper

antsy
1 *adj Eagerly desirous; excited and tense, as in "He was antsy over the idea"*

aching, all atwitter, bursting, busting, gung ho, hepped up, het up, hitchy, honked up, hopped up, horked, hot, hot-eyed, hot to trot, hurting, hyped-up, hyper, in a dither, in a doodah, in a flutter, in a lather, in a state, in a sweat, in a tizzy, itching, itchy, keen, keyed up, perishing, psyched, psyched up, ranged, rarin' to go, red-hot, spoiling, steamed up, wild, wired, worked up, yantsy

2 SEE **JITTERY**

ass
1 *n The buttocks; the posterior*

[Brit, pronounced "ahs"] arse, back porch, back seat, backside, behind, bibby, bippy, boogie, bottom, botty, bucket, [chiefly Brit] bum, buns, butt, butt end, caboose, cakes, can, cheeks, cupcakes, derriere, duff, duster, fanny, gazonga, gazoo, gazool, heinie, hind end, hindside, kazoo, keister, loaves, oil bags, part that goes over the fence last, patoot, patootie, poop, popo, prat, pratt, rear, rear end, rolls, rump, rusty-dusty, seat, seat of the pants, south side, stern, tail, tail bone, tail end, tokus, tush, tushy, wazoo

2 *n Sexual activity; sexual gratification, as in "I'm going to get myself a little ass tonight"*

boff, boom-boom, booty, bop, bouncy-bouncy, butt, cat, chunk, cooz, crack, cunt, diddling, frig, frigging, fuck, fucking, gash, ginch, ground rations, hard breathing, heavy breathing, hole, hooch, hootchie-cootchie, hump, humpery, hunk, in-and-out, in-out, jazz, jelly-roll, jig-jig, a lay, a make, meat, nooky, notch, party, phutzing, piece, piece of ass, piece of butt, piece of tail, pom-pom, (with a black woman) poontang, pop, push-

push, pussy, quim, ride, roll, roll in the hay, screw, screwing, shtup, stuff, tail, trade, trim, twat, zig-zig

☞ *Of course, many more such terms may be made by adding the "ing" gerund suffix to any appropriate verb at "fuck."*

3 *n The whole person; one's self, as in "Get your ass out of here!"*

backside, behind, bottom, buns, butt, can, duff, fanny, keister, patoot, rump, tail, tokus

4 SEE **ASSHOLE**

5 SEE **JERK**

as shit

adv phr
Exceedingly; to a great degree or extent, as in "That place is dirty as shit"

as all creation, as all get-out, as blazes, as can be, as hell, no end, to the max

☞ *These terms always follow the adjective being modified.*

asshole

1 *n The anus; the rectum*

A-hole, ass, back door, back way, behind, bibby, bippy, bottom, brown, brownie, bucket, [chiefly Brit] bum, bumhole, bung, bunghole, butt, butthole, cornhole, dirt chute, dirt road, exhaust pipe, gazoo, gazool, gig, giggy, heinie, hole, kazoo, keister, poop chute, poophole, poo-poo, porthole, rosebud, round brown, shitter, slop chute, wazoo, where the sun doesn't shine, wing-wang, winkie, ying-yang, yin-yang

2 *n A despicable person; a vile and filthy wretch*

A-hole, badass, bad baby, bad egg, bad job, bad lot, bastard, birdturd, blue meany, bugger, bum, bummer, cocksucker, crumb, cuntface, cunthead, dick, dickhead, dip, dipshit, dipstick, dirtbag, dirty bum, dirty rat, double-clutcher, fink, four-letter man, fuck, fucker, fuckhead, heel, heeler, horse's ass, hound, hound-dog, hyena, jerk, junkyard dog, louse, mama-eater, mama-fucker, mama-grabber, mama-jumper, mama-kisser, mama-lover, mama-nudger, mama-rammer, mammy-eater, mammy-fucker, mammy-grabber, mammy-jumper, mammy-kisser, mammy-lover, mammy-nudger, mammy-rammer, MF, momzer, mother, mother-eater, motherfucker, mothergrabber, mother-jumper, motherkisser, motherlover, mothernudger, motherrammer, mucker, muhfuh, peckerhead, piece of shit, pigfucker, pissant, pisshead, prick, punk, putz, rat, rat-fink, rat-fuck, rat's asshole, RF, ringtail, rotten egg, rotter, sao, schmuck, scum, scumbag, scum of the earth, scumsucker, scurve, scuzz, scuzzbag, scuzzo, shit, shitass, shitface, shithead, shitheel, shithook, shitstick, shtoonk, shyster, skunk, sleazebag, sleazeball, so-and-so, S O B, son of a bitch, son of a whore, stinker, sumbitch, turd, worm

☞ *Even though most of these terms are felt to specify a male referent, some of them are increasingly used of women. Many of them are nearly synonymous with those listed under "jerk." The distinction is that while one detests an asshole, one despises a jerk. One both detests and despises a sleazebag.*

the axe
n phr Dismissal; discharge, as in "I had no idea my boss was dissatisfied until I got the axe"

the air, the boot, the bum's rush, the chop, the chuck, the gate, a hatchet job, the heave-ho, the hook, the kiss-off, the old heave-ho, the pink slip, the sack, the sackeroo, one's walking papers, one's walking ticket

☞ *These terms are almost always used after "give" or "get."*

B

back
v To give one's support to an effort, team, person, etc, as in "She has an uncanny knack for backing the eventual winner"

back up, bet on, boost, cheer for, get behind, give a leg up, go to bat for, go to the mat for, like, plug for, put one's money on, root for, stand behind, stick up for

back-breaker
n A very hard task; a Herculean labor

ball-buster, bastard, bitch, bitch-kitty, bone-breaker, brute, bugger, bun-buster, butt-buster, grind, gut-buster, hard row to hoe, heavy sledding, killer, large order, pisser, son of a bitch, sumbitch, tough grind, whiz-bitch

back out
1 *v phr To cancel or renege on an arrangement; withdraw*
2 SEE **COP OUT**

back down, chicken out, cop out, crab, crawdad, crawfish, fink out, funk out, rat out, weasel out, welsh, wiggle out, worm out

bad man

n phr A villain or scoundrel, esp in a play or movie

bad actor, badass, bad baby, baddie, bad hat, bad hombre, black hat, bugger, hard-boiled egg, heavy, meanie, Mister Bad Guy, rat, rotten egg, varmint, wrong number, wrongo, wrong 'un

bad-mouth

1 *v To denigrate; belittle, as in "He bad-mouthed her all over town"*

dump on, give a roasting, knock, pan, poor-mouth, rap, rip, roast, run down, slag, slam, take a dig at, take a swipe at

2 SEE **KNOCK**

bad news

1 *n phr Difficulty; trouble, as in "Cross the street when you see him coming, he's bad news"*

bad medicine, bad scene, bad shit, deep doo-doo, deep shit, deep trouble, diffyewculty, double-trouble, headache, hot grease, hot water, hurrah's nest, mind-fucker, murder, Old Man Trouble, pain in the ass, pain in the neck, poison, sticky wicket, tough shit, tough stuff, tsuris

2 SEE **the DAMAGE**

a bad scene

n phr A misfortune; an unhappy situation or event, as in "Our vacation turned out to be a bad scene"

bad trip, bitch, bitch-kitty, bummer, bum trip, disaster, downer, down trip, fake-out, mind-fucker, pain in the ass, pain in the neck

bad trip
n phr An unpleasant drug experience, esp with a hallucinogen; any unpleasant experience

acid funk, bad head, bum bend, bummer, bum trip, downer, down trip, drag, flip, flip-out, freak-out, low

bag
1 *n A quantity or package of narcotics*

bale of hay, balloon, bar, big hog, bindle, bird's eye, biz, block box, bottle, brick, can, cap, card, cargo, cube, deck, deuce, deuce bag, dime bag, elbow, feed bag, finger, foil, full moon, gang, gram, half, half bundle, half load, half piece, hunk, jug, kee, keg, key, ki, kite, ky, lid, load, long, match, matchbox, matchhead, microgram, milligram, moon, nickel, nickel bag, O, Ohio bag, O Z, paper, piece pillow, quarter bag, quarter ounce, sack, short, short piece, sixteenth, spoon, stash, tens, tin

2 *n That which one prefers or is doing currently; one's specialty, as in "Looks like fun, but windsurfing's not my bag"*

bit, cup of tea, dish, dish of tea, flash, gimmick, groove, joint, kick, [Brit] line of country, meat, scene, shot, thing, turf

3 SEE **CHUCK**
4 SEE **FIRE**
5 SEE **RUBBER**
6 SEE **TITS**

baldie
n A bald person

cueball, skinhead, suedehead

a ball

n phr *A very good time* — a blast, a gas, Gas City, a groove, a picnic, a supergroove

ball-buster

1 n *Someone who saps or destroys masculinity* — ball-wracker, bitch, nut-cruncher

2 SEE **BACK-BREAKER**

balls

1 n *The testicles* — ballocks, cojones, diamonds, the family jewels, jingle-berries, nuts, rocks

2 SEE **BULLSHIT**

3 SEE **GUTS**

banger

1 n *A cylinder in a car engine, as in "One of its bangers only fires when it feels like it"* — barrel, bucket, hole, lung, squirrel

2 SEE **JALOPY**

bare-ass

adj *Nude; unclad* — as nature made one, b a, bare-assed, buck naked, buff, in one's birthday suit, in the altogether, in the buff, in the raw, in the state of nature, naked as a jaybird, naked as the day one was born, [esp Brit] starkers, without a stitch

barf

v *To vomit; regurgitate* — [esp Brit] be sick, blow grits, boff, call Earl's, cheese, chuck, do a Technicolor yawn, drive the big bus, dump, feed the fish, flash, flash one's hash, have the pukes, heave, oops, oops up, ork, pray to the porcelain god, puke, ralph, ralph up, rolf, shoot one's cookies, shoot one's lunch, [Brit] sick up, snap one's cookies, talk to the big white phone, talk to the seals, toss one's cookies, upchuck, urp, whoops

barrel

v To go very fast; speed, as in "He barrels around corners with his eyes closed"

ball the jack, barrel along, barrel ass, bat, blast, bucket, burn, burn rubber, burn the breeze, burn the road, burn up the highway, carry the mail, chogie, clip, cut, dust, floor, floorboard, floor it, fly, fly low, fog, fog it, go full blast, go hell-bent, go hell-bent for election, go hell for leather, go hell to split, go lickety-cut, go lickety-split, go like a bat out of hell, go like a blue streak, go like a streak, go like Billy Hell, go like blazes, go like blue blazes, go like greased lightning, go like nobody's business, go like sixty, go like the deuce, go like the devil, go to beat the band, go to beat the Dutch, go to town, haul ass, haul the mail, hell, hell along, highball, hightail, hightail it, honk, hotfoot, hump, let her rip, make tracks, nail it, pack the mail, pour it on, pour on the coal, put it to the wood, put the hammer down, put the pedal to the metal, rip-ass, run wide open, scat, scoot, scorch, skin along, smoke, step on it, step on the gas, storm, streak, swoop, tear, tool, turn on the afterburners, varoom, vroom, zing, zing along, zip, zoom, zoomaty

basket

n The male genitals, as in "Check out the basket on that body builder"

apparatus, balls and bat, belongings, business, equipment, jewelry, meat, nasty bits, private parts, privates, works

bat around

v phr To discuss, as in "We'll bat around the idea a little before we decide"

chew over, go over, hash, hash over, kick around, knock around, toss around

bean

n The head; the skull

attic, belfry, biscuit, block, brainbox, chump, coco, coconut, conk, crown, crumpet, dome, dreambox, gourd, headpiece, knob, knuckle, noddle, noggin, noodle, nut, onion, pate, pimple, potato, pumpkin, sconce, top story, upper story, wetware

bean counter

n phr A statistician or arithmetical clerk in government or business

gnome, number cruncher, numbers cruncher

bean-eater

n A person of Spanish-American background, esp a Chicano

bean, bean-bandit, beaner, bravo, chili-chomper, chucke, chuey, greaseball, grease-gut, greaser, Mescin, oiler, pachuco, pepper-belly, pinto bean, taco, taco-bender

beanpole

n A tall, thin person

beanstalk, broomstick, clothes pole, daddy longlegs, gangleshanks, hatrack, highpockets, long drink of water, stick, string bean

beat

1 v To surpass; outdo

beat all, beat all hollow, beat one's time, burn, clobber, come out on top, have it all over, lick, outpoint, put in the shade, run circles around, show up, skin, skunk, smear, sweep, take it all, take the cake

2 SEE **MOOCHER**

beat-up
adj Battered and damaged, esp by age and use, as in "Our beat-up car still gets us around town"

broken-down, clapped-out, dog-eared, ramshackle, ratty, seedy

beaver
n The pubic hair, esp female

beard, brillo, bush, muff, pubes

beef
1 *n A complaint; a grievance*

belch, bellyache, big stink, bitch, gripe, grouse, holler, howl, kick, squawk, stink, tale of woe

2 *v To complain; utter a grievance, as in "She beefed about the umpire's call"*

belch, bellow, bellyache, bitch, blow up a storm, cop an attitude, crab, cut a beef, give heat, gripe, grouch, grouse, growl, have an attitude, holler, howl, kick, kick up a fuss, kick up a storm, kvetch, make a fuss, make a stink, make a big stink, moan, piss, piss up a storm, put up a squawk, raise a fuss, raise a ruckus, raise Cain, raise sand, raise the roof, squawk, squeal like a stuck pig, yammer, yap, yell bloody murder, yell blue murder, yell one's head off

3 SEE **COCK**
4 SEE the **DAMAGE**
5 SEE **HASSLE**

a bee in one's **bonnet**
n phr A particular idea or notion, esp an eccentric one; an obsession, as in "He's had a bee in his bonnet ever since he went to that preacher's lecture"

a bee, a bug, a flea in one's nose, a maggot, a maggot in one's brain, a thing

beer bust
n phr A party where beer is the featured drink

beer blast, beerfest, brew-out, hopfest, kegger, keg party

belly
n The stomach

basket, bread basket, gut, kishkes, kitchen, labonza, middle, pantry, solar plexus, tum, tummy, tummy-tum-tum, tum-tum

belly laugh
n phr A very loud and hearty laugh; a guffaw

belly-buster, bellytickler, belly-whopper, belly-wow, big yuck, boff, boffo, boffola, button buster, gut-buster, horselaugh, knee-slapper, side-splitter

belly-whopper
1 n A dive in which one strikes the water stomach first
2 SEE **BELLY LAUGH**

belly-buster, belly-flop, belly-flopper, belly-smacker, chewallop, chewalloper, gut-buster

bennies

n Any
amphetamine pills

A, aimies, amp, amt, amy, B-29s, bam, bambita, bams, bean, beans, benz, black beauties, black bombers, black bottle, blue angel, bombita, bottles, box of L, brain ticklers, brownies, browns, bumble bees, businessman's lunch, cartwheels, chalk, Christinas, Christmas trees, coast-to-coasts, copilot, crank, crink, cris, cross-countries, crosses, crossroads, cross-tops, crystal, dexies, dexo, dominoes, double cross, drivers, dynamite stocks, eye-opener, fives, football, forwards, glass, goies, grads, green dragon, greenies, hearts, horseheads, in-betweens, jam, jam Cecil, jelly-babies, jelly beans, jolly beans, joy pellet, L A turnabouts, leapers, lid poppers, lightning, lip proppers, nuggets, orange peaches, pep-em-ups, pep pills, pixies, purple hearts, rhythms, rippers, road dope, roses, sky rockets, sparkle plenties, sparklers, speckled birds, speed, splach, splash, splivins, STP, stuka, tabs, thrusters, truck drivers, turnabouts, uppers, uppie, ups, wake-ups, West Coast turnabouts, whites

☞ *The great number of slang terms for narcotics probably reflects both a need for coded reference to an illegal substance and a desire to be chic and up-to-date, in addition to the need to distinguish varieties.*

best shot

n phr One's
maximum effort; the
best one can do

one's all, all one's got, all-out try, all one's worth, one's damndest, full court press, the works

bet one's **ass**
v phr To be absolutely sure of something; be confident, as in "I'd bet my ass he knew it all the time"

bet one's bippy, bet one's boots, bet one's bottom dollar, bet dollars to doughnuts, bet one's last nickel, bet one's life, bet one's neck, bet one's shirt, bet one's sweet ass, bet one's sweet life, bet the farm, bet the ranch, bet the rent, bet one's whiskers, make book

bet your ass
affirmation Absolutely; definitely, as in "Bet your ass he's the next winner"

bet the house, bet the rent, bet your bippy, bet your boots, bet your bottom dollar, bet your life, bet your shirt, bet your sweet ass, bet your whiskers, fucking ay, fucking ay right, fucking well told, I'll drink to that, I'll tell the world, natch, right on, seguro que, shitsure, sure as shit, U B B, word, yeah, yep, you ain't just flapping your gums, you ain't just whistling Dixie, you bet, you betcha, you better believe it, you're damn tootin', you're telling me, you said a mouthful, you said it

Bible-banger
n A strict religionist, esp a Protestant fundamentalist

amen snorter, Bible pounder, Bible-puncher, Bible-thumper, Christer, Holy Joe, knee-bender
☞ *This list is close to the one at "goody-goody."*

big deal
1 *n phr Something very important*
2 SEE **BIG SHOT**

BFD, biggie

big-league
adj Serious; important; professional, as in "This is a big-league deal we're putting together"

big, big-bore, big-time, double-barrel, four-star, front-page, hardball, heavy, heavyweight, hefty, high-power, large, major-league

the **big leagues**
n phr The more serious reaches of a profession, business, etc, as in "For accountants, the Big 8 firms are the big leagues"

the bigs, the big time, hardball, the major leagues

bigmouth
n A pretentious and deceitful talker; a know-it-all

armchair general, armchair strategist, bag of wind, big wind, blower, blowhard, bull artist, bullshit artist, bullshitter, bullshooter, bull-thrower, crapper, gasbag, gasman, gatemouth, ho-dad, ho-daddy, hot-air artist, loudmouth, Monday morning quarterback, paper tiger, popoff, satchel mouth, Spanish athlete, windbag, windjammer

big O
n phr Opium

auntie, black pill, black snake, black stuff, brew units, brick gum, brown hash, brown stuff, bunk, button, chicory, Chinese molasses, chocolate, cookie mud, cream, cutered pill, dopium, dream, dream beads, dream wax, elevation, fire-plug, foon, fun, ghow, glad stuff, goma, gow, gow crust, goynk, grease, green ashes, green mud, green powder, gum, hop, lemkee, lightning smoke, mahogany juice, midnight oil, molasses, munsh, O, Op, pan juice, pekoe, pen yen, piki, pill pillow, plack shit, poppy, poppy rain, poppy train, pox, puff, rooster brand, root tonic, sam how, san lo, sealing wax, son lo tar, yen chee, yen chiang, yen pock, yen shee suey

☞ *The great number of slang terms for narcotics probably reflects both a need for coded reference to an illegal substance and a desire to be chic and up-to-date, in addition to the need to distinguish varieties.*

big shot
1 *n phr A very important or self-important person; an influential person*

the berries, big bean, big bloke, big boy, big bug, big cheese, big deal, big do, big doolie, big enchilada, big fish, big frog, big gee, biggie, big gun, big guy, big hombre, big macher, big man, big noise, big squeeze, big stuff, big timer, big wheel, boss, boss man, brass hat, the cheese, face card, the great one, heavy, heavyweight, higher-up, high muckety-muck, high-up, himself, his nibs, honcho, hoohaw, hotshot, macher, magoo, muck, mucky-muck, nabob, panjandrum, pooh-bah, shot, topsider, VIP, wheel

2 SEE **WHEELER-DEALER**

bike
n A motorcycle

hog, iron, sled

a bill
n phr A hundred dollars

C, century, C-note, C-spot, yard

billy club
n phr A police officer's nightstick

billy, hickory, rosewood, shill

bind
n A predicament

box, clutch, crunch, fine kettle of fish, fix, hell of a mess, hell of a note, hell to pay, hell to pay and no pitch hot, hobble, hole, hot spot, hot water, how-de-do, jam, mell of a hess, mess, pickle, pinch, pretty pickle, spot, [Brit] sticky wicket, tight spot, tough spot, unholy mess

☞ *This word is very often used in the expression "in a bind."*

binders
n The brakes of a car

anchors, cinchers

binge
n A spree; a carousal

bat, bender, booze-up, brannigan, bust, caper, guzzle, hell-bender, hooley, jag, randan, rip, shindy, soak, stew, tear, toot, twister, whooper-dooper, wingding

bingle
n A base hit in baseball

ace, B, bagger, base knock, dinger, tater

the **bird**
1 *n phr A rude flatulatory noise made in derision*

Bronx cheer, raspberry, razoo, the razz

2 *n phr An obscene, insulting gesture made with the middle finger*

the finger
☞ *This term is usually used after "get" or "give."*

bit
1 *n A prison sentence*

hitch, jolt, lag, piece, spot, stretch, time, trick

2 SEE **ACT**
3 SEE **BAG**

bitch

1 *n A woman one dislikes or disapproves of*

broad, cunt, witch

☞ *Female equivalents of the contemptuous terms for men, listed in this book under "asshole," are relatively rare. Contempt for females, in slang, stresses their putative sexual promiscuity and weakness rather than moral vileness and general odiousness. Some terms under "asshole," though, are increasingly used of women.*

2 SEE **BEEF**

3 SEE **HUMDINGER**

a bitch

1 *n phr An unhappy occurrence; a wretched circumstance, as in "Isn't it a bitch, his dying so young?"*

hell, a hell of a note, hell on wheels

2 *n Anything arduous or very disagreeable*

an all-nighter, a back-breaker, a bastard, a killer, no picnic, no tea party, a son of a bitch

3 SEE **BALL-BUSTER**

bitch box

n phr A public address system or loudspeaker

growler, squawk box

bite

1 *v To accept a deception as truth; be gullible, as in "He bit when I told him he'd won the lottery"*

be an easy mark, be a patsy, be a sucker, be easy, be green, eat up, fall for, gobble down, go for, gulp down, lap up, swallow; swallow hook, line, and sinker; swallow whole, take the bait

2 *n One's share of a sum*

cut, divvy, end, look-in, percentage, piece, rake-off, score, slice, split, takeout, taste, whack

3 SEE the **DAMAGE**

bite the bullet
v phr To accept the cost of a course of action, though it be painful

face the music, [Brit] grasp the nettle, pay the piper, stand up and take it, take it, take one's medicine, take the rap

blabbermouth
n A person who talks too much; a logorrheic person

babblemouth, babbler, bag of wind, barber, big breeze, bigmouth, big noise, big wind, blabber, blabberer, blabmouth, blah-blaher, blatter, blowhard, chatterbox, chatterer, chinwagger, ear-bender, flapjaw, gabber, gabblemouth, gabbler, gasbag, gatemouth, gibble-gabble, gum-beater, hot-air artist, jabberer, jawsmith, load of wind, loudmouth, motor-mouth, ratchet-jaw, ratchet-mouth, rattletongue, satch, satchelmouth, spieler, spouter, spouter-offer, tongue-wagger, windbag, windjammer, woofer, word-slinger, yapper, yenta

blackball
v To hold in strong disfavor; ostracize; reject

black, blacklist, put on the crap list, put on the ditch list, put on the shit list, shit-list, stink-list, thumb down, tin-can, turn thumbs down on

black eye
n phr An eye surrounded with darkened areas of contusion

goog, mouse, shiner

Black Maria
n phr A police van

blue liz, go-long, milk wagon, paddy wagon, pie wagon

blank check

n phr General freedom of action; carte blanche

free ticket

blankety-blank

adj or n A generalized euphemism substituted for a taboo or vulgar term, as in "Get your blankety-blank car out of my way"

bleep, bleeping, bliggey, so-and-so, you-know-what

blast

1 v To attack, esp with strong verbal condemnation; excoriate

crack down on, lambaste, lay into, let fly at, let have it, let loose on, light into, pile into, pitch into, plow into, rip into, roast, sail into, scorch, skin alive, sock, sock it to, tear into, tie into, wade into, whale, whale into

2 SEE **BALL**

3 SEE **BARREL**

4 SEE **CLOBBER**

5 SEE **FIX**

6 SEE **KICK**

7 SEE **PLUG**

8 SEE **WINGDING**

blind pig

n phr A saloon or club that operates illegally

after-hours club, blind tiger, bootleg joint, social club, speakeasy

☞ *Many of these terms were more current during the prohibition era than they are now.*

blind-side

v To attack by surprise; fool an opponent

blind-pop, bushwhack, sucker-punch

Blind Tom

n phr A sports official

guesser, hizzoner, ref, ump, whistle tooter, zebra

blood

n A black person

blood brother, blood sister, bro', brother, mamber, sister, soul brother, soul sister, youngblood
☞ *These terms are not per se offensive, unlike the terms under "nigger."*

blow

1 v To do fellatio

bite, dick-lick, eat, eat it, give cap, give cone, give good head, give head, gobble, go down and do tricks, go down on, hoover, lick, play the skin flute, suck, suck off

2 v To do cunnilingus

do it the French way, eat, eat furburger, eat fur pie, eat hair pie, eat it, eat seafood, French, go down and do tricks, go down on, have a box lunch, lick, slurp

3 v To spend money, esp extravagantly or foolishly, as in "He had a nice nest egg, but he blew it gambling at the track"

blow in, diddle away, dish out, drop, fool away, fork out, fork over, fribble away, fritter away, frivol away, lay out, piddle away, piss away, pour down the drain, pour down the rathole, shell out, shoot, throw away

4 *v To expose something secret; bare, esp a scandal, as in "He threatened to blow the whole nasty story unless they paid him"*

blow sky-high, blow the lid off, blow the whistle, blow wide open, give away, let it all hang out, show up, spill, spill one's guts, tattle, tell all

5 SEE **BLOW GRASS**
6 SEE **BLOW OFF**
7 SEE **FLUFF**
8 SEE **FUCK UP**
9 SEE **SNORT**
10 SEE **SPLIT**
11 SEE **SQUEAL**

blow grass
v phr To smoke marijuana

bang, beat the weeds, be in weeds, bend the head, bite one's lip, blast, blow, blow a stick, blow smoke, blow one's top, bounce the goof balls, break a stick, burn an Indian, burn the hay, bust, do, do a joint, do up, do your business, drag, drink Texas tea, drop a joint, fire up, get down, get it on, get off, get on, go loco, goof, hit, hit the hay, hoka toka, hump the sage, kiss Mary Jane, light up, pick up, poke, pot out, power hit, pull, send, send up, sip, smoke rings, straighten out, taste, tighten one's wig, toke, toke up, torch up, tote, trigger, turkey, turn on, waste

blow it with someone
v phr To make someone hostile or estranged; antagonize

blot one's copybook, break one's shovel, get on someone's list, get on someone's shit list, miss the boat, queer it

blow job
n phr An act of fellatio or cunnilingus

cap, French job, good head, hair pie, head, head job, hose job, job, knob job, lipstick on a dipstick, suck, suction, tongue job

blow off
1 *v phr To boast; brag*

big-mouth, big-talk, blow, blow one's bazoo, blow hard, blow off one's mouth, blow off one's trap, blow off one's yap, blow one's own horn, blow one's own trumpet, blow smoke, brag oneself up, bullshit, crack one's jaw, lay it on thick, loudmouth, loud-talk, mouth off, pat oneself on the back, pop off, pop off at the mouth, run off at the mouth, shoot off one's mouth, shoot the bull, shoot the crap, shoot the shit, sling it, sling the bull, spout, spout off, talk big, throw the bull, toot one's own horn, woof

2 SEE COP OUT

blow one's **top**
1 *v phr To become angry; fly into a fit*

become livid, blow a fuse, blow a gasket, blow one's cool, blow one's cork, blow one's stack, blow one's stopper, blow one's topper, blow up, blow one's wig, burn, burn up, cast a kitten, climb the wall, fall apart, flip, flip one's lid, flip out, flip one's raspberry, flip one's wig, fly off the handle, get one's back up, get one's dander up, get one's gauge up, get one's hair up, get hot under the collar, get in a swivet, [Brit] get in a wax, get into a lather, get into a snit, get into a state, get into a stew, get into a sweat, get one's Irish up, get mad, get pissed off, get one's shit hot, get sore, get the red ass, get the wind up, go ape, go off the deep end, go out of one's skull, go up the wall, have a bird, have a blowoff, have a blowup, have a catfit, have a conniption fit, have a cow, have a duckfit, have a fit, have a shit fit, have kittens, have pups, have steam coming out of one's ears, hit the ceiling, jump salty, lose one's cool, lose one's wig, pop one's cork, see red, shit a brick, shit bricks, simmer, sizzle, smoke, smolder, spit tacks, steam, stew, sweat, throw a fit, throw a hyper, turn purple

☞ *These terms share semantic territory with "make a scene," which should also be considered.*

2 SEE **FREAK OUT**

blowup
n A fit of anger; a rage

blowoff, catfit, conniption, conniption fit, duckfit, flare-up, hemorrhage, lather, stew, sweat, tantrum, tizzy, [Brit] wax

blow up
v phr To exaggerate the importance of; overemphasize, as in "They blew the thing up into a major scandal"

make a big deal, make a big production, make a big stink, make a federal case, pump up, run into the ground, work into the ground

☞ *These terms share semantic territory with "nitpick," which should also be considered.*

blubber
n Body fat

avoirdupois, beef, flab

blue movie
n phr A pornographic movie

adult movie, beaver, blue flick, dirty movie, flesh flick, fuck film, skin flick

the blues
n phr Depression; low spirits

blahs, [Brit] blue funk, doldrums, dumps, [Brit] funk, grumps, mulligrubs, the pip, red ass

bluff

v To use confident deception as a means of winning or succeeding, as in "He bluffed a throw to first to keep the runner from taking a large lead"

cheek it, fake it, shuck, vamp, wing, wing it

bobtail

n A dishonorable discharge from the armed forces

bob, DD, kick, yellow ticket

bone factory

1 *n phr A hospital*
2 SEE **BONEYARD**

bonehouse, butcher shop, croaker joint

boner

1 *n A blunder; an egregious mistake*

[Brit] balls-up, bitch-up, bloomer, bloop, blooper, bobble, bonehead play, bonehead trick, boo-boo, boot, clam, clinker, cross-up, dumbo, flub, flubdub, flub-up, flummox, foozle, foulup, fuck-up, goof, goof-up, howler, louse-up, miscue, muck-up, muff, screw-up, slip-up, snafu, whoops

2 SEE **GRIND**
3 SEE **HARD-ON**

boneyard

n A cemetery

bone factory, bone orchard, marble city, marble orchard

booby hatch
n phr A mental hospital

the bin, bughouse, cackle factory, cracker factory, crazy house, funny farm, funny house, laughing academy, loony bin, nut academy, nut box, nut college, nut factory, nut farm, nut foundry, nut hatch, nut house, rubber room

the book
n phr Figures and other materials concerning past performance, as in "The book on this guy is he'll take the easiest way out"

chart, dope, dope sheet, form, numbers, stats, track record

boondockers
n Heavy and sturdy shoes or boots

clodhoppers, shitkickers, stompers, wafflestompers

the boondocks
n phr Remote places; rural regions

the back country, the backwoods, the Bible Belt, the boonies, the brush, the bush, hickdom, the middle of nowhere, [Australian] the outback, the provinces, the rhubarbs, stick country, the sticks, the tall timbers, yokeldom

booze
n Any alcoholic drink, esp whiskey and other spirits; liquor

alky, the bottle, the cup that cheers, the demon rum, firewater, grog, hard stuff, hooch, John Barleycorn, joyjuice, juice, laughing soup, rum, the sauce, stuff

boss

1 *n The leader; the highest authority*

big boy, big cheese, big chief, big enchilada, big gee, big guy, big shot, boss man, chief cook and bottle-washer, godfather, governor, head cheese, himself, his highness, his nibs, honcho, kingfish, kingpin, main squeeze, the Man, man in the front office, man upstairs, Mister Big, number one, number-one boy, numero uno, old man, pooh-bah, skipper, top dog, top sawyer, topsider

2 *v To control; manage, as in "She bosses a Fortune 500 firm"*

be at the helm, be in the driver's seat, call the shots, crack the whip, handle the reins, have the last word, have the say-so, head up, mastermind, rule the roost, run, wear the pants

both hands

n phr A ten-year prison sentence

couple of fives back to back, double finn, sawbuck, tenner, ten-spot

the **bottom line**

n phr The decisive essentials; the grim reality, as in "Sales are the bottom line here"

the ball game, the clincher, the meat, the meat and potatoes, the name of the game, the nitty-gritty, the payoff, the score, the story, where the rubber meets the road

bounce

1 *v To eject by force; expel*

boot out, bum-rush, chuck, give the bum's rush, give one the gate, give the hook, give the old heave-ho, give the one-two-three, kick out, put the skids to, throw out on one's ass, throw out on one's ear, turn out

2 SEE **PIZZAZZ**

bracelets

n A pair of handcuffs

braces, clamps, cuffs, darbies, mitts, nippers, wristlets

brain wave
n phr A sudden, useful idea, as in "I thought for hours, then wham, a brain wave struck"

brainstorm, hot notion, idear, idee

the brass
n phr High officials; chiefs

big boys, big brass, biggies, the big money, brass hats, execs, front office, gold braid, honchos, lords of creation, muckety-mucks, our betters, people upstairs, power, powers that be, power structure, top brass

break out
1 *v phr To escape from prison or some other confining situation*

absquatulate, beat it, blow, blow town, breeze, broom, bust out, cheese it, clear out, crash out, crush out, duck out, dust, fly the coop, go over the wall, hightail, hit the hump, lam, make a break for it, make oneself scarce, powder, run out, [Brit] scarper, scram, skedaddle, skin out, skip, skip out, split, take a powder, take a runout powder, take it on the lam, vamoose

2 SEE **RUSTLE UP**

break up
v phr To laugh uproariously

bust a gut, cackle, crack up, die laughing, [Brit] fall about, fall out, har-har, pee one's pants, piss one's pants, split a gut, split a gut laughing, split one's sides, yuk

break someone **up**
v phr To cause laughter; amuse enormously

bowl over, convulse, fracture, kill, knock dead, lay in the aisles, lay low, mow down, panic, put in stitches, slaughter, slay, wow

brew
n Beer

the amber brew, barley broth, brewskie, froth, suds

brick-top

n A red-headed person

carrothead, carrot-top

briefed

adj Informed; prepared by instruction

brought up to speed, clued, clued in, filled in, pooped up, prepped, primed, put in the picture

broad

1 *n A woman*

babe, baby, baby doll, biddy, bim, bimbo, [Brit] bint, [esp Brit] bird, bit of fluff, bozette, bundle, bunny, butt, canary, chick, chickabiddy, chicken, chicky, chippy, cooz, cow, crack, cunt, cunt meat, cutie, dame, dearie, dish, doll, dollop, dolly, fem, femme, filly, fluff, frail, frau, gal, ginch, girlie, hammer, heifer, hen, hide, honey, honey-bun, honey-bunny, jane, jenny, job, klooch, lady, lassie, leg, mama, mare, mat, miss, missie, missis, missiz, moll, momma, mouse, pet, piece, pussy, pussycat, quail, rag and a bone and a hank of hair, rib, shemale, she-she, shouter, sis, sissy, sister, skeezer, skirt, slash, snatch, squab, squaw, stuff, sweet baby, sweetheart, sweet momma, sweet patootie, sweet stuff, sweet thing, tail, tart, tomato, toots, tootsie, twist, wench, witch, wool, wren

☞ *The semantic boundaries between "broad," "dish," and "floozy" are not easy to set. All three terms should be considered.*

☞ *Many women find many of these terms offensively sexist.*

2 SEE **DISH**

broke

adj Penniless; destitute

beat, bust, busted, clean, cleaned out, cold in hand, dead broke, dingy, down and out, down for the count, flat, flat-ass, flat broke, flat on one's ass, melted out, on one's ass, on one's ear, on the hog, on the rims, on the rocks, on one's uppers, O O F, oofless, piss-poor, shatting on one's uppers, short, [Brit] skint, stone broke, stony, stony cold broke, strapped, tap, Tap City, tapped, tapped out, thin, tight, wasted, wiped out, without a pot to piss in, without a red cent, without a sou, without one dollar to rub against another

brown-nose

1 *v To curry favor; toady*

apple-polish, back-scratch, back-slap, blow smoke, bootlick, brown, get in solid with, get next to, get on the right side of, honey up to, kiss ass, lick ass, play up to, polish apples, shine up to, suck, suck around, suck ass, suck up to, sweeten up, wipe someone's ass

2 *n A toady; a sycophant*

apple-polisher, ass-kisser, ass-licker, ass-sucker, ass-wiper, back-patter, back-scratcher, back-slapper, bootlicker, browner, brown-noser, bucker, earbanger, eggsucker, A K, kiss-ass, kiss-butt, stooge, suck-ass, suck-off, TL, TLer, tokus-licker, yes man

bruiser

n A big, strong man

big beef, big bozo, big bruiser, big horse, big hunk, big hunk of beef, big tuna, brute, heavy, heavyweight, hulk, jumbo, man mountain, moose, whale

brush up

v phr To improve, review, or perfect one's mastery, as in "You'd better brush up your math before you try for that job"

bone up, bone up on, brush up on, check up on, cram, cram up, fresh up, get up, get up on, polish up, sharpen up, shine up, smarten up

buck

1 *n A US dollar*

berry, bone, buckeroo, cartwheel, case note, cent, clanker, copeck, ducat, fish, frogskin, iron man, one-spot, peso, plaster, plunk, potato, rock, rutabaga, scoot, scrip, simoleon, single, skin, slab, smacker, snuff, toad skin

2 *v To resist; defy, as in "Be very careful if you intend to buck the mayor"*

fight, go up against, take on

buck private
n phr An Army private; a common soldier

buckass private, bullet bait, cannon fodder, dough, doughboy, doughfoot, GI, GI Joe, Joe, Joe Blow, Joe Shit the Ragman, Joe Snuffy, Joe Tentpeg, John Dogface, Private Slipinshits

buddy up
v phr To become friends

be buddy-buddy, be palsy-walsy, chum up, click, get chummy, hit it off, pal together, pal up, play footsie, team up

bug
1 *v To annoy, anger, pester, or harry*

aggravate, be in one's face, be on one's back, be on one's case, break chops, burn, chivvy, discombobulate, dog, drug, flake off, get, get someone down, get down on, get someone's goat, get in one's face, get in one's hair, get someone's nanny, get on someone's back, get on someone's case, get on someone's nerves, get to, get to someone, get under one's skin, get up someone's nose, give someone a bad time, give someone a hard time, give someone grief, give someone the needle, gravel, gripe, gripe one's ass, gripe one's balls, gripe one's butt, gripe one's cookies, gripe one's left nut, gripe one's middle kidney, gripe one's soul, hassle, hock, hound, jerk someone around, jerk someone's chain, jerk someone's strings, miff, needle, nudge, nudzh, peeve, pick on, push, push someone's button, rank, rank out, rattle someone's cage, rib, ride, rile, roust, shag, sound, yank someone's chain

2 *n A horse that has never won a race*

maiden

3 SEE **FAN**
4 SEE **HOT ROD**
5 SEE **NUT**

bugger

1 *v To do anal intercourse; sodomize*

assfuck, BF, boogie, brown, brownhole, bumfuck, bunghole, buttbang, buttfuck, cornhole, dick, do it the Greek way, Greek, pack fudge, pack some mud, part cheeks, pitch, punk, ream, split some buns, stretch some jeans

2 SEE **BACK-BREAKER**
3 SEE **BAD MAN**
4 SEE **SUCKER**

build

n One's physique, esp one's figure

bod, shape

built

adj Physically well-developed, esp in a sexually attractive way

built for comfort, built like a brick shithouse, constructed, curvaceous, hunky, stacked, well-built, well-upholstered

bulldoze

v To intimidate; overcome by force

bogart, buffalo, bullyrag, get tough with, gorilla, lean on, manhandle, railroad, roust, sandbag, snowball, steamroller, strong-arm

bullheaded
adj Obstinate

feisty, hardheaded, hardnosed, hardshell, hardshelled, mulish, pigheaded, set in one's ways, stiffnecked, stubborn as a bobtail mule, stubborn as an ox

bullshit
1 *n Nonsense; absurdities; pretentious or deceitful talk*

all that jazz, apple butter, applesauce, [Brit] balls, baloney, banana oil, beans, bilge, blah, blah-blah, blahs, blarney, blather, borax, bosh, BS, bull, bulldink, bullrag, bullshine, bunk, bushwah, cheese, claptrap, cowflap, cowplop, crap, crapola, crock, crock of shit, crud, dogshit, eyewash, fiddle-faddle, flamdoodle, flapdoodle, flubdubbery, flummadiddle, garbage, gas, gash, guff, gum-beating, hockey, hogwash, hoke, hokey-poke, hokey-pokey, hokum, holly-golly, hooey, hop, horsefeathers, horseshit, hot air, hully-gully, jabberjack, jazz, jiggerypokery, jive, jive-ass, kafooster, malarkey, marmalade, monkeydoodle, moonshine, mumbo-jumbo, mush, oil, phony-baloney, phonus-balonus, piece of shit, piffle, pile of shit, poppycock, rot, rubbish, schmegeggy, shit, shit for the birds, smoke, spinach, tommyrot, [Brit] tosh, trash, tripe, twiddle-twaddle, yack, yackety-yack, yap

2 *v To talk nonsense, esp with an intent to deceive*

blow off, blow off one's mouth, blow off one's trap, blow off one's yap, con, crap, fast-talk, fatmouth, guff, horseshit, jive, lay it on, lay it on with a trowel, mouth off, pile it up, pop off, run off at the mouth, shit, shoot the breeze, shovel the shit, shuck, shuck and jive, sling it, sling the bull, spread it, spread it on thick, spread it thick, sweet-talk, talk big, talk through one's hat, throw the bull, woof

3 SEE **BLOW OFF**
4 SEE **GAB**

bum

1 *n A vagrant; a derelict*

bag lady, bag woman, barrelhouse bum, bindle stiff, bo, bottle baby, Bowery bum, bummer, busthead, dock rat, drifter, floater, grifter, hobo, low-life, moocher, shopping bag lady, shopping cart lady, skell, Skid Row bum, speck bum, stewbum, stiff, stumblebum, vag, weary Willy, wino

2 *v To beg; cadge, as in "Where can I bum a cigarette?"*

chisel, dog it, drop the lug on, freeload, hit up, make a touch for, mooch, put the arm on, put the lug on, put the touch on, scrounge, scrounge up, shake down, sleaze, stick for, touch, touch up

3 SEE **ASS**
4 SEE **ASSHOLE**
5 SEE **CON**
6 SEE **CRUMMY**
7 SEE **GREEN AROUND THE GILLS**
8 SEE **HOOKER**

bum rap

n phr An unjustified condemnation or punishment

bad deal, bad rap, bum beef, bum deal, bum finger, frame, frame-up, lousy deal, phony rap, raw deal, RF, rotten deal, royal fucking, the shaft

bundle

1 *n A large amount of money, as in "That car must have cost a bundle"*

bale of hay, bankroll, barrel of money, big bankroll, big bucks, big money, bunch, bundle of dough, carload, chunk of cash, chunk of dough, cool million, deep pockets, gobs, hard coin, heaps of cash, heavy chips, heavy coin, heavy jack, heavy lettuce, heavy money, heavy sugar, important money, king's ransom, megabucks, mint, mintful, mucho dinero, nice hunk of change, nice hunk of jack, nice piece of change, nice piece of jack, package, [Brit] packet, piece of cash, piles, pretty penny, raft, rafts, real money, scads, serious money, tidy sum, wad, wads

2 SEE **BROAD**

bush
1 *adj Mediocre; second-rate*

bush-league, cut-rate, dime-a-dozen, fair-to-middling, garden variety, low-rent, narrow-gauge, of a sort, of sorts, one-horse, piddling, pissy-ass, the poor man's, run-of-the-mill, run-of-the-mine, scrub, small-beer, small-bore, small-potato, small-time, softball, a sort of a, so-so, tacky, tatty, tinhorn, two-bit

2 SEE **PIDDLY**

the bush leagues
n phr The mediocre and inferior reaches of business, entertainment, sports, etc

the minor leagues, the small time

bust
1 *v To arrest; take prisoner*

bag, claw, clip, collar, cop, flag, flake, grab, haul in, jab, knock, make a pinch, nab, nail, nick, pick up, pinch, pull in, put the arm on, put the claw on, put the collar on, put the sleeve on, roust, run in, sidetrack, stiff collar, gotcha, grab, pickup, pinch

2 *n An arrest*
3 SEE **BROKE**
4 SEE **CLOBBER**
5 SEE **SOCK**

bust one's **ass**

v phr To strive; make one's best effort, as in "She didn't exactly bust her ass to make me feel welcome"

bend over backwards, break a hamstring, break one's neck, buckle down, bust a gut, bust one's balls, bust one's buns, bust one's butt, bust one's chops, bust one's conk, bust one's cork, bust hump, bust one's hump, bust one's nuts, bust one's sweet ass, do one's damndest, give it one's all, give it one's best, give it one's best shot, go all the way, go for all the marbles, go for broke, go for it, go out of one's way, go the extra mile, go the full yard, go the limit, go the whole hog, go the whole nine yards, go to the wall, haul off, knock oneself out, knuckle down, lay oneself out, make a full-court press, put one's back into it, rare back, reach back, rupture oneself, shoot the works, split a gut, spread oneself, suck it up

butt

1 *n A cigarette*

cig, cigareete, cigaroot, ciggy, coffin nail, coffin tack, dope, dope stick, drag, fag, gasper, grette, grit, joint, pimp stick, root, skag, slim, smoke, square joint, straight, tailormade, toke, weed

2 *n The remainder of a smoked cigarette or cigar*

dinch, dincher, maggot, Navy, roach, seed, skag, snipe

3 SEE **ASS**

butterfingers

n A clumsy, unhandy person; a fumbler

bull in a china shop, clunker, duffer, flub, flubdub, flubup, foozler, fumble-fist, goof-up, hacker, klutz, lobster, lubber, lummox, muffer, schlep, schloomp, slob

butt in

v phr To intrude; meddle

barge in, burst in, bust in, charge in, check in, chime in, chisel in, come barging in, come busting in, crowd someone's act, cut in, elbow in, get into the act, horn in, jimmy in, kibitz, muscle in, nose in, poke one's face in, poke one's nose into, put one's oar in, put one's two cents in, put one's two cents' worth in, stick one's nose into, weigh in

button man
n phr A low-ranking member of the Mafia

button player, button soldier, soldier

buy
1 v To believe; accept

buy into, buy off on, down, eat up, fall for, go for, kid oneself, lap up, sign off on, stand still for, swallow; swallow hook, line, and sinker; take, tumble for

2 v To approve; acquiesce in

drink to, give one's OK to, go along with, OK, say amen to, shake hands on, sign off on, sit still for, stand still for, string along with, throw in with

buzz
n A telephone call

jingle, ring, tinkle

by ear
adv phr By instincts and feelings rather than calculation and thought

by guess and by God, by the seat of one's pants

C

Caddy
n A Cadillac car   boat, Cad, Jew canoe, Kitty

camel-jammer
n An Arab or other   raghead
Eastern or Middle
Eastern person

can
1 *n A toilet, as in*   [esp Canadian] biffy, bog house, bog shop, commode,
"No visit to this bar   convenience, crap can, crapper, donicker, flusher,
is complete without   head, jakes, jane, john, johnny, kazoo, latrine, lav, [Brit]
a trip to the can"   loo, pot, potty, shitcan, shithouse, shitter, throne,
                         throne room

2 SEE **ASS**
3 SEE **FIRE**

can of worms
n phr A complex   bad scene, bag of worms, mess, mish-mash, perplex,
situation; a   rigmatick, ringding-do
rigmarole

caper
n A crime, esp a   frolic, job, touch, trick
robbery

card sharp
n phr An expert card player, esp a dishonest one in gambling

card shark, crimp, dildock, mechanic, pasteboard shark, shark, sharp, sharpie, sharpster
☞ *This list does not distinguish the modes or types of such card players.*

carry
v To be armed, as in "Don't mess with her, she carries"

be heeled, be rodded, be rodded up, carry the difference, pack, pack heat

carry a lot of weight
v phr To have power and influence, as in "The clergy carry a lot of weight around here"

draw a lot of water, have clout, walk heavy
☞ *These terms share semantic territory with "boss," which should also be considered.*

cart
v To transport; take; carry

drag, hump, lug, pack, schlep, tote

carved in stone
adj phr Fixed; immutable

in cement, set in concrete

case dough
n phr Money set aside for emergencies, "just in case"

ace in the hole, backlog, holdout, mad money, nest egg, something in the sock, stake

catch

n A hidden cost, qualification, defect, etc, as in "Any time you see a car advertised at such a low price, you know there's a catch"

clinker, hitch, joker, kicker, snag, stinger

catch hell

v phr To be severely reprimanded or punished

catch hail Columbia, catch holy hell, catch it, catch it in the neck, catch merry hell, catch the devil, get it

catch redhanded

v phr To find or seize someone in the act of doing something forbidden; catch in flagrante delicto

catch cold, catch on the hop, catch with a smoking gun, catch with a smoking pistol, catch with one's hand in the cookie jar, catch with one's hand in the till, catch with one's pants down, catch with the goods, catch with the merchandise, have bang to rights, have cold, have dead to rights, land, nail

catch-22

n A situation with contradictory requirements, as in "I'm caught in the catch-22 of needing a job to gain experience and needing experience to get a job"

lose-lose situation, no-win situation

cauliflower ear
n phr A boxer's or wrestler's ear deformed by injuries and accumulated scar tissue

pretty ear

the chair
n phr The electric chair

hot seat, hot squat, Old Smoky, Old Sparky, the smoky seat

chapter
n A division of a sports contest, esp an inning of baseball

canto, chukker, stanza, waltz

cheat
v To be sexually unfaithful

bad time, chippy, get a little on the side, nosh, play around, step out on someone, two-time, yard

check out
v phr To examine; scrutinize; inspect

check, cop a gander at, dig, double-O, eye, eyeball, gander, get a load of, give a look at, give the once-over, give with the eye, glim, glom, grab a look at, have a gander at, have a looksee, kick the tires, make, once-over, pick up, pin, pipe, put the eye on, scope on, scope out, size up, [Brit] take a dekko at, take a gander at, take a hinge at, take a reading, take a squint at, [Brit] vet

check the plumbing
v phr To go to the toilet

answer a call of nature, go powder the face, go to the little boys' (or girls') room, go to the powder room, go to the throne room, see a man about a dog

☞ *This sort of euphemism was once a rich source of wit, including the classic "go to Cannes [the famous watering place]."*

cheeky
adj Impudent; impertinent; rude

bold as brass, cocky, flip, fresh, gutty, lippy, nervy, sassy, smart-alecky, smart-ass, snotty, wise-ass, wise-guy

cheesecake
1 *n Photography and performance featuring womens' legs, breasts, hips, etc*

calendar art, gow, jiggle, jiggly, leg art, pinup, T A, T and A, tit art, tits and ass

2 *adj Showing the semiclad female body*

calendar, flesh, girlie, jiggle, pinup, skin, T A, T and A, tits-and-ass

cherry
n A virgin, of either sex

canned goods

chestnut
n A trite old story, joke, song, etc

bromide, corny joke, Joe Millerism, oldie, old turkey, old wheeze, warmed-over cabbage, yawner

chew out
v phr To reprimand; scold

bawl out, bear down on, bite someone's head off, boil in oil, call down, call on the carpet, chew someone's ass out, climb, climb someone's frame, climb someone's hump, come down hard on, come down on, crack down on, crawl, cuss out, cut someone a new asshole, dress down, eat out, give a good talking to, give a piece of one's mind, [Brit] give a rocket, give hail Columbia, give hell, give holy hell, give it in the neck, give merry hell, give the business, give the deuce, give the devil, give the dickens, give the works, give what-for, go at, go up in someone's face, haul over the coals, jack up, jump all over, jump down someone's throat, jump on, jump on someone's meat, land on, lay down the law, lay into, let have it, light into, make it hot for, pile into, pin someone's ears back, pitch into, plow into, put on the rack, put the fear of God into, put the gakk on, put through the wringer, rack out, raise hell with, raise the dickens with, rake over the coals, rake up one side and down the other, read the riot act, ream, ream out, rip into, roast, sail into, tear into, tear off a strip, tee off on, tell a thing or two, tell off, wade into

chicken
1 *n A coward; a poltroon*

candy-ass, chicken-liver, fraidy-cat, jellyfish, lilyliver, Milquetoast, pucker-ass, scaredy-cat, sissy, weak sister, wimp, yellow-belly

2 *adj Cowardly; craven*

chicken-hearted, chicken-livered, gutless, lily-livered, milk-livered, mousy, pucker-assed, rabbity, sissified, sissy, weak-kneed, yellow

3 SEE **BROAD**
4 SEE **CHICKENSHIT**

chicken feed
n phr A small amount of money

buttons, chicken money, coffee and cakes, crumbs, hay, nickels and dimes, peanuts, small beer, small bread, small change, small potatoes, tin

chicken out
v phr To cancel or withdraw from an action because of fear; be intimidated

back out, chicken, funk, funk out, get cold feet, turn chicken, turn yellow

chickenshit
n Pettiness and meanness, esp in a bureaucracy, as in "The new tax law is mostly chickenshit"

birdshit, chicken, horseshit, Mickey Mouse, shit for the birds, small beer, small change, small potatoes, turkey-shit

chiller
n A horror film

chiller-diller, slash-and-gash film, slasher, slice-and-dice film, snuff film

Chink
n A Chinese or person of Chinese extraction

Buddhahead, Chinee, Chino, pong, rice-belly, slant-eyes

☞ *These terms are all offensive.*

chintzy
adj Stingy; parsimonious

cheap, chinching, chinchy, close, Scotch, skinflint, tight, tight as a drum, tight as Kelsey's nuts, tight as O'Reilly's balls, tight as Reilly's balls

chitchat
n Talk, esp relaxed and idle conversation

bibble-babble, blah-blah, blat, buzz, chin, chin-chin, chin music, chitter-chatter, gab, gabble, gas, gibble-gabble, guff, hot air, jaw, jive, [Brit] natter, prittle-prattle, tittle-tattle, yack, yackety-yack

choke up
v phr To become tense and ineffective under pressure, as in "Their team choked up when the pennant race heated up"

choke, clutch up, swallow the apple, swallow the olive, take the pipe, tense up

choppers
n The teeth

china, crockery, fangs, grinders, ivories, pearlies, snappers, tusks

chow
1 *n Food*

eats, feed, grits, groceries, grub, the nosebag, prog, ribs, scarf, scoff, scoffings, tuck, vittles

2 SEE SCARF

Christer
n A straitlaced person, esp a very pious one

Bibleback, bluenose, goody-goody, holier-than-thou, Holy Joe, Nice Nelly, plaster saint

chuck
v To discard; rid oneself of

axe, bag, boot, can, deep-six, ditch, dump, eighty-six, get shut of, give the deep six, give the heave-ho, junk, kiss goodbye, put the skids to, scarf, scrap, scrap-heap, shitcan, shuck, toss overboard, unload
☞ *These terms share semantic territory with "nix," which should also be considered.*

chummy
adj Very friendly

buddy-buddy, palsy-walsy

chutzpa
n Extreme brashness; arrogant presumption, as in "Telling off your boss takes a lot of chutzpa"

brass, cheek, cheekiness, cockiness, crust, face, freshness, gall, guts, innards, moxie, nerve, snottiness

cinch

1 *n An easy task; anything easy*

blowoff, breeze, cake, cakewalk, cherry pie, clay pigeon, duck soup, easy digging, easy meat, gravy, jelly, kid stuff, picnic, pie, piece of cake, pipe, pushover, setup, shoo-in, slope-out, snap, sure thing, tea party, turkey-shoot, walkaway, walkover, waltz

2 *n A certainty; something sure to happen, as in "It's a cinch he'll be there, if he knows what's good for him"*

cold pack, dead certainty, dead cinch, dead-sure thing, fuzzy, lead-pipe cinch, lock, mortal lock, natural, open-and-shut case, shoo-in, sure bet, sure shot, sure thing

cinched

adj Certain; sure; assured, as in "He had the race cinched minutes before it ended"

cold, dead cinched, in the bag, knocked, nailed down, on ice, open-and-shut, racked, sewed up, taped, wired, wired up

the circular file

n phr The wastebasket

the can, file 13, file 17, memory hole

clamp down

v phr To enforce laws and rules rigorously

read the riot act, throw the book at

classy

1 *adj Having or showing prestige; typical of high society*

cushy, dicty, fancy-Dan, fancy-schmancy, flossy, high-class, highfalutin', high-grade, high-hat, high-hatty, high-rent, high-tone, high-toned, high-tony, hoity-toity, la-de-da, luxo, plush, plushy, posh, red-carpet, ritzy, silk-stocking, snazzy, snitzy, spiffy, swank, swanky, swish, top-drawer, top-shelf, [Brit] upmarket, upper-crusty, upscale, zazz, zazzy

2 SEE **GREAT**

clean
1 *adj Free of drug use, as in "She's been clean for three years, ever since she was in rehab"*
off the habit, off the needle, turned off

2 *adj Innocent; unincriminated*
clean as a hound's tooth, clean as a whistle, clear, in the clear, lily white, off the hook, squeaky clean

clean up
v phr To earn or acquire much money; make a large profit, as in "They cleaned up when the two companies merged"
cash in, coin money, hit it big, line one's pockets, make a bundle, make a killing, make a mint, make big money, make megabucks, milk the cash cow, rake it in, shake the money tree

clean up one's act
v phr To correct one's behavior or attitude; act properly
act one's age, clean up one's shit, cut the comedy, cut the crap, cut the funny business, get one's act together, get it together, get on the ball, get one's shit together, get straight, get with it, pull up one's socks, shape up, shape up or ship out, slipper, sprout wings, straighten up and fly right, suck it up, take a brace, tie one's shoes, toe the mark

cliffhanger
n Something very suspenseful
close shave, narrow squeak, near shave, near thing, squeaker, white knuckle

clinch

1 *v To determine conclusively; finish definitively; win*

cinch, ice, make official, nail down, put away, put in the bag, put in the can, put on ice, sew up, wrap, wrap up

2 *n An embrace*

bear hug, bunny hug, clutch

a clip

n Each one; each occasion, as in "His friends' weddings cost him a few hundred dollars a clip"

a crack, a go, a per-each, a pop, a shot, a slug, a smack, a throw, a toss, a whack

clit

n The clitoris

button, little boy in the boat, man in the boat

clobber

1 *v To defeat, esp to defeat decisively; trounce*

banjax, beat all hollow, beat the bejesus out of, beat the daylights out of, beat the hell out of, beat the kishkes out of, beat the living shit out of, beat the shit out of, beat the socks off of, beat the stuffing out of, beat the tar out of, blank, blast, blitz, blow away, blow someone's door off, blow out of the water, bulldoze, bury, bushwhack, bust, butcher, catch someone's lunch, clean someone's clock, clean someone's plow, clean up on, clean up the floor with, coldcock, conk, cook someone's goose, crawl someone's hump, cream, crock, do a job on, do a number on, do for, do in, doughpop, do up, drub, dry-gulch, dump, dust off, eat for breakfast, eat someone's lunch, finish, finish off, fix, fix someone's hash, flatten, give the business to, give the works to, give someone what for, gorilla, go upside one's face, go upside one's head, hand someone his (or her) head, hang one on, have for breakfast, have someone's lunch, hit someone where he (or she) lives, ice, jack up, jolt, kayo, kick the shit out of, knock someone's block off, knock for a loop, knock someone galley west, knock someone into the middle of next week, knock someone's lights out, knock off, knock out, knock someone sky west, knock the daylights out of, lambaste, lather, lay out, let someone have it, lick, lick to a frazzle, liquidate, make hamburger of, make hash of, make mincemeat of, make someone say uncle, make short work of, massacre, massage, maul, meat-axe, mess up, mop up on, mop up the floor with, mow down, murder, nuke, paste, polish off, powder, pulverize, punch someone's lights out, punch someone out, put away, put the blocks to, put the skids to, roll over, romp over, rough up, rub out, run a game on, run a number on, sack, sandbag, scalp, schmear, schneider, scrag, scraunch, settle someone's hash, shellac, shoot down, shoot down in flames, shut out, sink, skin, skin alive, skunk, slaughter, slay, slug, smear, smoke, smother, snuff, snuff out, sock, steamroller, stomp, swallow with a glass of water, swamp, take, take downtown, take into camp, take out, take to the cleaners, tie one on, topple, trash, trim, trip, vamp, vamp on, waffle, wallop, waste, wax, whale, whipsaw, whitewash, whomp, whop, whup, wipe out, wipe up the floor with, work over, wreck, zap, zonk, zonk out

☞ *These terms share semantic territory with "sock," which should also be considered.*

2 SEE BEAT

clout
n Power; effective force; impact

bang, biff, drag, the goods, grease, jazz, jism, jolt, juice, kick, kick-ass, mohoska, moxie, muscle, oof, oomph, pizzazz, poop, pow, pull, punch, push, snap, sock, spunk, starch, steam, the stuff, suck, suction, umph, wallop, what it takes

cock

n The penis

apparatus, banana, bayonet, beef, belongings, [Latino] bicho, bone, business, club, creamstick, dang, dibble, dick, dicky, ding-dong, dink, dong, doodle, dork, dummy, flute, hairsplitter, hammer, hang-down, hog, horn, hose, hunk of meat, jang, jigger, jock, John, Johnny, johnson, John Thomas, joint, jones, joy knob, joy stick, knob, love-muscle, meat, member, middle leg, pecker, peenie, peter, pinga, poker, pole, pork, prick, prong, pud, putz, ramrod, reamer, reltney, rod, root, sausage, schmuck, shlang, shlong, short arm, shvantz, skin flute, sugar stick, third leg, tool, wang, weener, weenie, weinie, wiener, wienie, works, yang, yard, ying-yang

☞ *"Dingbat," "dingus," "doodad," "dofunny," "dojigger," "thingy," or any other of the numerous terms for something one does not know the name of or does not wish to name may be used as a euphemism for penis.*

☞ *"Penis" is one of the more prolific of slang concepts. Farmer and Henley's* Slang and Its Analogues *(1888–1904) lists about 200 English terms under the heading "cream-stick."*

cockeyed

1 *adj Askew; crooked, as in "His hat was cockeyed, his clothes disheveled"*

agee, agee-jawed, all anyhow, all nohow, antigodlin, askewgee, catawampus, crooked as a dog's hind leg, every which way, galley-west, haywire, lopper-jawed, popeyed, screwy, sigoggling, six ways to Sunday, skew-gee, skew-jawed, skygodlin, slonchways, slonchwise, wamper-jawed, weewaw, whopper-jawed, [Brit] wonky, yaw-ways

2 SEE **CRAZY**

cocksucker

1 *n A person who does fellatio, esp a male homosexual*
2 SEE **ASSHOLE**

come-freak, come-queen, dick-licker, eater, gobbler, goopgobbler, peter-eater, piccolo player, scumsucker, skin-diver

cock-teaser

n A person who arouses a man sexually and then denies the sex act

dick-teaser, prick-teaser, PT

☞ *Plausible compounds may be made by appending "teaser" to any term for penis.*

coke

n Cocaine

base, bernice, bernies flake, big bloke, big C, Billie Hoke, birdie powder, blinkie, bloke, blort, bounce powder, brute, burese, burnies, C, caballo, Cadillac, candy cee, Carrie Nation, Carry, Cecil, cee, chalk, Charley, cheese, chick, Cholly, c-jam, coca, coca paste, coconut, cola, cookie, Corine, crack, Doctor White, duct, dust, dynamite, flake, Florida snow, foo-foo dust, foolish powder, freebase, frisking powder, gin, girl, glad, gold, golden girl, goofy dust, H and C, happy dust, heaven dust, her, hocus, hot and cold, ice, incentive, jam, joy dust, joy flakes, joy powder, the Lady, Lady Snow, Lady White, the leaf, mayo, med mojo, monkey cocaine, mosquito, nose, nose candy, nose powder, nose stuff, number three, old Madge, old slave, paradise, perico, piece, pimp dust, pogo pogo, poison, powder, powder diamonds, racehorse, rane, rock, sleep, snort, snow, snowball, snow bird, snow caine, snow flakes, speedball, stuff, sugar, super blow, toot, tootonium, turkey, uptown, whiff, white, white cross, white death, white girl, white horse, white lady, white mosquito, white paste, white powder, white stuff, white tape, white tornado, wings, witch

☞ *The great number of slang terms for narcotics probably reflects both a need for coded reference to an illegal substance and a desire to be chic and up-to-date, in addition to the need to distinguish varieties.*

cold as hell
adj phr Very cold

cold as a bastard, cold as a bitch, cold as a welldigger's ass, cold as a welldigger's ass in the Klondike, cold as a witch's tit, cold as charity, cold as Kelsey's ass, cold enough to freeze the balls off a brass monkey, colder than hell

cold fish
n phr A person who lacks emotional warmth, compassion, sociability, etc

chilly mo, iceberg, ice maiden

the cold shoulder
n phr A snub; a contemptuous dismissal, as in "She tried to make it up to him, but he just gave her the cold shoulder"

the beady eye, the brush, the brush-off, the chill, the cold stare, the cut direct, the dead cut, the fish-eye, the freeze, the frost, the go-by, the hairy eyeball, the ice

collitch
n A college; a university

alma mammy, brainery, coll, U, varsity

come
1 v To have an orgasm; ejaculate semen or secrete other sexual fluids
2 SEE **CUM**

blow off, come off, drop one's load, get it off, get one's nuts, get one's nuts cracked, get one's nuts off, get one's rocks, get one's rocks off, go off, pop one's cookies, shoot, shoot one's load, shoot one's wad, spunk, spurt

come again
sentence Please repeat what you said

how's that?, let's have it again, run it by again, says which, say what

come down a peg
v phr To be humiliated; stop behaving in a haughty manner

climb down, come off one's perch, crawl in a hole and pull it in after, eat crow, eat dirt, eat humble pie, eat shit, get off one's high horse, land with a dull thud, pull in one's horns, sing another tune, take off one's high hat, tuck one's tail

come off
1 v phr To occur; happen, as in "What's coming off here?"
2 SEE **COME**

come down, cook, go, go down, go on

come on strong
v phr To begin and proceed vigorously; succeed brilliantly

be on a roll, come on, come on like gangbusters, hit the jackpot, make out like a bandit, pour it on, ring the bell, set the world on fire, turn on the heat

come out

v phr To become an acknowledged homosexual

come out of the closet, debut

come unglued

v phr To go out of control; deteriorate to chaos, as in "I couldn't keep the situation from coming unglued"

come unstuck, come unwrapped, go on the rocks, go to the dogs, go to hell, go to pieces, go to pot, go to smash
☞ *The term is often used of a person who has a traumatic emotional crisis, as in "I'm afraid Ruth came unglued after the cat got killed."*

con

1 v To cheat; swindle; deceive

bamboozle, beat, bite, blind-pop, blind-side, bum, bunco, burn, chisel, clip, cold haul, cream, curve, deke, diddle, dipsy-doodle, do a number on, doodle, do out, do over, doublecross, euchre, fake out, fast-talk, fiddle, fleece, flimflam, four-flush, fox, frig, fuck, futz, give someone a line, give someone the business, gouge, gyp, gyppo, hand someone a lemon, have, hook, hornswoggle, hose, hustle, hype, jerk someone's chain, jerk someone's string, make a patsy of, milk, murphy, play for a sucker, play the dozens on, pluck, pull a fast one, pull someone's chain, pull someone's string, pull the wool over someone's eyes, rattle someone's chain, ream, rip off, roll, rook, rope, rope in, run a game on, run a number on, scam, screw, sell, sell a bill of goods, shake down, shuck, skin, skunk out of, slicker, smuck, snooker, stick, stiff, sting, sucker, take, take someone downtown, take someone for a ride, take someone into camp, take someone to the cleaners, throw someone a curve, throw the hooks into someone, trim, yentz
☞ *This term is very often followed by "out of," as in "I conned him out of a couple of new tires."*
☞ *The distinction between "con" and "fuck" in its*

metaphorical sense is sometimes hard to draw, and both terms should be considered; "con" also shares semantic territory with "snow," which should be considered.

2 SEE SCAM

con

n A convict; a jail or prison inmate

jailbird, lagger, loser, stir bird, vic, yardbird

con man

n phr A confidence man; a swindler

biter, bunco, bunco artist, bunco steerer, burn artist, burner, chiseler, clip artist, cold decker, con artist, crook, diddler, dipsy-doodle, double-crosser, fiddler, flammer, fleecer, flimflam man, flimflammer, four-flusher, gouger, grifter, gyp, gyp artist, hoser, hustler, jackleg, rooker, scammer, shark, sharp, sharper, sharp-ie, shuffler, shyster, skinner, slicker, stinger, two-timer, yentzer

cookie

n A person of either sex; an individual, as in "He's not the cookie I'd pick for that assignment"

apple, article, baby, bird, breed of cat, cats, character, citizen, clown, cluck, critter, cuss, customer, dish, duck, egg, face, fart, fish, gent, gink, guy, head, hoot, item, jasper, job, jobbie, joker, number, party, piece of cheese, specimen

cook up

v phr To devise; fabricate

fudge, hoke up, hype up, put together, whomp up, work up

cool

1 adj Going well; in good condition, as in "I told the host we thought the party was cool"

all there, A-OK, cooking, copacetic, ducky, fonky, funky, grad, groovy, having one's stuff wired, hitting on all six, hotsy-dandy, hotsy-totsy, hunky, hunky-dory, in good shape, in great shape, in kelter, in kilter, in town, in whack, mellow, neat, OK, okey-dokey, rosy, sharp, toast, together, up to scratch, up to snuff, up to the mark

2 *adj Aloof and uninvolved; deliberately disengaged; totally relaxed*

beat, blip, chill, cooled-out, down, far out, fresh, gone, groovy, heavy, hep, hip, ice, illen, loose, loose as a goose, looseygoosey, mellow, nervous, out, pretty scary, rat-fuck, turned on, way out, weird, wiggy, wild, zero cool

3 SEE **GREAT**

4 SEE **LAID-BACK**

cooler

1 *n A solitary-confinement cell*

bing, hole, icebox, iso, oven, sol

2 SEE **the SLAMMER**

cool it

v phr To moderate one's behavior; to calm oneself

back off, chill out, cool out, give it a rest, go easy, hang it easy, hang loose, hold one's horses, hold it, hold one's water, keep one's pants on, keep one's shirt on, not blow a fuse, not blow a gasket, not get one's balls in an uproar, play it cool, pull in one's ears, pull in one's horns, pull one's punches, simmer down, stay loose, take a chill spill, take it easy, take the heat off

cop

1 *n A police officer; a constable*

arm, azul, big John, blue, bluebelly, bluebird, blueboy, bluecoat, blue man, [Brit] bobby, bull, cinder bull, cinder dick, copper, county mounty, dick, Dogberry, elbow, finest, finger, flatfoot, flathead, flatty, flic, fly ball, fly bob, fly bull, fly cop, fly dick, fly mug, fuzz, fuzzy, gazer, gendarme, goms, gumboot, gumfoot, gumheel, gumshoe, harness bull, harness cop, harness dick, jake, John Law, lajara, the law, the Man, muzzler, nab, nabs, narc, narco, oink, orange crush, ossifer, paddy, [Brit] peeler, pig, rubber heel, sam, screw, shamus, shoe,

Smokey Bear, Smokey the Bear, Smoky, stick man, uncle, yard bull

☞ *This list does not discriminate the various sorts of law enforcement officers, and hence should be used carefully. Several items share semantic territory with "dick."*

2 SEE **BUST**
3 SEE **SCORE**

cop out
1 *v phr To evade; intentionally fail to cope or act*

back out, blow it off, blow off, bog, chicken out, flick it in, fold, punk out, punt, rat out, shake, shine, tap dance, throw in the sponge, throw in the towel, waffle, weasel out, worm out

2 SEE **BACK OUT**

the cops
n phr The police; law enforcers in general

the finest, the fuzz, the heat, the Man

☞ *More such terms may of course be made by making plural expressions with "the" of the terms under "cop."*

corn
1 *n Sentimentality; maudlin emotionalism*

corn on the cob, drool, flapdoodle, glop, goo, hearts and flowers, mush, schmaltz, slobber, slop, slush, sob stuff

2 *n Old-fashioned and sentimental music*

Mickey Mouse, razzmatazz, ricky-tick, rooty-toot

corny
adj Sentimental; banal; pathetic

beery, cornball, corn-fed, drippy, gloppy, gluey, glutinous, gooey, goopy, gummy, gushy, hicksville, icky, moony, mushy, off the cob, on the cob, ricky-tick, rinky-dink, sappy, schmaltzy, sloppy, slushy, soppy, soupy, squishy, sticky, teary

cough up
v phr To pay; hand over

ante up, come across with, come through with, cough over, dig down for, dig up, dish out, dish up, fork out, fork over, fork up, kick in, lay down, plank down, plunk down, pony out, pony up, shell, shell out

one couldn't care less
sentence One simply does not care; one is sublimely indifferent

one could care less, one doesn't give a damn, one doesn't give a shit, ishkabibble, it makes one no difference, it's no skin off one's ass, it's no skin off one's butt, it's no skin off one's nose, mox nix aus, one should worry, tough shit, what do you want from me

a country mile
n phr A long distance

far piece, from hell to breakfast, good way, long chalk, smart piece, way to hell and gone

cowboy
n A violent and reckless criminal; a thug

dropper, gorilla, hood, hoodlum, lobo, plug-ugly, ugly customer, yegg

☞ *These terms share semantic territory with "goon" and "hit man," which should also be considered.*

cow college
n phr An agricultural college thought to be of humble distinction

cow tech, East Jesus State, old Siwash, Siwash

crack
1 n A joke, as in "That was a pretty dumb crack"

gag, one-liner, rib-tickler, wisecrack

2 SEE **COKE**

a crack

n phr An attempt, as in "I'll have a crack at the job"

a bash, a belt, a cut, a fling, a go, a hack, a hit, a kick at the cat, a lick, a riffle, a rip, a ripple, a shot, a smack, a stab, a try, a whack, a whop

cracker

n A rural Southerner

Arky, clay eater, good old boy, hillbilly, Okie, peck, peckerwood, redneck, white trash, wood, woodchuck, woolhat

crack up

v phr To suffer an emotional or mental breakdown; go into hysteria, depression, etc

blow one's cork, blow one's mind, blow one's stack, blow one's top, chase butterflies, crack, flip, flip one's lid, flip one's wig, freak out, go ape, go balmy, go bananas, go batty, go crackers, go off one's bean, go off one's chump, go off one's head, go off one's nut, go off one's rocker, go off the deep end, go off the track, go off the trolley, go out of one's gourd, go out of one's skull, go out of one's tree, go to pieces, lose one's marbles, slip a cog, wig out

☞ *These terms may be greatly multiplied by using "go" with many of the other terms for "crazy"; "schiz out" should also be considered.*

crap

1 *n Anything of shoddy quality; rubbish; trash*

bilge, borax, cruft, dogshit, doodle, dreck, El Cheapo, garbage, gook, junk, khazeray, a lemon, Mickey Mouse, piece of crap, piece of shit, poot, rinky-dink, rummage, schlock, shit, sleaze, spinach, tripe, truck, unkjay

2 SEE **BULLSHIT**
3 SEE **SHIT**

crash

1 *v To fail; suffer a disaster; become inoperative, as in "I was doing fine until the computer crashed"*

crash and burn, fry, go belly up, go down, go down in flames, go south, melt down, shut down

2 *n A disaster; a debacle, as in "His wife's leaving him precipitated an emotional crash"*

blowup, bust, cat's astrophe, crack-up, meltdown, smash, smashup, wash-up

3 SEE **SNOOZE**

crazy

1 *adj Insane; demented*

ape, apeshit, [Brit] around the bend, balmy, bananas, barmy, bats, batty, bent, [Brit] bonkers, bonzo, buggy, bughouse, bugs, bugsy, cockamamie, cockeyed, crack-brained, cracked, [Brit] crackers, crackpot, crackpotty, crazy as a bedbug, crazy as a coot, crazy as a loon, crazy as catshit, cuckoo, daffy, dick-brained, ding-dong, dippy, dopey, dotty, dumdum, a few cards short of a full deck, food for squirrels, fruitcakey, fruity, funny, ga-ga, gonzo, Gonzo City, goofy, goo-goo, half-baked, half there, having a screw loose, haywire, kooky, loco, loony, loony-tune, loopy, loose in the bean, loose in the upper story, lunch, lunching, lunchy, [Brit] mental, meshugah, nerts, nertsy, nobody home, not all there, not tightly wrapped, nuts, nutso, nutsy, nutty, nutty as a fruitcake, off, off one's bird, off one's chump, off one's head, off one's noodle, off one's nut, off one's onion, off one's rocker, off the wall, off one's trolley, out of one's gourd, out of one's head, out of one's skull, out of one's tree, out to lunch, pixilated, potty, psycho, queer, queer in the head, [Brit] round the bend, rowing with one oar in the water, rum-dum, sappy, scatty, schizo, schizoid, schizy, screwball, screwy, sick, sick in the head, sicko, sicksicksick, spaced out, squirrely, tetched, tetched in the head, tetchy, tomfool, up the wall, wacko, wacky, weird, wild-ass

2 SEE **GREAT**

creepy
1 *adj Frightening;*
terrifying

furry, hairy, scary, shivery

2 SEE **WEIRD**

croak
v To die, as in "One
minute she was
sitting there talking
to us, the next
minute she croaked"

belly up, bite the dust, bow out, buy it, buy the farm, buy the ranch, cash in one's checks, cash in one's chips, check out, conk off, conk out, cop it, exit, farm, give out, give up the ghost, go belly up, go home feet first, go home in a box, go to glory, go west, kick in, kick off, kick the bucket, pass out, peg out, pop off, push up daisies, slip one's cable, turn up one's toes

crooked dice
n phr Dice that
have been altered so
as not to roll true to
the mathematical
odds

bevels, bricks, busters, bust-outs, despatchers, door pops, flat passers, flats, fullams, hits, horses, low-fullams, misses, odds splitter, passers, phonies, pigs, repeaters, rollers, tats, uphills
☞ *The terms are mostly specific to a certain kind of alteration, and not generic "crooked dice."*

crowd
v phr To press or
importune

get on someone's back, get on someone's case, lean on, press, push, put the heat on, put the screws to, put the squeeze on

cruise
v To go about seeking sexual encounters, esp in bars or along streets

cat around, trade, troll

crummy
adj Of inferior quality; shoddy

awful, badass, bash, beastly, bum, bush-league, cheap, cheesy, cotton-pickin', crappy, cruddy, crumbun, dinky, dipshit, dog-ass, doggo, doggy, dud, for the birds, from hunger, gnarly, godawful, gross, grungy, half-assed, half-baked, hanky-pank, junk, junky, lousy, low-down, low-rent, low-ride, mangy, measly, Mickey Mouse, mouldy, no-account, no-good, piss, piss-poor, pissy, punk, putrid, raggedy-ass, raggedy-pants, rank, rat-ass, ratty, raunchy, rinky-dink, rotten, sad, scanky, schlock, schlocky, [esp Brit] scruffy, shitty, stinking, stinko, tacky, tatty, tickytacky, tinhorn, trashy, two-bit, ungodly, X-double-minus, yucky

cum
n Semen

come, cream, gism, goo, hockey, jism, jizz, juice, love juice, man oil, scum, spunk

cunt
n The vulva; the vagina

bearded clam, beaver, booty, box, cake, cat, chink, cho-cha, chooch, clam, cooch, couze, crack, cunny, doodle, [Brit] fanny, furburger, fur pie, futy, gash, gig, giggy, ginch, hair pie, hole, honeypot, hotbox, jam, jelly, jelly-roll, man-hole, meat, muff, nooky, notch, pit, poontang, pussy, quim, slit, slot, snatch, squirrel, stuff, trim, tuna, tuna fish, twat
☞ *"Dingbat," "dingus," "doodad," "dofunny," "dojigger," "thingy," or any other of the numerous terms for something one does not know the name of or*

does not wish to name may be used as a euphemism for vulva.

☞ *"Vulva, vagina" is one of the most prolific of slang concepts. Farmer and Henley's* Slang and Its Analogues *(1888–1904) lists about 700 terms under the heading "the monosyllable."*

cunt-lapper
n A person who does cunnilingus

clit-licker, muff-diver

curtains
n Death; disaster; the bitter end

bye-bye, the end of the line, hips, last roundup, lights out, the payoff, taps

cut
1 v To choose not to attend a class, examination, etc, as in "She decided to cut Econ that day"

bag, blitz, flush, shine, skip

2 v To treat with deliberate hauteur; snub

brush, brush off, chill, cold-shoulder, cut dead, freeze, freeze out, give the beady eye, give the brush, give the brush-off, give the chill, give the cold shoulder, give the fish-eye, give the fluff, give the go-by, give the hairy eyeball, high-hat, ice, ice out, kiss off, put on the frost, put on the high hat, put the chill on, put the freeze on, snoot, turn the cold shoulder

3 SEE **BITE**
4 SEE **CRACK**
5 SEE **DIVVY**
6 SEE **SPLIT**

cut a deal

v phr To make or conclude an arrangement; transact an agreement

crack a deal, deal, [Brit] do a deal, make a deal

cut no ice

v phr To have no influence or effect; make no difference

butter no parsnips, cut no shit, cut no smoke, make no diff, make no never-mind, not make a diff of bitterence

cut one's own throat

v phr To ruin or injure oneself, usu unintentionally, as in "A politician who argues in favor of legalizing drugs is just cutting his or her own throat"

commit suicide, cut oneself off at the knees, shoot oneself in the foot, snatch defeat from the jaws of victory

D

the damage

n A customer's bill or check, as in "You bought the theater tickets, so let me pay the damage at the restaurant"

the ante, the bad news, the beef, the bite, the grunt, the knock, the score, the tab, the tariff

damn

adj Cursed; accursed; wretched, as in "Give me the damn thing and I'll try to make it work"

all-fired, blame, blamed, blanked, blankety, blankety-blank, blasted, bleeding, bleep, bleeping, blessed, blinkety, blinkety-blink, blinking, [Brit] bloody, blooming, consarned, cotton-pickin', cussed, dadblame, dadblamed, dadblasted, dadburned, daddratted, dadgasted, dadgum, dadgummed, dagnabbed, damnationed, damned, dang, danged, darn, darned, dashed, dern, derned, deuce, diddle-damn, diddle-damned, dingbusted, dinged, dingswizzled, doggone, doggoned, double-clutching, doubledamned, dratted, effing, flipping, forking, frapping, freaking, frigging, frogging, fucking, gee-dee, godawful, goddamn, goddamned, goddarn, goddarned, goldamn, goldang, goldanged, goldarn, goldarned, goldern, goshawful, goshdamn, goshdamned, goshdang, goshdarn, goshdarned, goshdern, goshderned, goshganded, hell-fired, mother, motherfucking, mothering, pesky, [Brit] ruddy, stinking

☞ *These terms represent the most numerous and systematic euphemisms in slang. Damning someone's soul to hell, or asking God to do that, must never be uttered outright, perhaps for fear it might actually take place.*

dead to rights
adv phr With no possibility of escape or evasion; in flagrante delicto

cold, redhanded, with a smoking gun, with one's hand in the cookie jar, with one's hand in the till, with one's pants down, with the goods, with the merchandise

dealer
n A person who peddles drugs

bagman, big man, broker, 'cainer, candy man, connection, connector, cop man, cowboy, dope booster, dope peddler, dope pimp, dope runner, feed and grain man, fixer, good-time man, grog merchant, holder, hype, ice cream man, jobber, juggler, junker, junk peddler, missionary, mother, ounce man, peddler, push, pusher, righteous dealer, swing man, tambourine man, travel agent, viper

deck
1 n A package or portion of narcotics

bag, bale of hay, balloon, bar, big hog, bindle, bird's eye, biz, block box, bottle, brick, can, cap, card, cargo cube, deuce, deuce bag, dime bag, elbow, feed bag, finger, foil, full moon, gang, gram, half, half bundle, half load, half piece, hunk, jug, kee, keg, kite, lid, load, long, match, matchbox, matchhead, moon, nickel, nickel bag, O, Ohio bag, O Z, paper, piece, pillow, quarter bag, sack, short, short piece, spoon, tin, z

2 v To knock someone down, esp with the fist

belt over, bowl over, down, drop, flatten, floor, lay flat, lay out, lay out in lavender

desk jockey

n phr An office worker

paperweight, pencil driver, pencil pusher, pencil shover, pen pusher

dick

1 n A detective

bloodhound, D, deek, eagle-eye, eye, flatfoot, flattie, fuzz, gazer, gumshoe, gumshoe man, hawkshaw, house dick, narc, op, private eye, rubber-heel, Sherlock, Sherlock Holmes, sleuthhound, tec, undercover man

☞ *The list includes private detectives and specialized agents as well as police detectives. Several items share semantic territory with "cop."*

2 SEE COCK

dig

1 v To understand; comprehend

ace in, be with it, catch on, collar the jive, colly, flash on, get, get it straight, get the drift, get the hang of, get the idea, get the message, get the picture, get wise, get with it, grok, have it down, have it down pat, have it pegged, latch on, make, nail, pick up on, read, savvy, see where one is coming from, suss out, [Brit] tumble to, twig

2 v To like; admire; prefer

eat up, get a bang out of, get a boot out of, get a charge out of, get a kick out of, get a lift out of, get down with, get off on, go for, groove, groove on, wig

dirt

n Gossip; intimate or scandalous intelligence

buzz, D, jazz, juicy morsel, the latest, load of dirt, the lowdown, scuttlebutt, tittle-tattle

dirty

1 adj Dishonest; shady, as in "That was a dirty trick"

below the belt, crooked, crummy, dirty pool, foul, not cricket, raw, salty, shabby, sleazy

2 *adj Lewd; obscene*

blue, filthy, gamy, gully-low, hot, juicy, naughty, off-color, off-tone, racy, raunchy, raw, ripe, rough, spicy, steamy, X-rated

3 *adj Possessing narcotics*

carrying, holding

4 SEE **HOOKED**

5 SEE **LOADED**

dirty tricks

n phr Dishonest or underhanded practices; malicious tactics

dirty pool, dirty work, funny business, jiggery-pokery, monkey business, rough stuff, shady business, skullduggery

disc jockey

n phr A radio performer who plays and comments on phonograph records; also, the person who plays records at a discotheque

dee-jay, DJ, jock, pancake turner

dish

n A particularly attractive woman, esp one who is sexually attractive

angel, angelcake, angelface, babe, bathing beauty, beaut, beauty queen, beddy, [Brit] bird, bit of jam, broad, bunny, cack, cake, centerfold, charmer, cheesecake, chick, chiquita, cover girl, crack, [Brit] crumpet, cuddle-bunny, cupcake, cute chick, cutie, cutie-pants, cutie-pie, date bait, dazzler, dog, doll, dollface, dolly, dose, dreamboat, dream girl, eating pussy, eatin' stuff, eyeful, fetcher, fine hammer, flavor, fox, frail eel, frail job, furburger, fur pie, glamor girl, glamor puss, good-looker, hammer, head, honey, hot dish, hot number, hot patootie, hot sketch, knockout, looker, lovely, lulu, mink, morsel, nifty number, oomph girl, package, patootie, peach, peacharooney, peacherino, pin-up, pin-up girl, poppet, poundcake, quail, raving beauty, sex bunny, sex goddess, sex job, sex kitten, sex pot, sex queen, slash, slick chick, snapper, snugette, snuggy, stallion, stone fox, stunner, sweet patootie, table grade, ten, tomato

☞ *The semantic boundaries between "dish," "broad," and "floozy" are not easy to set. All three terms should be considered.*

ditsy
adj Silly; scatterbrained

addled, airbrained, airheaded, brack-brained, daffy, dippy, dipsy, dizzy, dopey, fluffheaded, ga-ga, giddy, goofy, goo-goo, kooky, loopy, potty, rattlebrained, scatty, zerking

ditz
n A silly person; a scatterbrain

addlebrain, addlehead, addlepate, airbrain, airhead, diddlehead, dizzy Lizzie, dumb Dora, fluffhead, giddy-brain, giddy Gertie, giddyhead, giddypate, jingle-brains, muddlehead, ninny, rattlebrain, Silly Billy, spoony

☞ *"Ditz" shares some semantic territory with "dope." The distinction is that one feels affection for a ditz and primarily contempt for a dope.*

dive
n Any disgusting or disreputable place, esp a cheap bar, nightclub, lodging house, or dance hall

barrel house, booze joint, boozer, boozery, bottleshop, crib, doggery, dramshop, dump, firetrap, gargle factory, gin dive, gin mill, grogshop, hellhole, hole, honky-tonk, hooch house, joint, juice-joint, layout, place, pot-house, rathole, shebang, spot, waterhole, watering hole, watering place

divvy

v To divide and share out receipts, profits, loot, etc

cut, cut the take, cut up, cut up the jackpots, cut up the melon, cut up the pie, cut up the pipes, cut up the touches, divvy out, divvy up, piece up, razor

do

1 *v To take or inject narcotics*

do up, slam, use

2 SEE **SHIT**

3 SEE **WINGDING**

doctor

v To alter or tamper with something dishonestly

do creative accounting, doctor up, fiddle, fiddle with, fuck with, fudge, juggle, juggle with, mess with

does a bear shit in the woods

question That was a stupid question; isn't the answer very obvious, as in "Do I feel rotten about losing my job? Does a bear shit in the woods?"

does a wooden horse have a hickory dick, does Howdy-Doody have wooden balls, is the pope Catholic, is the pope Polish

doll

1 *n Any notably decent, pleasant, generous person*

ace, fuzzy one, honey, light, living doll, Mr Nice Guy, one-way guy, prince, pussycat, sugar pants, sweetheart, sweetie

2 *n A capsule of a barbiturate drug*

amy, backward, bank bandit, barb, black beauty, black molly, blockbuster, blue, blunt, brain tickler, candy, Christmas roll, Christmas tree, courage pill, dolly, downer, gangster pill, GB, goofball, goofer, gorilla pill, green dragon, joy pellet, King Kong, King Kong pill, mighty Joe Young, nebbie, nemish, nemmie, nimby, peanut, pill, purple heart, Red, Red Devil, sleeper, softball, stum, stumbler, stupper, thrill pill, tooie, toole, truck driver, yellow jacket

☞ *The great number of slang terms for narcotics probably reflects both a need for coded reference to an illegal substance and a desire to be chic and up-to-date, in addition to the need to distinguish varieties.*

doll up
v phr To dress fancily and in one's best clothes

deck out, deck up, dog out, dog up, doll out, dress to kill, dress to the nines, dress to the teeth, dress up, dude up, dud up, fancy up, fig out, fig up, get up, gussy up, prank, primp, prink, put on one's best bib and tucker, put on one's glad rags, put on one's Sunday clothes, put on one's Sunday-go-to-meeting clothes, put on the dog, put on the style, rag out, rag up, rig out, rig up, ritz up, slick up, snazz up, spiff up, spruce up, swank it, swank up, [Brit] tart up, titivate, tog out, tog up, trick out, trick up

donnybrook
n A riotous scene, esp a general brawl

battle royal, brannigan, ding-dong, foofooraw, gin, hit-fest, hoedown, hoo-ha, kick-up, knock-down-drag-out, rhubarb, riot, row, row-de-dow, ruckus, ruction, rumble, rumpus, shemozzle, shindy, slugfest

☞ *Consider "free-for-all" also, and see the note there.*

dope
1 n A stupid or foolish person; an idiot

addlebrain, airbrain, airhead, applehead, bakehead, balloonhead, bananahead, basket case, beefwit, beetlebrain, birdbrain, blithering idiot, blockhead, blubberbrain, blubberhead, bohunk, bonehead, boob, booby, bozo, brack-brain, bubble-brain, bubblehead, buckethead, bulb, bunhead, cabbagehead, cheesehead, chickenhead, chowderhead, chucklehead, chump, clod, cluck, cluckhead, clunk, clunkhead, cokehead, coot, cretinoid, deadhead, dim bulb, dimwit, dingbat, dingding, ding-dong, dip, dipshit, dittybop, dodo, doo-doo head, dough-head, drop case, drop kick, drop shot, dufus, dufus-ass, dumbard, dumb bastard, dumbbell, dumb bunny, dumb cluck, dumb dodo, dumb Dora, dumb fuck, dumbhead, dumb jerk, dumbkopf, dumbo, dumb ox, dumbshit, dumdum, dummy, farmer, fart blossom, fatbrain, fathead, feeb, feeblo, flake, flathead, flub, flubdub, flub-up, four-letter man, gearbox, gearhead, gnatbrain, goney, goof, goofball, goofer, goofus, goofy, gooney, goop, gump, hummer, ivory-dome, jackass, jarhead, jellybean, jiggins, juggins, jughead, kluck, klutz, knothead, knucklehead, lamebrain, lardhead, lip mover, loogan, lummox, lump, lunch box, lunk, lunkhead, marble-dome, meatball, meathead, melonhead, Mickey Mouse, modoc, mope, mouthbreather, mullethead, musclehead, mush-head, mutt, mutthead, muttonhead, nincompoop, ninny, nitwit, noddy, noodle, noodlehead, nougat, numbhead, numbskull, oofus, peabrain, peahead, pinhead, pod person, pointed head, pointhead, pointy-head, poop, potatohead, puddinghead, pumpkinhead, putty-head, reject, retard, retardo, ring-ding, rockhead, rum-dum, sap, saphead, sapperoo, sappo, sausage, schlemiel, schlep, schloomp, schmegeggy, schmendrick, schmo, semolia, shit-for-brains, shovelhead, simp, slow coach, spastic, spazz, stupe, stupido, tackhead, tard, thickbrain, thickhead, thicko, thickskull, thickwit, troll, turkey, twimble, vegetable, watermelonhead, woodenhead, woodhead, yahoo, yap, yo-yo, zerk, zombie

☞ *"Dope" shares some semantic territory with "ditz." The distinction is that one feels primarily contempt for a dope, but some affection for a ditz.*

2 *n Any narcotic drug*

bang, bingle, birdie powder, birdie stuff, blanks, candy, caronotics, cotics, dizzy-wizzy, dreams, dry booze, dry grog, dummy, easing powder, fairy powder, feed, flea powder, fun medicine, ganger, garbage, geez, geezer, God's medicine, goods, gosneaks, grog, happy dust, happy flakes, happy powder, happy stuff, hash, heesh, hokus, hot stuff, ice cream, Lady White, leather dew, lemon, lemonade, locus, mahoska, merchandise, mojo, mooch, needle candy, nocks, nose candy, pot, powdered joy, reefer, shit, smoke, stuff, turkey

3 SEE **POOP**

dope den

n phr A place or party where marijuana is smoked

balloon room, ballroom, beat pad, blasting party, blast party, club, crash pad, dopatorium, doperie, pot

do the Dutch

v phr To commit suicide

do the Dutch act, take a D

double

n A person or thing that strongly or exactly resembles another; a duplicate

clone, dead ringer, living picture, look-alike, ringer, spit and image, spitting image

double cross

n phr A betrayal or cheating of one's own colleagues; an act of treachery and deceit

cross, cross-up, dipsy-doodle, double deal, double shuffle, double-time, double X, fast shuffle, sell-out, two-time, Wichita, XX

double-talk

n Language that cannot be understood, esp overly technical jargon

double Dutch, gobbledygook, Greek, jibber-jabber, monkey talk, mumbo-jumbo

dough

n Money; currency; wealth

beans, berries, billies, bit of change, bone, boodle, [chiefly Brit] brass, bread, bucks, cabbage, change, chips, clams, coin, coin of the realm, cold cash, cush, dib, dibs, dinero, do-re-mi, doubloons, ducats, feed, the filthy, filthy lucre, folding, folding cabbage, folding green, folding lettuce, folding money, frogskin, gee, geets, geetus, gelt, gold, gravy, green, greenbacks, green folding, green money, green stuff, happy-cabbage, hard cash, hunk of change, hunk of jack, jack, kale, kale-seed, kopecks, lean green, lettuce, long green, loot, lucre, mazuma, mean green, mezonny, mon, moo, moolah, mopus, the necessary, the needful, nuggets, ooftish, oofus, ooks, ookus, palm oil, pesos, piece of change, piece of jack, poke, potatoes, the ready, rivets, salve, scratch, shekels, simoleons, skins, spondulics, the stuff, sugar, tin, wampum, wherewithal, the wherewithal, whip-out

down

1 adj Depressed; melancholy

blah, blue, bummed, bummed out, down, down in the dumps, down in the mouth, dumpish, in a funk, in the doldrums, in the dumps, low-down, mopey, mopish, singing the blues

2 SEE **COOL**
3 SEE **GREAT**

drag

1 *n A dull, boring person*   crashing bore, deadass, deadfanny, deadneck, dead one, drip, dull tool, flat tire, headache, jerk, pain in the ass, pain in the neck, pill, wet blanket

2 SEE **BUTT**
3 SEE **CLOUT**
4 SEE **TOKE**

duck-squeezer

n An environmentalist; a conservationist   eagle freak, ecofreak, econut, greenie, tree-hugger, web-foot

dude

1 *n A dapper man, esp one who is ostentatiously dressed; a dandy*   alligator, Beau Brummel, buck, cake-eater, cat, city slicker, clothes horse, drugstore cowboy, fancy Dan, fancypants, fashion plate, flash-sport, gay-cat, hard-legs, hepcat, hotshot, jazz-bo, la-de-da, lady-killer, plate, sharpie, sheik, slicker, smooth article, smoothie, sport, stud, swell

2 SEE **GUY**
3 SEE **LADIES' MAN**

duffer

n A mediocre or downright poor performer, athlete, etc   dub, hacker, muffer, scrub, second-rater

dullsville

adj Boring; tedious   beige, blah, boh-ring, dead, deadsville, dragass, draggy, dragsville, dull as dishwater, hicksville, ho-hum, oofless, yawny

dumb

adj Stupid; mentally sluggish

beanheaded, beef-witted, beetleheaded, blockheaded, blubberbrained, blubberheaded, blunderheaded, blunt-witted, boneheaded, boobish, brainless, cabbage-headed, chowderheaded, chuckleheaded, clodpated, [Brit] clottish, clunkish, clunky, cretinoid, dead between the ears, dead from the neck up, dense, dim, dim-witted, dingy, dizzy, doodle-brained, dopey, dorky, down a quart, dufus, dufus-assed, dumb as a box of rocks, dumbbell, dumb-cluck, dumbheaded, dum-dum, dunderheaded, fatbrained, fatheaded, fat-witted, feather-brained, feather-headed, feeble in the head, fizz, flatheaded, flubdubbed, fool-headed, goofy, gormless, gunga, half-assed, half-baked, half-boiled, half-brained, half-there, jingle-brained, [Brit] joltheaded, jugheaded, klutzish, klutzy, knuckleheaded, lackbrained, lackwitted, lame, lamebrained, light upstairs, lumpish, lunch, lunching, lunchy, lunkheaded, lunky, meatheaded, missing some marbles, muddle-headed, mulletheaded, mushheaded, muttheaded, mutton-headed, nitwitted, not all there, not right bright, numb, numb-brained, numbheaded, numbskulled, ossified, peabrained, peaheaded, peanut-brained, pie-faced, pinheaded, pointy-headed, puddingheaded, pumpkin-headed, rum-dum, rummy, sapheaded, sappy, schleppy, scramble-brained, shady, shallow-brained, shallow-pated, shallow-witted, shitheaded, short-witted, soft, softheaded, soft in the head, sorry-ass, spastic, spazz, spazzy, swift, thick, thick-headed, thickskulled, thick-witted, thin in the upper crust, three bricks shy of a load, weak in the head, weak in the upper story, without all one's oars in the water, without all one's switches on, without brain one, with rocks in the head, woodenheaded

dump
1 *n Any unpleasant place; a repulsive venue*
2 SEE **DIVE**

firetrap, hellhole, hole, joint, rathole, shithole, shithouse

dust bunny
n phr A tuft of dust that accumulates under beds, tables, etc

beggar's velvet, dust kitty, ghost turd, house moss, kitten, slut's wool

Dutch rub
n phr The trick or torment of holding someone's head and rubbing very hard and painfully at a small area of scalp with the fist

barbershop quartet, noogie

dyke
n A lesbian

Amy-John, boondagger, bull, bulldagger, bulldyke, bulldyker, butch, diesel-dyke, fairy lady, fem, femme, lesbo, lez, lezzie, man, Mary, top sergeant
☞ *No distinction is made in this list between active and passive, aggressive and "feminine" lesbians.*

eager beaver
n phr An active, ambitious person

ball of fire, big-time operator, buster, bustler, cage rattler, fireball, flamer, go-getter, heller, holy terror, hot shot, human dynamo, hummer hustler, live wire, operator, piss-cutter, pisser, pistol, powerhouse, self-starter, spark plug, springbutt, stemwinder, striker, take-charge guy, young Turk

eagle day
n phr Pay day

when the eagle flies, when the eagle shits

easy as pie
adj phr Very easy

duck-soup, easy as can be, easy as could be, easy as falling off a log, easy as hell, easy as rolling off a log, like a turkey-shoot, like falling off a log, like shooting fish in a barrel, like stealing candy from a baby, no sweat, simple as ABC, soft

eat dirt
v phr To accept rebuke or harassment meekly; swallow one's pride, as in "Marine Corps recruits soon learn to eat dirt"

eat it, eat shit, lump it, pocket one's pride, take it, take shit

eat high on the hog

v phr *To live well and happily; prosper, as in "Once we win the lottery, we'll eat high on the hog"*

be fat dumb and happy, be in clover, be in fat city, be in hog heaven, be like pigs in shit, be sitting pretty, be up tight, eat high off the hog, eat high on the joint, have egg in one's beer, have it good, have it made, have the world by the balls, have the world by the curlies, have the world by the nuts, have the world by the short hairs, live high on the hog, live off the tit, piss on ice, shit in high cotton, sit fat, sit in the catbird seat, sit pretty

eat up

1 *v phr* *To accept; believe, esp something a bit dubious*

buy, eat, fall for, gobble up, stand still for, swallow

2 SEE **FLIP**

egghead

n *An intellectual; a thinker*

brain, conehead, conk-buster, double-dome, egg, high-brow, ivory-dome, longhair, pointed head, pointhead, pointy-head

excess baggage

n phr *A person or thing regarded as unnecessary and likely to impede*

[esp Brit] odd man out, one too many, square peg, third wheel

excuse me all to hell

sentence *I apol-ogize; please forgive me*

pardon me all to hell, pardon me for living
☞ *Always used ironically, when one believes an at-tack or accusation is unjustified.*

fall
v To be arrested; be imprisoned

break into jail, drop, fall out, take a fall, trip, tumble

falsies
n A pair of pads worn to give the appearance of large breasts

gay deceivers, props

fan
n A devotee or enthusiast, esp of a sport, team, etc

aficionado, booster, buff, bug, fiend, freak, groupie, hondo, junkie, nut, rooter

fart
1 v To expel gas from the anus; flatulate

break wind, buck snort, cut a fart, cut the cheese, lay a fart, lay one, let a fart, let wind

2 SEE **COOKIE**
3 SEE **GUY**
4 SEE **ZILCH**

a fat chance
n phr No chance at all

a Chinaman's chance, a snowball's chance in hell, not an earthly chance, not a prayer

fat city
n phr An ideal situation; paradise

cloud nine, cloud seven, Fiddler's Green, hog heaven, pig heaven

fatty
n An obese person

biggie, blimp, blubberpot, butterball, chub, chubbette, Crisco, elephant, fat, fat-ass, fat-guts, fats, fatso, fat stuff, five-by-five, heavyweight, hippo, jelly-belly, jumbo, lard-ass, lard-bucket, plumpie, porky, pudge, pudgy-wudgy, pus-gut, pustle-gut, tub, tubby, tub of guts, tub of lard, walrus, whale

fed-up
adj Satiated; surfeited

brassed off, browned off, crammed, fed to the gills, fed to the teeth, full up, have a bellyful, have a snootful, sick of, stuffed, turned off, up to here

a feed
n phr food

eats, grub, a hot, spread

feel
v To touch or caress sexually; fondle, as in "She slapped him hard when he felt her"

cop a feel, feel up, grope, handle, honk, mouse, paw, pet, play grab-ass, [Brit] play slap and tickle, rub

feisty
adj Truculent; irascible

cantankerous, crabby, crusty, cussed, dukes-up, fire-eating, grouchy, hardnosed, huffish, huffy, mean, miffy, ornery, salty, scrappy, [Brit] shirty, snarky, soreheaded, tetchy

figure
v To make sense; be plausible and reasonable, as in "It just doesn't figure that she would leave town"

compute, hang together, hold together, hold up, hold water, stack up, wash

fill someone in
v phr To inform; instruct, esp beforehand

brief, bring up to speed, clue, clue in, give the dope, give the info, give the lowdown, give the poop, give the scoop, keep posted, lay on, let in on, poop up, post, put in the picture, put someone wise, slip the info, smarten, smarten up, wise up

filthy with
adj phr Having much of; much endowed with, as in "She's filthy with talent"

loaded with, stinking with, up to here with, up to the ass with, up to the eyeballs with

fin
n A five-dollar bill; five dollars, as in "Lend me a fin till payday"

finiff, fiver, five-spot

fingerfuck
v To insert a finger into the vulva

diddle, finger, frig, play stink-finger, play stinky-pink, play stinky-pinky

finished

adj Ruined, esp occupationally; no longer able to function or compete

canned, dead, deep sixed, done for, had it, kaput, kicked out, out in the cold, out of it, out on one's ass, out on one's ear, sent to the showers, shot down
☞ *This list may be extended by using the participial form of verbs under "fire."*
☞ *These terms share semantic territory with "kaput," which should also be considered.*

fink

1 *n A traitor to one's race, class, sex, etc, as in "We elected him to represent us, and he turned out to be a fink"*
2 SEE **ASSHOLE**
3 SEE **SCAB**
4 SEE **SNITCH**

[all black] Afro-Saxon, Aunt Jane, Aunt Sally, fade, handkerchief-head, h n, house nigger, Mister Tom, Oreo, Tom, Uncle Tom; [both Native American] apple, Uncle Tomahawk; [Latino] Tio Taco; [sex] Aunt Tom

fire

v To discharge from a job; dismiss, as in "I was fired for coming in late every day for a month"

axe, bag, boot, bounce, bump, can, drop, give someone his (or her) running shoes, give someone his (or her) walking papers, give someone his (or her) walking ticket, give the axe, give the boot, give the bum's rush, give the chop, give the door, give the gate, give the hook, give the kissoff, give the old heave-ho, give the pink slip, [chiefly Brit] give the sack, kick, kiss off, pay off, pink-slip, [chiefly Brit] sack, send to the showers, show someone the door, show the gate, tie a can to, toss out

fish or cut bait
sentence Do one thing or another, but stop dithering; take action

get your finger out of your ass, piss or get off the pot, shit or get off the pot

a fix
1 *n phr A dose or injection of a narcotic*

bag, ball, bang, bing, blast, cushion, do-up, fix-up, goof-ball, hit, hype, jab, joy pop, joy prick, keek, knife in the arm, line, line shot, mainline, muscle, ping in the wing, ping-wing, pin shot, pop, prod, prop, set, short order, shot, skin pop, skin pump, ski-trip, tab, taste

☞ *This list does not distinguish among the various kinds of dose or method of dosage.*

2 *n phr A situation; a state of affairs, esp a tricky one, as in "Ollie certainly got us into quite a fix"*

a how-de-do, a how-do-you-do, a kettle of fish

fix someone
v phr To punish, esp in a spirit of retaliation, as in "He swore he'd fix her for sabotaging his project"

attend to, come down on, crack down on, do for, finish, fix someone's hash, fix someone's wagon, give it to someone in the neck, give someone the business, give someone the works, jump all over, let someone have it, lower the boom on, make it hot for, settle someone's hash, skin alive, sock it to, stick it to, take care of, wipe out, wreck

☞ *These terms share semantic territory with "clobber," which should also be considered.*

fix up
v phr To set in order

do up, neaten up, police up, red up, set to rights, [esp Brit] sort out

flack

1 *n Advertising or promotion; blatant publicity, as in "Most campaign information is little more than flack"*

bally, ballyhoo, buildup, bunk, crap, eyewash, flackery, flak, hoke, hokey-pokey, hokum, hoopla, hornblowing, hot air, hype, jive, moonshine, pitch, plugging, PR, promo, pub, puff, puffery, song and dance, spiel, whoopla

2 *n A publicity person or press agent*

drum-beater, flacker, gasman, hype artist, hyper, puff artist, shill, space bandit, tout

flak

1 *n Trouble; fuss; agitation*

botheration, fireworks, [esp Brit] flap, grief, heat, holly-golly, hoopla, how-de-do, pucker, racket, rhubarb, ruckus, rumpus, [Brit] shemozzle, static, stew, stink, tizzy, to-do

2 *n Severe criticism; angry blame*

agony, flack, grief, heat, static

flaky

adj Eccentric; unconventional, as in "My flaky uncle likes to do his gardening in the nude"

birdy, cracked, cranky, flake, funny, goofus, goofy, half-cracked, half-nuts, haywire, kinky, loopy, nutty, pix-ilated, queer, screwy, sproutsy, squirrely, wacked, wacko, wacky, weird, zerking

flat-out

1 *adv Unrestrained-ly; without reservation, as in "She flat-out told him to go away"*

all-out, all the way, one's ass off, ass over tincups, balls-out, balls to the wall, one's brains out, one's buns off, but good, clear to hell, for all one's worth, forty ways to Sunday, from hell to breakfast, from soup to nuts, from the ground up, full blast, hammer down, one's head off, head over heels, hell-bent-for-leather, hell-for-leather, hell-to-split, in spades, knock-down-drag-out, lickety-cut, lickety-split, like a dose of salts, like shit through a tin horn, six ways to Sunday, something awful, something fierce, till one is blue in the face, to a fare-thee-well, to beat the band, to beat the Dutch, to hell, to hell and gone, to the max, the whole hog, the whole nine yards, wide open

2 SEE **LICKETY-SPLIT**

flip

1 *v To respond enthusiastically; feel great excitement and pleasure, as in "Very few readers flipped over his first book"*

be bugs about, be ga-ga over, be turned on, eat up, flip out, freak, freak out, get a bang out of, get a rush out of, get high on, go ape over, go ape-shit over, go bananas over, gobble up, go for, go nuts over, go overboard for, rave about, wig, wig out

☞ *Many of these terms coincide with those for the effects of narcotics and for the onset of insanity.*

2 SEE **FREAK OUT**

the flip side

n phr The opposite side of a question, issue, matter, etc, as in "But the flip side is that such freedom becomes anarchy"

the B-side, the other side of the coin, the other side of the picture

floor it

1 *v phr To drive at full speed*

go flat-out, goose it, nail it, put the hammer down, put the pedal to the metal

2 SEE **BARREL**

floozy

1 *n A sexually promiscuous woman*

alley cat, bag, baggage, bar-girl, B-girl, bike, bimbo, broad, bum, chippy, cooz, demi-rep, dirtyleg, easy lay, easy make, easy ride, fast chick, fish, fox, gash, grassback, low rent, nice girl, nympho, piece, piece of ass, piece of tail, pig, pleaser, punchboard, push, pushover, puta, quickie, quick push, quiff, roundheel, roundheels, sex job, shack, shack job, shackup, snake, sweat hog, swinger, town bike, town pump, tramp, tube, whore ☞ *The semantic boundaries between "floozy," "broad," and "dish" are not always easy to set. All three terms should be considered.*

2 SEE **HOOKER**

flop

1 *n A failure, esp a total one*

blast, bomb, brodie, bust, clinker, clunker, [Brit] damp squib, dog, dud, Edsel, el foldo, fizz, fizzle, fliv, flivver, flopperoo, floppola, flukum, flummox, frost, gas, gasser, hurtburger, lead balloon, lemon, loser, stiff, turkey, washout

2 *v To fail*

bomb, bust, crap out, fall down on the job, fall flat on one's ass, fall on one's ass, fall on one's face, fizz, fizzle, flummox, fold, frost, go belly up, go down for the count, go kerplunk, go over like a lead balloon, go over like a turd in the punchbowl, go pfft, go south, lay an egg, pfft, pull an el foldo, run on empty, take a dive, tank, tap out, wash out ☞ *This list may be increased by using the negative form of terms under "hack it."*

3 SEE **SNOOZE**

flophouse

n A cheap and sordid rooming house or hotel

bughouse, cathouse, chinch pad, crib, crumb house, crumb jopint, doss house, fleabag, fleabox, fleahouse, fleatrap, flop joint, scratch house

fluff

1 *v To forget one's lines on stage*

ascend, balloon, blow, blow up, dry up, flub, go up in one's line, go up in the air, make an ascension

2 SEE **GOOF**

flunk

v To fail an examination, course, etc

bust, flag it, flush, flush it, tube it

fly right

v phr To be honest, dependable, etc

be on the level, be on the up and up, go legit, go straight, keep one's nose clean, pull up one's socks, straighten out, straighten up, straighten up and fly right, tie one's shoes, toe the mark, wipe one's nose

fogy

1 *n An old person; a senior citizen*

alter kocker, antique, dodo, foozle, fossil, geezer, mossback, oldster, old-timer

2 *n A conservative person*

die-hard, fud, fuddy-duddy, hardshell, stick, stick in the mud

fold

v To lose energy and effect; wilt; be defeated, as in "When he saw who they had as witnesses, he folded"

back down, bite the dust, burn out, call it a day, call it quits, cave, cave in, chuck it, conk out, crap out, expire, give in, give out, holler quits, knuckle under, peter out, poo out, poop out, pull an el foldo, run out of gas, run out of steam, say uncle, throw in one's cards, throw in the sponge, throw in the towel, toss in the sponge, toss in the towel

☞ *These terms share semantic territory with "go ker-flooey," which should also be considered.*

fool around with
v phr To handle or tamper with; have to do with, as in "I wouldn't fool around with that red switch if I were you"; also, to engage in sexual activity with, as in "He said he'd kill me if he caught me fooling around with his sister"

dick around with, dick with, diddle around with, diddle with, fart around with, fart with, fiddle around with, fiddle with, fool with, fuck around with, fuck with, futz around with, futz with, jack around with, mess around with, mess with, monkey around with, monkey with, muck around with, muck with, potchkie around with, potchkie with, putz around with, putz with, screw around with, screw with

forget it
interj An exclamation of pardon; a token of forgiveness

don't give it a second thought, it's nothing, makes no never mind, mox nix aus, no big deal, no biggie, no problem, no sweat

for keeps
adv phr Forever; permanently

forever and amen, for good, for good and all, till hell freezes over, till the cows come home

for kicks
adv phr For no definite or useful reason; for mere pleasure

for fun, for the hell of it, just for the hell of it

for openers
adv phr As a beginning; as a first move or suggestion

first off, for starters

for sure
adv phr Definitely; certainly; really, as in "We are beaten for sure"

but good, dead sure, for a fact, for certain, for real, no buts about it; no ifs, ands, or buts; no two ways about it, shitsure, sure as God made little green apples, sure as hell, sure as I live and breathe, sure as shit, sure as shootin', sure as the devil, sure as you're a foot high, sure-nuff, sure thing

frame
v To prepare and maneuver someone for swindling, tricking, incriminating, etc, as in "He insisted that they had framed him with a few accidental and trivial circumstances"

build, bum-beef, frame up, set up

freak out
v phr To have an unpleasant experience with a narcotic, esp a hallucinogen; to have a similar experience not due to drug use

blow one's top, flip, flip out, freak, go on a bad trip, have a bad trip

freebie

n Anything given or enjoyed free of charge, as in "My friend at the box office is usually good for a freebie"

comp, free lunch, free-o, giveaway

free-for-all

n A riotous scene, esp a general fight

barney, battle royal, brannigan, brawl, broil, dogfight, donnybrook, fracas, gin, knock-down-drag-out, melee, mix-up, rhubarb, riot, row, ruckus, ruction, rumble, rumpus, run-in, scrap, scrimmage, scuffle, set-to, shindy, tussle

☞ *Consider "donnybrook" also. The distinction may be only fanciful, but "donnybrook" seems to designate a boisterous scene, whereas "free-for-all" stresses the fighting.*

free gratis

adj phr Free of charge; nonpaying

[Brit] buckshee, cufferoo, cuffo, for free, for nothing, freebie, free gratis for nothing, on the arm, on the cuff, on the house

freeze up

v phr To panic; be paralyzed by fear

choke up, clank, clank up, funk, swallow the apple, take the pipe

French kiss

n phr A kiss in which the tongue of one person explores the oral cavity of another, and vice versa

soul kiss

frisk
v To search a person for weapons or contraband

body-shake, fan, frisk down, pad down, prat-prowl, prowl, shake, shake down, skin-search, strip-search, toss

Frog
n A French person or a person of French extraction

Frenchy, frog-eater, Froggy
☞ *These terms are likely to give offense.*

from scratch
adv phr From the very beginning

from square one, from the git-go, from the ground up, from the top, from the word go

front runner
n phr The leader and one most likely to win a contest, election, race, etc

best bet, favorite, hot favorite, hot horse, odds-on favorite

fruit salad
n phr A group of stroke victims or otherwise totally disabled patients

potato patch, rose garden, vegetable garden

fry
v To put or be put to death in the electric chair

burn, cook, jump, ride old Smoky, ride old Sparky, ride the lightning, roast, sizzle, squat hot, toast

fuck
1 v To do the sex act with or to; copulate

ball, bang, boff, [Brit] bonk, boogie, boom-boom, bop, buzz the brillo, crawl, dick, diddle, dip one's wick, do it, do the thing, eff, fork, frig, futy, futz, get one's ashes hauled, get one's banana peeled, get into someone's drawers, get into someone's pants, get it off with, get laid, get one's nuts cracked, get one's nuts off with, get one's nuts with, get off with, get over, get one's rocks off with, get one's rocks with, get some nookie, [Brit] get stuffed, give out, give someone the shaft, go all the way, go at it, go the limit, go to bed with someone, go to it, go to town, have someone, have a party, have one's end off, [Brit] have it off, horse, hose, hump, jam, jazz, jump, jump someone's bones, knock off, knock off a piece, lay, lay pipe, lay tube, make, make it, make out with, nail, off, party, perform, phutz, plank, play bouncy-bouncy, play hide-the-weenie, plow, pluck, poke, pop, pork, pound, prong, pump, put, put it to, put out, put the blocks to, raunch, ream, ride, roll, score, score with, scrag, screw, scrog, scrump, shaft, shag, shtup, sleep with someone, spread, spread for someone, [Brit] stuff, swing, tear off a piece, tear off a piece of ass, throw a fuck into, trick, trick out, work out, yentz

2 *v To maltreat; victimize, as in "If he's not careful to get everything in writing, those guys will fuck him"*

diddle, file, fork, frig, fuck over, fuck up, give the finger, give the shaft, grunge, hose, mess someone around, mess someone over, ream, screw, screw over, sell down the river, sell out, shaft, smuck, stiff, yank

a fuck
n An instance of the sex act

bang, boff, bop, frig, futz, horizontal bop, hump, jazz, lay, parallel parking, party, phutz, piece, piece of ass, piece of tail, poke, ride, roll, roll in the hay, screw, shag, some couze, some cunt, some jellyroll, some nookie, some twat

fuck book

n phr A pornographic book or magazine

stroke book

fucked-up

1 *adj Confused; chaotic*

all anyhow, all nohow, arsy-varsy, ass backwards, assed-up, balled-up, bassackwards, bollixed-up, bugged-up, buggered-up, cockeyed, every which way, flummoxed, fouled-up, fried, fubar, fubb, fucked-up like a Chinese fire call, fumtu, futzed-up, galley-west, gummed-up, gummixed-up, helter-skelter, higgledy-piggledy, hugger-mugger, kerflummoxed, messed-up, messy, mocus, mommixed-up, mucked-up, mussed-up, out in left field, ramble-scramble, screwed-up, screwy, skewgee, skimble-skamble, sky-west, sloppy, snafu, snafued, susfu, tarfu, untogether, up gefucked

2 SEE **ON THE BLINK**

fucking

1 *adj Utter; total, as in "Ain't it a fucking shame?"*

blinking, bloody, blooming, crying, damn, dern, frigging, plum, plumb, regular, stone

2 *adv Extremely; utterly, as in "Isn't that a fucking stupid thing to say?"*

bloody, damn, frigging, God-awful, goshawful, mighty, plum

fuck up

v phr To fail, esp by blundering; ruin one's prospects

be a loser, be shot down in flames, be thrown for a loss, bilge, bite the dust, blow, blow it, bomb, cave in, [Brit] come a cropper, crap out, crash, crash and burn, do an el foldo, drop the ball, fall flat on one's ass, fizzle, flop, fold, fold up, foozle, foul up, go belly up, go down the drain, go down the tube, goof, go under, go up the spout, gum up, keel over, lay an egg, lose out, miss the boat, muff, not cut it, not cut the mustard, not get to first base, not hack it, not make it, not make the grade, peg out, peter out, poop out, screw up, step on one's dick, step on it, step on one's schvantz, strike out, suck wind, take a bath, take the gas, take the pipe, whiff, wipe out

fuck-up
1 n A bungler, esp a chronic one
2 SEE SNAFU

bobbler, bonehead, dub, foozler, fumble-fist, goof, goofer, goof-up, goofus, screw-up, slob

fuck you
interj An exclamation of very strong defiance and contempt

bite moose; chuck you, Farley; chuck you, Farley, and your whole famn damily; cram it, drop dead, eat it, eat this, eff you, fork you, fubis, fuck you and the horse you rode in on, get lost, [Brit] get stuffed, go fly a kite, go fuck yourself, go impale yourself, go piss up a rope, go pound salt, go pound salt up your ass, go pound sand, go pound sand up your ass, go screw yourself, go shit in your hat, go soak your head, go suck eggs, go to hell, [Brit] I'm all right Jack, kiss my ass, piss on you, put it in your ear, ram it, read my lips, screw you, shit in your hat, shit on you, shove it, [Brit] sod you, so's your old man, stick it, stick it in your ear, stick it up your ass, stick it where the sun doesn't shine, stow it, stuff it, take a flying fuck, take a flying fuck at a rolling doughnut, take a flying fuck at a rubber duck, take it in the ear, up against the wall, up thine with turpentine, up your ass, up your butt, up your gazool, up your gig, up your giggy, up yours, you know what you can do with it, you know where you can stick it

☞ *These, along with "kiss my ass," constitute the most abusive and provocative nonethnic rejections available in US slang. The distinction between the two verbal assaults is not easy to draw, and both should be considered.*

full of piss and vinegar
adj phr Brimming with energy; very lively

chipper, feeling one's oats, feisty, full of beans, full of go, full of pep, full of prunes, full of steam, go-go, gung ho, hopped up, peppy, rambunctious, rarin' to go, snappy, starchy, tearing up the pea patch, zappy, zingy, zippy

full of shit
adj phr Wrong; mistaken; not to be credited, as in "Politicians are full of shit"

all wet, dead wrong, full of baloney, full of beans, full of bull, full of crap, full of prunes, full of shit as a Christmas goose, haywire, in the right church but the wrong pew

fur pie
n phr Cunnilingus

box lunch, French, the French way, furburger, hair pie, head

G

gab

1 *n Talk; speech*

blab, blat, buzz, chin, chin music, chinning, flapjaw, gas, gibble-gabble, guff, jabber, jawing, jibber-jabber, lip, noise, palaver, patter, prattle, rag-chewing, rap, rapping, talk-talk, talky-talk, tongue-wagging, yackety-yack, yacking, yap, yapping

2 *v To talk, esp idly or frivolously; chatter*

bat one's chops, bat one's gums, bat one's jaws, bat one's jowls, bat one's lip, bat the breeze, beat one's chops, beat one's gums, beat one's jaws, beat one's jowls, beat one's lip, blab, blat, breeze, bullshit, buzz, chin, fan, fat-mouth, flap one's chops, flap one's gums, flap one's jaw, flap one's jowls, flap one's lip, flip one's lip, gabble, gas, gibble-gabble, gum, hump one's chops, hump one's gums, hump one's jaw, hump one's jowls, hump one's lip, jabber, jaw, jibber-jabber, mouth off, [chiefly Brit] natter, palaver, pop off, rap, rattle, run off at the mouth, shoot off one's face, shoot off one's mouth, shoot the breeze, shoot the bull, shoot the shit, sound off, spiel, spout off, talk someone's ear off, talk up a storm, throw the bull, wag one's chin, warm someone's ear, woof, yack, yackety-yack, yack it up, yack-yack, yack-yack-yack, yammer, yap, yatata, yatter, yip

☞ *The many "yack" forms have "yak" spelling variants and variants in "yock" and "yuck."*

☞ *"Gab" shares semantic territory with "blow off" and "shoot the breeze," which should also be considered.*

gabby
adj Very talkative; garrulous and gossipy, as in "My taxi driver was the gabby sort"

all jaw, bigmouthed, flapjawed, full of wind, gassy, gimbaljawed, lippy, longwinded, motormouthed, satchelmouthed, talky, windy, yappy

gadget
n Any unspecified or unspecifiable usu small device or object; something one does not know the name of or does not wish to name

bitch, bugger, contraption, deedee, dingbat, dingus, doobob, doodad, doodle, doofunny, doohickey, doohinkus, doohinky, doojigger, doomajigger, doowhangam, doowhistle, doowillie, frobnitz, fucker, gidget, gigmaree, gilgadget, gilguy, gilhickey, gilhooley, gimmick, giz, gizmo, goofus, guy, hickey, hootenanny, hootmalalie, jigger, jimjick, kickshaw, little guy, mother, motherfucker, mucket, puppy, thingamajig, thingumabob, thingummy, thingy, whangdoodle, whatamahicky, whatchamacallit, whatsit, whoozis, widget, you-know-what

☞ *This is a partial list only. The terms may be multiplied enormously with variant spellings and with other spur-of-the-moment combinations of "do," "thing," and "what" with nonsense syllables. All told, these useful designators and euphemisms may potentially be the largest set of slang synonyms.*

gadgetry
n Ingenious or impressive devices, esp electronic or mechanical, as in "James Bond's gadgetry has saved his neck many times"

bells and whistles, gimmickry, gimmicks, Mickey Mouse

a gamble
n phr An uncertain venture; a matter of chance

chancy proposition, crap shoot, dicey proposition, horse race, iffy proposition, risky business, sporting proposition

gang bang
n phr An occasion when several males do the sex act serially with one woman

gang fuck, gang shag, train

gangster
n A member of a criminal gang; an organized-crime figure

button man, goombah, Mafioso, mobster, soldier

gay
1 *adj Homosexual, as in "Gay activists are pushing for antidiscrimination legislation"*

bent, fag, faggoty, faggy, fairy, fay, flaming, flitty, fruity, homo, kinky, lacy, light-footed, light on his feet, limp-wristed, Mary, nancy, Nelly, pansy, pink, queer, swish ☞ *"Gay" applies to both male and female homosexuals, but the other terms in this list are used nearly*

2 *n A male homosexual*

exclusively of males. Female homosexuals are characterized as "lez," "lezzie," "lesbo," "lizzy," or "dykey." angel, camp, capon, daisy, dilly dude, drag queen, dyna, fag, faggot, fairy, fay, fegelah, femme, flamer, flaming asshole, flaming fruitbar, flit, flower, flute, fluter, foop, fooper, freak, frit, fruit, fruitcake, girl, gump, home boy, homo, jackie, jocker, limp-wrist, maricon, Mary, mo, nancy, nancy boy, nelly, pansy, pato, pix, pogue, [Brit] poof, [Brit] poofter, [Brit] poove, punk, queen, queenie, queer, sissy, swish, three-letter man

get a kick out of
v phr To enjoy especially; delight in

dig, get a bang out of, get a charge out of, get off on, go for, groove on

get by
v phr To do acceptably well; neither succeed nor fail, but survive

cope, get along, get on, make out, manage, [Brit] muddle through, scrape along, scrape by, scruff, scruff along, scuffle, scuffle along, skin through, squeak by, squeak through

get down to brass tacks
v phr To talk seriously about essential things

cut the shit, get down to cases, get down to the nitty gritty, get to the bottom line, lay it on the line, level, talk turkey

get even
v phr To take revenge

even the score, get one's own back, get square, knot the score, return the compliment, settle accounts, settle the score, square accounts

get it in the neck

v phr *To be severely punished or injured, as in "If my girl doesn't stop whining she's going to get it in the neck"*

be shot down, be shot down in flames, be wiped out, get clobbered, get it, get one's lumps, get taken off at the knees, get the business

get it together

v phr *To arrange one's life and affairs properly; become organized*

bring this shit to a focus, get one's act together, get one's act together and take it on the road, get one's ducks in a row, get one's head together, get it all together, get one's shit together, get one's stuff together

get lucky

v phr *To enjoy good luck*

luck out, luck up

get me

question *Do you understand me?*

are we on the same wavelength, are you tuned in, catch, catch on, catch the drift, collar my jive, compree, comprenny, cool, coppish, dig, dig me, dontcha know, do you read me, get it, get the drift, get the message, get the picture, got it, got me, OK, read me, read my lips, right, savvy

get off someone's **back**

v phr *To leave alone; stop annoying or nagging*

back off, do not crowd someone, get off someone's case, get off someone's neck, get out of someone's face, let someone breathe

get on the ball
v phr To rally one's wits and energies; improve one's performance

get one's ass in gear, get one's finger out of one's ass, get one's head out of one's ass, get on the stick, get with it, pull up one's socks, spudge around, stir around, tie one's shoes

get on the bandwagon
v phr To join a popular trend, movement, etc

climb on the bandwagon, go along with the crowd, hop on the bandwagon, leap on the bandwagon

get the ax
v phr To be dismissed, discharged, etc

get the air, get the boot, get the bum's rush, get the hook, get the sack

get the lead out
v phr To hurry; get busy and play one's part

get a hump on, get a hustle on, get a move on, get one's ass, get one's ass in gear, get a wiggle on, get cracking, get cutting, get one's finger out of one's asshole, get going, get it on, get off one's ass, get off one's butt, get off one's dead ass, get off one's duff, get off the dime, get on one's horse, get on the stick, get the lead out of one's ass, hop to it, hump, hustle, hustle up, look alive, make it snappy, not stand around with one's finger up one's ass, pick 'em up and lay 'em down, pour it on, pour on the coal, quit fucking the dog, rustle one's bustle, shake a leg, shake it, shake it up, shake the lead out, show a leg, snap it up, snap to it, spudge around, step on it, stir one's stumps

ghetto box
n phr A large portable stereo radio and cassette player often carried and played loudly in public places

boogie box, box, coon box, ghetto blaster, thunderbox radio

gimmick
n Anything calculated to seize and rivet the attention, as in "We'll need a gimmick to sell it"

come-on, grabber, hook, pitch

gimpy
adj Having a limp or being lame

game, hoppy, limpy

gin mill
n phr A barroom; a saloon

boozer, fillmill, gargle factory, gin palace, gin parlor, groggery, grog-mill, guzzlery, guzzle shop, hoochery, waterhole, watering hole, watering place

give a miss
v phr To avoid; not choose, as in "I think I'll give that banquet a miss and just stay home"

give the go-by, pass up, skip, take a bye, take a rain check

give someone a pain in the ass
v phr To be distasteful, tedious, repellent, etc, as in "After the first few days that job gave me a pain in the ass"

frost someone's ass, get in someone's hair, give someone a pain, give someone a pain in the neck, give someone a swift pain in the ass, gripe someone's ass, gripe someone's balls, gripe someone's cookies, gripe someone's left nut, gripe someone's middle kidney, gripe someone's soul, miff, peeve, put someone's nose out of joint, rub one the wrong way

give someone a ring
v phr To call, esp on the telephone

give someone a blow, give someone a buzz, give someone a shout, [Brit] give someone a tinkle

give something a shot
v phr To have a try at; make an attempt

give something a crack, give something a go, give something a riffle, give something a rip, give something a ripple, give something a whack, have a crack at, have a go at, have a riffle at, have a rip at, have a ripple at, have a shot at, have a whack at, take a crack at, take a lick at, take a riffle at, take a rip at, take a ripple at, take a shot at, take a whack at

give someone a slap on the wrist
v phr To punish mildly

rap someone's knuckles

give five
v phr To greet with a handshake or a slapping of hands

give some skin, press the flesh, slap five, whip out

give someone **his (or her) walking papers**
v phr To dismiss or discharge; reject, as in "After the third time he cheated on her she gave him his walking papers"

give someone his (or her) running shoes, give someone his (or her) walking ticket, give someone the air

give the cold shoulder
v phr To snub; behave disdainfully

brush, brush off, chill, cold-shoulder, cut, cut dead, freeze, freeze out, give the beady eyeball, give the fish-eye, give the go-by, give the hairy eyeball, high-hat, put on the freeze, put on the frost, snoot, turn the cold shoulder, turn up one's nose, upstage

give someone **the finger**
v phr To make a contemptuous sign with the hand, middle finger extended

flip the bird, throw a bird

glad-hander
n A person who evinces a warmth and heartiness that is probably insincere; one who is designedly cordial

flesh-presser, handshaker, mitt-glommer, phony

glad rags
n phr One's best clothing

best bib and tucker, dress-ups, fancy rags, [Brit] full fig, Sunday best, Sunday-go-to-meeting clothes

glass arm
n phr A baseball pitcher's arm that is prone to injury and inflammation

crockery, putty arm

glass jaw
n phr A boxer's chin that cannot tolerate a hard punch

china chin

glitch
n A malfunction; a defect

bug, goof, hitch, kink, monkey-wrench in the works, screw-loose, slip-up, something screwy, wrinkle

glitzy
adj Blatantly scintillant; gaudy

day-glo, flashy, flossy, jazzy, loud, splashy, splurgy, zazz, zazzy

glob
n A mass of viscous matter

blob, gob

gloomy Gus
n phr A morose, melancholic person

crape-hanger, grinch, killjoy, party-poop, party-pooper, prophet of doom and gloom, turn-off, wet blanket

G-man
n An agent of the Federal Bureau of Investigation; a special agent

Feeb, Feebie, hard John

the **go-ahead**
n phr Permission or a signal to proceed; consent

the green light, the nod, the OK, permish, thumbs up

go back to square one
v phr To be forced to return to one's starting point; make a new beginning

be at jump street, be at square one, be at the git-go, go back and punt, go back to the old drawing board, scrub the slate clean, start from scratch, wipe the slate clean

go broke
v phr To become penniless; become insolvent

be cleaned out, be taken to the cleaners, be washed out, be washed up, be wiped out, go belly up, go bust, go to the cleaners, lose one's shirt, take a bath, tap out, wash out

go crazy
v phr To become insane; lose one's mind, as in "War is enough to make anyone go crazy"

blow one's cork, blow one's stack, blow one's top, crack up, flip, flip one's lid, flip out, flip one's wig, freak out, go ape, go apeshit, [Brit] go around the bend, go balmy, go bananas, go barmy, go bats, go batty, go bent, [Brit] go bonkers, go bonzo, go buggy, go bughouse, go bugs, go bugsy, go cockamamie, go cockeyed, go crackbrained, go cracked, [Brit] go crackers, go crackpot, go crackpotty, go crazy as a bedbug, go crazy as a coot, go crazy as a loon, go crazy as catshit, go cuckoo, go daffy, go dingdong, go dippy, go dopey, go dotty, go dumdum, go fruitcakey, go fruity, go funny, go ga-ga, go gonzo, go Gonzo City, go goofy, go half-baked, go half there, go haywire, go kooky, go loco, go loony, go loony-tune, go loopy, go lunchy, go mental, go meshugah, go nerts, go nertsy, go nuts, go nutso, go nutsy, go nutty, go nutty as a fruitcake, go off, go off one's chump, go off one's nut, go off one's rocker, go off the wall, go off one's trolley, go out of one's gourd, go out of one's skull, go out of one's tree, go potty, go psycho, go queer, go queer in the head, [Brit] go round the bend, go rum-dum, go scatty, go schizo, go schizy, go screwball, go screwy, go squirrely, go tetched, go tetched in the head, go up the wall, go wacko, go wacky, go weird, go wild-ass, lose one's gourd, nut up, schiz out, slip one's trolley, snap, wig out

☞ *These terms are very often used loosely or figuratively.*

gofer
n A low-ranking subordinate

bench warmer, best boy, bottom man on the totem pole, doormat, gal Friday, go-for, gopher, grunt, guy Friday, hired help, lightweight, little shot, low-level Munchkin, low man on the totem pole, man Friday, peon, scrub, second fiddle, second-stringer, spear-carrier, stooge, third-stringer, utility infielder

go for
1 v phr To choose; prefer, as in "She always goes for the best wine"
2 SEE DIG

come down for, give the nod to, plump for, push, push for, vote for

go for it

v phr To stake everything on a taxing try; take a risk

bet the farm, bet the house, bet the ranch, go for all the marbles, go for broke, go for the fences, go for the long ball, shoot the works, shoot one's wad

☞ *This term was widespread in the 1980s as an exhortation and was probably related to the contemporary obsession with sports and physical fitness.*

go into one's **dance**

v phr To begin a prepared line of pleading, persuasion, selling, seduction, etc, as in "She's quiet most of the time, but put her with a client and she'll go into her dance"

do one's number, go into one's act, go into one's dog and pony show, go into one's song and dance

go kerflooey

v phr To cease to function; break down; collapse

belly up, bust down, cash in, conk out, crap out, crash, fizzle, fizz out, get out of commission, get out of kilter, get out of whack, give out, give up the ghost, go belly up, go blooey, go down, go down the chute, go down the drain, go down the tubes, go flooey, go haywire, go kablooey, go kaput, go on the blink, go on the bum, go on the fritz, go up in smoke, go up the spout, gronk out, hit the skids, [Brit] pack up, peg out, poop out, pot out, tap out

gold mine
n phr A very profitable venture; a lucrative business

bonanza, gravy train, license to print money

goner
n A person or thing that is doomed beyond hope of saving

cooked goose, dead duck, dead meat, dead pigeon, dead rabbit, gone case, gone coon, gone gander, gone goose

goo
n Any viscous and unappealing fluid or mixture; anything slimy and nasty

glop, gook, goop, goozlum, guck, gumbo, gunk, jism, muck, mung, sludge, stickum

good guy
n phr A decent person; a reliable and admirable citizen, as in "It's hard to believe a good guy like him could be a spy"

ace, good egg, good head, good Joe, good sport, Mr Nice Guy, one-way guy, prince, regular fellow, regular guy, righteous egg, right gee, right guy, square dealer, square John, square shooter, supergopher
☞ *These terms, like "guy," are now used also of women.*

goody-goody
n A prim and ostentatiously virtuous person

bluenose, goody, goody two-shoes, holier-than-thou, Nice Nelly, old maid
☞ *This list is close to the one at "Bible-banger." Slang does not take virtue at the ideal evaluation.*

goof

1 *v To make a mistake; blunder, as in "The right fielder really goofed on that play"*

blot one's copybook, blow, blow it, bobble, boot, [Brit] drop a brick, drop one's bucket, drop the ball, [Brit] duff, flub, flub the dub, fluff, foozle, foul up, fuck up, get egg on one's face, goof up, louse up, make a blooper, make a boner, make a boo-boo, make a mess, muck up, pull a bloomer, pull a blooper, pull a bonehead play, pull a boner, pull a boo-boo, put one's foot in it, put one's foot in one's mouth, screw up, slip a cog, step on one's dick, trip up

2 SEE FUCK UP

go off half-cocked

v phr To make a premature response, esp an angry one

be quick-draw, be too quick on the draw, be too quick on the trigger, go off at the half-cock, shoot from the hip

goof off

1 *v phr To avoid work; shirk duty*

bunny-fuck, coast, conk off, dog it, dope off, drag-ass, drag one's ass, drag one's feet, drag it, dragtail, drag one's tail, fake off, fall down on the job, featherbed, float, flub, flub the dub, fluff off, fuck off, fuck the dog, goldbrick, goof around, hump the hound, jerk off, lay down on the job, lie on one's oars, lollygag, screw off, screw the pooch, sit on one's ass, sit on one's hands, skate, slack, sluff, [Brit] snurge, soldier, spin one's wheels, whip the dog

2 *v phr To pass time lazily and pleasantly; idle about, as in "I'm just going to goof off on this vacation"*

ass around, bat around, beat around, boogaloo, boogie, bum around, cat around, cruise around, cut didoes, cut up, dick, dick around, diddle, diddlybop, doodle, fart around, fiddle around, fiddlefart, fiddlefart around, fool around, fuck around, fuck off, fuck the dog, futz around, goof around, hack around, hang, hang around, hang out, horse, horse around, hump the hound, jack around, jerk off, kick, kick around, knock around, laze around,

[Brit] lollop around, lollygag, mellow out, mess around, Mickey Mouse around, monkey around, mooch around, [Brit] muck about, noodle, piddle around, play around, poot around, putz around, rail it, rat around, rat-fuck, schloomp, schloomp around, screw around, shuck, sit on one's ass, sit on one's butt, sit on one's duff, smoke and joke, stall around, suck around, veg, veg out

goof-off

n A person who regularly and chronically avoids work; a shirker

bunk lizard, coffee cooler, feather merchant, fluff-off, fuck-off, goldbrick, goldbricker, lard-ass, [Brit] layabout, lazybones, piker, sack artist, screw-off, slacker

gook

1 *n An Asian or person of Asian extraction*
2 SEE **GOO**

dink, goo-goo, slant-eye, slope, slopie, zip
☞ *These offensive terms are applied most often to Vietnamese and other Southeast Asians.*

goon

n A rough, intimidating man, esp a paid ruffian; a thug

ape, bad baby, biff-guy, big tuna, bimbo, bozo, bruiser, cowboy, dropper, enforcer, gorill, gorilla, greaser, hard-boiled egg, hard case, heavy, heavy man, hood, hoodlum, hooligan, jaboney, knuckle-dragger, lobo, loogan, mugger, muscle, muscle man, muscler, persuader, plug-ugly, pretty boy, pug, rough customer, roughneck, shtarker, sidewinder, starker, strong-arm, strong-arm man, tough, tough baby, tough guy, tough mug, ugly customer, yegg

goon squad

n phr A group of ruffians, esp in the hire of a labor union, a corporation, etc

beef squad, strong-arm squad

goose

v To goad or otherwise stimulate to activity; energize

get someone off his (or her) dead ass, give a hotfoot, jazz up, juice up, perk up, poke, switch on, turn on
☞ *Other terms may be made by recalling that to "goose" is to cause someone to "get the lead out."*

goose bumps
n phr Gooseflesh

duck bumps

goosy

adj Sensitive; touchy, as in "He was inclined to be goosy about his business affairs"

miffy, prickly, quick on the draw, quick on the trigger, quick on the uptake, tetchy, thin-skinned

go over the hill
v phr To go absent without leave from a military unit

break barracks, go AWOL, hit the hump, take French leave

go over with a bang
v phr To succeed brilliantly; be enthusiastically approved

ace it, be a gas, be a gasser, be a hit, be a smash, be a smash hit, bring down the house, click, click big, come on like gangbusters, connect, go great guns, go like a house afire, go over, go over like a million bucks, go places, go to town, hit, [Brit] hit for six, hit it, hit pay dirt, hit the jackpot, kill them, knock someone's socks off, knock them dead, knock them out, lay them in the aisles, make it, make it big, make out like a bandit, pan out, put them away, put them in the aisles, put them on the floor, slaughter them, slay them, stop the show, strike oil, wow them

go public
v phr To reveal; be open about, as in "After a few weeks they thought they ought to go public with their report"

come out of the closet, take it to the street

go straight
v phr To renounce a life of crime and iniquity; reform, as in "Some people go straight even with little or no rehabilitation"

go legit, slipper, walk the straight and narrow, wipe one's nose

go through the mill
v phr To have practical experience of something; be thoroughly seasoned

earn one's ticket, pay one's dues, win one's wings

go to bat for
v phr To defend; take sides with

back up, go to the wall for, ride shotgun for, stand behind, stand up for, stick up for, stump for

go to hell

1 *v phr* To deteriorate; be on the road to ruin, as in *"The air quality in our town would go to hell if they built that shopping center here"*

come apart at the seams, come unglued, come unstuck, go downhill, go down the chute, go down the drain, go down the tubes, go to hell in a bucket, go to hell in a handbasket, go to perdition, go to pot, go to the dogs, go to wrack and ruin, go up the spout, hit the skids

2 SEE **FUCK YOU**

grab

v To acquire; gather

bag, catch, collar, cop, corral, dig up, drag down, get one's hands on, get hold of, get one's hooks into, glom on to, grab off, grub up, hook, knock down, land, latch on to, nab, nail, net, pull down, rake up, round up, scare up, scrape up, snag

grab-ass

n Sexual dalliance short of copulation; caressing, as in *"They played grab-ass for an hour before consummating their affair"*

bush patrol, canoodling, a feel, a feel-up, a grope, groping, hanky-panky, a love-up, lovey-dovey, slap and tickle

grabby

1 *adj* Captivating; very attractive, as in *"Get a load of that grabby hunk"*

catchy, hooky

2 *adj* Greedy; acquisitive; selfish

hoggish, hoggy, piggish, piggy

grand
n A thousand dollars

big one, G, gee, horse, K, ten yards, thou

grand slam
n phr A decisive and total victory

clean sweep, landslide, sweep, wipe-out

grandstand
v To play or perform in a brilliant and spectacular way, esp for the approval of an audience

grandstand it, hot dog, make a circus play, make a grandstand play, play to the gallery, profile, profile for the fans, showboat, show off, style

grandstander
n A person who habitually grandstands

glory-grabber, grandstand player, gunner, hot dog, showboat, showoff

gravy
n Money or other valuables beyond what one earns; a bonus

cake, easy money, easy pickings, found money, jelly, pie, velvet

grease monkey
n phr A mechanic, esp an automotive mechanic

greaseball, greasehound

grease someone's **palm**
v phr To bribe

cross someone's palm, oil someone's palm

greasy spoon

n phr A small,
cheap restaurant,
lunch room, or diner

beanery, bean wagon, chili joint, dog wagon, doughnut factory, doughnut foundry, doughnut house, doughnut joint, dump, eatery, grease joint, grease pit, grease trough, ham-and-eggery, ham joint, hashery, hash foundry, hashhouse, one-arm, one-arm joint, quick and dirty, quick and filthy, sloppy Joe's

great

adj Excellent;
wonderful

A-1, ace-high, aces, ah tuff, A-OK, awesome, bad, baddest, [Brit] bang on, bang-up, bangy, [Canadian] beauty, the berries, bio, bionic, bitchen, blip, blue-chip, boffo, [Australian] bonzer, boo, boss, brutal, bully, bumpin', champ, chewy, chill, chilly, class, classy, cock, cocky, cool, corking, crack, crackerjack, cracking, crazy, Cugat, dandy, darling, deadly, deadly boo, def, delish, devoon, dishy, divine, dope, double bitchen, down, dreamy, drooly, ducky, dynamite, elegant, endsville, evil, fab, fabby, faboo, fancy, fantabulous, far in, far out, fiendish, fiendish back, fierce, flash, fly, four-O, frabjous, frantic, fresh, froody, funky, gear, ginchy, gingerpeachy, gnarly, gone, gorgeous, the greatest, grooby, groovy, hando, hard, hash, heavenly, heavy, hellacious, high-class, high-rent, hipper-dipper, hot, hotsy-totsy, hounds, humdinging, hyper, ice, immense, intense, irie, jammy, jim-dandy, keen, key, kicky, killer, the kind, knockout, marvy, mean, mezz, mighty, the most, the mostest, nasty, neat, nifty, nitro, not too shabby, the nuts, on the beam, outasight, out of sight, out of this world, peacharooney, peachy, peachy-keen, plummy, potent, pretty radical, primo, rad, rattling, regular, righteous, ripping, ritzy, royal, scrumptious, serious, sexy, shag, sharp, skookum, slick, slurpy, smashing, smooth, snazzy, socko, solid, some kind of, something else, spanking, spiffy, stoking, stunning, super, superbo, super-duper, superfly, sweet, swell, swell-elegant, tawny, terrific, thrashing, thumping, the ticket, tickety-boo, tip-top, tits, toast, too much, top-drawer, top-hole, top-notch, tops, totally bitchen, tough, tubular, unreal, upscale, vicious, wailing, way out, weird, wicked, wig, wiggy, wild, [Brit] wizard, world-class, yummy, zero cool

☞ *The large number and rapid obsolescence of these terms reflects the use of slang as a sign of up-to-the-minute consciousness, of newness and glitter, of this day's "image."*

green around the gills
adj phr Sick; miserable; nauseated, as in "His cooking will make you feel green around the gills"

blah, blue around the gills, bum, crummy, off one's feed, out of sorts, pasty, peaked, peaky, punk, rocky, seedy, shaky, sick as a dog, sick as a pig, under the weather, wonky

greenhorn
n An inexperienced person; a newcomer; a neophyte

boot, buckwheater, cheechako, greeny, jaboney, Johnny-come-lately, [Brit] new boy, new kid on the block, rookie, rube, tenderfoot

grind
n A diligent student

bone, boner, dexter, dweeb, eager beaver, gradehound, greasy grind, grunt, gweebo, nerd, poler, sunshine girl, throat, tool, ween, weenie, wonk

groupie
1 *n A young woman who seeks to share the glamor of famous persons, esp rock-and-roll musicians, by offering help and sexual favors*
2 SEE **FAN**

bunny, star-fucker

grunt
1 *n An infantry soldier; a rifleman*
2 SEE the **DAMAGE**
3 SEE **GOFER**
4 SEE **GRIND**
5 SEE **SHIT**

blisterfoot, crunchie, dogface, dough, doughboy, doughfoot, line dog, line doggie, paddlefoot

gut course
n phr An easy college course

[Canadian] bird course, cinch, crib course, crip course, gut, lead-pipe course, Mickey Mouse course, pipe course, ride, setup, sluff course

guts
1 *n Courage; intrepidity*

balliness, balls, ballsiness, brass balls, [Latino] cojones, ginger, gravel, grit, intestinal fortitude, moxie, nerve, spizzerinctum, spunk, stuff

2 *n The insides of a person, machine, etc; the viscera*

innards, kishkes, tripes

gutsy

adj Courageous; bold, as in "Picking an ex-con to head the department was a gutsy move"

ballsy, braver than Dick Tracy, dead game, gritty, gutty, nervy, spunky, stand-up

guy

n A man; a male person

apple, bean, bloke, boy, bozo, brother, bub, bucko, bud, bug, bugger, buster, cat, chap, character, chief, chum, clown, codger, cookie, cove, cuss, daddy, daddy-o, doc, dog, duck, dude, duffer, egg, fart, fella, feller, fucker, galoot, gazabo, gee, geezer, gent, gink, giz, gizmo, he-male, hombre, huckleberry, jamoke, jasper, Joe, [esp Brit] Johnny, joker, lad, man-jack, mister, monkey, mug, schmo, scout, shaver, son of a bee, son of a bitch, son of a gun, son of a so-and-so, sport, squirt, stiff, storch, stud, sucker, sumbitch, walyo

☞ *"Guy" is now often used for women, esp in the plural. This may or may not be a consequence of feminist consciousness.*

guzzle

v To drink liquor, as in "He always likes to guzzle on payday"

bend the elbow, booze, chug-a-lug, crook the elbow, down a few, fight a bottle, gargle, hang a few on, have a dram, have a gargle, have a nip, hit the booze, hit the bottle, hit the sauce, juice, knock back, knock off, lap, lap up, liquor up, slug down, slurp, souse, splice the main brace, swig, swill, tank, tank up, tip the elbow, toss off, wet one's goozle, wet one's whistle

H

hack it
v phr To succeed; cope successfully

breeze home, bring down the house, bring home the bacon, click, come out on top, come through, come up trumps, connect, cut it, cut the mustard, deliver the goods, fly, get home free, get off the ground, get places, hack, hit pay dirt, hit the mark, make a go of it, make it, make out like a bandit, make the cut, make the grade, make the riffle, play, pull it off, put it across, put it over, ring the bell, score, strike oil, turn the trick, win out

☞ *These terms are most often used in the negative.*

hairy
1 *adj Difficult; arduous and dangerous, as in "Driving racing cars is a hairy line of work"*
2 SEE **CREEPY**

brutal, furry, heavy, hefty, mean, no cinch, no picnic, no snap, rough, rough as a cob, rugged, sticky, tough, tricky, wicked

half-assed

1 *adj Slipshod; careless, as in "He's a nice guy, but his work is always half-assed"*

half-baked, hit-or-miss, messy, skewgee, slam-bang, slapbang, slapdash, sloppy, sorry, sorry-ass

2 SEE **DUMB**

3 SEE **PIDDLY**

ham

v To overact; be self-dramatizing and overemotional, as in "Give her an audience and she starts to ham"

chew the ham, chew up the scenery, emote, ham it up

ham-handed

adj Awkward; undextrous

all thumbs, butterfingered, ham-fisted, klutzy, schleppy

hand it to someone

v phr To pay a compliment; praise someone for a success

hand someone a bouquet, hand someone a posy, pat someone on the back, take off one's hat to, throw bouquets at

hang on

v phr To accuse of; inculpate for, as in "How many charges can we hang on this guy?"

drop on, fasten on, finger for, paste on, pin on, point the finger at someone for, rap with

hang out with

v phr To associate with; consort with, as in "I don't like to hang out with drunkards"

be buddy-buddy with, be palsy-walsy with, buddy up with, buddy with, chum around with, chum with, gang up with, hang around with, hang with, have truck with, hook up with, join up with, line up with, pal up with, pal with, string with, team up with, throw in with, train with

hang tough

v phr To endure in a difficult plight; show pluck and persistence

grin and bear it, gut it out, hang in, hang in there, hang on, hold out, keep on trucking, macho it out, ride it out, stand the gaff, stick, stick in there, stick it out, take it, take it on the chin, tough it out

hard-on

n A penile erection

blue-veiner, bone, bone-on, boner, charge, horn, prong-on, stiff one

hash

n Hashish

Afghani, African black, bambalacha, black, black hash, black oil, black Russian, blond, blue cheese, candy, charas, cherry Leb, chocolate, chunk, citroli, dope smoke, green Moroccan, heavy hash, heesh, hog, honey oil, Indian oil, Indian rope, Leb, Lebanese, lightning hash, mud, Nepalese hash, Nepalese temple balls, Nepalese temple hash, oil, one, the one, Pakistani hash, powder, quarter moon, red Lebanese, red oil, sealing wax, sheesh, shishi, smash, sole, son of one, temple balls, temple bells, temple hash

☞ *The great number of slang terms for narcotics probably reflects both a need for coded reference to an illegal substance and a desire to be chic and up-to-date, in addition to the need to distinguish varieties.*

hash mark

n phr A service stripe, worn on the sleeve to mark each four-year period of military service

bean stripe, hash stripe, ignorant stripe

hassle

1 *n A disagreement; a quarrel; a fight, as in "I don't want any hassle with you over this"*

barney, beef, blowup, brush, donnybrook, duel, dust, dustup, fireworks, flare-up, fracas, fraction, go, hoe-down, knock-down-drag-out, mix-up, one-on-one, pissing contest, pissing match, punch-out, rhubarb, row, ruckus, ruction, rumpus, run-in, scrap, set-to, shindy, [Brit] slanging match, spat, tangle, tiff

2 *v To quarrel; actively disagree; fight*

bicker, bump heads, duel, go at it, go round and round, go toe to toe, go to it, go to the mat, have a barney, have a pissing contest, have a pissing match, have a run-in, have a shindy, [Brit] have a slanging match, kick up a row, lock horns, make the fur fly, mix, mix it up, put on the gloves, row, ruckus, rumpus, scrap, set to, slug it out, spar, spat, tangle, tangle assholes, throw leather, thump, tiff, trade punches, wrangle

3 SEE **BUG**

hate someone's guts

v phr To detest; strongly dislike

be down on, hate like poison, hate like sin, have a hard-on for, have it in for, have no use for, not be seen dead with, not give a shit for, not give someone the time of day, not piss on someone's gums if his (or her) teeth were on fire, not piss up someone's ass if his (or her) guts were on fire, take a scunner at

have a ball
v phr To enjoy oneself thoroughly; frolic; celebrate

ball, boogie-woogie, cut loose, cut up, enjoy, get behind, get one's cookies, get down, get it on, get one's jollies, get one's kicks, get naked, get off, get one's rocks, go places and do things, go to town, groove, have lots of laughs, jam, jive and juke, kick out the jams, kick up one's heels, let oneself go, let loose, let off steam, live it up, make whoopee, paint the town red, party, raise a ruckus, raise hell, raise the roof, rat-fuck, whoop it up

have a field day
v phr To be very successful, esp at the expense of an opponent

fatten up, lunch up

have a hair up one's ass
v phr To be very irascible and touchy, as in "I wouldn't talk to him today, he has a hair up his ass"

be feisty, have a bug up one's ass, have a bug up one's nose, have a chip on one's shoulder, have a hair up one's nose, have a short fuse

have a hole in one's head
v phr To be stupid

be a quart low, be overdosed on dumb pills, blither, dither, drool, have a few buttons missing, have a few marbles missing, have a hole in one's wig, have a loose shingle, have a screw loose, have one's head up one's ass, have rocks in one's head, have shit for brains, have three bricks shy of a load, not find one's way to first base, not have a clue, not have all one's switches on, not have both oars in the water, not have brain one, not have brains enough to come in out of the rain, not have brains enough to walk and chew gum at the same time, not know one's ass from one's elbow, not know one's ass from third base, not know shit from Shinola, not play with a full deck

☞ *Hundreds of these expressions may be made by combining "be," "have," "not have," etc, with the terms for "dumb."*

☞ *Many of these terms share semantic territory with "not know shit from Shinola," which stresses ignorance rather than stupidity, and should also be considered.*

have a lech for
v phr To be especially desirous of; crave greatly

be antsy for, be crazy about, be ga-ga over, be high on, be hipped on, be nuts about, be stuck on, be sweet on, go for, go for in a big way, have a case on, have a crush on, have a hard-on for, have a mash on, have a thing for, have a weakness for, have a yen for, have eyes for, have hot nuts for, have hot pants for, have hot rocks for, have it bad for, have the hots for

☞ *This phrase is often used generally or figuratively.*

have a load on
v phr To be drunk

feel no pain, have a bag on, have an edge on

☞ *Hundreds of these terms may be made by combining "be" with the terms for "plastered."*

have balls
v phr To be courageous; be daring, as in "You gotta have balls to be in this line of work"

have brass balls, have cast-iron balls, have guts, have no nerves, have the nerve

have someone **by the balls**

v phr To have a decisive advantage over, as in "With evidence of his infidelity we really have him by the balls"

have by the curlies, have by the knickers, have by the nuts, have by the short hairs, have over a barrel, have the bulge on, have the drop on, have where the hair is short, hold the trump hand, hold the whip hand

have something **cinched**

v phr To be sure of a favorable outcome; be sure of success or victory, as in "After the second inning rally the Tigers had it cinched"

have a lock on, have hacked, have iced, have it made, have knocked, have made, have taped, have wired

have hot pants

v phr To be lustful; be sexually excited and desirous

cream one's jeans, have a hard-on, have a lech, have blue balls, have hot nuts, have hot rocks, have lead in one's pencil, have the hots, have the urge to merge, lech, lech after

have it both ways

v phr To hold and esp to profit from two contrary positions, as in "I'd like to support both candidates, but you can't have it both ways"

have your cake and eat it, work both sides of the street

have someone's number

v phr To know and understand someone thoroughly, including deep motives and likely actions

be onto someone, be wise to someone, have someone's measure, have someone pegged, have someone sized up, have someone taped, have someone's wavelength, know what makes someone tick, read someone, read someone like a book

have the rag on

v phr To menstruate

come around, fall off the roof, fly the red flag, have Baker flying, have the curse

one's head off

adv phr At full tilt; mightily, as in "He had to holler his head off before they did anything"

one's ass off, one's brains out, one's buns off

heavy

1 *adj Important; consequential, as in "They were into heavy talk, no trivia"*
2 SEE **BAD MAN**

big, heavyweight, hefty, high-powered, large

heeled

1 *adj Armed; carrying a weapon*
2 SEE **LOADED**

carrying, carrying a rod, carrying the difference, packing heat, rodded, rodded up, [Brit] strapped

heist

1 *n A robbery*

bag job, boost, burn, caper, crib crime, crib job, five-finger discount, holdup, job, knockover, lift, pinch, rip-off, rustle, short heist, stickup, sting

2 *v To steal; rob; burglarize, as in "They heisted nearly five million in cash"*

bag, boost, burgle, burn, buzz, clip, crab, crack, crash, get busy, get paid, go south with, highjack, hoist, hold up, hook, hug, hustle, jackroll, jump, kick over, kipe, knock off, knock over, lift, loid, make, mooch, move, mug, nab, [Brit] nick, nip, pinch, pluck, put the grab on, rip off, roll, rumble, rustle, scarf, scoff, scoop, score, smooch, snaffle, snatch, snitch, stick up, swipe, take off, tip over, yoke

☞ *This list does not take account of the various types and modes of thievery.*

heist man

n phr A professional thief or holdup man; a robber, burglar, pickpocket, etc

booster, box man, cannon, cat bandit, cracksman, creeper, derrick, dip, dunnigan, file, fingersmith, five finger, five fingers, fork, gee whiz, goniff, gopher, grifter, gun, hijacker, holdup man, iceman, knucker, knucksman, lift, lifter, lush roller, lush worker, moll-buzzer, mugger, nabber, off artist, pennyweighter, pete-man, peter man, roller, rustler, safecracker, second-story man, stickup man, wire, yegg, yoker

☞ *This list includes thieves using various techniques, locales, etc. It is a curious fact that US slang lacks a widespread generalized term for "thief."*

hell around

v phr To lead a life of low pleasure, as in "I like to hell around with my pals till we can barely stand up"

bust loose, go on the loose, hell, knock around, let oneself go, tear around, tear-ass around, tom-cat around, whoop it up, whore around

hell breaks loose

sentence The situation deteriorates; trouble strikes

all hell breaks loose, it's every man for himself, it's Katie bar the door, the roof caves in, the roof falls in, the shit hits the fan, things come unstuck

a hell of a

adj phr Very remarkable, awful, admirable, distressing, etc, as in "We had a hell of a time when that pipe ruptured"

a bitch of a, a helluva, one bitch of a, one hell of a, some, some kind of a

he-man

1 n An aggressively masculine man

caveman, hairy-chest, hunk, macho, man's man, mensch Gregs

2 adj Very masculine; blatantly virile

hairy-chested, hunky, macho, two-fisted

3 SEE HUNK

hero

n A long sandwich of cheeses, sausage, etc, made from a loaf of bread cut lengthwise

grinder, hero sandwich, hoagie, poor boy, sub, submarine, submarine sandwich, torpedo

☞ *These terms are regionally distributed, hence not all are used in all parts of the US.*

hick

n A rural person; a rustic

apple-knocker, Arky, brush ape, chawbacon, Clem, clodhopper, clover-kicker, dark, gully-jumper, hayseed, hayseeder, Herkimer Jerkimer, hillbilly, honyock, honyocker, hoosier, jasper, jay, jaybird, jerk-off, John

Farmer, joskin, local yokel, nose-picker, Okie, plow jockey, pumpkin roller, redneck, Reuben, rube, shit-kicker, SK, sodbuster, stump-jumper, woodhick, yap, yokel

hideaway
n A hiding place; a place to escape attention or discovery

[Brit] bolt-hole, funk hole, hideout, hidey-hole, hole-up, scatter

hide out
v phr To conceal oneself; take cover

hole in, hole up, lay doggo, lay low, play possum, sit tight, tunnel

high
1 *adj Intoxicated with narcotics; drugged*

all lit up, amok, amuck, backed up, baked, basted, beaming, beaten, belted, bent, bent out of shape, blasted, blind, blitzed, blitzed out, blocked, blown out, bombed, bombed out, bonged out, boxed, buzzed, called, capped out, charged, charged up, coasting, coked, coked out, coked up, cooked up, crazy, delirious, destroyed, doped, doped up, dragged, drifty, fired, flattened, flipped, flipping, floating, flying, flying high, flying in the clouds, foxy, fractured, frazzled, fried, fried to the gills, frosted, frosty, frosty frozen, frozen, full, full blast, full of junk, fuzzy, gassed, geared, geared up, geed up, geezed, geezed up, getting a rolling buzz, getting a rush, glazed, gone, gonged, goofed, gorked, gorked out, gowed, gowed up, grifado, grooving, halvahed, heaped, hopped, hopped up, horsed, in, in a nod, in a session, in a zone, in flight, in orbit, in the air, in the pocket, in transit, jacked-up, jagged, jailhouse high, jolted, junked, junked up, keyed up, knocked out, leaping and stinking, loaded, locked, luded out, maxed, mohasky, muggled, muggled up, noddy, numbered out, on, on a bean trip, on a cloud, on a dope jag, on a joy ride, on cloud nine, on the gow, on the nod, on the stuff, ossified, out, out of it, overamped, overcharged, overdosed, packed up, passed out, polluted, poppied, potted, pottle-dripped, purring like a kitten, ripped, running amok, sent, set on one's ass, shot up, singing, sleighriding, smashed, snowed, snowed in, snowed up, spaced, spaced out, spacey, spiked, sprung, stoned, stoned to the eyes, straight, strung out, switched on, tall, tea'd up, there, torn up, totaled, tranqued, tripped out, tripping, trippy, turned on, twisted, up, wasted, way out, weirded out, whipped, wigged out, wiggy, wingy, wiped out, wired, wrecked, zipped, zoned, zoned out, zonked, zonked out, zonkers

2 *n The exhilarated or exalted feeling produced by a narcotic; a narcotic intoxication*

belt, blast, boot, buzz, charge, drag, flash, head, hit, jolt, kick, rush, splash, thrill, tingle, trip, zing

3 SEE **PLASTERED**

high-powered
adj Powerful; strong and effective, as in "She's a high-powered executive these days"

double-distilled, dynamite, hefty, high-geared, stem-winding, stronger than pig-shit, thumping

hike
1 *v To increase; raise, as in "They threaten to hike the rent next month"*

boost, crank up, heist, hike up, jack up, jump up, kite, pick up, step up, up

2 *n An increase; a raising or rising*

boost, jump, uptick

a hit

1 *n Anything sensational or exciting, esp a conspicuous success*

barn-burner, blast, blockbuster, blood-curdler, boffo, bomb, bombshell, breath-taker, eye-popper, flabbergaster, gangbusters, gas, gasser, gut-thumper, heart-stopper, jarrer, jolter, one for the book, phenom, riot, rip snorter, rouser, sensaysh, smash, smash-hit, snorter, sockdolager, sockeroo, something else, something to write home about, staggerer, standout, stunner, winner

2 SEE a FIX

hitchhike

v To get free rides by standing beside a road and signaling drivers

hitch, hitch a lift, hitch a ride, thumb, thumb a lift, thumb a ride

hit it off

v phr To like one another; get along very well, as in "We hit it off the first time we met"

click, have great chemistry

hit man

n phr A gunman, esp a professional assassin

apache, blaster, blotter, bumpman, button man, croaker, driller, dropper, enforcer, gorilla, gun, gunman, gunpoke, gunsel, hatchet man, hired gun, hitter, iceman, plugger, ratboy, rod, rod boy, rodman, rubber, torpedo, trigger, trigger man

hold someone's
feet to the fire
*v phr To punish
severely and
publicly; make an
example of; crucify,
as in "The teacher
swore he'd hold my
feet to the fire if I
acted like that
again"*

let turn in the wind, nail to the cross, nail to the wall, stick it to

homer
v To hit a home run

hit a dinger, hit for the circuit, hit one out of there, make a circuit clout, park one, park it in the bleachers, power a homer

honest-to-God
1 *adj Genuine;
authentic; real*

aces, all wool and a yard wide, big as life, card-carrying, copper-bottomed, eighteen-carat, flat-ass, for real, for serious, for-sure, honest-to-goodness, honest-to-Pete, kosher, legit, McCoy, natural-born, no buts about it; no ifs, ands, or buts; no-shit, O G, on the level, on the up-and-up, really-truly, regular, simon-pure, solid, stone, straight, sure-enough, sure-thing, up-and-up

2 *adv phr Really;
truly*

I kid you not, I shit you not, no bull, no kidding, no shit, you better believe

honey
1 *n Beloved person;
sweetheart*

angel, angelface, babe, baby, baby-doll, babykins, bubbele, bubbie, buttercup, child, dearie, doll, doll-baby, dove, dreamboat, duckling, ducks, ducky, duckywucky, dumpling, heartthrob, hon, honey-bunch, honey-bunny, honey-child, honeypie, lamb, lambkins, lamby-pie, lollypop, love, lover, lovey, pet, poopsy,

poopsy-woopsy, precious, snooks, snooksy-wooksy, snookums, snooky, sugar, sugar-bun, sugar-pants, sweetheart, sweetie, sweetie-pants, sweetie-pie, sweetkins, sweetness, sweet patootie, sweet potato, sweets, toots, tootsie, tootsie-pie, tootsy-wootsy

☞ *These terms are very often used as an endearment in address, as in "Yes, honey, I'll be home soon."*

2 SEE **HUMDINGER**

honk

1 *v To sound the horn of a car*   beep, oogah, toot

2 SEE **FEEL**

hooked

adj Addicted to narcotics   bamboozled, dipped, dirty, from Mount Shasta, gow-headed, having a monkey on one's back, hung out, hung up, in business, narkied, on, on the horse, on the mojo, on the monkey wagon, on the needle, on the pipe, on the stuff, pasted, poppy-headed, riding the poppy train, riding the witch's broom, shoveling the black stuff, strung, strung out, up against it

hooker

1 *n A prostitute*   ass peddler, bat, B-girl, bim, bimbo, [Brit] bona roba, bum, butt peddler, call girl, cat, chippy, commercial beaver, dirtyleg, fille de joie, flatback, flesh peddler, floozy, ho, kelsey, lady of the evening, ler, notch girl, [Brit] Piccadilly commando, piece of trade, pro, pross, prossie, prosty, puta, putana, quiff, Sadie, Sadie Thompson, saleslady, sidewalk susie, skank, skeezer, tail peddler, working broad, working girl

☞ *Terms for a male prostitute do not abound, e.g., "call boy" and "male model," though many of the basically female terms can be used.*

2 SEE **SNORT**

hoopla

1 *n A clamorous commotion*

brouhaha, fireworks, flap, foofooraw, fuss, hoo-ha, how-de-do, racket, ruckus, rumpus, [Brit] shemozzle, shindy, to-do

2 SEE **FLAK**

horny

adj Sexually excited and desirous

antsy, goatish, hard, hard up, hot, hot as a three-dollar pistol, hot to trot, hunky, itching, itchy, rammy, randy, rooty, sexy, steamed, turned on

horse

n Heroin

ack-ack, antifreeze, Aunt Hazel, Aunt Noral, bad bundle, balot, big boy, big H, big Harry, black gold, black tar, blue sky, bonita, boy, bozo, brown, brown Rhine, brown rock, brown stuff, brown sugar, caballo, caca, China white, China white goods, Chinese, cobics, corgy, courage pills, crap, crown crap, deck, dog food, dogie, dopoe, downtown, dugee, dynamite, dyno, ferry dust, foolish powder, gammot, George smack, goldfinger, H, hairy, halvah, H and C, Harry, Hazel, H-cap, Henry, hero, him, hocus, hook, horse radish, hot and cold, jeegee, jive dojee, Jones, joy dust, joy flakes, joy powder, kenkoy, Lady H, matsakaw, mayo, McCoy, merchandise, Mexican mud, muscle, oil, old Steve, oroy, pack, piece, poison, powder, pulborn, pure, rat poison, red, red chicken, red rock, rock, salt, scag, scar, scat, schlechts, schlock, schmack, schmeck, schmeek, scott, shit, shriek, skid, slag, sleeper, smack, smeck, snow, sugar, syrup, tinik, TNT, Tootsie Roll, tragic magic, white nurse, white stuff, witch, witch Hazel

☞ *The great number of slang terms for narcotics probably reflects both a need for coded reference to an illegal substance and a desire to be chic and up-to-date, in addition to the need to distinguish varieties.*

horse around

v phr To joke and caper pleasurably; indulge in horseplay

carry on, cavort, cut capers, cut didoes, cut up, fart around, feel one's oats, fool around, frivol, kick up one's heels

the **horselaugh**

n phr A loud, nasty, and dismissive laugh at someone

the merry ha-ha

horse opera

n phr A cowboy movie; a western

bang-bang, giddyapper, horse opry, oateater, oater, oat opera, sagebrusher

horseplay

n Boisterous fun; uninhibited jollification

capers, didoes, high-jinks, monkeyshines, shenanigans

hot

1 *adj Very popular; very much courted and desired; very successful, as in "Clark Gable was a very hot movie star in his day"*

big, in, large, the rage, the thing

2 *adj Performing very well; enjoying a winning impetus*

in a bubble, in a zone, on a roll, on one's game

3 SEE **HORNY**

hot damn

interj An exclamation of delight, gratification, relish, etc

hot diggety, hot diggety damn, hot diggety dog, hot diggety doggety, hot dog, hot poo, hot shit, hot spit, hot ziggety, shit on wheels

hot pants

n phr Strong sexual desire; lust

blue balls, a hard-on, horniness, hot nuts, hot rocks, the hots, a lech, stonies

hot rod

n phr A car specially modified and fitted with a powerful or rebuilt engine so as to be much faster than one of the same stock design

A-bomb, bomb, bug, can, destroker, destroke rod, dragster, gow, gowed-up job, gow job, hauler, hopped-up job, hot iron, juiced-up jalopy, juiced-up job, rod, set of wheels, souped-up job, soup job, stepped-up job, street job, stroker, stroke rod

hot shot

n phr An especially gifted and effective person; an achiever

ball of fire, best thing since sliced bread, crowd-pleaser, fast burner, fireball, flash, go-getter, greatest thing since sliced bread, hot dog, hot dogger, hot number, hot rock, hot shit, hot stuff, hustler, no slouch, piss-cutter, pisser, pistol, shit on wheels, whiz, whiz kid, winner, wiz, world-beater

house-cleaning

n A reorganization of a business or government department, esp with dismissal of incompetent or dishonest employees

shake-up

a howl

n Something very funny; a hilarious show, occasion, etc

a boff, a boffo, a boffola, a hoot, a knee-slapper, a laff, a laff riot, a laugh, a laugh and a half, a laugher, a panic, a rib-tickler, a riot, a scream, a side-splitter, a stitch, a yuk, a yuk-yuk

how's tricks

sentence Hello; how are you?

hi ya, hi y'all, howdy, how goes it, how're you doing, how's every little thing, how's the world treating you, how's things, how's your hammer hanging, how they hanging, how you was, long time no see

hubby

n A husband

the lord and master, man, the man of the house, the mister, the old man, the worser half

humdinger

n Something remarkable, wonderful, superior, etc

ace, aceroo, aces, the article, barn-burner, bear, bear-cat, beaut, beauty, the best thing since sliced bread, a bitch, a bitch-kitty, blinger, the cat's balls, the cat's eyebrows, the cat's meow, the cat's nuts, the cat's pajamas, the cat's whiskers, champ, champion, the cheese, corker, crackerjack, daisy, dandy, darb, dill, dilly, dinger, doozy, the goods, a groove, honey, hooper-doo, hooperdooper, hot poo, hot shit, hot spit, hot stuff, hummer, jim-dandy, joe-darter, kick, killer, killer-diller, kill-out, knockout, lily, lollapalooza, lulu, the McCoy, the most, the nuts, oner, peach, peacherino, peacheroo, phenom, pip, pipperoo, pippin, piss-cutter, pisser, pistol, the real George, ringtailed snorter, ripsnorter, snorter, sockdolager, sockeroo, some punkins, something, something else, something to write home about, stemwinder, the stuff, stunner, sweetheart, tops, the tops, whiz, whizbang, winner, wow, wowser

hung
adj Having impressive male genitals

endowed, hung like a bull, hung like a horse, hung like a stallion, hung like a stud, well-endowed, well-hung

hungry
adj Very ambitious; threateningly self-improving, as in "The new employee's not just a hard worker, she's hungry"

bucking, [Brit] dead keen, eager, going for the jugular, lean and mean, on the make

hunk
1 *n An attractive man, esp one who is sexually attractive*

Adonis, beefcake, caveman, centerfold, collar ad, dreamboat, glamor puss, Greek god, he-man, hunk of beef, hunkorama, macho, pin-up boy, sex pot, smooth article, smoothie

2 SEE **HE-MAN**

hunky
1 *n A foreigner, esp an Eastern European laborer*

bohunk, ginzo

2 SEE **SEXY**

3 *adj Handsome; sexually attractive, as in "She was studying the hunky fellow at the next table"*

funky, laid out, Studley

4 SEE **HE-MAN**

hustle

1 *v* To work as a prostitute

2 SEE **CON**

3 SEE **GET THE LEAD OUT**

4 SEE **HEIST**

cruise, cruise for trade, go on track, hook, peddle ass, red-light, turn tricks

iffy
adj Uncertain; risky　　[Brit] dicey, fifty-fifty, fluky, touch-and-go

I'll be damned
sentence and interj
May I be
maltreated,
confounded,
accursed, etc; an
exclamation of
surprise or
determination

I'll be, I'll be a dirty name, I'll be a dirty word, I'll be a monkey's uncle, I'll be a son of a bitch, I'll be a son of a gun, I'll be blowed, I'll be cow-kicked, I'll be danged, I'll be darned, I'll be ding-swizzled, I'll be dipped, I'll be dipped in shit, I'll be fucked, I'll be hanged, I'll be hornswoggled, I'll be jiggered, I'll be jig-swiggered, I'll be switched

☞ *In every expression, "I'll be" may be replaced with "I'm."*

in
adj Successful, as in
"After one more
all-out try he was
in"

[Brit] home and dry, home free, in like Flynn, out of the woods

in a fog
adj phr In a
confused state;
disoriented; dazed

in a haze, in a muddle, in a zone, mooning, moony, nodding, noddy, spaced, spaced out, spacey

the in group
n phr An exclusive group or clique of influential persons

insiders, old-boy network, old boys' system, those in the know, those in the loop

in hog heaven
adj phr In a position of ease and affluence; richly contented

fat, dumb, and happy; in clover, in fat city, in pig heaven, on top of the world, on velvet, pissing on ice

innards
n The viscera

guts, insides, kishkes, meatware, stuffings, tripes

in place
adv phr Available; effectuated or installed, as in "She has all her support systems in place"

aboard, on deck, on line, on tap

in stir
adv phr In prison

abroad, away, inside, out of circulation, out of town, up the river
☞ *This list may be greatly extended by making phraes with "in" or "in the" and terms under "the slammer."*

in the bag
adj phr Certain; as sure as if prearranged, as in "His election is in the bag"

all tied up, cinched, dead sure, iced, racked, taped, tied up, wired, wired up

in the driver's seat
adj phr In the position of authority and advantage; in control

in the catbird seat, sitting fat, sitting pretty

in the groove
adj phr Performing well and spontaneously; working seemingly without effort

getting down, getting off, grooving, in the pocket, in the zone, jamming, on the beam, winging

in the pipeline
adj phr Being prepared, processed, or worked on; imminent

in the hopper, in the works, on the fire

in there
adj phr Making a great effort; coping energetically, as in "The marketing department is always in there, finding new ways to sell our products"

in there pitching, on the spot, on top of it, right in there, right there

into
prep Currently interested in; practicing or absorbed in, as in "That year he was into Chinese cooking"

doing, hepped on, inta, wired into

it's a new ball game
sentence The situation has entirely altered; a new beginning must be made

all bets are off, back to the old drawing board, it's a whole 'nother thing, we're back at square one

it takes two to tango
sentence This cannot happen or have happened without more than one person or party, as in "She says that the divorce was all his fault, but it takes two to tango"

it's a two-way street, it's not a one-way street

izzatso
interj An exclamation of disbelief or defiance

applesauce, balls, baloney, bullshit, come off it, don't give me that shit, don't make me laugh, get out of here, the hell you say, hooey, in a pig's ass, like fun, no shit, says which, says who, says you, tell it to Sweeney, tell it to the Marines, who you kidding, you're full of hops, you're full of shit, you wouldn't shit me

J

Jack
n Mister; Sir; you there

Brother, Bub, Bud, Buddy, Buster, Butch, Chief, Dad, Daddy, Daddy-O, Doc, Fella, Guy, Hombre, Joe, Mac, Man, My Man, pal, Skipper, Sport

☞ *These are terms of address used by one man to another, either amiably or edged with hostility. They merge ordinary nicknames with terms for "man" and "fellow."*

jack off
v phr To masturbate

bang the bishop, beat one's dummy, beat one's log, beat one's meat, beat off, beat the hog, bring oneself off, choke the gopher, cuff one's meat, fist-fuck, flog one's meat, flong one's dong, fuck off, get oneself off, give oneself a hand job, jerk one's gherkin, jerk off, play with oneself, pound one's meat, pound one's peenie, pull oneself off, pull one's pud, rub off, screw off, stroke, [Brit] toss off, [Brit] wank, [Brit] wank off, whack off

jail bait
n A girl below the legal age of sexual consent

San Quentin pigeon, San Quentin quail

jalopy

n A car

ark, banger, beater, boat, boiler, bucket, bucket of bolts, buggy, bus, buzz-buggy, buzz-wagon, cage, chariot, clunk, clunker, cochecito, crate, four-wheeler, gas-guzzler, goat, grinder, heap, hoopy, iron, jitney, job, junker, junk-heap, lemon, lizzie, lunker, puddle jumper, ride, set of wheels, sheen, short, strugglebuggy, trans, transportation, tub, tuna wagon, vet, wheels, winter rat, wreck, zoom buggy

☞ *Many of these are used especially of old and ruinous cars, but they may be used appropriately of any car.*

Jane

n An average woman

Jane Doe, Jane Q Citizen, Jane Q Public, plain Jane

jazzed-up

adj Made faster, more exciting, fascinating, etc, as in "They promise a jazzed-up version of Uncle Remus"

gassed-up, goosed-up, hopped-up, jazzed, pepped-up, pumped-up, punched-up, revved-up, souped-up, zazzed-up

jazz up

v phr To make faster, more exciting, more stimulating, etc

gas up, goose, goose up, hop up, hype up, jack up, jazz, jim-jam, juice up, jump up, pep up, pump up, punch up, put balls on, put hair on, rev up, zazz up

jazzy

adj Exciting; stimulating

peppy, punchy, zappy, zazzy, zingy, zippy

Jeez

interj An exclamation of emphasis, surprise, disbelief, impatience, irritation, pain, etc

ay caramba, begorra, bless me, bless my soul, [Brit] blimey, boy, boy-howdy, brassafrax, brother, burbage, by cracky, by damn, by gad, by gee, by George, by golly, by jiminy, by jingo, by Jove, by thunder, chit, Chrisakes, Christ Almighty, Christ-on-a-crutch, [Brit] crikey, dammit, damn, damnation, dear me, doggone, for cat's sakes, for crying in the grog, for crying out loud, for goodness' sakes, for gosh sake, for heaven's sakes, for Pete's sake, for pity's sakes, for the love of Mike, for the love of Pete, gadzooks, gee, gee-whillikers, gee-whiz, George, glory hallelujah, God Almighty, goldamn, golly, golly gee, good gracious, goodness sakes alive, good night, [Brit] gorblimey, gosh all fishhooks, gosh almighty, goshdarn, gracious, gracious sakes alive, great leaping Jesus, great Scott, gunga, hail Columbia, heavens, heavens sakes, heavens to Betsy, hell, hell's bells, hey, hey-man, hijo, holy cats, holy cow, holy gee, holy hell, holy mackerel, holy Moses, holy shit, holy smokes, hoo-boy, hoo-ha, how about that, I declare, I swan, Jeepers, Jeepers Creepers, jeezy-peezy, Jesus, Jesus H. Christ, Judas priest, jumping Jehosaphat, jumping Jesus, law, leaping lizards, Lord have mercy, Lordy, man, man alive, my glory, my God, my gosh, my lands, ouch, poo, rats, sakes alive, shee, shee-it, sheesh, sheet, shit, shoot, suffering cats, ye gods, ye gods and little fishes, yikes, yipe, yipes

☞ *This interesting term represents both euphemism and blasphemy, and could be extended almost indefinitely.*

jerk

1 *n A tedious and ineffectual person, esp a man; a fool*

ass, bimbo, boob, bozo, chump, clown, cluck, corn dog, creep, dexter, dildo, dill, dingbat, dink, dipshit, dipstick, dolf, dork, drip, drizzle, drizzlepuss, drool, dud, dumdum, dummy, dweeb, eightball, fathead, fishball, foul ball, fuckhead, funk, fuzznuts, geek, geekoid, gink, goobatron, goober, goof, goon, grind, groover, grunch, grunge, gug, gumby, gump, gweebo, headache, Herkimer Jerkimer, hoakie, ho-dad, horse's ass, huckleberry, jackass, jack-off, jag, jag-off, Jerk McGee, jerk-off, joker, kink, kinko, klutz, lame, lop, lummox, lunk, lunkhead, meatball, Melvin, mince, mutt, nebbish, nerd, numbnuts, ook, outz, pain, pain in the ass, pain in the neck, peckerhead, pill, pinhead, plonk, pogue, poop, poor slob, poot, poot-butt, pud, punk, ringtail, sad apple, sap, saphead, scag, schlemiel, schlep, schlepper, schmo, schnook, schtoonk, shit-ass, shrimp, simp, skag, slob, snarf, squirt, stick, stiff, sucker, turkey, twerp, [Brit] twit, weenie, wimp, wonk, worm, yap, yo-yo, zhlub, zod

2 SEE **DRAG**

jerk town
n phr A small town crossroads, East Jesus, filling station, jerkwater town, mudhole, noplaceville, one-horse town, one-stoplight town, podunk, tank town, whistle stop, wide place in the road

the jet set
n phr Wealthy, the beautiful people, the glitterati
glamorous people

a jiffy
n phr A very short as long as it takes to say Jack Robinson, the bat of a eye,
time; an instant a bit, a flash, half a mo, a hoop and a holler, a jif, a jiff, a jiffin, a jiffing, less than no time, a mo, no time, no time at all, a sec, a shake, a tick, a twink, a twinkling, two hoops and a holler, two shakes, two shakes of a lamb's tail, a wink

jiggers
interj An exclamation of alarm and warning, as in "Jiggers, here comes the boss"

cheese it, chickie

the jitters
n phr Fidgety nervousness; uneasy restlessness

the all-overs, butterflies, the dithers, the fantods, the fidgets, the heebie-jeebies, the jeebies, the jimjams, the jumps, the leaping heebies, the quivers, the screaming meemies, the shakes, shpilkes, the willies, the wim-wams

jittery
adj Nervous; anxious

all of a doodah, all shook, all shook up, antsy, bouncing off the walls, clutched, clutchy, edgy, fretty, hitchy, hot and bothered, hyper, in a pucker, in a state, in a stew, in a sweat, in a swivet, in a tizzy, in the anxious seat, itchy, jumpy, nervous as a cat on a hot tin roof, nervous as a dog shitting razorblades, on edge, shook, shook up, uptight, wired, worried stiff, yantsy

jock
n An athlete

jockstrap, strap

Joe Blow
n phr Any man; the average man

every Tom Dick and Harry, ham-and-egger, Joe Schmo, Joe Six-Pack, Joe Storch, Joe Zilch, John, John Doe, Johnny, John Q Citizen, man on the street, one of the boys, one of the guys, ordinary guy, ordinary Joe, poor fish, poor John, Richard Roe, square John, Storch, zilch

Joe College

n phr A young man whose dress and manner betoken the nonacademic aspects of college life

Joe Yale, key, white shoe

joint

1 *n A marijuana cigarette*

ace, bam, bammy, belt, birdwood, bomb, bomber, boo reefer, booster stick, burnie, butt, canceled stick, cartucho, cattail, ceck, cigar, cocktail, dinky dow, doobie, double header, dream stick, dynamiter, fat jay, fatty, funny cigarette, gage butt, gasper, gold leaf special, gonga smudge, goober, good butt, goof butt, gooly butt, gow, gyve, hay butt, hot stick, J, jay, jay smoke, jive, jolt, J smoke, kick stick, killer, killer stick, leno, log, mezz, mezz roll, miggle, mighty mezz, ming, mooter, muggle, muggles, nail, nose burner, number, pin, pinner, reefer, riff, roach, root, skoofus, skrufus, spliff, splim, splint, stack, stencil, stick, stick of gage, stick of tea, tea, tea bag, tea-stick, thing, thirteen, thriller, thumb, torch, torpedo, tube, twist, vonce, weed, zol

☞ *The great number of slang terms for narcotics probably reflects both a need for coded reference to an illegal substance and a desire to be chic and up-to-date, in addition to the need to distinguish varieties.*

2 SEE **BAG**
3 SEE **COCK**
4 SEE **DIVE**
5 SEE the **SLAMMER**
6 SEE **WORKS**

jumped-up

adj Inflated, esp by artifice; made more imposing

jacked-up, puffed-up

junkie

1 *n A narcotics user or addict*

acidhead, ad, bangster, channel swimmer, coke freak, cokehead, cokey, cubehead, dip, dope fiend, dopehead, dopenik, doper, dopester, dreamer, druggie, drughead, feeblo, fiend, flier, freak, glassy-eye, goof, gowhead, gowster, grasshopper, hashhead, head, hog, hophead, hop merchant, hopster, hype shooter, jabber, junker, junk hawk, junk hog, junk hound, junk man, liner, mainliner, mainline shooter, meth freak, meth head, narco, needle fiend, needle jabber, needle nipper, needle pusher, needle rusher, pillhead, pill-popper, pinhead, pinjabber, pothead, puller, reefer, sleighrider, smack freak, smackhead, smecker, snowbird, space cadet, speedball, speedo, stoner, student, unkjay, vein shooter, weed eater, weedhead, zone, zoner

☞ *This list is not confined to any particular manner of injection or consumption, nor to any particular narcotic.*

2 SEE FAN

K

kaput

1 *adj Ruined; wrecked; inoperative*

all washed up, ausgespielt, belly-up, blooey, buggered, burned out, clobbered, cooked, dead, dead in the water, dead meat, dished, done for, down and out, down for the count, down the chute, down the drain, down the pipe, down the tube, down the tubes, finished, floored, flummoxed, frazzled, fried, in the bag, in the dumper, in the tub, kayoed, laid out, one's name is mud, NG, nuked, on the rocks, on the skids, out of business, out of luck, out of the box, out on one's ass, out the window, pfft, played out, shit out of luck, shot, shot down in flames, snakebit, snake-bitten, S O L, south of the border, sunk, tapped out, toast, totaled, Tubesville, up the spout, washed up, wasted, whipped, wiped out

☞ *This list may be extended by using participial forms of terms under "go kerflooey."*

☞ *These terms share semantic territory with "out of luck," which should also be considered.*

2 SEE **FINISHED**

keep one's **cool**

v phr To stay unruffled; be calm, as in "It's hard to keep your cool when you lose your job"

go with the flow, keep a tight asshole, keep cool, keep one's hair on, keep one's pants on, keep one's shirt on, not bat an eye, not blink an eye, not blow a fuse, not blow a gasket, not get one's balls in an uproar, not get one's shit hot, not lose one's cool, not turn a hair

kibitzer

n A person who gives intrusive advice; a meddler

backseat driver, buttinsky, nark, Nosy Parker, Paul Pry, snoop, woppitzer, yenta

a kick

n A delightful sensation; a thrill, as in "Seeing her again was quite a kick"

bang, belt, biff, blast, boot, buzz, charge, drive, flash, flip, groove, head, hit, jolt, large charge, lift, punch, rush, toot, up, upper, wallop, zing

kick ass

v phr To punish; assert authority; discipline harshly

attend to, bear down on, climb, climb one's frame, come down on, crack down on, fix, give hell, give it to, give merry hell, jump, jump all over, kick ass and take names, kick booty, let someone have it, light into, lower the boom, make it hot for, pitch into, put the wood to, read the riot act, settle someone's hash, skin alive, stack asses, strafe, throw the book at

kick back

v phr To relax; rest and restore oneself

catch one's breath, ease up, knock off, lay back, lay chilly, lay up, mellow out, put one's feet up, take a break, take a breather, take a load off, take a load off one's feet, take five, take it easy, take ten, take time out, unkink, unlax, unwind, walk cool, wind down

kick in

v phr To give, pay, contribute

ante up, come across with, dish out, dish up, feed the kitty with, fork out, fork over, fork up, hand over, pony up, put out, shell out, slip, weigh in with

kicks

1 *n* Pleasure; gratification

bangs, cookies, [esp Brit] fun and games, happies, jollies, knocks, what turns you on

2 *n* Shoes

ends, kickers, leathers

kid

1 *n* A child

blister, boychick, brat, carpet rat, crumbcatcher, crumbcrusher, crumbgrinder, crumbsnatcher, curtain climber, drape ape, godfer, grommet, holy terror, house ape, imp, kiddo, kiddy, legbiter, little bugger, little devil, little dickens, little monkey, little pest, little pisher, little punk, little rascal, little shaver, mud lark, Munchkin, pisher, poot-butt, punk, punk kid, pup, puppy, rug ape, rug rat, slasher, snotnose, sprout, squirt, toddler, yard rat, young punk, young 'un

2 *v* To joke; jest; banter

crack funny, crack wise, jive, josh, make a funny, shuck, shuck and jive, wisecrack

3 *v* To fool; deceive, as in "That can't be true; you're kidding me"

give someone leg, goof on someone, have someone on, jack someone around, jerk someone around, jerk someone's chain, jerk someone off, pull someone's leg, put someone on, spoof, yank someone's chain

4 SEE **SNOW**

kid around

v phr To jest and banter; tease

boogaloo, boogie, fool around, jape, jive, josh, kid, lark, shuck, shuck and jive

kike
n A Jew

clipped dick, eagle-beak, Goldberg, Hebe, hooknose, Ike, Ikey, mockie, sheeny, Yid, zip top

☞ *These terms are deeply offensive.*

kinky
1 *adj Sexually deviant*
2 SEE **FLAKY**
3 SEE **GAY**

bent, far out, freaky, funky, funny, oddball, offbeat, off the wall, queer, rat fuck, strangioso, weird

kiss my ass
sentence I invite you to perform or submit to a humiliating act

bite my ass, bite this, cram it, fuck you, [Brit] get stuffed, go fuck yourself, ram it, screw you, shove it, [Brit] sod you, stick it, stick it in your ear, stick it up your ass, stick it where the sun doesn't shine, stuff it, up your ass, up yours, you know what you can do with it, you know where you can stick it

☞ *The distinction between "kiss my ass" and "fuck you" (also a main entry in this book) is not easy to draw. For a full repertory of powerful insults one should consider both.*

knock
1 *n A disparaging comment; an insult*

brickbat, bringdown, dig, ding, dirty crack, dirty dig, dump, dumping, nasty crack, pan, put-down, rank-out, rap, razz, rip, shot, slam, slap, slap in the face, sock, spitball, swipe

2 *v To criticize harshly, often unfairly; complain of; carp at*

bad-mouth, bring down, burn, dig at, dis, down, dump all over, dump on, jab, joan, lambaste, pan, pimp, poor-mouth, put down, put the shit on, rank out, rap, razz, rib, ride, rip, rip on, roast, run down, shoot on, slag, slag off, slam, slap, spitball, take a dig at, take a potshot at, take a swipe at, trash, zing

3 SEE **BAD-MOUTH**

knocked up
adj phr Pregnant

expecting, having a bun in the oven, in the family way, on the hill, preggers, preggy, prego, puffed, pumped, that way, wearing her apron high

knock off
1 *v phr* To stop, esp to stop working; desist, as in "I think I'll knock off early today"
2 SEE **KICK BACK**

bag it, belay, break off, call it a day, call it quits, can it, caulk off, check it in, come off, cut out, drop it, go to the showers, hang it up, lay down one's tools, lay off, [Brit] pack in, [esp Brit] pack it in, [esp Brit] pack up, secure, shut up shop, stow it, take a break, take five, take ten

knock out
v phr To make someone unconscious, esp with a blow

chill, coldcock, cork, cream, deck, drop, duke someone out, finish, flatten, kayo, knock cold, knock cuckoo, knock someone's lights out, knock stiff, knock the day-lights out of, K O, lay out, lay out cold, lay out in lavender, put on the floor, put out like a light, stiffen

knock something **out**
v phr To make or produce, esp rather quickly, as in "I couldn't find time to knock the invitation out myself"

cobble up, knock something together, throw something together, whomp up

knock up
v phr To make pregnant

bump, fix up, get in trouble, put a bun in the oven

know one's **onions**
v phr To be competent and authoritative, esp in one's work; have impressive skill

have all the moves, have been around, have been through the mill, know all the answers, know all the moves, know all the tricks, know a thing or two, know backwards and forwards, know one's beans, know one's business, know from A to Z, know from the ground up, know one's stuff, know the ins and outs, know the ropes, know the score, know one's way around, know what it's all about, know what's what, know where it's at, not be born yesterday

kraut
n A German or person of German extraction

Boche, Dutchie, Dutchman, Fritz, Fritzie, Heinie, Hun, Jerry, krauthead, squarehead
☞ *These terms are considered offensive.*

kvetch
n A complainer, esp a chronic malcontent

beefer, bellyacher, bitcher, crab, crank, gripe, griper, grouch, grouchbag, groucher, grouse, grouser, grumbler, heat merchant, moaner, [Brit] moaning Minnie, picklepuss, sorehead, sourpan, sourpuss

L

ladies' man
n phr A man who pursues and otherwise devotes himself to women to an unusual degree

bad dude, bad-mother swinger, buck, cake-eater, Casanova, cat, chaser, Don Juan, drugstore cowboy, dude, God's gift to women, heartbreaker, hotshot, hound dog, lady-killer, Lothario, lounge lizard, lover-boy, make-out artist, masher, operator, playboy, poodle-faker, Romeo, sheik, skirt-chaser, smooth article, smoothie, smooth operator, sport, stud, studhammer, tomcat, wolf, woman-chaser

laid-back
adj Relaxed; unhurried

breezy, cas, chilly, cool, cooled out, easy, easy-going, mellow

latrine lawyer
n phr A soldier who is argumentative and authoritative among his peers with respect to his superiors, to rules and regulations, and to justice and expediency; a noisy meddler

clubhouse lawyer, forecastle lawyer, guardhouse lawyer, jailhouse lawyer, sea lawyer
☞ *While the entry term refers to soldiers, the modifiers in the list indicate similar types among other male groupings.*

a laugh
n phr Something very funny; a laughing matter

[Brit] a giggle, a hoot, a howl, a killer, a laugh and a half, a riot, a scream, a stitch

laundry list
n phr A bill of items to be obtained, requested, discussed, etc, as in "Once she has the microphone we'll have to listen to her whole laundry list of issues"

shopping list, want list, wish list

lay it on the line
v phr To speak candidly and straightforwardly; be plain

get down to brass tacks, go the hang-out road, lay it on the table, let one's hair down, let it all hang out, level, make no bones, pull no punches, put one's cards on the table, put it on the line, spill, spill one's guts, talk straight from the shoulder, talk turkey, tell it like it is

lay off
interj An exclamation of annoyance and warning

back off, butt out, get lost, get out of my hair, go fly a kite, go jump in the lake, go peddle your papers, go soak your head, keep your nose out of this, stick to your knitting, take a walk

lean on someone
v phr To put pressure on, esp with violence or the threat of it, as in "If he doesn't pay us today, we'll have to lean on him"

high-pressure, pressure, put the blocks to, put the heat on, put the squeeze on, twist someone's arm, work on

leatherneck

n A US Marine   devil dog, gyrene, jarhead, seagoing bellhop

letdown

n A disap-   [Brit] bringdown, comedown, [Brit] damp squib, dud,
pointment; a failure   dull thud, false alarm, flash in the pan, frost, lemon,
of expectation   misfire, nine days' wonder

let oneself **go**

v phr To behave in   break out the jams, bust loose, cut loose, go hog wild,
an unrestrained   kick out the jams, kick over the traces, let 'er rip, let
manner; be   one's hair down, let it all hang out, let loose, loosen up,
uninhibited   pull out all the stops

let it all hang out

v phr To speak   get it off one's chest, get it out of one's system, go the
candidly; abandon   hang-out road, let one's hair down, let it out, level, not
all concealment   bottle it up, open up, spill one's guts, spill it, spit it out,
tell it like it is, unload

**a lick and a
promise**

n phr A hasty job;   a once-over, a once-over lightly
*a cursory
performance, as in
"It's quitting time,
so all I can offer is a
lick and a promise"*

lickety-split

adv Very rapidly; at   all out, balls to the wall, flat-out, full blast, full steam,
full speed   hammer down, hell-bent, hell-bent for election, hell-
for-leather, in high gear, in overdrive, lickety-cut, like
a bat out of hell, like a blue streak, like a house afire, like
a scared rabbit, like a streak, like Billy Hell, like crazy,
like greased lightning, like hell, like mad, like sixty, like

thunder, on the double, to beat the band, to beat the devil, to beat the Dutch, wide open

lid

n A hat

bonnet, chapeau, Stetson

lightweight

n An inconsequential person; a trivial person

also-ran, busher, bush-leaguer, doormat, dud, eightball, featherweight, half-pint, limp-dick, little shot, loser, man with a paper ass, nebbish, no bargain, nobody, nobody to write home about, no great shakes, nonentity, nonstarter, no prize package, nothing to write home about, not much of a bargain, palooka, peanut, pip-squeak, pissant, poor fish, poor slob, punk, sad apple, sad sack, schlemazel, second-stringer, slob, small potatoes, small-timer, third-rater, tinhorn

☞ *These terms share semantic territory with "loser" and with "wimp," which should also be considered.*

like hell

1 *adv phr To an extreme degree; exceedingly, as in "This blister hurts like hell"*

one's ass off, one's brains out, hand over fist, one's head off, in a big way, in spades, in the worst way, like a house afire, like all creation, like all get-out, like anything, like Billy Hell, like blazes, like blue blazes, like blue hell, like everything, like it had gone out of style, like nobody's business, like sin, like sixty, like the deuce, like the devil, like the dickens, like there was no tomorrow, something awful, something fierce, to beat anything, to beat hell, to beat the band, to beat the deuce, to beat the devil, to beat the dickens, to beat the Dutch, to the max

2 *adv phr Never; not at all, as in "Like hell we did"*

fat chance, I'll be damned if, I'll be fucked if, in a pig's ass, in a pig's ear, in a pig's eye, like fun, like shit, my ass, my eye, nohow, no way, no way Jose, there's no way

limey
n An English person, esp a man

beefeater, Brit, John Bull, lime-juicer
☞ *Strictly speaking, "Brit" applies to any native or citizen in Great Britain, hence to the Welsh, Scots, Cornish, Manx, etc, as well as the English. Both US and British usage tends to be somewhat loose on this point.*

line
n A try at persuasion; a piece of advocacy

applesauce, fast line, jive, line of chatter, line of hooey, pitch, routine, snow job, song, song and dance, spiel
☞ *These terms share semantic territory with "bullshit," which should also be considered.*

little bitty
adj phr Very small; tiny

banty, bitsy, bitsy-witsy, bitty, bitty-witty, dinky, eentsy-weentsy, half-pint, inky-dinky, itsy-bitsy, itsy-witsy, itty-bitty, knee-high, little bitsy, peanut, peewee, piddling, piddly, pint-size, pocket-size, poky, runty, teentsy, teentsy-weentsy, teeny, teeny-weeny, two-by-four, vestpocket, weenchy, weentsy

loaded
1 adj Very rich; affluent

big rich, bloated, dirty, dirty with money, fat, filthy, filthy rich, filthy with money, flush, heeled, holding, in the bucks, in the chips, in the dough, in the money, loose, lousy, lousy rich, made of money, nigger rich, on the gravy boat, on the gravy train, oofy, rolling in it, six feet up a bull's ass, stinking, stinking rich, well-heeled

2 SEE **HIGH**
3 SEE **PLASTERED**

loan shark
n phr An underworld usurer

juice dealer, shy, shylock

long johns

n phr *Long winter underwear*

BVDs, John Ls, long-handle underwear, longies, long ones, woolies

long shot

n phr *A person, horse, project, etc, that seems unlikely to win*

dark horse, fooler, sleeper

loser

1 n *A person or thing that fails, esp habitually*

also-ran, boho, born loser, bust, clinker, dog, dud, dull tool, eightball, foul ball, lemon, never-was, nonstarter, pig-meat, poor slob, sad apple, sad sack, schlemiel, schmendrick, schmo, schnook, slob, total loss, turkey, wipe-out

2 SEE **FLOP**

lousy with

adj phr *Abundant with, as in "The place was lousy with retired couples"*

alive with, awash in, crawling with, loaded with, mangy with

lude

n *A dose or capsule of methaqualone*

Canadian quail, lemon, quack, quad, quas, soap, soaper, super soaper, wall banger

lush

n *A heavy drinker; an inebriate*

bar-fly, booze-fighter, booze-freak, boozehound, boozer, bottle-man, dipso, drunk, elbow bender, geek, ginhead, ginhound, guzzler, hooch-hound, juicehead, loadie, lusher, lushwell, oryide, rumbag, rumhound, rummy, rumpot, shikker, soak, sot, souse, sponge, stew, stewbum, wino

M
n Morphine

bang, barmecide, big M, birdie powder, birdie stuff, coby, cube, cube juice, em, glad stuff, goma, gonga dust, happy medicine, hard stuff, hell dust, hocus, joy dust, joy flakes, Marmon, Miss Emma, Miss Emma Jones, Miss Morph, moocah, morph, morphina, Mr Morpheus, number thirteen, piece, Red Cross, sister, sugar, sweet Jesus, sweet Morpheus, tab, uncle, white cross, white death, white goddess, white linen, white merchandise, white nurse, white powder, white silk, white stuff, white tape, wings, witch

mack
n A pimp

mackman, player, [chiefly Brit] ponce

make a killing
v phr To get a large, quick profit; win hugely

clean up, feather one's nest, hit the jackpot, make a bundle

make a scene

v phr To create a disturbance; exhibit noisy indignation; make a public outburst, as in "He made quite a scene when they told him he couldn't use his credit card"

carry on, cast a kitten, cut up, get into a swivet, get into a tizzy, have a conniption fit, have a cow, have a duckfit, have a fit, have a shit fit, have a tantrum, kick up a fuss, kick up a racket, kick up a row, kick up a stink, kick up a storm, make a how-de-do, make a stink, make a to-do, make fireworks, make waves, piss up a storm, raise a fuss, raise a hullaballoo, raise a ruckus, raise a stink, raise a storm, raise Cain, raise hell, raise sand, raise the devil, raise the roof, rattle cages, rock the boat, shit a brick, spit tacks, tear up the peapatch

☞ *These terms share semantic territory with "blow one's top," which should also be considered.*

the McCoy

n phr A person or thing of excellent quality; just what is wanted

the article, gem, the goods, mensch, real guy, the real McCoy, the right sort, the right stuff, sweetheart, the tops

☞ *Most of the terms at "humdinger" may be used in this sense. A person designated "the McCoy" is not precisely the same as a "good guy," because the former has more to do with sterling moral qualities than with simple geniality.*

meat wagon

n phr An ambulance

fruit wagon

Mick

n An Irishman or -woman or person of Irish extraction

bog-hopper, bog-trotter, harp, Mickey, mulligan, paddy

☞ *These terms are offensive.*

Mickey Finn
n phr A strong hypnotic or barbiturate dose, esp of chloral hydrate, put secretly into a drink

knockout drops, little Michael, little Mickey, mickey, peter

mish-mash
n A mixture; a miscellany, esp with ill-matching components

dog's breakfast, grab-bag, mess, odds and ends, rag-bag

mitt
n A hand

biscuit hook, bunch of fives, duke, fist, five, fiver, flapper, flipper, glom, glommer, hook, lunch hook, meathook, paw, some skin

mob scene
n phr A crowded occasion or place

fannybumper, Grand Central Station, sardine can

moneybags
n A wealthy person

bloated plute, Croesus, Daddy Warbucks, deep pockets, fat cat, jillionaire, lord of creation, Mister Moneybags, plute, [Brit] warm man

monicker
n A person's name

front name, handle, label, tag

monkey business
n phr Dubious behavior; dishonesty; deception

funny business, hank, hanky-pank, hanky-panky, hocus-pocus, hokey-poke, hokey-pokey, skullduggery

monster
adj Very large; huge

God-size, humongous, jumbo, king-size, moby, walloping, whacking, whambang, whopping

moocher
n A parasite; a habitual beggar and drone

beat, bum, bummer, cadger, deadbeat, deadhead, freeloader, moke, momzer, mooch, panhandler, schnorrer, scrounger, [Brit] spiv, sponge, sponger

moonlight
v To work at a job in addition to one's regular job

daylight, double, double in brass

the most
1 *n phr The superior person or thing; the best of all*

A number 1, A-1, the berries, burner, the cat's, the cat's balls, the cat's eyebrows, the cat's meow, the cat's nuts, the cat's pajamas, the cat's whiskers, the champ, the champion, the greatest, the mostest, oner, something else, too much, the tops

2 SEE **HUMDINGER**

mug shot
n phr A photograph of a person's face, esp the front and side views made for police records

art, mug

mule

1 *n An obstinate person*

bitter-ender, bulldog, bullethead, bullhead, diehard, donkey, hammerhead, hardhead, hardnose, hard nut to crack, pighead, stiffneck

2 SEE **PANTHER PISS**

mung

n Anything nasty; filth; ordure

crap, glop, grunch, grunge, muck, prut, scrunge, scunge, scuzz, scuzzo

☞ *These terms share semantic territory with "goo," which should also be considered.*

neck
v To kiss, embrace, and caress; dally amorously

boodle, box tonsils, canoe, canoodle, cuddle, do homework, fling woo, go on bush patrol, grab on, lollygag, love up, make out, park, perch, pet, pitch woo, play kissie, play kissie-kissie, play kissy-face, play kissy-facey, play kissy-poo, play lickey-face, play smacky lips, play snuggle-bunnies, play tonsil hockey, smash mouth, smooch, spoon, suck face, swap spit

nigger
n A black person

blackbird, blood, blue, blue-gum, blue-skin, boogie, boot, bro, brother, burrhead, chocolate drop, chungo bunny, clink, cluck, coon, darky, dinge, eightball, geechee, groid, hardhead, Hershey bar, hod, inky-dink, jarhead, jig, jigaboo, jit, jungle bunny, kinky-head, mayate, nig, niggra, peola, schvartze, scuttle, shade, shad-mouth, shadow, skillet, smoke, spade, spook, zig, zigaboo
☞ *All these terms will give deep offense if used by nonblacks.*

night spot
n phr A nightclub

boite, club, lounge, nitery, room, trap

nit-pick

v To quibble over trivia; cavil

chop logic, pick nits, split hairs

☞ *These terms share semantic territory with "blow up," which should also be considered.*

nix

v To veto; reject

bag, kill, negative, not buy, not sign off on, put the kibosh on, thumb down, turn down cold, turn thumbs down

☞ *These terms share semantic territory with "chuck," which should also be considered.*

no fooling

sentence I am speaking seriously and honestly

I kid you not, I'm not just whistling Dixie, I shit you not

nope

negation No; never

forget you, negative, nix, no deal, no dice, no go, no sale, no sirree, no soap, nothing doing, not on your life, not on your tintype, no way, no way Jose, uh uh

no shit

interj An exclamation of happy credulity, as in "They bought my story? No shit"

no jive, no kidding, you wouldn't shit me

not give a damn

v phr To be indifferent to or contemptuous of; not care one whit

not give a dang, not give a darn, not give a dern, not give a flying fuck, not give a fuck, not give a hill of beans, not give a hoot, not give a rat's ass, not give a shit, not give diddly-damn, not give diddly-shit, not give spit, not give squat

☞ *This set may be enlarged enormously by substituting nearly any word for "shit" (that is, excrement) or "a shit," or any word for "zilch" (that is, nothing) in the formula.*

☞ *The terms share semantic territory with "one couldn't care less," which should also be considered. The distinction is one of impact, the terms above being much stronger than the others.*

not know shit from Shinola

v phr To be very ignorant; be hopelessly ill-informed; be stupid

know from nothing, not know one's ass from a hole in the ground, not know one's ass from first base, not know one's ass from one's elbow, not know beans, not know bubkes, not know diddly, not know diddly-damn, not know diddly-poo, not know diddly-poop, not know diddly-shit, not know diddly-squat, not know diddly-squirt, not know diddly-whoop, not know from nothing, not know shit, not know squat, not know zilch, not know zip, not know zippo

not worth a damn

adj phr Valueless; worthless

not worth a bucket of warm spit, not worth a plugged nickel, not worth a shit, not worth beans, not worth bubkes, not worth shit, not worth spit, not worth the powder to blow it to hell

☞ *The number of terms may be increased enormously by using nearly any word for "shit" (that is, excrement) or any word for "zilch" (that is, nothing) in the formula.*

nudnik

n An annoying person; a pest; a nuisance

nudge, pain, pain in the ass, pain in the neck, schlepper

nut

1 *n A crazy or very eccentric person; a lunatic*

bat, batty, bug, butterfly case, coot, crackbrain, crackpot, crazy, cuckoo, cupcake, daffydill, ding, ding-a-ling, dingbat, dip, flake, food for squirrels, freak, fruit, fruitcake, full-mooner, gonzo, goof, goofball, headcase, kook, loon, loonball, loony, loony-tune, loony-tunes, mental job, meshugana, nutball, nutbar, nutcake, nutcase, nutter, psycho, screwball, screw-loose, section eight, sickie, sicko, space cadet, space-out, squirrel, squirrel-food, wack, weirdie, weirdo, wombat

☞ *The semantic boundary between "eccentric person" and "insane person" is not easy to draw, so one should also see the entry for "oddball."*

2 SEE **BEAN**
3 SEE **FAN**

O

oddball

1 *n An eccentric person; a strange one*

bird, character, crank, creep, cueball, cupcake, dilly dude, ding-a-ling, dingbat, ding-dong, ferret, flake, foul ball, freak, fruit, fruitcake, geek, goober, goof, goofball, kook, nut, odd fish, odd stick, pod person, queer customer, queer duck, queer fish, [Brit] rum one, [Brit] rum customer, screwball, screw-loose, sickie, sicko, space cadet, space-out, spastic, spazz, spook, squirrel, twink, vert, wack, wacko, weirdie, weirdo, wombat, zod, zombie, zone, zoner

☞ *The semantic boundary between "eccentric person" and "insane person" is not easy to draw, so one should also see the entry for "nut."*

2 SEE **KINKY**

off one's feed

adj phr Not feeling or looking well; indisposed

not up to snuff, off color, peaked, peaky, poorish, punk, under the weather

OK

affirmation Yes; I agree; I accept that

copacetic, definitely, hokey-dokey, ok, okay, oke, okey-doke, okey-dokey, okle-dokle, right, rightio, righto, right on, right you are, Roge, Roger, Roger-dodger, sure enough, sure nuff, sure thing, yeah, yeah man, yep, yes indeedy, yes sirree, yes sirree Bob, you bet, you betcha, yowzah, yup

☞ *These terms share semantic territory with "bet your ass," which should also be considered.*

the OK

n phr Permission; consent, as in "After they thought it over they gave me the OK to start"

the go, the go-ahead, the green light, the nod, the okay, thumbs up

old bag

n phr An old woman; a female senior citizen

hag, no spring chicken, old bat, old battle-ax, old broad, old dame, old doll, old girl, old hag, old heifer, old hen, old witch

old fart

n phr An old man; a male senior citizen

alter kocker, codger, crock, dodo, duffer, fogy, fossil, futz, gaffer, geezer, gramps, old bird, old boy, old buzzard, old codger, old duffer, old fossil, old futz, old geezer, old poop, oldster, old-timer, pappy, pappy guy

old woman

n phr One's wife; one's helpmate

ball-and-chain, bedmate, better half, frau, good wife, little woman, mat, missumis, old lady, squaw, trouble and strife, wifie

the **once-over**

n phr A look or glance of inspection; scrutiny

[Brit] dekko, the eye, gander, hinge, a load of, looksee, peek, peep, quick-over, slant, squint, [Brit] vetting

on **hold**

adv phr In postponement or abeyance

in a holding pattern, in cold storage, in mothballs, in the deep freeze, in the icebox, on ice, on the back burner, on the shelf

on someone's **shit list**

adv phr Ill-regarded by; hated and menaced by

in someone's bad books, on someone's get-lost list

on the **ball**

adj phr Skillful, alert, and effective; aware and effectual

on the stick, with it

on the **blink**

adj phr Not functioning; not operating; out of repair, as in "We can't process your order. Our computer's on the blink"

ausgespielt, blooey, buggered-up, bum, bust, busted, conked out, down, flooey, fritzed, fucked-up, haywire, jimmied-up, kerflooey, loused-up, off, on the bum, on the fritz, out of commission, out of kilter, out of whack, [Brit] packed-up, shot, snafu, snafued

on the cuff
adv phr On credit, as in "He bought a couple of new suits on the cuff"

jawbone, on the arm, on the finger, on tick

on the double
adv phr Quickly; immediately, as in "I want that thing here and I want it on the double"

at the double, chop-chop, double-quick, hubba-hubba, immediately if not sooner, in a whoosh, in nothing flat, most rickety-tick, PDQ, pronto, [Brit] quickstep, toot sweet

on the level
adj phr Fair; even; equable, as in "Are you sure this deal is on the level? Won't somebody get shafted?"

[Australian] fair dinkum, level, on the legit, square

on the nose
adj phr Precisely right; exact, as in "His stock-market prediction was on the nose"

dead nut, on the bean, on the bull's-eye, on the button, on the dot, on the money, right on, slap on

on the QT
adv phr Secretly; quietly; not for publication, as in "I'll tell you this on the QT"

between you and me, between you and me and the bedpost, entre nous, hush-hush, off the record, strictly between us, under one's hat, under wraps

on the sauce
*adj phr Drinking
liquor, esp heavily*

boozing, guzzling, on the bottle, on the juice, on the shikker

on someone's
wavelength
*adv phr In
agreement; in
harmony*

grokking, hearing someone, on the same wavelength, tuned in

open one's **yap**
*v phr To speak; say
something, as in
"When they asked
her why, she didn't
open her yap"*

open one's face, open one's head, peep, pipe, pipe up, put one's oar in, put one's two cents in, put one's two cents' worth in, sing, sing out, warble

out
adj Unconscious

dead to the world, down for the count, out cold, out like a light, out of it

out of one's **depth**
*adj phr In a
situation where one
cannot cope, esp
because of
inexperience or
incapacity*

in deep water, in over one's head, outclassed, out of one's league, over one's head

out of luck

adj phr Having little chance of success; in great difficulty, as in "If you want to pay by check, I'm afraid you're out of luck"

behind the eight ball, between a rock and a hard place, dead in the water, down on one's luck, hard put, hard up, in a bind, in a box, in a fix, in a hole, in a jam, in a mess, in a pickle, in a tight spot, in bad shape, in deep shit, in deep trouble, in deep water, in Dutch, in hot grease, in hot water, in the soup, on the hook, on the hot seat, on the ropes, on the spot, out of one's depth, shit out of luck, shot down in flames, S O L, sunk, up against it

☞ *These terms share semantic territory with "kaput," which should also be considered.*

P

pad
n One's room or dwelling

cave, coop, crash pad, crib, cubby, diggings, digs, hangout, hideout, hive, hutch, kip, layout, roost, setup, squat

paint the town red
v phr To carouse

bar-hop, bat, binge, booze, cut up, go on a bat, go on a bender, go on a binge, go on a tear, paint the town, [Brit] pubcrawl, raise hell, tear

pal
n A friend, esp a very close male friend

ace, asshole buddy, bosom buddy, buckwheat, bud, buddy, buddy-boy, buddy-buddy, buddyroo, buttfuck buddy, [Brit] butty, chum, [Australian] cobber, [Brit] cock, goombah, Holmes, homeboy, homey, landsman, main man, mellow, paesan, paisano, pally, palsy-walsy, pard, pardner, road dog, sidekick, walkboy

palsy-walsy
adj Very friendly

chummy, dovey, footsie, footsie-wootsie, huggy-huggy, kissy-huggy, like that, lovey-dovey, pally, thick, thick as thieves

panhandle
v To beg, esp by accosting people on the street

batter, ding, plingstem

panic
1 *v To become frightened; take alarm*

break out in assholes, flip, fudge one's undies, funk, get spooked, get the wind up, push the panic button, shit bullets, shit green, shit one's pants, suck air, sweat bullets

2 SEE **BREAK** someone **UP**

panther piss
n phr Inferior or bootleg liquor

bayou blue, bellywash, boilermaker's delight, bugjuice, busthead, cane corn, choke-dog, coffin varnish, corn juice, corn mule, dishwater, firewater, gage, goggle-eye, King Kong, Kong, lightning, moon, moonshine, moony, moose milk, mountain dew, mule, paint remover, panther, panther sweat, pig iron, pig sweat, popskull, prairie dew, redeye, rotgut, scrap iron, screech, sheep-dip, shellac, shine, shoe polish, snake poison, stump liquor, swipe, tangle-foot, tangle-leg, third rail, tiger sweat, varnish, varnish remover, white lightning, white mule, wild cat

paperhanger
n A person who passes counterfeit money

bill-poster, paper-layer, paper-pusher, pusher

park
v To put; place, as in "Where did you park the scissors?"

hide, stash

party hat
n phr The array of lights on the roof of a police car or emergency vehicle

cherry, gumball, Mickey Mouse ears

pass out
v phr To lose consciousness

go out, go out like a light, go under, hear the birdies sing, hit the canvas, zonk, zonk out

pasteboard
1 *n A ticket of admission*

board, ducat, duck, dukie, tab

2 *n A playing card*

board, book, broad, devil book, flat, rag

patsy
n A victim; a dupe

alvin, angel, boob, chicken, chump, clay pigeon, cousin, doormat, douchie, dumbjohn, easy make, easy mark, fall guy, fish, goat, goofus, gork, jay, [esp Brit] jiggins, [esp Brit] juggins, lamb, mark, monkey, mooch, [esp Brit] mug, pigeon, prune, pushover, schnook, setup, sitting duck, storch, sucker, tool, vic, yap, yold

pay dirt
n phr Profit

payoff, percentage, score, swag, take, velvet

pay one's dues
v phr To serve and suffer such that one earns what one gets, as in "No one gets very far in this line of work without paying his dues"

earn one's wings, go through the mill, have one's ticket punched

pay off
1 *v phr To be profitable*

pan out

2 SEE **FIRE**

pearl-diver

n A person who washes dishes, esp in a restaurant

bubble dancer

peepers

n The eyes

baby blues, blinkers, daylights, glimmers, glims, lamps, [Brit] mince pies, oglers, optics, peekers, peeps, pincers

peg

1 *v To identify; classify*

button down, finger, make, nail, nail down, pigeonhole, pin, pin down, put down for, spot as, tab

2 *v To throw*

chuck, chunk, let fly, shy, trun

pete

n A safe; a strongbox

box, can, crib, peet, pete-box, peter

Philly

n Philadelphia

the big Pretzel, Phil, Quakertown, Sleepy Town

phony

1 *adj False; counterfeit*

bogue, bogus, fake, hoked-up, hokey, hyped-up, phonus balonus, phony as a three-dollar bill, plastic, plug, plugged, pseudo, pumped-up, queer, stiff

2 *n Something false or counterfeit*

fake, falsy, fritzer, phonus balonus, phony baloney, puton

3 *n A person who affects some identity, role, nature, etc; a poseur; an impostor*

actor, bluffer, boogerboo, fake, fakeroo, four-flusher, fraud, glad-hander, handshaker, ho-dad, humbug, pseud, quack

pick-me-up

n A person or thing, esp a drink or snack, that invigorates; a stimulant

kick in the ass, pepper-upper, perker-upper, picker-upper, shot in the arm, shot in the ass

pick up the tab

v phr To pay; assume the expense, as in "I'll pick up the tab for the new park"

ante up, come across, cough over, cough up, dig down for, dish out, dish up, fork out, pay the freight, pick up the check, pop for, shell out for, spring for

piddly

adj Meager; trivial; paltry, as in "How could he expect her to accept such a piddly offer?"

bush, bush-league, chickenshit, diddly, five-and-dime, half-assed, half-pint, jeasly, jerkwater, measly, Mickey Mouse, narrow-gauge, peanut, peewee, penny ante, penny pool, pint-size, pippy-poo, pissant, pissy, pissy-ass, [esp Brit] poky, rinky-dink, runty, small-beer, small-bore, small-change, small-potato, small-time, softball, tinhorn, tinpot, two-bit, two-blink, two-by-four

piece

1 *n A share; a portion; a financial interest, as in "He settled for a small salary and a piece of the gross"*

piece of the racket, slice, slice of the melon, taste

2 SEE **ASS**

3 SEE **ROD**

pig

1 *n A glutton*   chow hound, gobbler, greedy-guts, hog, khazer, table finisher

2 SEE **COP**

3 SEE **FLOOZY**

pig out

v phr To overeat; eat greedily, as in "When I get off this diet, I'm going to pig out on cake and ice cream"   be a khazer, cram, dive in, eat like a horse, fork it in, gobble, hog it, hog it down, make a pig of oneself, pitch in, pork out, scarf out, shovel it in, stuff oneself

pimpmobile

n Any very fancy and usu large car   cuntmobile, hog, nerdmobile, rapemobile, rape wagon, sex wagon

pinko

n A person of liberal or left-wing opinions   commie, lefty, [Brit] lib-lab, parlor pink, pink, radiclib

pins

n The legs, as in "Check out her pins"   gams, hind legs, pegs, shanks, stems, sticks, stumps, trotters, underpinnings, wheels

piss

1 *v To urinate*   dangle one's hose, flash, leak, make a pit stop, pee, pee-pee, piddle, pump bilge, pump ship, take a leak, take a whizz, tinkle, wee-wee, whizz

2 *n Urine*   pee, pee-pee, wee-wee, whizz

3 SEE **BEEF**

a piss
n phr An act of urination

a leak, a pee, a piddle, a tinkle, a whizz

pissed off
adj phr Angry; indignant

bent out of shape, boiling, boiling mad, browned off, burned up, burning, chapped, cranky, dandered, drug, edged, fighting mad, fit to be tied, hacked, hacked off, het up, hopping mad, hot, hot and bothered, hot under the collar, huffy, in a huff, in a lather, in a lava, in a pucker, in a stew, in a sweat, in a swivet, in a tizzy, [Brit] in a wax, lathered, livid, mad, mad as a hornet, mad as a wet hen, miffed, miffy, on a tear, p'd, peed, peeved off, pissed, p o'd, pushed out of shape, raving mad, red-assed, red-necked, riled up, [Brit] shirty, sore, sore as a boil, steamed, steamed up, steaming, stuffy, t'd off, tearing mad, tee'd off, ticked, ticked off, torqued, [Brit] waxy

piss someone **off**
v phr To make someone angry; arouse keen indignation

burn someone's ass, burn someone's butt, burn someone off, burn someone up, frost, get a rise out of, get someone's back up, get someone's dander up, get someone's Irish up, hack someone, make someone hot under the collar, make someone mad, make someone sore, miff, pee someone off, piss, put someone's back up, [Brit] put someone's monkey up, put someone's nose out of joint, raise someone's dander, rile, steam, tee someone off, tick someone off

piss-off
n Anger; indignation, as in "He didn't conceal his piss-off at what they had done"

bile, burn, dander, Irish, mad, miff, pucker, R A, the redass, stew

piss-ugly
adj Very ugly;   ugly as cat-shit
repulsive

the pits
n phr The most   the armpit, the asshole, Barf City
loathsome place or
situation
imaginable, as in
"She says her
university is the
pits"

pizzazz
n Energy; vitality,   bang, biff, bounce, drive, get-up-and-go, ginger, gism,
as in "If he had   hustle, jazz, kick, kick-ass, mohoska, moxie, oof, oomph,
more pizzazz he'd   pep, pepper, piss and vinegar, poop, pow, punch, push,
be unbeatable"   snap, spizzerinctum, spunk, starch, steam, zap, zing,
zip, zippo, zizz, zowie

plastered
adj Drunk;   (very drunk) alkied, aped, bagged, basted, behind the
intoxicated with   cork, blind drunk, blitzed, blitzed out, bloated, blotto,
alcohol   blowed away, blue, boiled, bombed, boozed, boozed
up, boozy, borahco, bottled, boxed, bunned, buzzed,
buzzy, caged, canned, canned up, clobbered, cockeyed, cooked, corked, corned, crashed, crocked,
cronk, crumped out, dead drunk, dead to the world,
decks awash, discouraged, drunk as a boiled owl,
drunk as a coot, drunk as a fiddler's bitch, drunk as a
lord, drunk as a skunk, edged, embalmed, faced, faint,
far gone, feeling good, feeling no pain, flooey, flying
high, fractured, fried, fried to the gills, fuzzled,
gassed, ginned, ginned up, glassy-eyed, glazed, gone,
gonged, grogged, had one too many, half-bagged, half-
corned, half-crocked, half in the bag, half-lit, half-

screwed, half seas over, half-shaved, half-shot, half-slewed, half-snaped, half-sprung, half-stewed, half under, happy, having a bun on, having a load on, having an edge on, having a skinful, having a snootful, having a snoot full, having one too many, high, high as a kite, hooched up, illuminated, impaired, in a bad way, in color, in one's cups, in the bag, juiced, juiced up, knocked out, laid out, lathered, liquored, liquored up, lit, lit up, lit up like a Christmas tree, loaded, looped, looping, lubricated, lushed, lushed up, mashed, muddled, obfuscated, oiled, on the shikker, organized, ossified, overtaken, petrified, pickled, pie-eyed, [Brit] pissed, plonked, plotzed, polluted, poopied, potted, reeling, ripe, ripped, riproaring drunk, roaring drunk, rocky, rummed up, saturated, sauced, schnockered, screwy, scronched, seeing pink elephants, shaved, shikker, shitfaced, shot, slewed, sloshed, slugged, smashed, snozzled, snuffy, soaked, soused, sozzled, spiffed, spifflicated, sprung, squiffed, squiffy, squiffy-eyed, stewed, stewed to the gills, stiff, stinking, stinking drunk, stinko, stitched, stoned, swacked, swacko, swizzled, swozzled, tangle-footed, tangle-legged, tanked, tanked up, tanky, three sheets to the wind, tight as a tick, tuned, under the influence, under the table, up to the ears, up to the eyeballs, up to the gills, waxed, wiped, wiped out, woozy, zonked, zonked out, zonkers

☞ *"To the ears," "to the gills," or "to the eyeballs" may be added to most of the adjectives as an intensifier; "half" may precede these adjectives as a moderating adverb.*

(slightly drunk) buzzy, happy, having a buzz, having a buzz on, having a slight edge, mellow, mildly impaired, pinked, pleasantly plastered, rosy, tiddly, tipsy, woozy

☞ *"Drunk" is one of the most prolific of slang concepts, probably because drunkenness has proffered the most persistent need of euphemism, both clever and defensive. Benjamin Franklin took note of this when he published a compilation of 225 terms for "drunk" (some fifteen of which are still current) as* The Drinker's Dictionary *in January 1737.*

platter
n A phonograph record

disc, plate

play ball
v phr To cooperate; collaborate; acquiesce, as in "They suggested bribery, but he wouldn't play ball"

go along, play, play along, play the game, stand still for

playboy
n A person devoted to partying and pleasure; a bon vivant

fun-seeker, gadabout, gay bird, gay dog, good time Charlie, man-about-town, sport

play dirty
v phr To use unethical, illegal, or injurious means; chicane

bend the rules, hit below the belt, play dirty pool, pull something funny, pull funny business, stack the cards, stretch the rules

play games
v phr To maneuver and manipulate cunningly; toy and gamble

angle, diddle around, fuck around, jockey, mess around

play hardball
v phr To be serious and determined to the point of callousness

go for the jugular, not play games, not play penny ante, play for keeps, play rough

play hooky
v phr To stay away from work and duty, esp from school

juke

play it safe
v phr To choose a cautious line of behavior; avoid much risk, as in "He played it safe and brought travelers' checks on vacation"

be on the safe side, cut one's losses, hedge one's bets, play safe

play second fiddle
v phr To be in an inferior position; lack power or will to lead

suck hind tit, take a back seat

play up to
v phr To ingratiate oneself with, esp by friendly flattery

buddy up to, butter up, make up to, play kissie with, run after, shine up to, suck up to

plug

1 *v To shoot or shoot at with a firearm*

blast, blaze away at, give a dose of lead poison to, let fly at, let loose at, let moonlight into, open up on, peg, perforate, plunk, pop at, pot, puncture, smoke, take a crack at, take a pop at, take a potshot at, zap

2 *v To progress or propel haltingly but doggedly, as in "I plugged at this book for many moons"*

hump and bump, plug along, plug away

3 *n A recommendation, as in "We would welcome plugs for this book"*

blurb, boost, build-up, plugola, puff, puff job, push

plug into

v phr To discover and exploit to one's advantage; tap

buy into, get aboard, get on board, tie into

poker face

n phr An expressionless face

deadpan, straight face

pooch

n A dog

bowwow, dorg, Fido, hound, man's best friend, mutt, pup, pup-dog, puppy, puppy-dog, purp, Rover

the poop

1 *n Information; data, as in "Give me the poop on our competition overseas"*

the dirt, the dope, [Brit] the gen, the goods, the info, the lowdown, the pif, the scoop, scuttlebutt, the skinny, the word

2 SEE **SHIT**

pooped
adj Very tired; exhausted

all in, all shot, one's ass is dragging, ausgespielt, bagged, beat, beat out, beat to the ankles, beat to the ground, beat to the socks, blitzed, blitzed out, bone-tired, burned out, bushed, chewed, clanked, crapped out, dead, dead on one's feet, dog-tired, done, done in, done to a frazzle, dragged out, fagged, fagged out, feeped out, frazzled, fried, fucked out, had it, knocked out, on one's last legs, out on one's feet, paled, paled out, played out, plumb tuckered, poohed, poohed out, pooped out, punch-drunk, ready to drop, run ragged, shot, tapped out, one's tail is dragging, tuckered, tuckered out, worn to a frazzle

pop someone's **cherry**
v phr To terminate someone's virginity

cherrypop, cop someone's cherry

popeyed
adj Having protruding eyes; exophthalmic

bugeyed, goggle-eyed, googly-eyed, gotch-eyed

porn
n Pornography

porno, raunch, rough stuff

pot
n Marijuana; cannabis sativa

Acapulco gold, Acapulco red, Angola black, ashes, Aunt Mary, baby, baby buds, bam, bambalacha, bammy, bang, bay, Bethesda gold, bhang, birdwood, black Columbus, black gold, black gungeon, black moat, black mold, black mole, black monte, black mota, blank, block mo, blue de hue, blue sage, blue-sky blond, bo bo, bo bo bush, boo, brand X, Breckenridge green, brifo, broccoli, buddha, buddha sticks, bull jive, bunk, bush, busy, butter flower, Cambodian trip weed, Cam red, Canadian black, canned goods, charge, chiba chiba, Chicago black, Chicago green, chira, churus, Colombian, Columbus black, conga, conga brown, Congo mataby, dagga, dew, ding, dirt grass, Dona Juanita, doobie, dope, dope smoke, dynamite, faggot, fennel, fu, funny stuff, gage, Gainesville green, gangster, ganja, garbage, gash, gates, gear, giggle smoke, gold, gold leaf, goof butt, grass, grass weed, greefa, green griff, greta, gunny, happy gas, happy grass, hay, hemp, herb, herbs, HOG, hooch, hot jay, ice bag, ice pack, incense, Indian, Indian hay, Indian hemp, Indian weed, jahooby, Jamaican, jay, Jersey green, jingo, jive, Johnson, joy smoke, J smoke, juane, juanita, juanita weed, ju ju, kaif, kanjac, keef, Kentucky blue, Kona gold, laughing grass, laughing tobacco, leaves, leper grass, Lipton's punk, loco weed, love weed, lozerose, lozies, M, mach, Mach Picchu, Maggie, Manhattan silver, Manhattan white, Mary, Mary and Johnny, Mary Ann, Mary Jane, Mary Warner, Mary Weaver, Mary Werner, Maui, Maui wowie, megg, mesca, Mex, Mexican, Mexican brown, Mexican green, Mexican red, the might mezz, MJ, M O, modams, mohasky, mojo, mooca, mootah, mooter, mootie, mu, mud, murder weed, musta, muta, New York white, noble weed, Oaxacan, one-toke weed, Panama gold, Panama red, patyo de gayina, pleiku pink, pod, powder, PR, Punta Rojas, ragweed, railroad weed, Rangoon, red, red gunyon, reefer, reefer weed, righteous bush, rocket, s, salt and pepper, Santa Maria gold, Santa Maria red, sativa, sausage, sess, shit, shuzit, sinsemilla, smoke, snop, stinkweed, straw, stuff, supremo, sweet lunch, sweet Mary, T, tea, Tennessee blue, Texas tea, Thai stick, Thai weed, Thunder weed, viper weed, wacky tobaccy, wacky weed, Wahegan, weed, wheat, wild weed, yerba, yesca, Zacatecas purple, zoom

☞ *The great number of slang terms for narcotics probably reflects both a need for coded reference to an illegal substance and a desire to be chic and up-to-date, in addition to the need to distinguish varieties.*

potbelly
n A protuberant stomach; a paunch

ballast, bay window, beer belly, bulge, corporation, fallen chest, German goiter, gut, jelly-belly, labonza, middle-age spread, Milwaukee goiter, Milwaukee tumor, pooched-out belly, porch, pot, potgut, pus-gut, pustle-gut, spare tire

pothead
n A user of marijuana, esp a heavy user

blower, blow top, bo-bo jockey, dopehead, doper, dopester, freak, Fu Manchu, goof, gouger, gowster, grass eater, grasshead, grasshopper, green, griefer, hay burner, hayhead, head, hophead, junkerman, lover, lusher, mugglehead, oiler, pot lush, puller, reefer, reefer hound, roach bender, tea blower, teahead, tea hound, teo, T-man, toker, twister, weed eater, weedhead, weed hound, weed twister

pow
1 *interj An imitation of a blow, collision, explosion, etc, used for sudden emphasis or to show sudden understanding, as in "And pow, there he was" or "Pow, the thing fell apart"*
2 SEE CLOUT

bam, bang, biff, bingo, blam, blap, blooey, bop, boppo, kerblooey, kerboom, kerplunk, kerthump, powie, smack, smacko, socko, whack, wham, whambang, whammo, zap, zowie

prissy
adj Overfastidious;
primly censorious

choosy, finicky, fusspotty, fussy, pernickety, persnickety, picky, prunish

private eye
n phr A private
detective

eye, op, peeper, tin star

pro
1 *n A serious*
performer or
practitioner; a
professional
2 SEE **HOOKER**

big boy, big girl, big lady, big man, suit
☞ *These terms mark the contrast between child and adult performance.*

proposition
v To invite or
request sexual favors

come on to, george, hit on, lay the make, make a move on, make a pass, mash, pass, pitch, put a move on, put the make on, put the moves on, throw a pass

prowl car
n phr A police
squad car

cherry top, cruiser, fuzz tub

psych someone **up**
v phr To arouse
someone
emotionally,
spiritually,
mentally, etc, to a
maximum effort;
raise to a state of
keen readiness and
capability

gear, gear someone up, pump someone up

pumped
adj In a state of excited preparedness and heightened keenness; keyed up

charged up, cranked up, geared, geared up, jazzed, leaning forward in the saddle, psyched, psyched up, pumped up, rarin' to go

punch-drunk
adj Dazed; exhibiting brain damage from repeated blows to the head

punchy, slap-happy, slug-nutty

punch line
n phr The last line or part of a joke, which makes it funny

gag line, kicker, payoff, punch, snapper, sock line, zinger

puss
n The face

beezer, clock, dial, gills, kisser, map, mask, mug, mush, pan, phiz

pussyfoot
v To be careful and hesitant; avoid direct and immediate action

beat around the bush, play it close to the chest, play it close to the vest, pussyfoot around, take it easy, take one step at a time, tap-dance, tiptoe, walk on eggs, walk on eggshells

pussy-whipped
adj Dominated by a woman, esp one's wife; hen-pecked

cunt-struck, whipped

PUT UP OR SHUT UP

a **put-on**
n phr A deception;
a trick

a con, a leg-pull, a number, a spoof

put on the ritz
v phr To make a
display of wealth
and luxury

dog it, give oneself airs, put on, put on airs, put on class, put on frills, put on swank, put on the dog, put on the high hat, ritz it, swank it

put the bite on
v phr To make a
request, esp for
money; importune

drop the lug on, hit, hit up, put the arm on, put the bee on, put the claw on, put the lug on, put the sleeve on, put the sting on, put the touch on, shake down, tap, touch, touch up

put-up job
n phr A pre-
arranged matter and
outcome; a contrived
affair, as in "It
wasn't a real
election, it was a
put-up job"

boat race, the fix, rigged fight, setup, tank job, wired job

put up or shut up
sentence Support
your statements,
boasts, opinions, etc,
with something
tangible

let's see the color of your money, put your money where your mouth is, talk is cheap

quickie

n A very quick sex act

bunny fuck, quick one, ram-bam thank you ma'am, wham-bam thank you ma'am

R

rabbi

n A patron and influential political friend, esp of a police officer

Chinaman

racket

n An occupation or concern, esp an illegal or somewhat shady one

dodge, game, graft, line, [Brit] line of country, number, scam

rack up

v phr To achieve; score or earn a total of, as in "The first year they racked up a 40% profit"

pile up, stack up

razzle-dazzle

n Adroit deception, as in "They were able to make their case without resort to razzle-dazzle"

dipsy-do, dipsy-doodle, double shuffle, fancy footwork, fast footwork, fast shuffle, flamdoodle, [Brit] gammon, hanky-pank, hanky-panky, hokey-pokey, hokum, jive, quick shuffle, razzmatazz, ring-a-ding, ring-a-ding-ding, smoke and mirrors

redneck
1 *n A bigoted and conventional person; a loutish ultraconservative*

Archie Bunker, hard-hat, neanderthal, no-neck

2 SEE **CRACKER**

rehash
v To review; discuss again; repeat

recap

rejigger
v To alter or readjust; tinker with, as in "I think we had better rejigger those cost estimates"

doctor, doctor up, fine-tune, fix up, rehaul, retool, revamp, trouble-shoot

ride the arm
v phr To collect a taxi fare without using the meter

arm it, highflag

rig
v To prearrange or tamper with a result or process, as in "It looked like a real rescue, but the whole thing was rigged"

cold deck, fake, fake up, fix, hold a boat race, put up, satchel, set up, stack, stack the cards, stack the deck, tank

roach clip

n phr A tweezerlike clip for holding a marijuana cigarette stub

airplane, crutch, Jefferson airplane, roach holder, roach pick

rocky

adj Dazed; weak and unsteady; confused, as in "I was a little rocky from lack of sleep"

dopey, foggy, fuddled, fuddleheaded, groggy, muzzy, out of it, out on one's feet, punchy, woozy

rod

1 *n A pistol*

artillery, belly gun, boomstick, bulldog, bulldozer, cannon, equalizer, fire stick, gat, hardware, heat, heater, hogleg, iron, jammies, John Roscoe, the noise, noise tool, oscar, pea shooter, persuader, piece, popper, roscoe, Saturday night special, shooting iron, sixgun, snubby, snug, zip gun

2 SEE COCK

rookie

n A newcomer; a novice; a tyro

boot, cruit, dumbjohn, fish, greenhorn, greeny, jellybean, John, Johnny-come-lately, [Brit] new boy, poggie, pogue, raw recruit, rook, snotnose, tenderfoot, wetnose, yardbird

rootin'-tootin'

adj Boisterous; rowdy; vigorous, as in "They had a rootin'-tootin' party going on"

harum-scarum, knock-down-drag-out, rambunctious, rampageous, riproaring, riprorious, rock 'em–sock 'em, rough-and-tumble, row-dow, rowdy-dow, rowdy-dowdy, slam-bang

rough up
v phr To hit and pummel; attack viciously

beat on, bushwhack, give the business, give the works, gorilla, haze, hit on, manhandle, massage, mess up, punish, stiff, stiff-arm, stomp, strong-arm, work over

roust
v Esp of police officers, to harass

chivvy, hassle, jack up, jam, lean on, take on, yank

rubber
n A condom

bag, Coney Island whitefish, fishskin, Frenchie, French letter, French safe, French tickler, Manhattan eel, pro, raincoat, rubber boots, safe, safety, scumbag, shower cap, skin

rubberneck
v To stare; gape

gander, gawk, gawp, goggle, goof at, rubber, take a gander

rug
n A toupee

divot, door mat, muff, sky rug

rumble
1 *n A fight between street gangs*

dance

2 *n A police search or raid*

bust-up, knockover, roust, tipover

3 SEE **HEIST**

run it up the flagpole
v phr To try out an idea, concept, etc, as in "Seems like a good idea, but let's run it up the flagpole first"

put one toe in first, run it up the flagpole and see if anybody salutes, test the water, try it on, try it on for size

rustle up

v phr To produce or provide, esp hastily, as in "With two minutes' warning I had to rustle up an alibi"

break out, knock out, promote, rassle up, rustle, scare up, scrape up, scrounge, scrounge up, whomp up

S

sack time
n phr Sleep

beauty sleep, beddy-bye, blanket drill, bunk fatigue, bunk habit, bye-bye, doss, kip, pad duty, rack duty, rack time, sack, sack drill, sack duty, shuteye, winks, Zs

sass
n Impudence; impertinent responses, as in "Just do what I say and don't give me any sass"

back-chat, back-talk, cheek, guff, lip, sauce

sawbones
n A physician or surgeon

bone-bender, bones, butcher, croaker, medic, medico, pill-bag, pill-peddler, pill-pusher, pill-roller

sawbuck
n A ten-dollar bill; ten dollars

dime-note, saw, tenner, ten-spot

scab

n A nonunion worker, esp one who attempts to break a strike

blackleg, boll weevil, fink, jackleg, rat, scissorbill

scads

n A large quantity or amount; many many

all kinds of, and then some, bags, barrels, bunches, a bundle, bundles, enough to choke a horse, a fistful, a flock, forty-'leven, gobs, hatfuls, a heap, heaps, a helluva lot, a jillion, jillions, lashings, loads, lots, a mess, more than you can shake a stick at, no end of, oceans, oodles, packs, piles, a power, a raft, rafts, seventy-leven, a shit-house full, a shit-load, a shitpot, a sight, a skillion, slathers, a slew, slews, a stack, stacks, umpteen, wads, a zillion, zillions

scalper

n A person who buys tickets to be sold at prices higher than is legally permitted

digger

scam

n A swindle; a confidence game; a fraud

bill of goods, bite, boiler room, bucket shop, bunco, bunco game, burn, the C, clip, clip game, con, the con, con game, con job, diddle, diddling, dipsy-do, dipsy-doodle, dodge, double cross, double shuffle, fast one, fast shuffle, fiddle, flam, flimflam, frigging, fucking, gig, grift, gyp, hanky-panky, hoke, hokey-pokey, hosing, hustle, hype, murphy, number, the old army game, racket, razzle-dazzle, razzmatazz, reaming, ripoff, rooking, runaround, sell, shakedown, shell game, skin game, skinning, slicker game, slickering, snow job, sting, sucker game, suckering, suck-in

☞ *Technically this list combines several types of fraud, but most of these terms can be used in the general sense.*

scarecrow
n An ugly person

bad broad, bag, bat, beast, beasty, board, buffarilla, clock stopper, cow, dog, doggy, double-bagger, douche-bag, Elsie, faggot, fright, gargoyle, geech, hag, hatchet-face, hatchet-puss, hog, horror, mess, no bargain, no prize package, picklepuss, scrag, scuzz, sight, skag, skank, skunk, snake, sourpuss, sweat hog, tusker, two-bagger, vinegar-puss, witch

☞ *This list makes no distinction of gender, although some of the terms are specific to ugly women.*

scared shitless
adj phr Very frightened; terrified

fudging one's undies, goose-bumpy, goose-fleshy, in a funk, scared spitless, scared stiff, scared to death, shitting one's drawers, shitting one's pants, spooked, white-knuckled

scare the shit out of
v phr To frighten very much

make someone's hair curl, put the fear of God into, scare shitless, scare spitless, scare stiff, scare the bejesus out of, scare the living shit out of, scare the pants off, scare the tar out of, scare witless, spook, throw a scare into

scarf
v To eat

chaw, chow, chow down, fall to, feed one's face, garbage down, get around, gorm, gorp, graze, grease down, grit, grub up, inhale, munch out, munch up, pitch in, polish off, put away, put it away, put on the feed bag, scarf up, scoff, snorf, stoke up, tuck away, tuck in

schlocky

adj Inferior; shoddy; cheap and gaudy

bargain-basement, cheapie, cheapo, cheapshit, cheesy, chintzy, crapoid, crappy, cruddy, crummy, dime-a-dozen, dimestore, five-and-dime, hanky-pank, junk, junky, low-rent, low-ride, Mickey Mouse, Model-T, NG, no-account, no-count, no-good, punk, south of the border, tacky, tatty, tinpot, trashy, two-bit

schmooz

n A conversation, esp a long and amiable one

blabfest, bull session, chatfest, chaw, chawfest, chin, chinfest, chin-wag, confab, gabfest, gam, gas, gum-beating, hash session, heart-to-heart, jaw, jawfest, jive session, palaver, pow-wow, rag-chew, rag-chewing, rap, rapping, rap session, RF session, set, talkfest, tongue-wag, visit

schnozz

n The nose

bazoo, beak, beezer, bill, boke, boko, bugle, honker, horn, muzzle, nozzle, proboscis, schnozzle, schnozzola, smeller, snoot, snout, snozzle, trumpet

score

1 v To buy or get narcotics

be put straight, cap, connect, cop, cop a buy, cop a fix, cop a match, deal, get through, hit, make a buy, make a meet, make the man, pick up, prime the pump

2 n Loot; booty

bacon, boodle, bundle, cop, goods, haul, hot stuff, pickin's, swag, take

screwed

adj Victimized; maltreated, as in "She really got screwed when she bought that car"

conned, diddled, frigged, fucked, fucked over, had; laid, relaid, and parlayed; screwed over; screwed, blued, and tattooed; shafted, shat on, shit on, suckered, taken, taken into camp, taken to the cleaners, yentzed ☞ *Other such terms may be made from the appropriate forms of the verbs "con" and "fuck."*

screw up

1 *v phr To spoil something, esp by bungling; confuse and ruin*

ass up, [Brit] balls up, ball up, bitch, bitch up, blow, blow high as a kite, blow it, bollix, bollix up, boot, bugger, bugger up, cook, crab, crock, crumb, crumb up, dish, dutch, finish, flummox, foul up, fritz, fuck up, goof up, gummix up, gum up, hash up, jigger, jimmy up, kibosh, louse up, make a hash of, make a mess of, make a muddle of, mess up, mommix, mommix up, muck up, muff, mung, mung up, pickle, play hell with, play merry hell with, plumber, put the kibosh on, queer, send to hell in a handbasket, shoot down, shoot down in flames, sink, snafu, snarl up, wipe out

☞ *The phrase "the works" or "the deal" may be added to nearly all these terms for fullness.*

2 SEE **FUCK UP**

scrub

v To cancel; eliminate; erase

abort, axe, bag, belay, blow, blow off, can, chuck, cut, deep-six, ditch, drop, kill, knock off, scrap, scratch, scrub, shit-can, spike, wash out, wooden-stake

scrunch

v To squeeze; consolidate, as in "We managed to scrunch all my stuff into one suitcase"

ooch, oonch, scooch, scrooch, scrooge, scrunch up

scut work

n phr Tedious work needing little thought or skill; drudgery

bullwork, dogwork, donkeywork, grunt labor, grunt work, scud, scut, shitwork

security blanket
n phr A thing or person that provides a sense of safety and emotional comfort; a talisman

blue blanket, rabbit's foot, sugar tit

set someone **back**
v phr To cost, as in "That book will set you back twenty-two bucks"

[Brit] knock someone back, move someone back, put someone back, stand

sexy
1 *adj Sexually attractive*

dang, foxy, ginchy, humpy, hunky, luscious, sesky, slinky, slutty, steamy, sultry, twisty, va-va-voom, voomy, zoftig
☞ *These synonyms apply primarily to women. "Sexy" itself applies, and the equivalent for males is "hunky."*

2 SEE GREAT

shades
n Sunglasses

peepers, sunshades

the shaft
n phr Unfair or cruel treatment, as in "They promised to help us, but they gave us the shaft instead"

a bad deal, a bum deal, a fucking, a hosing, a lousy deal, a raw deal, a rotten deal, a royal fucking, a screwing, a shafting, the shit end of the stick, the shitty end of the stick, the short end of the stick

the shakes
n phr Delirium tremens

the clanks, the creeps, the DTs, the heebie-jeebies, the horrors, the jimjams, the jumps, the screaming mee-mies, the snozzlewobblies

shave
v To reduce; decrease, as in "We had to shave expenses by ten percent"

chisel down, cut, drop, knock down, scale down, skinny down

shill
1 *n An associate of an auctioneer, gambler, hawker, etc, who pretends to be a member of the audience and stimulates it to desired action*

blind, booster, bunco-steerer, capper, come-on, come-on man, doker, front, heel, nark, Peter Funk, pigeon, plant, seat-man, shillaber, shiller, steerer, stick, stooge

2 SEE **BILLY CLUB**
3 SEE **FLACK**

shit
1 *n Feces; excrement*

business, caca, crap, do, doo-doo, dreck, hockey, number two, poo, poop, poo-poo, poot, squat, turd

2 *v To defecate*

crap, do one's business, do number two, drop one's load, dump a load, grunt, make, pinch a loaf, poo, poop, squat, take a crap, take a dump, take a shit

3 SEE **ASSHOLE**
4 SEE **BULLSHIT**
5 SEE **HORSE**
6 SEE **ZILCH**

a shit
1 *n phr A bowel movement*

a crap, a dump, a poo, a poop, a squat

2 SEE **ASSHOLE**

shit list
n phr A usu fancied list of persons one does not wish to associate with or favor

drop-dead list

the shits
n phr Diarrhea; loose bowels

the Aztec two-step, Basra belly, the craps, Delhi belly, the GIs, the GI shits, gyppy tummy, Hong Kong dog, Johnny Trots, Montezuma's revenge, the quickstep, the runs, the trots, turista

shooting gallery
n phr A place where a narcotics user can get a dose or injection

launching pad, needle park

shoot the breeze
1 *v phr To chat amiably and casually; converse*

bat one's chops, bat one's gums, bat one's jaw, bat one's jowls, bat one's lip, bat the breeze, beat one's chops, beat one's gums, beat one's jaw, beat one's jowls, beat one's lip, bullshit, chew the fat, chew the rag, chin, chinjaw, chop one's teeth, confab, fan, flap one's chops, flap one's gums, flap one's jaw, flap one's jowls, flap one's lip, gab, gas, have a chinfest, have a gabfest, have a talkfest, hump one's chops, hump one's gums, hump one's jaw, hump one's jowls, hump one's lip, jaw, mouth off, [Brit] natter, palaver, patter, pop off, rap, run off at the mouth, schmooz, shoot the bull, shoot the crap, shoot the fat, shoot the shit, sound off, wag the tongue, yack, yackety-yack

2 SEE **BULLSHIT**
3 SEE **GAB**

shoot up
v phr To take an injection or other dose of narcotic

back-track, back up, bang, boot, broach, bust the main-line, cave, cave-dig, ditch, douche, do up, down, drill, drop, flush, gate, geez, get off, get with it, give wings, go in the gutter, gutter, hit, hit the sewer, hit up, hop up, hype, jab, jab a vein, jack, jack off the spike, jack up, jerk off, jolt, kick the gong around, laugh and scratch, line, lip the dripper, main, mainline, pipe, pit, pop, raise a welt, register, send it home, sewer, shoot, shoot gravy, skin pop, spike up, splash, take off, tap, tie off, tie up

the shorts
n phr Lack of money; a shortage of funds

not a pot to piss in, financial embarrassment, not one dollar to rub against another, the tights

shorty
n A person of short stature

duckbutt, dusty butt, featherweight, half-pint, little drink of water, little squirt, midget, peanut, peewee, pip-squeak, runt, sawed-off runt, shrimp, squirt

show up
v phr To arrive; be present

blow in, bob up, breeze in, buzz in, check in, clock in, drag in, drop in, fall by, fall down, fall out, fall up, get in, hit town, make the scene, pop up, pull in, punch in, put in an appearance, ring in, roll in, show, sign in, time in, tool in, turn up, weigh in

shrink

n A psychiatrist, psychoanalyst, or other psychotherapist

bug doctor, couch doctor, guru, headpeeper, headshrinker, nut doctor, shrinker

shut up

1 v phr To be quiet; stop talking

belt up, bottle it, button one's face, button one's lip, button up, caeto, clam up, cut the mouth, drink one's beer, dry up, dummy up, hang up, keep one's mouth shut, keep one's trap shut, not let out a peep, not say boo, pipe down, rest one's jaw, ring off, save one's breath, shush, shut one's bazoo, shut one's face, shut one's shit, shut one's trap, shut one's yap, sign off, stow it, stow the gab, zip one's lip, zip one's mouth
☞ *All these terms in the imperative, and the following interjections, may be used as stern or angry commands.*

2 interj Be silent; hold your tongue

at ease, bag your head, belay that, bottle it, can it, cork it, cut it out, cut the chat, cut the shit, knock it off, pack it up, save your breath, shet ep, shush your mouth, shut your ass, stow it

shyster

n A lawyer, esp an unscrupulous one

ambulance chaser, fixer, lip, mouthpiece, tongue

sissy

1 n An effeminate male

cream puff, cupcake, daisy, fancy-pants, flower, lily, Lord Fauntleroy, mama's boy, nance, nancy, pansy, pantywaist, Percy, Percy-boy, Percy-pants, sis, sissy-pants, softy, tootie fruity, weak sister
☞ *These terms share semantic territory with "wimp," which should also be considered.*

2 SEE GAY

sit tight

1 *v phr* *To wait*
patiently; be patient

hang around, hang on, hold one's horses, hold it, hold
the phone, keep one's hair on, keep one's pants on,
keep one's shirt on, not hold one's breath, stay put

2 *v phr* *To retain*
one's position; refuse
to shift, as in "The
landlord offered me
a thousand dollars
to move, but I'm
going to sit tight"

die hard, hold out, stand one's ground, stand pat, stay
put, stick to one's guns, take one's stand

the **slammer**

n phr *A jail or*
prison

the academy, the bastille, the big, the big cage, the big
house, the big joint, the big school, the bing, the board-
ing school, the brig, the bucket, the caboose, the cage,
the calaboose, the calabozo, the can, the cannery, the
clink, the clinker, the coalhole, the college, the collitch,
the cooler, the coop, the fed pen, the hole, the hoosegow, the icebox, the joint, the jug, the lockup, the mill,
the pen, the pogey, the pokey, the pound, the quad, the
slam, the state pen, the stir, the tank

sleazebag

n *A disgusting*
person, esp a smelly,
filthy one; a moral
and physical sloven

chili-bowl, creep, crud, crumb, crumb-bun, dip, dirtbag, dirtball, douchebag, filthbag, fishball, geek, mess,
pus-bag, scum, scumbag, scumsucker, scurve, scut,
scuzzbag, scuzzo, sleaze, sleazeball, slimebag, slimeball, slimebucket, slob, sludgeball, weirdo, zhlub
☞ *Many of these terms are synonymous with those*
found under "asshole" and "jerk." The distinction is
that while one despises a jerk and detests an asshole,
one both despises and detests a sleazebag.

sleep around

v phr To be sexually promiscuous

fool around, play around, play musical beds, swing

smack

1 *adv Exactly; precisely, as in "Smack on the hour of three, she came"*

bam, [esp Brit] bang, bung, plonk, plump, plunk, slam-bang, slap, slap-bang, smack dab, spang, square

2 SEE **HORSE**

smart-ass

1 *n An impudent and officious person; a wiseacre*

armchair general, armchair strategist, bigmouth, ho-dad, know-it-all, smart aleck, smart guy, smartmouth, smarty, smartypants, wise apple, wise-ass, wise guy, wisenheimer

2 *adj Impudent; disrespectfully frivolous, as in "That sort of smart-ass remark is going to get you in trouble"*

cheeky, cute, flip, flip-lipped, sassy, smart, smart-alecky, smartmouth, wise, wise-ass

the **smart money**

n phr The predictions, expectations, and bets of those who know best

the educated money, the hip gee, the wise money

smarts

n Intelligence; competence

brains, brain stuff, gray matter, know-how, moxie, savvy, something on the ball, the stuff, what it takes

smidgen
n A small amount

cunt-hair, dab, dablet, lick, little bit, mite, skinch, skosh, smitch, tad, wee bit

a smoke
n An act of smoking tobacco, esp a cigarette, as in "He said he was just going out for a smoke"

a burn, a butt, a cig, a coffin-nail, a drag, a fag, a gasper, a puff, a pull

smoke out
v phr To discover

get a line on, sniff out, suss out, [Brit] winkle out

smoothie
1 n A sophisticated and seductively pleasant person
2 SEE **LADIES' MAN**

old smoothie, slicker, smooth article, smooth citizen, smooth number, smooth operator, smooth potato

snafu
n A very confused situation; chaos

[Brit] balls-up, Chinese fire call, Chinese fire drill, [Brit] dog's dinner, fine how-de-do, flummox, foozle, foul-up, fuck-up, goat fuck, goat rope, goat screw, goof-up, hell of a mess, hurrah's nest, mell of a hess, mess, Mickey Mouse, mix-up, muss, pretty kettle of fish, rat's nest, sapfu, screw-up, shitstorm, stew, tuifu, unholy mess

snappy
1 adj Stylish; modish, as in "She had on a snappy new skirt"
2 SEE **ZINGY**

chic, classy, dressy, flossy, hip, mod, snazzy, trendy

sneakers

n Rubber-soled sports shoes

JC water-walkers, sneaks, tennies, tenny runners

snitch

n A police informer or spy

bat carrier, beefer, boogie, canary, cheese bun, cheese eater, copper, dime-dropper, dimer, faded boogie, finger, fink, geepo, nark, nightingale, nose, pigeon, rat, ratter, shamus, shiever, singer, snitcher, snitch jacket, squawk, squeaker, squeal, squealer, stool, stoolie, stool pigeon, tipster, weasel, whistle-blower, whistler, zuch

snooty

adj Snobbish; haughty and disdainful; supercilious

dicty, high and mighty, highfalutin', high-hat, high-hatty, hincty, hoity-toity, la-de-da, sniffy, snobby, snotty, standoffish, stuck-up, top-hat, uppish, uppity

snooze

v To sleep; go to sleep; go to bed

bag it, bag some Zs, cap out, catch Zs, caulk off, collar a nod, conk off, conk out, cop some Zs, cork off, crap out, crash, crawl into the hay, cut some Zs, cut Zs, dope off, doss, ear, fall out, flack out, flake out, flop, get some blanket drill, get some bunk fatigue, get some rack, get some sack time, get some shuteye, go beddie-bye, hit the great white biscuit, hit the hay, hit the pad, hit the sack, hit the trees, kip, pad down, pad out, pile up some Zs, pound one's ear, rack, rack out, roll in, sack out, saw logs, saw wood, stack some Zs, take a power nap, take forty winks, turn in, Z, Zee, [Brit] zizz

a snooze

n phr A nap; a doze; sleep

cat nap, forty winks, a kip, rack duty, rack time, sack drill, sack time, shuteye, some Zs, wink, [Brit] zizz, [Brit] zizzy

snort

1 *n A drink of liquor*

ball, bump, bumper, drag, dram, a finger, gargle, geezer, glug, guzzle, hook, hooker, jigger, jolt, kick, nip, peg, pull, shot, slug, slurp, snifter, spot, suck, swallow, swig, tot

2 *v To inhale cocaine*

blow, blow Charley, blow coke, get your nose cold, go on a sleigh ride, horn, kiss, scoop, see Steve, short, sniff, snowmobile, snozzle, toot, whiff

snow

v To deceive, esp with smooth persuasion; mislead

bamboozle, blow smoke, [Brit] bowl a googly, buffalo, deal from the bottom of the deck, diddle, dipsy-doodle, do a number, do a snow job, double shuffle, fake out, fast-shuffle, fast talk, flimflam, give a bum steer, give someone a line, give someone the business, have someone on, hornswoggle, humbug, hustle, hype, jerk someone's chain, jerk someone's string, kid, play for a sucker, pull a fast one, pull someone's chain, pull one's leg, pull someone's string, pull the wool over someone's eyes, put it over on, put someone on, put one over, rattle someone's chain, rope in, run a game, run a number, sell a bill of goods, slicker, snooker, snow-job, spoof, string along, sucker, take for a ride, take in, throw a curve, throw curves, use smoke and mirrors

☞ *These terms share semantic territory with those at "con," which should also be considered.*

snuff

v To kill; murder

blast, blot, blot out, blow away, blow out, bump, bump off, burn, burn down, bury, bushwhack, chill, clip, cut down, cut off, do in, drop, dry-gulch, dump, erase, finish off, fix, frag, get, give the business, give the heat, give the works, go out in the country with, grease, gun down, hit, ice, iron out, knock off, lay out, liquidate, off, polish off, push, push across, push off, put away, put on ice, rub, rub out, scrag, send to kingdom come, send west, set over, settle, settle someone's hash, snuff out, spoil, take care of, take for a ride, take off, take out, waste, wipe out, zap, zing

soap opera

n phr A radio or television daily dramatic series showing the painful, passionate, and riveting amours and disasters of more or less ordinary people

soap, soaper, sudser, suds scenario, washtub weeper

sock

1 v To strike, esp with the fist; punch, as in "The dispute got serious when she socked him"

bang, bash, belt, biff, blap, blast, boff, bonk, bop, brain, bust, clip, clock, clonk, clout, club, clunk, coldcock, conk, cork, crack, crown, ding, duke, dust, dust someone's jacket, fire on, give five to, give it to, give someone the works, go upside someone's face, go upside someone's head, hammer, hang a left on, hang a right on, haul off and land one, haul off on, hit on, hit upside someone's face, hit upside someone's head, hit someone where he (or she) lives, knock someone's block off, land a haymaker, land one, larrup, lather, lay one on, let someone have it, lower the boom, nail, paste, plant one on, poke, pop, pot, put the slug on, rock, rock and sock, slam, slug, smack, smear, soak, swat, tag, tan, thump, thwack, wallop, whack, wham, whang, whomp, whop ☞ *Many of these terms share semantic territory with "clobber," which should also be considered.*

2 n A blow, esp with the fist; a punch

bam, bang, bash, belt, biff, blap, bloop, blooper, bolo, bonk, bop, bust, clip, clout, crack, ding, haymaker, jab, klop in the chops, knock, knuckle sandwich, lam, the leather, lick, poke, pop, pow, roundhouse, shot, slam, smack, smash, swack, swat, swipe, thump, thwack, wallop, whack, wham, whop, zetz

3 SEE **KNOCK**

softie
n A person who is amiably compliant

easy mark, old softie, pushover, soft touch, squish ☞ *A "softie" is not a "dupe" or "patsy," but a kind person who wishes to please.*

soft-pedal
v To make less prominent; de-emphasize

belittle, play down, pull one's punches

soft soap
n phr Flattery; cajolement

applesauce, banana oil, blarney, bull, butter, eyewash, grease, grease job, oil, salve, soap, sweet talk

soft-soap
1 *v To flatter; cajole, as in "We all started soft-soaping him about his speech"*

blarney, build someone up, bull, bullshit someone, butter someone up, dish out the applesauce, dish out the baloney, fatmouth, feed someone a line, give someone a grease job, grease, honey up, lay it on thick, lay it on with a trowel, schmear, scratch someone's back, shoot someone a line, spread it on thick, sweeten someone up, sweet-talk

2 SEE **STROKE**

southpaw
n A left-handed person

cockeye, forkhander, lefty, portsider, sidewheeler, wrongarmer

so what
interj An exclamation of indifference, as in "So you got a bonus check, so what"

big deal, do tell, hoo-ha, so what else is new, what else is new, you wouldn't shit me

spare tire
n phr A usu fatty surplus about the waist

bulge, corporation, love handles, middle-age spread

specs
n Spectacles

cheaters, glims, goggles, windows

spell out
1 v phr To explain; clarify, as in "I didn't get it the first time, so they spelled it out for me"

break something down, brief, bring someone up to speed, clue, clue in, connect the dots, cue someone in, cut a take, cut it up, decode, draw a map, draw a picture, fill someone in, kick apart, lay out, poop someone up, put in plain English, [Brit] put someone in the picture, put in words of one syllable, run down, sort out, straighten someone out

2 v phr To make precise; specify clearly, as in "Next we must spell out the exact terms of what you get"

button down, nail down

split
v To leave; depart

air out, amscray, ankle, ankle along, bag ass, bail, beat it, blast off, blaze, blow, blow away, boogie, book, book it, boot and saddle, bop off, breeze, breeze off, broom, bugger off, bug out, bunk, burn, burn rubber, butt out, buzz, buzz off, catch one's lid, chase oneself, chase along, check out, cheese it, clear out, clock out, cruise, cut, cut a, cut and run, cut ass, cut out, diddy now, dig out, drag ass, drag one's freight, drag it, duck out, dust, ease, ease on out, ease out, fade, fade away, fade out, flake off, fly the coop, fuck off, get going, get lost, get moving, get off the block, get off the dime, get on one's horse, get the hell out, git, go south, haul one's ashes, haul ass, haul it, head out, highball, hightail, hightail it, hike, hit out, hit the bricks, hit the road, hit the trail, hoof, hoof it, hook it, hop it, lam, light, light out, make like a banana split, make like a paper doll and cut out, make like a sheepherder, make like a tree and leave, make oneself scarce, make tracks, mosey, mosey along, nix out, patch out, peel out, [esp Brit] piss off, pop off, powder, pull one's freight, pull out, punch out, rabbit, rabbit-foot, ramble, rip off, [Brit] scarper, scoot, scram, screw, set sail, shag, shag ass, shemozzle, shove off, shuffle along, skate, skedaddle, skiddoo, skin out, skip, skip out, sky out, sky up, slide, slope, split the scene, take a douche, take a hike, take a powder, take a runout powder, take it on the lam, take off, take off like a bat out of hell, take off like a bigass bird, toddle along, toddle off, trot, truck, truck along, up stakes, vamoose, waltz off, warp out

☞ *Most of these, in the imperative, serve as more or less brusque commands.*

spoof
1 *v* To lampoon, as in, "They loved to spoof his dancing style"
2 SEE **KID**
3 SEE **SNOW**

send up

spook

1 *v To frighten;*
scare

bring scunnion, bring smoke, funk, give a turn, give the shakes, scare shitless, scare spitless, scare stiff, scare the hell out of, scare the life out of, scare the pants off of, scare the shit out of, scare to death, scare witless

2 SEE **NIGGER**

spotlight

v To single out
prominently;
emphasize

brightline, feature, give top billing to, headline, highlight, play up, shout up

square

1 *adj Conventional*
and conformistic in
behavior and
attitudes

Barbie-Doll, bogus, burbed-out, buttondown, buttoned down, clonish, drippy, drizzly, droid, four-square, fuddy-dud, fuddy-duddy, gray-flannel, groovy, hung-up, icky, Ken, kosher, L7, lame, plastic, ranky dank, squaresville, squeaky-clean, straight, straight-arrow, stuffy, swingin', uncool, unhep, unhipped, whitebread, white-bready, Wonder Bread

2 *n A conventional*
and conformistic
person

Babbitt, Barbie Doll, citizen, clone, clyde, cornball, cube, drip, drizzle, drizzlepuss, droid, Elk, flat hoop, flat tire, four-square, fuddy-dud, fuddy-duddy, jeff, Ken, nine-to-fiver, shim, Zelda, zoid

square deal

n phr Fair and
equal treatment;
honest dealing

even break, fair shake, good deal

squeal

v To be an informer, esp for the police; tattle, as in "He thought he'd gotten away with it, but his friend squealed"

beef, belch, blab, blow, blow the gaff, blow the whistle, canary, chirp, dime, drop a dime, drop the dime, eat cheese, finger someone, fink, go stool, holler, leak, mark, mouth on someone, nark, peach, put the claw on someone, put the finger on someone, rat, rat on, sell out, sing, sing out, snitch, spill one's guts, spill the beans, squawk, stool, talk, tell tales out of school, trick, weasel

squeezebox

n An accordion

groanbox, pushbox, stomach Steinway, windbox

stake someone to

v phr To give to someone, esp as a treat or gift, as in "Her dad staked her to a new car when she graduated"

blow someone to, come through with, deal out, dish out, dole out, hand out, slip someone, spot someone, stand someone

stall

v To delay; temporize; procrastinate

beat around the bush, buy time, drag one's feet, hem and haw, hold off, play for time, pussyfoot, stall around, stall for time, stooge around, tap-dance, waffle

standoff

n A balanced contest; a stalemate; a deadlock

dead heat, Mexican standoff, photo finish, six of one and half a dozen of the other, toss, toss-up, wash

stanza

n A period, an inning, a round, or some other division of a game or bout

canto, chapter, chukker, frame, heat, session, verse, waltz

stash

v To conceal; store or hoard, as in "I stashed my money in a safe place"

rathole, sock away, squirrel, squirrel away, stash away

stick it

1 *interj* An exclamation of defiance at something offered or suggested, as in "He can take his apology and stick it"
2 SEE **FUCK YOU**

cram it, put it in one's ear, ram it, shove it, stow it, stuff it

☞ *These expressions may be intensified by adding "up one's ass" or "in one's ear" or "where the sun doesn't shine."*

stick one's **neck out**

v phr To put oneself at risk; invite trouble, as in "If you tell them the truth you'll be sticking your neck out"

ask for it, chance it, go out on a limb, lead with one's chin, put one's ass on the line, stretch one's luck, take a flyer

stick out like a sore thumb

v phr To be very conspicuous; stand out starkly

be as plain as the nose on your face, be plain as a pikestaff, glare, hang out, have a high profile, hit one in the eye, shout, speak for itself, stare one in the face, stick out all over, stick out a mile

stick to one's
knitting
*v phr To attend
strictly to one's own
affairs; not meddle*

butt out, keep hands off, keep one's nose out, keep off
the grass, leave it be, let sleeping dogs lie, let well
enough alone, mind one's own business

sticky-fingered
*adj Inclined to
steal; larcenous*

light-fingered

stiff
n A corpse

crowbait, dead meat, fly-bait, goner, worm-food

stir-crazy
*adj Insane,
stuporous,
hysterical, or
otherwise affected
mentally by
imprisonment*

coop-happy, stir-bugs, stir-daffy, stir-simple

stone
1 *adv Utterly;
totally*
2 SEE
HONEST-TO-GOD

clean, dead, deadass, flat-ass, from A to Z; lock, stock,
and barrel; plum, plumb, teetotally, wall-to-wall

straight
1 *adj Legitimate;
honest and proper*

by the book, clean, [Australian] dinkum, fair and
square, kosher, legit, on the legit, on the level, on the
square, on the up-and-up, square, straight-arrow, up-
and-up, up front

2 *adj Honest and
reliable; upright*

frontal, legit, on the legit, on the level, on the square,
on the up-and-up, out-front, straight-ahead, straight-

	arrow, straight from the shoulder, straight-shooting, straight-up, up-and-up, up-front
3 *n A person who does not use narcotics*	apple, brown shoes, do-righter, John, lame duck, square, square apple
4 *n A heterosexual man*	breeder, citizen, vanilla
5 *adj Heterosexual*	right-handed
6 SEE **SQUARE**	

the straight dope

n phr The truth; the unvarnished facts	chapter and verse, [Brit] the gen, the gospel, the gospel truth, the honest-to-God truth, the lowdown, the pif, the scam, the skinny, the straight goods, the straight of it, the straight poop, the straight scoop, the straight skinny, straight talk, the veritable cack, warts and all, where it's at, the whole story

stripper

n A strip-tease dancer	ecdysiast, grinder, peeler

stroke

1 *v To compliment; flatter and comfort, as in "Just stroke them a little, and they'll tend to agree with you"*	give warm fuzzies, massage someone's ego, soft-soap
2 *n Comforting and flattering praise; what one wants to hear*	ego massage, soft soap, sweet talk, warm fuzzies
3 SEE **JACK OFF**	

stuck-up

adj Haughty and conceited; snobbish

bigheaded, blown up, chesty, cocky, hatty, high-hat, high-hatty, hincty, hincty-ass, puffed up, stuck on oneself, swelled up, swellheaded, too big for one's britches, uppity

stud

1 n A sexually promiscuous and prodigious man

Casanova, chaser, cocksman, Don Juan, gash hound, heavycake, horndog, horny bastard, hot-nuts, hound dog, jelly-roll, lover-boy, make-out artist, masher, meathound, pistol Pete, rooster, skirt-chaser, stallion, studhammer, tom-cat, wolf, woman-chaser

2 SEE **DUDE**

3 SEE **LADIES' MAN**

suck

1 v To be disgusting or extremely reprehensible; be of wretched quality, as in "This play really sucks"

blow, rot, smell, stink, stink on ice, stink to high heaven, suck eggs, suck rope

2 SEE **BLOW**

sucker

1 n Any specified object, esp one that is prodigious, troublesome, effective, etc, as in "He just couldn't get that sucker working"

baby, bastard, bugger, cocksucker, fucker, momma, mother, motherfucker

☞ *It is odd to find only one overtly affectionate term in this cluster.*

2 SEE **PATSY**

sugar daddy
n phr A man who provides money, esp one who supports a mistress

daddy, John, old man, poppa, Santa Claus, sugar papa

Sunday punch
n phr A very hard blow

blockbuster, dynamite punch, haymaker, jolt, kayo, kayo shot, money punch, payoff punch, powerhouse punch

swabby
n A US Navy sailor

bluejacket, gob

swank
n Elegance; stylishness, as in "She took him to dinner at a place with lots of swank"

class, high tone, ritz, snazz, spiff

sweat
v To worry; fret

fuss, graum, lose sleep, stew

swell
1 *n An aristocrat; a rich and important person*

blue-blood, high-hat, nob, [Brit] toff, upper-cruster

2 SEE **GREAT**

swing
1 *v To be sexually promiscuous*

play musical beds, shack up, sleep around

2 SEE **FUCK**

swivet

n A fit of angry agitation, as in "He had a swivet when he realized they'd lost"

blowoff, blowup, catfit, conniption fit, duckfit, lather, pucker, snit, state, stew, tizzy, [Brit] wax, wingding

T

tab

n A promise to pay; written acknowledgment of a debt   IOU, marker

tail

1 *n A person who follows another for surveillance*   plaster, shadow, shagger

2 SEE **ASS**

take

n The proceeds of an event, performance, period of operation, etc, as in "Our take this quarter won't even cover our costs"   gate, gross, handle, haul, loot, score

take a beating
v phr To suffer a financial loss, esp to go bankrupt

be whitewashed, be wiped out, crack up, do an el foldo, drop a bundle, get it in the neck, go broke, go down for the count, go on the rocks, go to the cleaners, go to the wall, go under, take a bath, take it on the chin, tap out ☞ *These terms share semantic territory with "go ker-flooey," which should also be considered.*

take a crack at
v phr To make an attempt; have a try

get one's feet wet, give a fling, give a go, give a whirl, go at, have a crack, have a go, have a rip, have a ripple, have a shot, have a whack, make a stab, take a lick

take a dive
v phr To lose a prize-fight or other contest intentionally

dive, go in the tank, tank, throw

take care of numero uno
v phr To be primarily concerned with one's own profit, security, etc, as in "She doesn't worry about anyone else, she just takes care of numero uno"

feather one's nest, line one's nest, take care of number one

take someone **down a peg**
v phr To deflate or reduce, esp a pompous or vainglorious person

bring down, cut down to size, cut off at the knees, cut off someone's water, knock someone off his (or her) perch, prick someone's balloon, put a tuck in someone's tail, put someone's nose out of joint, put the skids to, send away with a flea in his (or her) ear, settle someone's hash, take down a notch, take the shine out of, take the starch out of, take the wind out of someone's sails, tell where to get off, tell where to head in, turn off someone's water

take it
v phr To accept and endure what one has deserved or pledged, as in "He can dish out abuse when it's called for but he sure can't take it"

bite the bullet, face the music, face up to it, grin and bear it, hang tough, hunker down, stand for it, stand the gaff, stand up and be counted, stay the course, stay the pace, stick it out, stick with it, take heat, take it on the chin, take it standing up, take one's lumps, take one's medicine, take the rap, tough it out

take on
v phr To challenge and oppose; accept combat with

buck, cross, go eyeball to eyeball with, go one on one with, go to bat against, go toe to toe with, go up against, stand up to, take a run at

talk someone **into**
v phr To persuade; actively influence

con, high-pressure, hook in, iggle, jaw, jawbone, pressure, sell, sell on, twist someone's arm

tan
1 *v To thrash; punish by spanking*

baste, burn someone's tail, dust someone's britches, dust someone's jacket, dust someone's pants, dust someone's trousers, fan someone's tail, give a dose of strap oil, lambaste, larrup, lather, paddle, paddlewhack, swinge, take it out of someone's hide, take the strop to, take to the woodshed, tan someone's hide, warm someone's seat, whale

2 SEE **SOCK**

tear-jerker
n A sentimental story, movie, song, etc

hard-luck story, sob story, sob stuff, tale of woe, weeper, weepie

tech
n A technician or engineer

techie, toolie

teenybopper
n A teenager or preteenager; an adolescent

bubble-gummer, the bubblegum set, grommet, teen, teener, the teen tribe, teenybop, teeny-rocker, tween-ager

that's the way the cookie crumbles
sentence Such is life; such are the mysterious ways of fate

c'est la vie, go figure, so what else is new, that's life, that's show biz, that's show business, that's the luck of the draw, that's the way the ball bounces, there you are, there you go, welcome to the club, what goes around comes around, win a few lose a few, you can't win them all

threads
n Clothing; dress

drapes, duds, fig, get-up, rags, rig-out, set of drapes, set of threads, togs, trappings, turnout, vines, weeds

ticker
n The heart

old ticker, pump, pumper

tickled
adj Pleased, as in "I was tickled that they had asked me"

happy as a clam, [Brit] happy as a sandboy, happy as can be, pleased as Punch, stoked, tickled pink, tickled silly, tickled to death, tickled to pieces

tightwad

n A parsimonious person; a miser

cheapskate, nickel-nurser, nickel-squeezer, penny-pincher, piker, pinchgut, pinchpenny, Scotsman, Scrooge

tin

n A police officer's badge

button, buzzer, potsy

tip

n A piece of information, as in "The cops got a tip about a drug deal"

hot tip, pointer, steer, tipoff

tits

1 n A woman's breasts

apples, bags, bazongas, bazooms, bazoonjies, big brown eyes, boobies, boobs, breastworks, cans, chi-chi, coconuts, globes, headlights, hooters, jugs, knockers, lungs, mangoes, maracas, melons, muffins, pair, snorbs, titties

2 SEE GREAT

toddle

v To walk, as in "After the party she toddled home"

amble, ankle, ankle along, bop, diddy-bop, ease, foot it, go by ankle express, hike, hit the sidewalk, hoof, hoof it, hoss it, leg it, march, mosey, mosey along, ooze, pad, percolate, pound the pavement, press the bricks, ride shank's mare, ride shank's pony, sashay, shag, shank it, shuffle, stump it, traipse, waltz

toke

1 n A sucking or inhalation of a lighted cigarette, cigar, etc, esp a marijuana cigarette
2 SEE **BUTT**

drag, puff, pull

Tommy gun

n phr A submachine gun

burp gun, chopper, typewriter

tootsies

n The feet

barkers, dogs, footsies, footsie-wootsies, hoofs, pedal extremities, puppies, pups, tootsie-wootsies, trotters

top-kick

n A first sergeant

first man, first shirt, first soldier, top, top sergeant

total

v To wreck; ruin, as in "She totaled the car not five minutes from home"

pile up, rack up, smack up, smash up, stack up, trash, waste, wipe out

tough

adj Severe and uncompromising; pugnacious and menacing, as in "Don't try any monkey business with them, they are very tough people"

butch, hard, hard as nails, hard-ass, hard-assed, hardnose, hardnosed, hard-rock, kick-ass, raw, rough-ass, shit-kicking, stompass

tough shit
sentence That's bad luck; that's a shame   tough break, tough luck, tough nibs, tough noogies, tough rocks, tough tiddy, tough titty, TS

trendy
adj Following new trends in fashion, art, literature, etc; anxiously au courant   faddy, go-go, a go-go, hep, in, up-to-datey, with it

the tube
n Television; a television set   boob tube, eye, idiot box, one-eyed monster, [Brit] telly, video

umpty-umpth
adj Of a large and unspecified ordinal number, as in "I promised for the umpty-umpth time"

jillionth, umptieth, zillionth

Uncle Sam
n phr The US Government

Mister Whiskers, Uncle Sammy, Uncle Sugar, Uncle Whiskers

undies
n Underwear

drawers, skivvies, unmentionables

up front
1 *adv phr In advance; before any deductions or further payments, as in "She said she would want half her fee up front"*

in front, off the top

2 SEE **STRAIGHT**

the upper crust
n phr The social aristocracy; the elite

the best people, the blue-bloods, the class, the classes, the cream, the First Families, the four hundred, the high-hats, the nobs, the quality, the smart set, the swells

upstairs
adv In the brain or mind; mentally, as in "She was a little feeble upstairs"

brain-wise, in the noodle, in the upper story

up the creek
adj phr In trouble; beleaguered; in a dilemma

between a rock and a hard place, between the devil and the deep blue sea, in a corner, in a fix, in a hole, in a hot place, in a hot spot, in a jam, in a mess, in a mess of trouble, in a pickle, in a pinch, in a tight corner, in a tight hole, in a tough spot, in deep doo-doo, in deep shit, in deep trouble, in deep water, in Dutch, in over one's head, in the soup, jammed up, on the hot seat, on the spot, out of one's depth, out on a limb, painted into a corner, stymied, sucking canal water, under the gun, up against it, up shit creek, up shit creek without a paddle, up to one's ass in alligators, up to one's ass in rattlesnakes

up to one's ass
adj phr Overwhelmed; oversupplied; surfeited

asshole deep, awash in, knee deep, rolling in, snowed under, swimming in, up to one's ass in alligators, up to one's ass in rattlesnakes, up to one's eyeballs, up to one's eyebrows, up to here

up to here

adv phr In great quantity; to a surfeit, as in "I've taken insults up to here, and that's enough" and then some, coming out one's ears, till one can taste it, to spare, up the ass, up the kazoo, up to the eyeballs, up to the eyebrows

V

vanilla
*adj Unadorned;
simple; basic, as in
"It was a vanilla
treatment of a very
complex matter"*

plain vanilla, your basic

vibes
*n What emanates
from a person,
situation, etc,
inherently, and is
especially felt
between persons, as
in "She and I shared
vibes right from the
first"*

chemistry, karma, vibrations

W

walk

1 *v* To break off negotiations, a relationship, etc, as in "The delegates said they'd walk if that rule went in"

take a walk, walk out

2 *v phr* To go on strike

hit the bricks, stage a walkout, walk out

walk out on

v phr To abandon or relinquish, as in "They walked out on the project before it really had a chance"

break off, chuck, cut one's losses, drop, duck out on, give the kiss off, kiss off, leave flat, leave in the lurch, leave out in the cold, quit cold, run out on, skip out on, take a walk, throw over, throw overboard, toss up, waltz out on

warble

v To sing

belt out, canary, chirp, croon, groan, line out, pipe, wail, yodel

☞ *This list does not distinguish types or styles of singing.*

warm body
n phr A person regarded as merely such

anything that breathes, bench-warmer, chair-warmer, cipher, nebbish

way to go
interj An exclamation of delighted congratulation

attaboy, attagirl, aw right, congrats, go man go, good deal, good shit, hey, looking good, nice going, right on, take a bow, that'll do it, that's my boy, that's my girl

weasel
v To evade and equivocate; use deceptive language, as in "I asked him to help, but he just stood there weaseling"

duck, duck and weave, hem and haw, sidestep, tap dance, [Brit] waffle

weird
adj Abnormal in a sinister way; alarmingly strange

creepy, double-gaited, far out, fruity, funny, kinky, oddball, off the wall, psycho, queer, sick, sicko, sickroom, sicksicksick, spazzy, strangioso, wacko, wacky, way out, weird-ass, wigged out, wiggy, zerking
☞ *These terms share semantic territory with "flaky" and "crazy," which should also be considered.*

whammy
n The evil eye; a crippling curse

double whammy, hex, the Indian sign, jinx, triple whammy

what's-his-name
n An unspecified or unspecifiable person

what's-his-ass, what's-his-face, whoozis, whoozit

what's up

sentence What is happening; what is the question, problem, etc

buzza, hello Joe whaddaya know, sappnin, what cooks, what do you say, what gives, what goes, what say, what's been shaking, what's buzzin' cousin, what's cooking, what's doing, what's going down, what's happening, what's shaking, what's the deal, what's the dope, what's the good word, what's the scam, what's up doc, wuzzup, zup

wheeler-dealer

n A person busy with many affairs, esp officiously and conspiratorially

big macher, big shot, big-time operator, ganze macher, macher, operator, wire-puller

when the chips are down

adv phr When the time of decision or confrontation has come, as in "He always turns and runs when the chips are down"

in a pinch, in the clutch, in the crunch, in the squeeze, when it comes to the short strokes, when push comes to shove, when the balloon goes up, when the chips are on the table

where one is at

n phr One's viewpoint or attitudes; one's value system, as in "We must get the criminal justice system working, that's where I'm at"

where one's head is at, where one is coming from

white shoe
n phr A typical Ivy League student

Joe Yale, key, shoe, white buck

whitey
n A white person; a Caucasian

(all black unless otherwise labeled) [Latino] Anglo, blue-eyed devil, bright skin, buckra, Charley, Chuck, dap, devil, face, fay, [Chinese] ghost, gray, hack, hardhead, hay-eater, hincty, honky, jeff, kelt, keltch, maggot, the Man, marshmallow, Mr Charley, Mr Eddie, ofay, paddy, pale, paleface, patty, peck, peckerwood, pink, silk, vanilla, white meat, wood, yakoo

the whole shebang
n phr Everything; the totality

the boodle, the business, the devil and all, the kit and boodle, the kit and caboodle; lock, stock, and barrel; the megillah, the schmear, the shebang, the shooting match, the smear, the whole bag of tricks, the whole ball of wax, the whole business, the whole enchilada, the whole kit and caboodle, the whole megillah, the whole nine yards, the whole schmear, the whole shooting match, the whole show, the whole works, the works, you name it

whomp up
1 *v phr To make, devise, or build, esp hastily; improvise, as in "I'm sure we can whomp up something for dinner"*
2 SEE **COOK UP**

bash out, bat out, [Brit] cobble together, fake up, hammer out, rig up, whip out

whorehouse

n A brothel

call house, call joint, cathouse, crib, house of ill fame, house of ill repute, joy house, juke house, maison joie, massage parlor, notcherie, notch-house, rap club, rub parlor, sporting house

wimp

n An ineffectual person; a soft, silly person; a weakling

baby, big baby, bimbo, candy ass, Caspar Milquetoast, chicken, cookie-pusher, cream puff, cry baby, daisy, doormat, drip, drone, drool, dweeb, Ethel, feather-weight, flower, fraidy-cat, goody-goody, gutless wonder, ho-dad, jellyfish, jerk, lily, limp-dick, limp dishrag, lizzy, loser, mama's boy, milktoast, Milquetoast, neb, nebbish, nervous Nellie, nobody, nothing, ook, pantywaist, Percy, puppy, pushover, pussycat, putz, sad apple, sad sack, scaredy-cat, schlemiel, schmendrick, schmo, tootie fruity, turkey, weak sister, wuss, wussy ☞ *These terms share semantic territory with "light-weight" and "sissy," which should also be considered.*

wimpish

adj Weak and soft; effeminate; timorous, as in "The voters tend to despise wimpish responses"

candy-ass, candy-assed, chicken-hearted, chicken-liv-ered, drippy, gutless, lily-livered, milk-livered, mousy, pansified, paper-assed, rabbity, sissified, soft-ass, wimpo, wimpoid, wimpy

wing

n An arm

fin, flapper, flipper, fluke, soupbone

wingding

n A party or other usu noisy celebration

bash, [Brit] bean-feast, blast, blowoff, blowout, brawl, bust, clambake, [Brit] do, fest, festa, fiesta, fight, get-together, gig, hoedown, hoodang, hoo-ha, jamboree, jollification, kick-up, rally, [esp Brit] rave-up, ruckus, rumpus, shindig, shindy, struggle, whoopdedoo, wing, wingdinger

wing it
v phr To improvise; extemporize, as in "I didn't know all my lines, so I had to wing it some"

ad lib, cheek it, fake, fake it, play it by ear, shuck, vamp, vamp till ready, wing

win the porcelain hairnet
v phr To deserve a spectacularly useless reward; merit nothing but something absurd, as in "For that brilliant idea you win the porcelain hairnet"

win the barbwire garter, win the cast-iron overcoat, win the fur-lined bathtub, win the hand-painted door-mat, win the solid gold chamber pot

wise me up
sentence Tell me what you know

beam me aboard, beam me aboard Scotty, bring me up to speed, clue me in, [Brit] put me in the picture
☞ *Other such requests may be framed by using terms under "spell out."*

wise up
v phr To become shrewdly aware; apprehend reality

be beamed aboard, get next, get next to oneself, get smart, get the message, get the picture, get wise, get wise with oneself, get with it, pull your head out, pull your head out of your asshole, smarten up, tie one's shoes, use one's bean, use one's head, use one's noodle

with flying colors
adv phr In a bold and assured way; grandly, as in "She didn't just win, she won with flying colors"

high, wide, and handsome; in a walk, in spades, never looking back, with a bang, with bells on, with knobs on, without mussing a hair, with tits on

with it
adj phr Cognizant; in touch; stylish and au courant, as in "Whatever the now trend is, I'm not with it"

alive with the jive, cool, down with it, go-go, groovy, hep, hepped, hep to the jive, hip, hipped, in the groove, into it, jivey, light, mellow, mod, on the ball, on the beam, plugged in, really into it, right there, sharp, solid, state of the art, switched on, there, trendy, turned on, wise

the woods are full of something
sentence The thing indicated is in plentiful supply, as in "The woods are full of stand-up comics these days"

they are a dime a dozen, they are cut-rate, they are going for peanuts, they are thick on the ground, we have them and then some, we have them coming out our ears, we have them to burn, we have them to spare, we have them up the kazoo

wop
n An Italian or person of Italian extraction

dago, dino, Eytie, ginzo, greaseball, greaser, Guinea, spaghetti, walyo
☞ *These terms will give deep offense if used by persons outside the ethnic group.*

work
v To succeed; come to fruition

click, come off, fly, gel, get off the ground, get to first base, go over, make it, play, play in Peoria, swim, take fire, take off, work out

working stiff

n phr An ordinary working person prole, stiff

work out

v phr To amend, repair, finish, etc, by careful effort, as in "It doesn't look promising, but we can work it out" iron out, sort out

works

n The apparatus for injecting or otherwise using narcotics artillery, bayonet, Bay State, biz, bong, boojie, cannon, collar, cook, cooker, cooking spoon, cotton, dinghiyen, dingus, dope gun, dripper, dropper, energy gun, engine, factory, fake, fakealoo, fit, G, gasket, gimmick, gimmicks, glass, glass gun, gun, hard nail, harpoon, head kit, hit spike, hop gun, horse and wagon, hype stick, ickey, jabber, Job's antidote, Johnson and Johnson, joint, kit, layout, light artillery, luer, machine, machinery, monkey drill, monkey pump, Mr Twenty-six, nail, needle, outfit, pin gun, point, prick, quill, rig, safety, satch cotton, set, sharp, spike, spike and dripper, spike and jolt, spoon, stabber, stem, tie, tools, Yale

☞ *This list does not take account of the various types and purposes of apparatus.*

☞ *The great number of slang terms for narcotics probably reflects both a need for coded reference to an illegal substance and a desire to be chic and up-to-date, in addition to the need to distinguish varieties.*

wow

v To delight extremely; impress powerfully and favorably, as in "She really wowed the opening-night audience"

bowl over, carve, choke someone up, crack them up, fracture, give a bang, give a boot, glaze someone over, go over, go over big, go over in a big way, go over like a million bucks, kill, knock someone cold, knock someone dead, knock someone for a loop, knock someone's lights out, knock someone out, knock someone's socks off, lay someone in the aisles, lay someone low, mow someone down, murder, put someone away, ring someone's bell, send, slaughter, slay, tickle the piss out of, tickle the shit out of, turn someone on

wrap up

v phr To complete; finish, as in "Let's wrap up this deal and go to lunch"

be through with, button up, call in one's chips, call it a day, call it quits, clean up, close out, close up, drop the curtain, fold up, mop up, pack in, pack up, polish off, put in the box, put the lid on, ring down the curtain, sew up, tie up, wind up, wrap

Y

yap

1 *n The mouth*   bazoo, chaps, chops, clam shells, clam trap, fish trap, flytrap, gills, gob, head, kisser, kissing trap, mug, mush, talk-trap, tater trap, trap

2 SEE **GAB**

3 SEE **JERK**

young squirt

n phr An adolescent male; a youth   poot-butt, punk, punk-kid, pup, snotnose, squirt, young punk

yours truly

pron phr I; me; myself, as in "Yours truly will take care of that"   little me, little old me; me, myself, and I; my lonesome, your Uncle Dudley

yuck
interj An exclamation of disgust and revulsion, as in "Yuck, did you see that he was eating pickles with ice cream?"

barf me out, ech, eeyuck, feh, gross me out, phew, ugh, yecch

yucky
adj Disgusting; loathsome

the armpits, Barf City, barfy, bletcherous, bogue, bum, cheesy, cocksucking, crapoid, crappy, crasty, creepy, creepy-crawly, cruddy, crummy, dirty, disgusto, fucking, fungus-faced, funky, gee, goat-smelling, godawful, greeby, grim, grody, gross, grotty, groudy, grungy, hairy, icky, messy, nasty, the pits, pukey, putrid, ratty, raunchy, rotchy, rotten, scroungy, scumsucking, scuzzy, shitty, sick, sicko, sicksicksick, skanky, sleaze-bag, sleazeball, sleaze-bucket, sleazo, sleazoid, sleazy, stinking, suck-off, tacky, vomitrocious, vomity, wormy, yecchy, Yucko City, zooey

Z

zero in

v phr To aim at or concentrate on a specific thing, person, etc; single out, as in "You have to zero in on the problem before you can start to solve it"

draw a bead, get down to cases, home in, narrow down on, pin down, pinpoint, spot, spotlight

zilch

1 *n Nothing; a minimal amount; an iota*

beans, Billy be damn, bubkes, a bucket of warm spit, [Brit] bugger-all, chopped liver, a damn, diddly, diddly-damn, diddly-poo, diddly-poop, diddly-shit, diddly-squat, diddly-squirt, diddly-whoop, dink, doodle-shit, doodly, doodly-shit, doodly-squat, dry spit on a hot day, a duck egg, a fart, a fig, a fuck, [Brit] fuck-all, a goose egg, a hill of beans, a hoot, a hooter, a hoot in hell, jack-shit, nada, nit, nix, one red cent, one thin dime, a plugged nickel, poo, poop, a rap, a rat's ass, a red cent, a row of pins, shit, a shit, shit-all, spit, squat, squirt, [Brit] sweet Fanny Adams, a thin dime, two hoots in hell, two whoops in hell, a whoop, zero, zip, zippo, zot, zotz

2 SEE **ZIT**

zingy

adj Full of energy and vigor

chipper, full of ginger, full of go, full of pep, full of piss and vinegar, gingery, gutsy, peppy, perky, punched-up, punchy, snappy, zappy, zippy

zit

n A minor skin lesion; a pimple; a blackhead

doohickey, goober, goophead, hickey, pip, zilch

zombie

n A mentally numb or dead person; a machinelike person

clone, plastic person, pod person

INDEX

Given a particular slang term or a concept in standard language, this index makes it possible to find the term's or the concept's slang synonyms in all their senses throughout the book.

In a typical index entry, the first line contains a slang word or phrase. Listed under it, in **boldface type,** are the main entries in the book where the word or phrase is cited as a synonym.

For example, the index entry for the slang word "ace" shows that "ace" appears in the book as a synonym for **angel dust, bingle, doll,** etc.

A second kind of index entry makes it possible to trace slang synonyms with only a concept in mind. These entries are headed by a nonslang term (for example, "agreement" and "body") and list the text entries where collections of synonyms express shades of this concept.

Finally, to make sure the index's coverage of the slang vocabulary is complete, all the main entry terms in the book appear in the index in their alphabetical positions. They may appear under an identical or near-identical head; **ace** is itself a main entry in the book, and this is signaled in the index entry by the appearance of the boldface **ace** with its three senses suggested. If there is no similar index head (as with **AC-DC**), the main entry term is given alone.

The index follows the same alphabetizing principles as the main text. In determining alphabetical position, the following were ignored: initial articles ("the," "a," and "an") and the nonspecific pronouns ("one," "one's," "oneself," "someone," "someone's," and "something"). For example, the index entry "throw someone a curve" immediately follows "throw a curve," and "one's head off" follows "headline."

A
  acid
  bennies

abandon
  walk out on

aboard
  in place

A-bomb
  hot rod

abort
  scrub

abroad
  in stir

absence
  play hooky

absorbed in
  into

absquatulate
  break out

abundant
  lousy with

the academy
  the slammer

Acapulco gold
  pot

accordion
  squeezebox

accuse
  hang on

AC-DC, "bisexual"

ace
  ace, "do well"
  ace, "expert"
  ace, "prison sentence"
  angel dust
  bingle
  doll
  good guy
  humdinger
  joint
  pal

ace-high
  great

ace in
  dig

ace in the hole
  case dough

ace it
  ace
  go over with a bang

aces
  great
  honest-to-God
  humdinger

achieve
  rack up

aching
  antsy

acid, "LSD"

acid funk
  bad trip

acidhead
  junkie

ack-ack
  horse

acquire
  grab

act, "imitation"

active person
  eager beaver

actor
  phony

act properly
  clean up one's act

addict
  junkie

addicted
  hooked

addlebrain
  ditz
  dope

addled
  ditsy

ad lib
  wing it

admire
  dig

Adonis
  hunk

adult movie
  blue movie

advance payment
  up front

affirmation
  OK

Afghani
  hash

aficionado
  fan

African black
  hash

Afro, "hair style"

Afro-Saxon
  fink

after-hours club
  blind pig

an age
  ages

agee
  cockeyed

aggravate
  bug

agony
  flak

agreement
  back out
  cut a deal
  on someone's wavelength

agricultural college
  cow college

A-hole
asshole

aimies
bennies

the air
the axe

airbrain
ditz
dope

airbrained
ditsy

airhead
ditz
dope

airheaded
ditsy

air out
split

airplane
roach clip

alcohol
beer bust
binge
blind pig
booze
brew
gin mill
guzzle
have a load on
lush
on the sauce
panther piss
plastered
the shakes
snort

alert
on the ball

alive with
lousy with

alive with the jive
with it

alkied
plastered

alky
booze

one's all
best shot

all anyhow
cockeyed
fucked-up

all atwitter
antsy

all bets are off
it's a new ball game

alley cat
floozy

all-fired
damn

all hell breaks loose
hell breaks loose

alligator
dude

all in
pooped

an all-nighter
a bitch

all nohow
cockeyed
fucked-up

all of a doodah
jittery

all one's got
best shot

all out
lickety-split
flat-out

all-out try
best shot

the all-overs
the jitters

all shook up
jittery

all shot
pooped

all that jazz
bullshit

all there
cool

all the way
flat-out

all thumbs
ham-handed

all tied up
in the bag

all washed up
kaput

all wet
full of shit

all wool and a yard wide
honest-to-God

alma mammy
collitch

aloof person
cold fish

also-ran
lightweight
loser

alter kocker
fogy
old fart

alvin
patsy

the amber brew
brew

ambidextrous
AC-DC

ambitious
hungry

amble
toddle

ambulance
meat wagon

ambulance chaser
  shyster

amend
  work out

amen snorter
  Bible-banger

amoeba
  angel dust

amok
  high

amount
  little bitty
  scads
  shave
  smidgen

amp
  bennies

amphetamines
  bennies

amscray
  split

amuck
  high

amuse
  break someone up

amy
  bennies
  doll

Amy-John
  dyke

anchors
  binders

and then some
  up to here

angel
  angel, "patron"
  dish
  gay
  honey
  patsy

angelface
  dish
  honey

angel hair
  angel dust

anger
  blowup
  pissed off
  piss someone off
  piss-off

angle
  play games

Anglo
  whitey

Angola black
  pot

angry
  blow one's top

angry fit
  swivet

ankle
  split
  toddle

Annie Oakley, "free ticket"

annoy
  bug
  give someone a pain in the
    ass

annoyance
  nudnik

antagonize
  blow it with someone

the ante
  the damage

ante up
  cough up
  kick in
  pick up the tab

antifreeze
  horse

antigodlin
  cockeyed

antique
  fogy

antsy
  antsy, "excited"
  horny
  jittery

anus
  asshole

any person
  warm body

A-OK
  cool
  great

A-1
  great
  the most

apache
  hit man

ape
  crazy
  goon

aped
  plastered

apeshit
  crazy

apology
  excuse me all to hell

apparatus
  basket
  cock

apple
  cookie
  guy
  straight

apple butter
  bullshit

applehead
  dope

apple-knocker
  hick

apple-polish
  brown-nose

apples
  tits

applesauce
  bullshit
  izzatso
  line
  soft soap

approve
  buy

Arab
  camel-jammer

Archie Bunker
  redneck

aristocracy
  the upper crust

aristocrat
  swell

ark
  jalopy

Arky
  cracker
  hick

arm
  cop
  wing

armchair general
  bigmouth
  smart-ass

armed
  carry
  heeled

arm it
  ride the arm

the armpits
  the pits
  yucky

around the bend
  crazy

arrangement
  cut a deal

arrest
  bust
  fall

arrive
  show up

arse
  ass

arsy-varsy
  fucked-up

art
  mug shot

article
  cookie

the article
  humdinger
  the McCoy

artillery
  rod
  works

ashes
  pot

Asian
  gook

askew
  cockeyed

askewgee
  cockeyed

ask for it
  stick one's neck out

ass
  ass, "buttocks"
  ass, "sexual activity"
  ass, "the whole person"
  asshole
  jerk

ass around
  goof off

assassin
  hit man

ass backwards
  fucked-up

assfuck
  bugger

as shit, "very"

asshole, "anus"
asshole, "disliked person"

the asshole
  the pits

asshole buddy
  pal

asshole deep
  up to one's ass

one's ass is dragging
  pooped

ass-kisser
  brown-nose

associate
  hang out with

ass over tincups
  flat-out

ass peddler
  hooker

athlete
  jock

attaboy
  way to go

attack
  blast
  blind-side

attagirl
  way to go

attempt
  best shot
  a crack
  fish or cut bait
  a gamble
  give something a shot

take a crack at
  work
attend to
  fix someone
  kick ass
attic
  bean
attitude
  feisty
  have a hair up one's ass
  where one is at
attractive man
  hunk
  hunky
attractive woman
  dish
Aunt Hazel
  horse
auntie
  big O
Aunt Jane
  fink
Aunt Mary
  pot
Aunt Noral
  horse
Aunt Sally
  fink
Aurora Borealis
  angel dust
ausgespielt
  kaput
  on the blink
  pooped
authentic
  honest-to-God
authority
  in the driver's seat
available
  in place

average man
  Joe Blow
average woman
  Jane
avoid
  give a miss
avoid work
  goof off
avoirdupois
  blubber
awareness
  wise up
awash in
  lousy with
  up to one's ass
away
  in stir
awesome
  great
awful
  crummy
aw right
  way to go
axe
  chuck
  fire
  scrub
the axe, "dismissal"
ay caramba
  Jeez
the Aztec two-step
  the shits
azul
  cop
B
  bingle
b a
  bare-ass
Babbitt
  square

babbler
  blabbermouth
babe
  broad
  dish
  honey
baby
  broad
  cookie
  honey
  pot
  sucker
  wimp
baby blues
  peepers
baby doll
  broad
  honey
back, "support"
back-breaker, "hard job"
a back-breaker
  a bitch
back-chat
  sass
the back country
  the boondocks
back down
  back out
  fold
backed up
  high
backlog
  case dough
back off
  cool it
  get off someone's back
  lay off
back out
  back out, "renege"
  chicken out
  cop out

back porch
  ass

back-scratch
  brown-nose

back-scratcher
  brown-nose

back seat
  ass

backseat driver
  kibitzer

backside
  ass

back-slapper
  brown-nose

back-talk
  sass

back to the old drawing
    board
  it's a new ball game

back-track
  shoot up

back up
  back
  go to bat for
  shoot up

back way
  asshole

the backwoods
  the boondocks

bacon
  score

bad
  great

badass
  asshole
  bad man
  crummy

bad broad
  scarecrow

bad bundle
  horse

baddest
  great

baddie
  bad man

bad dude
  ladies' man

bad egg
  asshole

badge
  tin

bad hat
  bad man

bad head
  bad trip

bad hombre
  bad man

bad job
  asshole

bad lot
  asshole

bad luck
  tough shit

bad man, "villain"

bad medicine
  bad news

bad-mother swinger
  ladies' man

bad-mouth
  bad-mouth, "denigrate"
  knock

bad news, "trouble"

the bad news
  the damage

bad rap
  bum rap

bad scene
  bad news
  can of worms

a bad scene, "misfortune"

bad shit
  bad news

bad time
  cheat

bad trip
  a bad scene
  **bad trip, "drug
    experience"**

bag
  bag, "narcotics quantity"
  bag, "preference"
  bust
  chuck
  cut
  deck
  fire
  a fix
  floozy
  grab
  heist
  nix
  rubber
  scarecrow
  scrub

bag ass
  split

baggage
  floozy

bagged
  plastered
  pooped

bagger
  bingle

bag it
  knock off
  snooze

bag job
  heist

bag lady
  bum

bagman
  dealer

bag of wind
  bigmouth
  blabbermouth
bag of worms
  can of worms
bags
  tits
bag some Zs
  snooze
bag woman
  bum
bag your head
  shut up
bail
  split
baked
  high
bakehead
  dope
bald person
  baldie
bale of hay
  bag
  bundle
  deck
ball
  a fix
  fuck
  have a ball
  snort
  a ball, "happy occasion"
ball-and-chain
  old woman
ballast
  potbelly
ball-buster
  back-breaker
  ball-buster, "emasculating person"

balled-up
  fucked-up
the ball game
  the bottom line
ballocks
  balls
ball of fire
  eager beaver
  hot shot
balloon
  bag
  deck
  fluff
balloonhead
  dope
balloon room
  dope den
balls
  balls, "testicles"
  bullshit
  guts
  izzatso
balls and bat
  basket
ballsiness
  guts
balls to the wall
  flat-out
  lickety-split
balls up
  screw up
balls-up
  boner
  snafu
ballsy
  gutsy
ball the jack
  barrel
ball up
  screw up

ball-wracker
  ball-buster
bally
  flack
ballyhoo
  flack
balmy
  crazy
baloney
  bullshit
  izzatso
balot
  horse
bam
  bennies
  joint
  pot
  pow
  smack
  sock
bambalacha
  hash
  pot
bambita
  bennies
bamboozle
  con
  snow
bamboozled
  hooked
bammy
  joint
  pot
bams
  bennies
banana
  cock
bananahead
  dope

banana oil
  bullshit
  soft soap
bananas
  crazy
bang
  blow grass
  clout
  dope
  a fix
  fuck
  a fuck
  a kick
  M
  pizzazz
  pot
  pow
  shoot up
  smack
  sock
bang-bang
  horse opera
banger
  banger, "engine cylinder"
  jalopy
bang on
  great
bangs
  kicks
bangster
  junkie
bang the bishop
  jack off
bang-up
  great
banjax
  clobber
bank bandit
  doll
bankroll
  angel
  bundle

bankruptcy
  take a beating
banty
  little bitty
bar
  bag
  deck
  gin mill
barb
  doll
barber
  blabbermouth
barbershop quartet
  Dutch rub
Barbie Doll
  square
barbiturate
  doll
bare-assed
  bare-ass
barf, "vomit"
Barf City
  the pits
  yucky
bar-fly
  lush
barfy
  yucky
bargain-basement
  schlocky
barge in
  butt in
bar-girl
  floozy
bar-hop
  paint the town red
barkers
  tootsies
barley broth
  brew

barmecide
  M
barmy
  crazy
barn-burner
  a hit
  humdinger
barney
  free-for-all
  hassle
barrel
  banger
barrel along
  barrel
barrel ass
  barrel
barrel house
  dive
barrelhouse bum
  bum
barrel of money
  bundle
base
  coke
baseball
  chapter
  homer
baseball hit
  bingle
bash
  a crack
  crummy
  sock
  wingding
bash out
  whomp up
basket
  basket, "male genitals"
  belly
basket case
  dope

Basra belly
 the shits

bassackwards
 fucked-up

bastard
 asshole
 back-breaker
 sucker

a bastard
 a bitch

baste
 tan

basted
 high
 plastered

the bastille
 the slammer

bat
 barrel
 binge
 hooker
 nut
 paint the town red
 scarecrow

bat around
 bat around, "discuss"
 goof off

bat carrier
 snitch

bat one's gums
 gab
 shoot the breeze

bathing beauty
 dish

the bat of a eye
 a jiffy

bat out
 whomp up

bats
 crazy

batter
 panhandle

battered
 beat-up

bat the breeze
 gab
 shoot the breeze

battle royal
 donnybrook
 free-for-all

batty
 crazy
 nut

bawl out
 chew out

bay
 pot

bayonet
 cock
 works

bayou blue
 panther piss

Bay State
 works

bay window
 potbelly

bazongas
 tits

bazoo
 schnozz
 yap

bazooms
 tits

bazoonjies
 tits

the beady eye
 the cold shoulder

beak
 schnozz

beaming
 high

beam me aboard
 wise me up

bean
 bean, "head"
 bean-eater
 bennies
 guy

bean-bandit
 bean-eater

bean counter, "clerk"

beaner
 bean-eater

beanery
 greasy spoon

bean-feast
 wingding

beanheaded
 dumb

beanpole, "tall person"

beans
 bennies
 bullshit
 dough
 zilch

beanstalk
 beanpole

bean stripe
 hash mark

bean wagon
 greasy spoon

bear
 humdinger

beard
 beaver

bearded clam
 cunt

bear down on
 chew out
 kick ass

bear hug
 clinch

beast
 acid
 scarecrow

beastly
 crummy

beasty
 scarecrow

beat
 beat, "surpass"
 broke
 con
 cool
 moocher
 pooped

beat all hollow
 beat
 clobber

beat around
 goof off

beat around the bush
 pussyfoot
 stall

beat one's chops
 gab
 shoot the breeze

beat one's dummy
 jack off

beaten
 high

beater
 jalopy

beat one's gums
 gab
 shoot the breeze

beat it
 break out
 split

beat off
 jack off

beat on
 rough up

beat out
 pooped

beat pad
 dope den

beat the bejesus out of
 clobber

beat the daylights out of
 clobber

beat the hell out of
 clobber

beat the hog
 jack off

beat the weeds
 blow grass

beat one's time
 beat

beat to the ground
 pooped

beat-up, "battered"

Beau Brummel
 dude

beaut
 dish
 humdinger

the beautiful people
 the jet set

beauty
 great
 humdinger

beauty queen
 dish

beauty sleep
 sack time

beaver
 beaver, "pubic hair"
 blue movie
 cunt

beddy
 dish

beddy-bye
 sack time

bedmate
 old woman

beef
 beef, "complain"
 beef, "complaint"
 blubber
 cock
 hassle
 squeal

the beef
 the damage

beefcake
 hunk

beefeater
 limey

beefer
 kvetch
 snitch

beef squad
 goon squad

beefwit
 dope

beef-witted
 dumb

a bee in one's bonnet,
 "obsession"

beep
 honk

beer
 brew

beer belly
 potbelly

beer party
 beer bust

beery
 corny

beetlebrain
 dope

beetleheaded
 dumb

beezer
 puss
 schnozz
beg
 bum
 panhandle
beggar's velvet
 dust bunny
 house moss
begin again
 go back to square one
beginning
 for openers
 from scratch
begorra
 Jeez
behavior
 flaky
 fly right
 play it safe
behind
 ass
 asshole
behind the cork
 plastered
behind the eight ball
 out of luck
beige
 dullsville
belay
 knock off
 scrub
belay that
 shut up
belch
 beef
 squeal
belfry
 bean
believe
 buy

belittle
 soft-pedal
bellow
 beef
bells and whistles
 gadgetry
belly, "stomach"
bellyache
 beef
bellyacher
 kvetch
belly-buster
 belly laugh
 belly-whopper
belly laugh, "laugh"
belly up
 croak
 go kerflooey
 kaput
belly-whopper
 belly laugh
 belly-whopper, "dive"
belongings
 basket
 cock
beloved person
 honey
below the belt
 dirty
belt
 high
 joint
 a kick
 sock
a belt
 a crack
belted
 high
belt out
 warble

belt over
 deck
belt up
 shut up
bench warmer
 gofer
 warm body
bender
 binge
bend over backwards
 bust one's ass
bend the elbow
 guzzle
bend the rules
 play dirty
bennies, "amphetamines"
bent
 crazy
 gay
 high
 kinky
bent out of shape
 high
 pissed off
benz
 bennies
bernice
 coke
berries
 dough
the berries
 big shot
 great
 the most
berry
 buck
be sick
 barf
best bet
 front runner

best bib and tucker
glad rags

best boy
gofer

best clothing
glad rags

the best people
the upper crust

best shot, "attempt"

best thing since sliced bread
hot shot
humdinger

bet
bet one's ass

bet one's boots
bet one's ass

bet dollars to doughnuts
bet one's ass

Bethesda gold
pot

bet on
back

betrayal
double cross

better half
old woman

bet the farm
bet one's ass
go for it

bet the ranch
bet one's ass
go for it

between a rock and a hard
place
out of luck
up the creek

between you and me
on the QT

bet your ass, "definitely"

bevels
crooked dice

BFD
big deal

B-girl
floozy
hooker

bi
AC-DC

Bibleback
Christer

Bible-banger, "religionist"

the Bible Belt
the boondocks

Bible-thumper
Bible-banger

bicker
hassle

biddy
broad

biff
clout
a kick
pizzazz
pow
sock

big
big-league
heavy
hot

big as life
honest-to-God

big boy
big shot
boss
horse
pro

big boys
the brass

big bozo
bruiser

big brass
the brass

big breeze
blabbermouth

big brown eyes
tits

big bucks
bundle

big bug
big shot

big C
coke

the big cage
the slammer

big cheese
big shot
boss

big chief
boss

big D
acid

big deal
**big deal, "important
matter"**
big shot
so what

big enchilada
big shot
boss

biggie
big deal
big shot
fatty

biggies
the brass

big girl
pro

big gun
big shot

big guy
big shot
boss

big H
  horse

big Harry
  horse

bigheaded
  stuck-up

big hog
  bag
  deck

the big house
  the slammer

big John
  cop

the big joint
  the slammer

big lady
  pro

big-league, "important"

the big leagues, "top rank"

big M
  M

big macher
  big shot
  wheeler-dealer

big man
  big shot
  bruiser
  dealer
  pro

big money
  bundle

the big money
  the brass

bigmouth
  bigmouth, "pretentious talker"
  blabbermouth
  blow off
  smart-ass

bigmouthed
  gabby

big noise
  big shot
  blabbermouth

big O, "opium"

big one
  grand

bigoted person
  redneck

the big Pretzel
  Philly

big rich
  loaded

the bigs
  the big leagues

the big school
  the slammer

big shot
  big shot, "important person"
  boss
  wheeler-dealer

big stink
  beef

big stuff
  big shot

big-talk
  blow off

big-time
  big-league

the big time
  the big leagues

big-time operator
  eager beaver
  wheeler-dealer

big tuna
  bruiser
  goon

big wheel
  big shot

bike
  bike, "motorcycle"
  floozy

bile
  piss-off

bilge
  bullshit
  crap
  fuck up

bill
  schnozz

a bill, "hundred dollars"

Billie Hoke
  coke

billies
  dough

bill of goods
  scam

bill-poster
  paperhanger

billy
  billy club

Billy be damn
  zilch

bim
  broad
  hooker

bimbo
  broad
  floozy
  goon
  hooker
  jerk
  wimp

the bin
  booby hatch

bind, "predicament"

binders, "brakes"

bindle
  bag
  deck

bindle stiff
bum

bing
cooler
a fix
the slammer

binge
binge, "spree"
paint the town red

bingle
bingle, "baseball hit"
dope

bingo
pow

bint
broad

bionic
great

bippy
ass
asshole

bird
broad
cookie
dish
oddball
the bird, "derisive noise"
the bird, "obscene
gesture"

birdbrain
dope

bird course
gut course

birdie powder
coke
dope
M

bisexual
AC-DC

bit
act

bag
bit, "prison sentence"

a bit
a jiffy

bitch
back-breaker
a bad scene
ball buster
beef
bitch, "disliked person"
gadget
screw up

a bitch
a bitch, "effort"
a bitch, "misfortune"
humdinger

bitch box, "public address
system"

bitchen
great

bitcher
kvetch

bitch-kitty
back-breaker
a bad scene
humdinger

a bitch of a
a hell of a

bitch up
screw up

bitch-up
boner

bite
bite, "be credulous"
bite, "share"
blow
con
scam

the bite
the damage

bite someone's head off
chew out

bite one's lip
blow grass

bite moose
fuck you

biter
con man

bite the bullet
bite the bullet, "accept
consequences"
take it

bite the dust
croak
fold
fuck up

bite this
kiss my ass

bit of change
dough

bit of fluff
broad

bit of jam
dish

bitsy
little bitty

bitter-ender
mule

biz
bag
deck
works

blab
gab
squeal

blabberer
blabbermouth

blabfest
schmooz

black
  blackball
  hash
black beauty
  bennies
  doll
blackbird
  nigger
black eye, "bruised eye"
black gold
  horse
  pot
black hash
  hash
black hat
  bad man
blackleg
  scab
blacklist
  blackball
Black Maria, "police van"
black moat
  pot
black mold
  pot
black mole
  pot
black molly
  doll
black monte
  pot
black mota
  pot
black oil
  hash
black person
  blood
  nigger
black pill
  big O

black Russian
  hash
black snake
  big O
black stuff
  big O
black tabs
  acid
black tar
  horse
black whack
  angel dust
blah
  bullshit
  down
  dullsville
  green around the gills
blah-blah
  bullshit
  chitchat
blahs
  the blues
  bullshit
blam
  pow
blame
  damn
blamed
  damn
blank
  clobber
  pot
blank check, "license"
blanked
  damn
blanket drill
  sack time
blankety
  damn

blankety-blank
  blankety-blank,
    "euphemism"
  damn
blanks
  dope
blap
  pow
  sock
blarney
  bullshit
  soft soap
blast
  barrel
  blast, "attack"
  blow grass
  clobber
  a fix
  flop
  high
  a hit
  a kick
  plug
  snuff
  sock
  wingding
a blast
  a ball
blasted
  damn
  high
blaster
  hit man
blasting party
  dope den
blast off
  split
blat
  chitchat
  gab
blather
  bullshit

blatter
blabbermouth

blaze
split

blaze away at
plug

bleeding
damn

bleeping
blankety-blank
damn

blessed
damn

bless my soul
Jeez

bletcherous
yucky

bliggey
blankety-blank

blimey
Jeez

blimp
fatty

blind
high
shill

blind drunk
plastered

blind pig, "illegal saloon"

blind-side
blind-side, "attack"
con

blind tiger
blind pig

Blind Tom, "sports official"

blinger
humdinger

blinkers
peepers

blinkety-blink
damn

blinkie
coke

blinking
damn
fucking

blip
cool
great

blister
kid

blisterfoot
grunt

blither
have a hole in one's head

blithering idiot
dope

blitz
clobber
cut

blitzed out
high
plastered
pooped

bloated
loaded
plastered

bloated plute
moneybags

blob
glob

block
bean

block box
bag
deck

blockbuster
doll
a hit
Sunday punch

blocked
high

blockhead
dope

blockheaded
dumb

block mo
pot

bloke
coke
guy

blond
hash

blood
blood, "black person"
nigger

blood brother
blood

blood-curdler
a hit

bloodhound
dick

blood sister
blood

bloody
damn
fucking

blooey
kaput
on the blink
pow

bloomer
boner

blooming
damn
fucking

blooper
boner
sock

blort
coke

blot
 snuff

blot one's copybook
 blow it with someone
 goof

blot out
 snuff

blotter
 acid
 hit man

blotto
 plastered

blow
 blow, "expose secrets"
 blow, "perform cunnilingus"
 blow, "perform fellatio"
 blow, "spend extravagantly"
 blow grass
 blow off
 break out
 fluff
 fuck up
 goof
 screw up
 scrub
 snort
 split
 squeal
 suck

blow a fuse
 blow one's top

blow a stick
 blow grass

blow away
 clobber
 snuff
 split

blow coke
 snort

blow one's cool
 blow one's top

blow one's cork
 blow one's top
 crack up
 go crazy

blowed away
 plastered

blower
 bigmouth
 pothead

blow grass, "smoke marijuana"

blow grits
 barf

blowhard
 bigmouth
 blabbermouth

blow hard
 blow off

blow high as a kite
 screw up

blow in
 blow
 show up

blow it off
 cop out

blow it with someone, "antagonize"

blow job, "cunnilingus"
blow job, "fellatio"

blow one's mind
 crack up

blown out
 high

blown up
 stuck-up

blowoff
 blowup
 cinch
 swivet
 wingding

blow off
 blow off, "boast"
 bullshit
 come
 cop out
 scrub

blow off one's mouth
 blow off
 bullshit

blowout
 wingding

blow out
 snuff

blow out of the water
 clobber

blow one's own horn
 blow off

blow smoke
 blow grass
 blow off
 brown-nose
 snow

blow one's stack
 blow one's top
 crack up
 go crazy

blow the gaff
 squeal

blow the lid off
 blow

blow the whistle
 blow
 squeal

blow someone to
 stake someone to

blow top
 pothead

blow one's top
 blow grass
 blow one's top, "be angry"
 crack up

freak out
go crazy

blow town
break out

blowup
blowup, "rage"
crash
hassle
swivet

blow up
blow one's top
blow up, "exaggerate"
fluff

blow up a storm
beef

blow wide open
blow

blubber, "fat"

blubberbrain
dope

blubberbrained
dumb

blubberhead
dope

blubberheaded
dumb

blubberpot
fatty

blue
cop
dirty
doll
down
nigger
plastered

blue acid
acid

blue angel
bennies

blue around the gills
green around the gills

blue balls
hot pants

bluebird
cop

blue blanket
security blanket

blue-blood
swell
the upper crust

blueboy
cop

blue cheer
acid

blue cheese
hash

blue-chip
great

bluecoat
cop

blue de hue
pot

blue dot
acid

blue-eyed devil
whitey

blue flag
acid

blue flick
blue movie

blue funk
the blues

blue-gum
nigger

blue heaven
acid

bluejacket
swabby

blue liz
Black Maria

blue man
cop

blue meany
asshole

blue mist
acid

a blue moon
ages

blue movie, "pornographic film"

bluenose
Christer
goody-goody

blue Owsley
acid

the blues, "depression"

blue sage
pot

blue-skin
nigger

blue sky
horse

blue-sky blond
pot

blue splash
acid

blue-veiner
hard-on

bluff, "deceive"

bluffer
phony

blunder
boner
fuck up
goof

blunderheaded
dumb

blurb
 plug
bo
 bum
board
 pasteboard
 scarecrow
boast
 blow off
boat
 Caddy
 jalopy
bobble
 boner
 goof
bobbler
 fuck-up
bobby
 cop
bo bo
 pot
bo-bo jockey
 pothead
bobtail, "military discharge"
bob up
 show up
Boche
 kraut
bod
 build
body
 ass
 asshole
 balls
 basket
 bean
 beaver
 belly
 black eye
 blubber
 build
 built

cauliflower ear
choppers
clit
cock
cum
cunt
falsies
fart
fatty
glass arm
glass jaw
goose bumps
hard-on
have the rag on
hung
innards
knocked up
mitt
peepers
pins
piss
a piss
poker face
potbelly
puss
schnozz
spare tire
stiff
ticker
tits
tootsies
wing
yap
zit
body-shake
 frisk
boff
 ass
 barf
 belly laugh
 fuck
 a fuck
 sock

a boff
 a howl
boffin
 ace
boffo
 ace
 belly laugh
 great
 a hit
 a howl
boffola
 belly laugh
 a howl
bog
 cop out
bogart
 bulldoze
bog-hopper
 Mick
bog house
 can
bog-trotter
 Mick
bogue
 phony
 yucky
bogus
 phony
 square
boho
 loser
boh-ring
 dullsville
bohunk
 dope
 hunky
boiled
 plastered
boiler
 jalopy

boiler room
scam

boiling mad
pissed off

boil in oil
chew out

boisterous
horse around
horseplay
rootin'-tootin'

boite
night spot

boko
schnozz

bold
cheeky

bollix
screw up

bollixed-up
fucked-up

bollix up
screw up

boll weevil
scab

bolo
sock

bolt-hole
hideaway

bomb
flop
fuck up
a hit
hot rod
joint

bombed
high
plastered

bomber
joint

bombita
bennies

bombshell
a hit

bonanza
gold mine

bona roba
hooker

bone
buck
cock
dough
grind
hard-on

bone-bender
sawbones

bone-breaker
back-breaker

bone factory
bone factory, "hospital"
boneyard

bonehead
dope
fuck-up

boneheaded
dumb

bonehead play
boner

bonehouse
bone factory

bone-on
hard-on

boner
boner, "blunder"
grind
hard-on

bones
sawbones

bone-tired
pooped

bone up on
brush up

boneyard, "cemetery"

bong
works

bonged out
high

bonita
horse

bonk
fuck
sock

bonkers
crazy

bonnet
lid

bonus
gravy

bonzer
great

bonzo
crazy

boo
great
pot

boob
dope
jerk
patsy

boobies
tits

boobish
dumb

boo-boo
boner

boobs
tits

boob tube
the tube

booby
 dope

booby hatch, "mental hospital"

boodle
 dough
 neck
 score

the boodle
 the whole shebang

boogaloo
 goof off
 kid around

boogerboo
 phony

boogie
 ass
 bugger
 fuck
 goof off
 kid around
 nigger
 snitch
 split

boogie box
 ghetto box

boogie-woogie
 have a ball

boojie
 works

book
 ace
 pasteboard
 split

the book, "performance record"

book it
 split

boom-boom
 ass
 fuck

boomstick
 rod

boondagger
 dyke

boondockers, "boots; shoes"

the boonies
 the boondocks

boo reefer
 joint

boost
 back
 heist
 hike
 plug

booster
 fan
 heist man
 shill

booster stick
 joint

boot
 boner
 chuck
 fire
 goof
 greenhorn
 high
 a kick
 nigger
 rookie
 screw up
 shoot up

the boot
 the axe

boot and saddle
 split

bootleg joint
 blind pig

bootlicker
 brown-nose

boot out
 bounce

boots
 boondockers

booty
 ass
 cunt

booze
 booze, "liquor"
 guzzle
 paint the town red

boozed up
 plastered

booze-freak
 lush

boozehound
 lush

booze joint
 dive

boozer
 dive
 gin mill
 lush

booze-up
 binge

boozing
 on the sauce

boozy
 plastered

bop
 ass
 fuck
 a fuck
 pow
 sock
 toddle

bop off
 split

boppo
 ace
 pow

borahco
 plastered

borax
  bullshit
  crap
boring
  dullsville
boring person
  drag
born loser
  loser
borrowed
  on the cuff
bosh
  bullshit
bosom buddy
  pal
boss
  big shot
  boss, "leader"
  boss, "manage"
  great
botheration
  flak
both hands, "prison sentence"
bottle
  bag
  deck
the bottle
  booze
bottle baby
  bum
bottled
  plastered
bottle it
  shut up
bottle-man
  lush
bottles
  bennies

bottleshop
  dive
bottom
  ass
  asshole
the bottom line, "decisive elements"
bottom man on the totem pole
  gofer
bounce
  bounce, "eject"
  fire
  pizzazz
bounce powder
  coke
bounce the goof balls
  blow grass
bouncing off the walls
  jittery
bouncy-bouncy
  ass
Bowery bum
  bum
bowl a googly
  snow
bowl over
  break someone up
  deck
  wow
bow out
  croak
bowwow
  pooch
box
  bind
  cunt
  ghetto box
  pete

boxed
  high
  plastered
box lunch
  fur pie
box man
  heist man
box of L
  bennies
box tonsils
  neck
boy
  guy
  horse
  Jeez
boychick
  kid
boy-howdy
  Jeez
bozette
  broad
bozo
  dope
  goon
  guy
  horse
  jerk
bracelets, "handcuffs"
braces
  bracelets
brack-brain
  dope
brack-brained
  ditsy
brag oneself up
  blow off
brain
  egghead
  sock
brainbox
  bean

brainery
 collitch

brainless
 dumb

brains
 smarts

one's brains out
 flat-out
 one's head off
 like hell

brainstorm
 brain wave

brain stuff
 smarts

brain tickler
 doll

brain ticklers
 bennies

brain wave, "idea"

brain-wise
 upstairs

brakes
 binders

brand X
 pot

brannigan
 binge
 donnybrook
 free-for-all

brashness
 chutzpa

brass
 chutzpa
 dough

the brass, "leaders"

brassafrax
 Jeez

brass balls
 guts

brassed off
 fed-up

brass hat
 big shot

brass hats
 the brass

brat
 kid

bravo
 bean-eater

brawl
 donnybrook
 free-for-all
 wingding

bread
 dough

bread basket
 belly

break a hamstring
 bust one's ass

break a stick
 blow grass

break barracks
 go over the hill

break chops
 bug

break something down
 spell out

break into jail
 fall

break one's neck
 bust one's ass

break off
 knock off
 walk
 walk out on

break out
 break out, "escape"
 rustle up

break out in assholes
 panic

break out the jams
 let oneself go

break up, "laugh"

break someone up, "amuse"

break wind
 fart

breasts
 tits

breastworks
 tits

breath-taker
 a hit

Breckenridge green
 pot

breeder
 straight

breed of cat
 cookie

breeze
 break out
 cinch
 gab
 split

breeze home
 hack it

breeze in
 show up

breeze off
 split

breezy
 laid-back

brew, "beer"

brew-out
 beer bust

brewskie
 brew

brew units
 big O

bribe
 grease someone's palm

brick
  bag
  deck

brickbat
  knock

brick gum
  big O

bricks
  crooked dice

brick-top, "red-head"

brief
  fill someone in
  spell out

briefed, "informed"

brifo
  pot

the brig
  the slammer

brightline
  spotlight

bright skin
  whitey

brillo
  beaver

bringdown
  knock
  letdown

bring down
  knock
  take someone down a peg

bring down the house
  go over with a bang
  hack it

bring home the bacon
  hack it

bring scunnion
  spook

bring up to speed
  fill someone in
  spell out

Brit
  limey

bro'
  blood
  nigger

broach
  shoot up

broad
  bitch
  broad, "woman"
  dish
  floozy
  pasteboard

broccoli
  pot

brodie
  flop

broil
  free-for-all

broke, "penniless"

broken-down
  beat-up

broker
  dealer

bromide
  chestnut

Bronx cheer
  the bird

broom
  break out
  split

broomstick
  beanpole

brothel
  whorehouse

brother
  blood
  guy
  Jeez
  nigger

Brother
  Jack

brought up to speed
  briefed

brouhaha
  hoopla

brown
  asshole
  brown-nose
  bugger
  horse

brown dots
  acid

browned off
  fed-up
  pissed off

brown hash
  big O

brownhole
  bugger

brownie
  asshole

brownies
  bennies

brown-noser
  brown-nose

brown Rhine
  horse

brown rock
  horse

browns
  bennies

brown shoes
  straight

brown stuff
  big O
  horse

brown sugar
  horse

bruised eye
  black eye

bruiser
  bruiser, "big man"
  goon
brush
  cut
  give the cold shoulder
  hassle
the brush
  the boondocks
  the cold shoulder
brush ape
  hick
brush off
  cut
  give the cold shoulder
the brush-off
  the cold shoulder
brush up on
  brush up
brutal
  great
  hairy
brute
  back-breaker
  bruiser
  coke
BS
  bullshit
the B-side
  the flip side
B-29s
  bennies
bub
  guy
Bub
  Jack
bubbie
  honey
bubble-brain
  dope

bubble dancer
  pearl-diver
bubble-gummer
  teenybopper
bubblehead
  dope
bubkes
  zilch
buck
  buck, "defy"
  buck, "dollar"
  dude
  ladies' man
  take on
buckass private
  buck private
bucker
  brown-nose
buckeroo
  buck
bucket
  ass
  asshole
  banger
  barrel
  jalopy
the bucket
  the slammer
buckethead
  dope
bucket of bolts
  jalopy
a bucket of warm spit
  zilch
bucket shop
  scam
bucking
  hungry
buckle down
  bust one's ass

buck naked
  bare-ass
bucko
  guy
buck private, "soldier"
buckra
  whitey
bucks
  dough
buckshee
  free gratis
buck snort
  fart
buckwheat
  pal
buckwheater
  greenhorn
bud
  guy
  pal
Bud
  Jack
buddha
  pot
Buddhahead
  Chink
buddy
  pal
Buddy
  Jack
buddy-boy
  pal
buddy-buddy
  chummy
  pal
**buddy up, "become
    friends"**
buddy up to
  play up to

buddy up with
  hang out with
buff
  bare-ass
  fan
buffalo
  bulldoze
  snow
buffarilla
  scarecrow
bug
  bug, "annoy"
  bug, "racehorse"
  fan
  glitch
  guy
  hot rod
  nut
a bug
  a bee in one's bonnet
bug doctor
  shrink
bugeyed
  popeyed
bugged-up
  fucked-up
bugger
  asshole
  back-breaker
  bad man
  bugger, "sodomize"
  gadget
  guy
  screw up
  sucker
bugger-all
  zilch
buggered-up
  fucked-up
  kaput
  on the blink

bugger off
  split
bugger up
  screw up
buggy
  crazy
  jalopy
bughouse
  booby hatch
  crazy
  flophouse
bugjuice
  panther piss
bugle
  schnozz
bug out
  split
bugs
  crazy
build
  build, "physique"
  frame
buildup
  flack
  plug
build someone up
  soft-soap
built, "well developed"
bulb
  dope
bulge
  potbelly
  spare tire
bull
  bullshit
  cop
  dyke
  soft soap
bull artist
  bigmouth

bulldagger
  dyke
bulldink
  bullshit
bulldog
  mule
  rod
bulldoze
  bulldoze, "intimidate"
  clobber
bulldozer
  rod
bulldyke
  dyke
bullet bait
  buck private
bullethead
  mule
bullheaded, "obstinate"
bull in a china shop
  butterfingers
bull jive
  pot
bullrag
  bullshit
bull session
  schmooz
bullshine
  bullshit
bullshit
  blow off
  bullshit, "nonsense"
  bullshit, "speak nonsense"
  gab
  izzatso
  shoot the breeze
bullshit someone
  soft-soap
bullshit artist
  bigmouth

bullwork
  scut work
bully
  great
bullyrag
  bulldoze
bum
  ass
  asshole
  bum, "beg"
  bum, "vagrant"
  con
  crummy
  floozy
  green around the gills
  hooker
  moocher
  on the blink
  yucky
bum around
  goof off
bum bend
  bad trip
bumble bees
  bennies
bum deal
  bum rap
  the shaft
bum finger
  bum rap
bumfuck
  bugger
bumhole
  asshole
bummed out
  down
bummer
  asshole
  a bad scene
  bad trip
  bum
  moocher

bump
  fire
  knock up
  snort
  snuff
bumper
  snort
bump heads
  hassle
bumpin'
  great
bumpman
  hit man
bump off
  snuff
bum rap, "injustice"
the bum's rush
  the axe
bum trip
  a bad scene
  bad trip
bun-buster
  back-breaker
bunch
  bundle
bunch of fives
  mitt
bunco
  con
  con man
  scam
bunco artist
  con man
  shill
bundle
  broad
  bundle, "wealth"
  score
bung
  asshole
  smack

bunghole
  asshole
  bugger
bungler
  fuck-up
bunhead
  dope
bunk
  big O
  bullshit
  flack
  pot
  split
bunk habit
  sack time
bunk lizard
  goof-off
bunned
  plastered
bunny
  broad
  dish
  groupie
bunny fuck
  goof off
  quickie
bunny hug
  clinch
buns
  ass
burbed-out
  square
burese
  coke
burgle
  heist
burn
  barrel
  beat
  blow one's top
  bug
  con

fry
  heist
  knock
  piss-off
  scam
  snuff
  split

a burn
  a smoke

burn an Indian
  blow grass

burn artist
  con man

burn down
  snuff

burned out
  kaput
  pooped

burned up
  pissed off

burner
  con man
  the most

burnie
  joint

burnies
  coke

burning
  pissed off

burn out
  fold

burn rubber
  barrel
  split

burn the breeze
  barrel

burn the hay
  blow grass

burn the road
  barrel

burn up
  blow one's top

burn someone up
  piss someone off

burn up the highway
  barrel

burp gun
  Tommy gun

burrhead
  nigger

burst in
  butt in

bursting
  antsy

bury
  clobber
  snuff

bus
  jalopy

bush
  beaver
  bush, "mediocre"
  piddly
  pot

the bush
  the boondocks

bushed
  pooped

busher
  lightweight

bush-league
  bush
  crummy
  piddly

bush-leaguer
  lightweight

the bush leagues,
    "mediocrity"

bush patrol
  grab-ass

bushwah
  bullshit

bushwhack
  blind-side
  clobber
  rough up
  snuff

business
  basket
  cock
  shit

the business
  the whole shebang

businessman's lunch
  bennies

bust
  binge
  blow grass
  broke
  bust, "arrest" (*v* and *n*)
  clobber
  crash
  flop
  flunk
  loser
  on the blink
  sock
  wingding

bust a gut
  break up
  bust one's ass

bust one's butt
  bust one's ass

bust down
  go kerflooey

busted
  broke
  on the blink

buster
  eager beaver
  guy

Buster
  Jack

busters
  crooked dice

busthead
  bum
  panther piss

bust hump
  bust one's ass

bust in
  butt in

busting
  antsy

bustler
  eager beaver

bust loose
  hell around
  let oneself go

bust out
  break out

bust-outs
  crooked dice

bust the mainline
  shoot up

bust-up
  rumble

busy
  pot

busy bee
  angel dust

busy person
  wheeler-dealer

butch
  dyke
  tough

Butch
  Jack

butcher
  clobber
  sawbones

butcher shop
  bone factory

but good
  flat-out
  for sure

butt
  ass
  asshole
  broad
  butt, "cigarette"
  butt, "cigarette stub"
  joint

a butt
  a smoke

buttbang
  bugger

butt-buster
  back-breaker

butt end
  ass

butter
  soft soap

butter-and-egg man
  angel

butterball
  fatty

buttercup
  honey

butterfingered
  ham-handed

butterfingers, "clumsy
    person"

butterflies
  the jitters

butter flower
  pot

butterfly case
  nut

butter no parsnips
  cut no ice

butter up
  play up to

butter someone up
  soft-soap

buttfuck
  bugger

buttfuck buddy
  pal

butthole
  asshole

butt in, "intrude"

buttinsky
  kibitzer

buttocks
  ass

button
  big O
  clit
  tin

button buster
  belly laugh

buttondown
  square

button down
  peg
  spell out

buttoned down
  square

button one's lip
  shut up

button man
  button man, "mobster"
  gangster
  hit man

button player
  button man

buttons
  chicken feed

button soldier
  button man

button up
  shut up
  wrap up
butt out
  lay off
  split
  stick to one's knitting
butt peddler
  hooker
butty
  pal
buy
  buy, "approve"
  buy, "believe"
  eat up
buy into
  buy
  plug into
buy it
  croak
buy narcotics
  score
buy the farm
  croak
buy time
  stall
buzz
  buzz, "telephone call"
  chitchat
  dirt
  gab
  heist
  high
  a kick
  split
buzza
  what's up
buzz-buggy
  jalopy
buzzed
  high
  plastered

buzzer
  tin
buzz in
  show up
buzz off
  split
buzz the brillo
  fuck
buzz-wagon
  jalopy
buzzy
  plastered
BVDs
  long johns
by ear, "instinctively"
bye-bye
  curtains
  sack time
by George
  Jeez
by guess and by God
  by ear
by the book
  straight
by the seat of one's pants
  by ear
C
  a bill
  coke
the C
  scam
caballo
  coke
  horse
cabbage
  dough
cabbagehead
  dope
cabbageheaded
  dumb

caboose
  ass
the caboose
  the slammer
caca
  horse
  shit
cack
  dish
cackle
  break up
cackle factory
  booby hatch
Cad
  Caddy
cadger
  moocher
Cadillac
  angel dust
  Caddy
  coke
caeto
  shut up
cage
  jalopy
the cage
  the slammer
caged
  plastered
cage rattler
  eager beaver
'cainer
  dealer
cake
  cinch
  cunt
  dish
  gravy
cake-eater
  dude
  ladies' man

cakes
 ass
cakewalk
 cinch
the calaboose
 the slammer
calendar art
 cheesecake
California sunshine
 acid
call down
 chew out
called
 high
call girl
 hooker
call house
 whorehouse
call it quits
 fold
 knock off
 wrap up
call joint
 whorehouse
call on the carpet
 chew out
call the shots
 boss
calm oneself
 cool it
Cambodian trip weed
 pot
camel-jammer, "Arab"
camp
 gay
can
 ass
 bag
 can, "toilet"
 chuck
 deck

fire
 hot rod
 pete
 scrub
the can
 the circular file
 the slammer
Canadian black
 pot
Canadian quail
 lude
canary
 broad
 snitch
 squeal
 warble
cancel
 chicken out
 scrub
canceled stick
 joint
candid speech
 let it all hang out
candy
 acid
 doll
 dope
 hash
candy ass
 wimp
candy-ass
 chicken
 wimpish
candy cee
 coke
candy man
 dealer
cane corn
 panther piss
can it
 knock off
 shut up

canned
 finished
 plastered
canned goods
 cherry
 pot
canned up
 plastered
the cannery
 the slammer
cannon
 heist man
 rod
 works
cannon fodder
 buck private
can of worms, "complex
  situation"
canoodle
 neck
canoodling
 grab-ass
cans
 tits
cantankerous
 feisty
canto
 chapter
 stanza
cap
 bag
 blow job
 deck
 score
caper
 binge
 caper, "robbery"
 heist
capers
 horseplay

capon
  gay
cap out
  snooze
capped out
  high
capper
  shill
car
  hot rod
  jalopy
  pimpmobile
card
  bag
  deck
card-carrying
  honest-to-God
card shark
  card sharp
careless
  half-assed
caress
  feel
caressing
  grab-ass
cargo
  bag
cargo cube
  deck
carload
  bundle
caronotics
  dope
carouse
  paint the town red
carpet rat
  kid
Carrie Nation
  coke
carrot-top
  brick-top

carry, "armed"
Carry
  coke
carry a lot of weight, "have
    influence"
carrying
  dirty
  heeled
carry on
  horse around
  make a scene
carry the difference
  carry
carry the mail
  barrel
cart, "transport"
carte blanche
  blank check
cartucho
  joint
cartwheel
  buck
cartwheels
  bennies
carve
  wow
carved in stone,
    "unchangeable"
cas
  laid-back
Casanova
  ladies' man
  stud
case dough, "emergency
    money"
case note
  buck
cash cow
  angel

cash in
  clean up
  go kerflooey
cash in one's chips
  croak
Caspar Milquetoast
  wimp
cast a kitten
  blow one's top
  make a scene
cat
  ass
  cunt
  dude
  guy
  hooker
  ladies' man
cat around
  cruise
  goof off
catawampus
  cockeyed
cat bandit
  heist man
catch
  catch, "hidden element"
  get me
  grab
catch one's breath
  kick back
catch cold
  catch redhanded
catch it
  catch hell
catch one's lid
  split
catch someone's lunch
  clobber
catch on
  dig
  get me

catch on the hop
  catch redhanded

catch the devil
  catch hell

catch the drift
  get me

catch-22, "contradiction"

catchy
  grabby

catch Zs
  snooze

catfit
  blowup
  swivet

cathouse
  flophouse
  whorehouse

cat nap
  a snooze

cats
  cookie

the cat's
  the most

cat's astrophe
  crash

the cat's meow
  humdinger
  the most

cattail
  joint

cauliflower ear, "damaged ear"

caulk off
  knock off
  snooze

caution
  pussyfoot

cave
  fold
  pad
  shoot up

cave in
  fold
  fuck up

caveman
  he-man
  hunk

cavort
  horse around

Cecil
  coke

ceck
  joint

cee
  coke

cemetery
  boneyard

cent
  buck

centerfold
  dish
  hunk

century
  a bill

certain
  cinched
  in the bag

certainly
  for sure

certainty
  cinch

c'est la vie
  that's the way the cookie crumbles

the chair, "electric chair"

chalk
  bennies
  coke

challenge
  take on

champ
  great
  humdinger

the champ
  the most

chance it
  stick one's neck out

chancy
  a gamble

change
  dough

channel swimmer
  junkie

chaotic
  fucked-up

chap
  guy

chapeau
  lid

chapped
  pissed off

chaps
  yap

chapter
  chapter, "game division; baseball inning"
  stanza

chapter and verse
  the straight dope

character
  cookie
  guy
  oddball

charas
  hash

charge
  hard-on
  high
  a pot

charged up
 high
 pumped

charge in
 butt in

charges
 the damage

chariot
 jalopy

Charley
 coke
 whitey

charmer
 dish

chart
 the book

chase along
 split

chase butterflies
 crack up

chaser
 ladies' man
 stud

chat
 shoot the breeze

chatfest
 schmooz

chatterbox
 blabbermouth

chaw
 scarf
 schmooz

chawbacon
 hick

chawfest
 schmooz

cheap
 chintzy
 crummy

cheapie
 schlocky

cheapskate
 tightwad

cheat, "philander"

cheaters
 specs

check
 check out

check in
 butt in
 show up

check it in
 knock off

check out
 check out, "examine"
 croak
 split

**check the plumbing, "use a
 toilet"**

check up on
 brush up

cheechako
 greenhorn

cheek
 chutzpa
 sass

cheek it
 bluff
 wing it

cheeks
 ass

cheeky
 cheeky, "rude"
 smart-ass

cheer for
 back

cheese
 barf
 bullshit
 coke

the cheese
 big shot
 humdinger

cheese bun
 snitch

cheesecake
 cheesecake, "seminude"
 cheesecake, "seminudity"
 dish

cheese eater
 snitch

cheesehead
 dope

cheese it
 break out
 jiggers
 split

cheesy
 crummy
 schlocky
 yucky

chemistry
 vibes

cherry
 cherry, "virgin"
 party hat

cherry Leb
 hash

cherry pie
 cinch

cherrypop
 pop someone's cherry

cherry top
 acid
 prowl car

chestnut, "trite story"

chesty
 stuck-up

chewallop
 belly-whopper

chew someone's ass out
  chew out
chewed
  pooped
chew out, "reprimand"
chew over
  bat around
chew the fat
  shoot the breeze
chew up the scenery
  ham
chewy
  great
chiba chiba
  pot
chic
  snappy
Chicago black
  pot
chi-chi
  tits
chick
  broad
  coke
  dish
chicken
  broad
  chicken, "coward"
  chicken, "cowardly"
  chicken out
  chickenshit
  patsy
  wimp
chicken feed, "little money"
chickenhead
  dope
chicken-hearted
  chicken
  wimpish
chicken out
  back out

chicken out, "withdraw
    from fear"
  cop out
chickenshit
chickenshit, "petty spirit"
  piddly
chicory
  big O
chief
  acid
  guy
Chief
  Jack
chief cook and
    bottle-washer
  boss
child
  honey
  kid
chili-bowl
  sleazebag
chili-chomper
  bean-eater
chili joint
  greasy spoon
chill
  cool
  cut
  give the cold shoulder
  great
  knock out
  snuff
the chill
  the cold shoulder
chiller-diller
  chiller
chill out
  cool it
chilly
  great
  laid-back

chilly mo
  cold fish
chime in
  butt in
chin
  chitchat
  gab
  schmooz
  shoot the breeze
china
  choppers
china chin
  glass jaw
Chinaman
  rabbi
a Chinaman's chance
  a fat chance
China white
  horse
chin-chin
  chitchat
chinch pad
  flophouse
chinchy
  chintzy
Chinee
  Annie Oakley
  Chink
Chinese
  Chink
  horse
Chinese fire drill
  snafu
Chinese molasses
  big O
chinfest
  schmooz
chinjaw
  shoot the breeze
chink
  cunt

Chink, "Chinese person"

chin music
 chitchat
 gab

chinning
 gab

Chino
 Chink

chintzy
 chintzy, "stingy"
 schlocky

chin-wag
 schmooz

chipper
 full of piss and vinegar
 zingy

chippy
 broad
 cheat
 floozy
 hooker

chips
 dough

chiquita
 dish

chira
 pot

chirp
 squeal
 warble

chisel
 bum
 con

chisel down
 shave

chiseler
 con man

chisel in
 butt in

chit
 Jeez

chitchat, "conversation"
chitter-chatter
 chitchat

chivvy
 bug
 roust

chloral hydrate
 Mickey Finn

chocha
 cunt

chocolate
 big O
 hash

chocolate drop
 nigger

chogie
 barrel

choke
 choke up

choke-dog
 panther piss

choke the gopher
 jack off

choke up
 choke up, "panic"
 freeze up

choke someone up
 wow

Cholly
 coke

chooch
 cunt

choose
 go for

choosy
 prissy

the chop
 the axe

chop-chop
 on the double

chop logic
 nit-pick

chopped liver
 zilch

chopper
 Tommy gun

choppers, "teeth"

chops
 yap

chop one's teeth
 shoot the breeze

chow
 chow, "food"
 scarf

chowderhead
 dope

chow down
 scarf

chow hound
 pig

Christ Almighty
 Jeez

Christer
 Bible-banger
 Christer, "pious person"

Christinas
 bennies

Christmas roll
 doll

Christmas tree
 doll

Christmas trees
 bennies

chubbette
 fatty

chuck
 barf
 bounce
 chuck, "throw away"
 peg

scrub
  walk out on

Chuck
  whitey

the chuck
  the axe

chucke
  bean-eater

chuck it
  fold

chucklehead
  dope

chuckleheaded
  dumb

chuck you, Farley
  fuck you

chuey
  bean-eater

chug-a-lug
  guzzle

chukker
  chapter
  stanza

chum
  guy
  pal

chum around with
  hang out with

chummy
  chummy, "friendly"
  palsy-walsy

chump
  bean
  dope
  jerk
  patsy

chum up
  buddy up

chum with
  hang out with

chungo bunny
  nigger

chunk
  ass
  hash
  peg

churus
  pot

chutzpa, "brashness"

cigar
  joint

cigarette
  butt
  a smoke

cigarette stub
  butt

cigarrode
  angel dust

ciggy
  butt

cinch
  cinch, "certainty"
  cinch, "easy task"
  clinch
  gut course

cinched
  cinched, "certain"
  in the bag

cinchers
  binders

cinder bull
  cop

cipher
  warm body

the circular file,
      "wastebasket"

citizen
  cookie
  square
  straight

citroli
  hash

city slicker
  dude

CJ
  angel dust

c-jam
  coke

clam
  boner
  cunt

clambake
  wingding

clamp down, "enforce"

clamps
  bracelets

clams
  dough

clam shells
  yap

clam trap
  yap

clam up
  shut up

clank
  freeze up

clanked
  pooped

clanker
  buck

the clanks
  the shakes

clank up
  freeze up

clapped-out
  beat-up

claptrap
  bullshit

class
  great

swank
the upper crust

classy
classy, "prestigious"
great
snappy

claw
bust

clay eater
cracker

clay pigeon
cinch
patsy

clean
broke
clean, "innocent"
clean, "narcotics-free"
stone
straight

clean as a whistle
clean

clean someone's clock
clobber

cleaned out
broke

clean sweep
grand slam

clean up
clean up, "profit"
make a killing
wrap up

clean up one's act, "act
    properly"

clean up the floor with
clobber

clear
clean

clear light
acid

clear out
break out
split

clear to hell
flat-out

Clem
hick

clerk
bean counter

click
buddy up
go over with a bang
hack it
hit it off
work

click big
go over with a bang

cliffhanger, "suspense"

climb
chew out
kick ass

climb down
come down a peg

climb one's frame
kick ass

climb on the bandwagon
get on the bandwagon

climb the wall
blow one's top

clinch, "conclude"
clinch, "embrace"

the clincher
the bottom line

clink
nigger

the clink
the slammer

clinker
boner
catch

flop
loser

the clinker
the slammer

clip
barrel
bust
con
heist
scam
snuff
sock

a clip, "each one"

clip artist
con man

clip game
scam

clipped dick
kike

clique
the in group

clitoris
clit

clobber
beat
clobber, "defeat"

clobbered
kaput
plastered

clock
puss
sock

clock in
show up

clock out
split

clock stopper
scarecrow

clod
dope

clodhopper
  hick

clodhoppers
  boondockers

clodpated
  dumb

clone
  double
  square
  zombie

clonk
  sock

close
  chintzy

close out
  wrap up

close shave
  cliffhanger

close up
  wrap up

clothes horse
  dude

clothes pole
  beanpole

clothing
  boondockers
  doll up
  glad rags
  kicks
  lid
  long johns
  sneakers
  threads
  undies

clottish
  dumb

cloud nine
  fat city

clout
  clout, "power"
  sock

clover-kicker
  hick

clown
  cookie
  guy
  jerk

club
  cock
  dope den
  night spot
  sock

clubhouse lawyer
  latrine lawyer

cluck
  cookie
  dope
  jerk
  nigger

cluckhead
  dope

clue
  fill someone in
  spell out

clued in
  briefed

clue me in
  wise me up

clumsy
  ham-handed

clumsy person
  butterfingers

clunk
  dope
  jalopy
  sock

clunker
  butterfingers
  flop
  jalopy

clunkhead
  dope

clunky
  dumb

clutch
  bind
  clinch

clutched
  jittery

clutch up
  choke up

clutchy
  jittery

clyde
  square

C-note
  a bill

the coalhole
  the slammer

coast
  goof off

coasting
  high

coast-to-coasts
  bennies

cobber
  pal

cobble up
  knock something out
  whomp up

cobics
  horse

coby
  M

coca
  coke

cocaine
  coke

cochecito
  jalopy

cock
  cock, "penis"

great
pal

cockamamie
crazy

cockeye
southpaw

cockeyed
cockeyed, "askew"
crazy
fucked-up
plastered

cockiness
chutzpa

cocksman
stud

cocksucker
asshole
cocksucker, "fellator"
sucker

cocksucking
yucky

cocktail
joint

cock-teaser, "sexual arouser"

cocky
cheeky
great
stuck-up

coconut
bean
coke

coconuts
tits

codger
guy
old fart

coffee
acid

coffee and cakes
chicken feed

coffee cooler
goof-off

coffin-nail
butt
a smoke

cognizant
with it

coin
dough

coin money
clean up

coin of the realm
dough

cojones
balls
guts

coke, "cocaine"

coked
high

coked up
high

cokehead
dope
junkie

cola
coke

cold
cinched
cold as hell
dead to rights

cold cash
dough

coldcock
clobber
knock out
sock

cold deck
rig

cold decker
con man

cold fish, "aloof person"

cold haul
con

cold in hand
broke

cold pack
cinch

cold-shoulder
cut
give the cold shoulder
the cold shoulder, "snub"

collar
bust
grab
works

collar ad
hunk

collar a nod
snooze

collar the jive
dig
get me

college
collitch

the college
the slammer

college man
Joe College

college student
white shoe

collitch, "college"

the collitch
the slammer

colly
dig

Colombian
pot

Columbo
angel dust

Columbus black
  pot

come
  come, "experience orgasm"
  cum

come a cropper
  fuck up

come across
  pick up the tab

come across with
  cough up
  kick in

come again, "repeat"

come apart at the seams
  go to hell

come around
  have the rag on

come barging in
  butt in

comedown
  letdown

come down
  come off

come down a peg, "be humiliated"

come down hard on
  chew out

come down on
  chew out
  fix someone
  kick ass

come-freak
  cocksucker

come off
  come
  come off, "happen"
  knock off
  work

come off it
  izzatso

come off one's perch
  come down a peg

come on
  come on strong

come-on
  gimmick
  shill

come on like gangbusters
  come on strong
  go over with a bang

come-on man
  shill

come on strong, "succeed brilliantly"

come on to
  proposition

come out of the closet
  come out
  go public

come out on top
  beat
  hack it

come-queen
  cocksucker

come through
  hack it

come through with
  cough up
  stake someone to

come unstuck
  come unglued
  go to hell

come up trumps
  hack it

coming out one's ears
  up to here

commercial beaver
  hooker

commie
  pinko

commit suicide
  cut one's own throat

commode
  can

commotion
  hoopla

communications
  give someone a ring

comp
  Annie Oakley
  freebie

competence
  know one's onions

complain
  beef

complainer
  kvetch

complaint
  beef

complete
  wrap up

complex situation
  can of worms

compliant person
  softie

compliment
  hand it to someone

comprehend
  dig
  get me
  have someone's number

compute
  figure

con
  bullshit
  con, "convict"
  con, "swindle"
  a put-on
  scam
  talk someone into

con artist
  con man

conceal
  stash

conceited
  stuck-up

conclude
  clinch

condom
  rubber

conehead
  egghead

Coney Island whitefish
  rubber

confab
  schmooz
  shoot the breeze

confidence
  bet one's ass

conflict
  hassle

conformist
  square

confused
  in a fog

confusion
  snafu

conga
  pot

con game
  scam

Congo mataby
  pot

congratulation
  way to go

con job
  scam

conk
  bean
  clobber
  sock

conk-buster
  egghead

conked out
  on the blink

conk off
  croak
  goof off
  snooze

conk out
  croak
  fold
  go kerflooey
  snooze

con man, "swindler"

connect
  go over with a bang
  hack it
  score

connection
  dealer

connector
  dealer

connect the dots
  spell out

conned
  screwed

conniption fit
  blowup
  swivet

consarned
  damn

conservative person
  fogy

conspicuous
  stick out like a sore thumb

constructed
  built

contented
  in hog heaven

contentious person
  latrine lawyer

contradiction
  catch-22

contraption
  gadget

contribute
  kick in

convenience
  can

conversation
  chitchat
  schmooz

convict
  con

convulse
  break someone up

cooch
  cunt

cook
  come off
  fry
  screw up
  works

cooked
  kaput
  plastered

cooked goose
  goner

cooked up
  high

cooker
  works

cook someone's goose
  clobber

cookie
  coke
  cookie, "any person"
  guy

cookie mud
  big O

cookie-pusher
  wimp

cookies
  kicks

cooking
  cool

cooking spoon
  works

cook up, "devise"

cool
  cool, "disengaged"
  cool, "good"
  get me
  great
  laid-back
  with it

cooler, "jail"

the cooler
  the slammer

cool it, "calm oneself"

cool million
  bundle

cool out
  cool it

coon
  nigger

coon box
  ghetto box

a coon's age
  ages

coop
  pad

the coop
  the slammer

cooperate
  play ball

cooperation
  it takes two to tango

coop-happy
  stir-crazy

coot
  dope
  nut

cooz
  ass

broad
  floozy

cop
  bust
  cop, "police officer"
  grab
  score

copacetic
  cool
  OK

cop a feel
  feel

cop a gander at
  check out

cop an attitude
  beef

cop someone's cherry
  pop someone's cherry

cope
  get by

copeck
  buck

copilot
  bennies

coping
  in there

cop it
  croak

cop man
  dealer

cop out
  back out
  cop out, "evade"

copper
  cop
  snitch

coppish
  get me

the cops, "police"

cop some Zs
  snooze

copulation
  fuck
  a fuck
  gang bang

corgy
  horse

Corine
  coke

cork
  knock out
  sock

corked
  plastered

corker
  humdinger

corking
  great

cork it
  shut up

cork off
  snooze

corn, "old-fashioned music"
corn, "sentimentality"

cornball
  corny
  square

corn dog
  jerk

corned
  plastered

corn-fed
  corny

cornhole
  asshole
  bugger

corn juice
  panther piss

corny, "sentimental"

corny joke
  chestnut

corporation
potbelly
spare tire

corpse
stiff

corral
grab

cost
set someone back

cotics
dope

cotton
works

cotton-pickin'
crummy
damn

couch doctor
shrink

cough over
cough up
pick up the tab

one couldn't care less, "be indifferent"

counterfeit
paperhanger

a country mile, "distance"

county mounty
cop

couple of fives back to back
both hands

courage
guts
gutsy
have balls

courage pill
doll
horse

cousin
patsy

couze
cunt

cove
guy

cover girl
dish

cow
broad
scarecrow

coward
chicken

cowboy
cowboy, "criminal"
dealer
goon

cowboy movie
horse opera

cow college, "agricultural college"

cowflap
bullshit

cow tech
cow college

cozmos
angel dust

crab
back out
beef
heist
kvetch
screw up

crabby
feisty

crack
ass
broad
coke
crack, "joke"
crack up
cunt
dish
great
heist
sock

a crack
a clip
a crack, "attempt"

crack a deal
cut a deal

crackbrain
nut

crackbrained
crazy

crack down on
blast
chew out
fix someone
kick ass

cracked
crazy
flaky

cracker
acid
cracker, "Southerner"

cracker factory
booby hatch

crackerjack
great
humdinger

crackers
crazy

crack funny
kid

crack hand
ace

cracking
great

crack one's jaw
blow off

crackpot
crazy
nut

cracksman
heist man

crack the whip
 boss

crack up
 break up
 crack up, "collapse
  emotionally"
 go crazy
 take a beating
 wow

crack-up
 crash

crack wise
 kid

cram
 brush up
 pig out

cram it
 fuck you
 kiss my ass
 stick it

crammed
 fed-up

crank
 bennies
 kvetch
 oddball

cranked up
 pumped

crank up
 hike

cranky
 flaky
 pissed off

crap
 bullshit
 crap, "inferior things"
 flack
 horse
 mung
 shit

a crap
 a shit

crap can
 can

crape-hanger
 gloomy Gus

crapoid
 schlocky
 yucky

crapola
 bullshit

crap out
 flop
 fold
 fuck up
 go kerflooey
 snooze

crapped out
 pooped

crapper
 bigmouth
 can

crappy
 crummy
 schlocky
 yucky

the craps
 the shits

crap shoot
 a gamble

crash
 crash, "disaster"
 crash, "fail disastrously"
 fuck up
 go kerflooey
 heist
 snooze

crashed
 plastered

crashing bore
 drag

crash pad
 dope den
 pad

crasty
 yucky

crate
 jalopy

crave
 have a lech for

crawdad
 back out

crawl
 chew out
 fuck

crawling with
 lousy with

crazy
 crazy, "insane"
 great
 high
 nut

crazy about
 have a lech for

crazy house
 booby hatch

cream
 ace
 big O
 clobber
 con
 cum
 knock out

the cream
 the upper crust

cream one's jeans
 have hot pants

cream puff
 sissy
 wimp

creamstick
 cock

cream up
 ace

credulity
  bite
creep
  jerk
  oddball
  sleazebag
creeper
  heist man
the creeps
  the shakes
creepy
  creepy, "terrifying"
  weird
  yucky
cretinoid
  dope
  dumb
crib
  dive
  flophouse
  pad
  pete
  whorehouse
crib course
  gut course
crib crime
  heist
crikey
  Jeez
crime
  ace
  bit
  both hands
  button man
  caper
  con
  con man
  cooler
  cowboy
  crooked dice
  fall
  gangster
  grease someone's palm

heist
heist man
hit man
in stir
jail bait
loan shark
paperhanger
pete
racket
rig
scalper
scam
score
the slammer
snuff
sticky-fingered
criminal
  cowboy
  gangster
crimp
  card sharp
crink
  bennies
crip course
  gut course
cris
  bennies
Crisco
  fatty
cristal
  angel dust
criticism
  flak
criticize harshly
  knock
critter
  cookie
croak, "death"
croak, "die"
croaker
  hit man
  sawbones

croaker joint
  bone factory
crock
  bullshit
  clobber
  old fart
  screw up
crocked
  plastered
crockery
  choppers
  glass arm
crock of shit
  bullshit
Croesus
  moneybags
cronk
  plastered
crook
  con man
crooked
  dirty
crooked dice, "altered dice"
crook the elbow
  guzzle
croon
  warble
cross
  double cross
  take on
cross someone's palm
  grease someone's palm
crossroads
  bennies
  jerk town
cross-tops
  bennies
cross-up
  boner
  double cross

crowbait
  stiff

crowd
  crowd, "press"
  mob scene

crowd someone's act
  butt in

crowd-pleaser
  hot shot

crown
  bean
  sock

crown crap
  horse

crud
  bullshit
  sleazebag

cruddy
  crummy
  schlocky
  yucky

cruft
  crap

cruise
  cruise, "search for sexual
    opportunities"
  hustle
  split

cruise around
  goof off

cruiser
  prowl car

cruit
  rookie

crumb
  asshole
  screw up
  sleazebag

crumbcrusher
  kid

crumb house
  flophouse

crumbs
  chicken feed

crumbun
  crummy

crumb up
  screw up

crummy
  crummy, "inferior"
  dirty
  green around the gills
  schlocky
  yucky

crumped out
  plastered

crumpet
  bean
  dish

crunch
  bind

crunchie
  grunt

crush out
  break out

crust
  chutzpa

crusty
  feisty

crutch
  roach clip

cry
  blubber

cry baby
  wimp

crying
  fucking

crystal
  angel dust
  bennies

C-spot
  a bill

cubby
  pad

cube
  acid
  bag
  M
  square

cubehead
  junkie

cube juice
  M

cuckoo
  crazy
  nut

cuddle
  neck

cuddle-bunny
  dish

cueball
  baldie
  oddball

cue in
  spell out

cuff one's meat
  jack off

cuffo
  free gratis

cuffs
  bracelets

Cugat
  great

cum, "semen"

cunnilingus
  blow
  blow job
  cunt-lapper
  fur pie

cunt
  ass

bitch
broad
cunt, "vulva"

cuntface
asshole

cunt-hair
smidgen

cunthead
asshole

**cunt-lapper, "performer of
    cunnilingus"**

cunt meat
broad

cuntmobile
pimpmobile

cunt-struck
pussy-whipped

cupcake
**dish
nut
oddball
sissy**

cupcakes
**acid
ass**

cup of tea
bag

curse
whammy

cursed
damn

curtain climber
kid

curtains, "death"

curvaceous
built

curve
con

cush
dough

cushion
a fix

cushy
classy

cuss
**cookie
guy**

cussed
**damn
feisty**

cuss out
chew out

customer
cookie

cut
**barrel
bite**
cut, "fail to attend"
cut, "snub"
**divvy
give the cold shoulder
scrub
shave
split**

cut a deal, "agree"

cut a fart
fart

cut and run
split

cut someone a new asshole
chew out

cut a take
spell out

cut capers
horse around

cut dead
**cut
give the cold shoulder**

cut didoes
**goof off
horse around**

cut down
snuff

cut down to size
take someone down a peg

cute
smart-ass

cutie
**broad
dish**

cutie-pie
dish

cut in
butt in

cut it
hack it

cut it out
shut up

cut it up
spell out

cut loose
**have a ball
let oneself go**

cut one's losses
**play it safe
walk out on**

cut no ice, "be ineffective"

cut off
snuff

cut off at the knees
take someone down a peg

cut out
**knock off
split**

**cut one's own throat,
    "disable oneself"**

cut-rate
bush

cut some Zs
snooze

cut the chat
  shut up
cut the cheese
  fart
cut the crap
  clean up one's act
cut the mouth
  shut up
cut the mustard
  hack it
cut the shit
  get down to brass tacks
  shut up
cut up
  divvy
  goof off
  have a ball
  horse around
  make a scene
  paint the town red
cut Zs
  snooze
cyclones
  angel dust
D
  acid
  dick
  dirt
dab
  smidgen
dab hand
  ace
Dad
  Jack
dadblamed
  damn
daddy
  guy
  sugar daddy
Daddy
  Jack

daddy longlegs
  beanpole
daddy-o
  guy
Daddy-O
  Jack
Daddy Warbucks
  moneybags
dadgasted
  damn
daffy
  crazy
  ditsy
dagga
  pot
dagnabbed
  damn
dago
  wop
daisy
  gay
  humdinger
  sissy
  wimp
the damage, "charges"
damaged ear
  cauliflower ear
dame
  broad
dammit
  Jeez
damn
  damn, "cursed"
  fucking
  Jeez
a damn
  zilch
one's damndest
  best shot

damp squib
  flop
  letdown
dance
  rumble
dander
  piss-off
dandered
  pissed off
dandy
  great
  humdinger
dang
  cock
  damn
  sexy
danged
  damn
dangle one's hose
  piss
dap
  whitey
dapper man
  dude
darb
  humdinger
darbies
  bracelets
dark
  hick
dark horse
  long shot
darky
  nigger
darling
  great
darn
  damn
date bait
  dish

day-glo
  glitzy

daylight
  moonlight

daylights
  peepers

dazed
  punch-drunk
  rocky

dazzler
  dish

DD
  bobtail

dead
  dullsville
  finished
  kaput
  pooped
  stone

deadass
  drag
  stone

deadbeat
  moocher

dead broke
  broke

dead cinch
  cinch

dead cut
  the cold shoulder

dead drunk
  plastered

dead duck
  goner

deadfanny
  drag

dead from the neck up
  dumb

dead game
  gutsy

deadhead
  dope
  moocher

dead heat
  standoff

dead in the water
  kaput
  out of luck

dead keen
  hungry

deadlock
  standoff

deadly
  great

dead meat
  goner
  kaput
  stiff

deadneck
  drag

dead nut
  on the nose

dead one
  drag

dead on one's feet
  pooped

deadpan
  poker face

dead pigeon
  goner

dead ringer
  double

dead sure
  for sure
  in the bag

dead-sure thing
  cinch

deadsville
  dullsville

dead to rights,
  "inescapably"

dead to the world
  out
  plastered

dead wrong
  full of shit

deal
  cut a deal
  score

dealer, "narcotics seller"

deal from the bottom of the
    deck
  snow

deal out
  stake someone to

dearie
  broad
  honey

dear me
  Jeez

death
  croak
  curtains

debut
  come out

deceive
  bluff
  kid
  snow

decent person
  doll
  good guy

deception
  monkey business
  a put-on
  razzle-dazzle

deck
  bag
  deck, "knock down"
  deck, "narcotics quantity"
  horse
  knock out

deck out
  doll up

decode
  spell out

decrease
  shave

deeda
  acid

deedee
  gadget

dee-jay
  disc jockey

deek
  dick

de-emphasis
  soft-pedal

deep pockets
  bundle
  moneybags

deep shit
  bad news

deep-six
  chuck
  scrub

deep sixed
  finished

deep trouble
  bad news

def
  great

defeat
  clobber

defecation
  shit
  a shit

defend
  go to bat for

defiance
  izzatso
  stick it

definitely
  bet your ass
  OK

deflate
  take someone down a peg

defy
  buck

deke
  con

dekko
  the once-over

delay
  stall

Delhi belly
  the shits

delight
  hot damn
  wow

delirious
  high

delirium tremens
  the shakes

delish
  great

deliver the goods
  hack it

delysid
  acid

demi-rep
  floozy

demon rum
  booze

denigrate
  bad-mouth

dense
  dumb

depart
  go over the hill
  split

depressed
  down

depression
  the blues

derisive noise
  the bird

dern
  damn
  fucking

derrick
  heist man

derriere
  ass

desk jockey, "office worker"

despatchers
  crooked dice

destroker
  hot rod

destroke rod
  hot rod

destroyed
  high

detective
  dick
  private eye

deteriorate
  come unglued
  go to hell

deterioration
  hell breaks loose

Detroit pink
  angel dust

deuce
  bag
  damn
  deck

deuce bag
  bag
  deck

developed
  built

deviant sex
  kinky

device
 gadget
 gadgetry
 gimmick

devil
 whitey

the devil and all
 the whole shebang

devil book
 pasteboard

devil dog
 leatherneck

devil dust
 angel dust

devise
 cook up
 whomp up

devoon
 great

devotee
 fan

dew
 pot

dexies
 bennies

dexter
 grind
 jerk

dial
 puss

diamonds
 balls

diarrhea
 the shits

dib
 dough

dibble
 cock

dice
 crooked dice

dicey
 a gamble
 iffy

dick
 asshole
 bugger
 cock
 cop
 dick, "detective"
 fuck
 goof off

dick around with
 fool around with

dick-brained
 crazy

dickhead
 asshole

dick-lick
 blow

dick-licker
 cocksucker

dick with
 fool around with

dicky
 cock

dicty
 classy
 snooty

diddle
 con
 fingerfuck
 fuck
 goof off
 scam
 snow

diddle around
 play games

diddle around with
 fool around with

diddle away
 blow

diddled
 screwed

diddle-damn
 damn

diddlehead
 ditz

diddler
 con man

diddle with
 fool around with

diddling
 ass
 scam

diddly
 piddly
 zilch

diddlybop
 goof off

diddy-bop
 toddle

diddy now
 split

didoes
 horseplay

die
 croak
 fry

diehard
 fogy
 mule

die hard
 sit tight

die laughing
 break up

diesel-dyke
 dyke

difficult
 hairy

dig
 check out
 dig, "admire"

dig, "comprehend"
get a kick out of
get me
knock

dig down for
cough up
pick up the tab

digger
scalper

diggings
pad

dig me
get me

dig out
split

digs
pad

dig up
cough up
grab

dildo
jerk

dildock
card sharp

dilly
humdinger

dilly dude
gay
oddball

dim
dumb

dim bulb
dope

dime
squeal

dime-a-dozen
bush
schlocky

dime bag
bag
deck

dime-dropper
snitch

dime-note
sawbuck

dime of buzz
angel dust

dimer
snitch

dimestore
schlocky

dimwit
dope

dim-witted
dumb

dinch
butt

dinero
dough

ding
knock
nut
panhandle
pot
sock

ding-a-ling
nut
oddball

dingbat
dope
gadget
jerk
nut
oddball

dingbusted
damn

ding-dong
cock
crazy
donnybrook
dope
oddball

dinge
nigger

dinged
damn

dinger
bingle
humdinger

dinghiyen
works

dingswizzled
damn

dingus
gadget
works

dingy
broke
dumb

dink
cock
gook
jerk
zilch

dinkum
straight

dinky
crummy
little bitty

dinky dow
joint

dino
wop

dip
asshole
dope
heist man
junkie
nut
sleazebag

dipped
hooked

dipper
angel dust

dippy
  crazy
  ditsy
dipshit
  asshole
  crummy
  dope
  jerk
dipso
  lush
dipstick
  asshole
  jerk
dipsy
  ditsy
dipsy-doodle
  con
  con man
  double cross
  razzle-dazzle
  scam
  snow
dip one's wick
  fuck
direct speech
  lay it on the line
dirt
  dirt, "gossip"
  the poop
dirtbag
  asshole
  sleazebag
dirt chute
  asshole
dirt grass
  pot
dirt road
  asshole
dirty
  dirty, "dishonest"
  dirty, "obscene"

dirty, "possessing
    narcotics"
  hooked
  loaded
  yucky
dirty bum
  asshole
dirty crack
  knock
dirtyleg
  floozy
  hooker
dirty movie
  blue movie
dirty pool
  dirty
  dirty tricks
dirty rat
  asshole
dirty tricks, "dishonest
    practices"
dirty with money
  loaded
dirty work
  dirty tricks
dis
  knock
disabled persons
  fruit salad
disappointment
  letdown
disaster
  a bad scene
  crash
disc
  platter
disc jockey, "radio
    performer"
discombobulate
  bug

discouraged
  plastered
discover
  smoke out
discuss
  bat around
disengaged
  cool
disgusting
  suck
  yucky
disgusting person
  sleazebag
dish
  bag
  broad
  cookie
  dish, "attractive woman"
  screw up
dished
  kaput
dish of tea
  bag
dishonest
  dirty
  put-up job
  rig
dish out
  blow
  cough up
  kick in
  pick up the tab
  stake someone to
dishwasher
  pearl-diver
dishwater
  panther piss
dishy
  great
disliked person
  asshole
  bitch

jerk
nudnik
on someone's shit list
scarecrow
shit list
sleazebag

dismiss
fire

dismissal
the axe
get the ax
give someone his (or her)
    walking papers

disparage
knock

disreputable place
dive

distance
a country mile

disturbance
make a scene

ditch
chuck
scrub
shoot up

dither
have a hole in one's head

the dithers
the jitters

ditsy, "scatterbrained"

dittybop
dope

ditz, "scatterbrain"

dive
belly-whopper
dive, "disreputable place"
take a dive

dive in
pig out

divide
divvy

divine
great

divot
rug

divvy
bite

divvy up
divvy

dizzy
ditsy
dumb

DJ
disc jockey

do
blow grass
do, "use narcotics"
shit
wingding

D O A
angel dust

do a deal
cut a deal

do a number on
clobber
con

doc
guy

Doc
Jack

dock rat
bum

doctor up
doctor
rejigger

Doctor White
coke

do one's damndest
bust one's ass

dodge
racket
scam

dodo
dope
fogy
old fart

does a bear shit in the
    woods, "flippant
    answer"

dog
bug
dish
flop
guy
loser
pooch
scarecrow

dog-ass
crummy

Dogberry
cop

dog-eared
beat-up

dogface
grunt

dogfight
free-for-all

dog food
horse

doggery
dive

doggo
crummy

doggone
damn
Jeez

doggy
crummy
scarecrow

dogie
horse

dog it
bum

goof off
put on the ritz

dog out
doll up

dogs
tootsies

a dog's age
ages

dog's breakfast
mish-mash

dog's dinner
snafu

dogshit
bullshit
crap

dog-tired
pooped

dog up
doll up

dog wagon
greasy spoon

dogwork
scut work

do in
clobber
snuff

doing
into

do it
fuck

doker
shill

doldrums
the blues

dole out
stake someone to

dolf
jerk

doll
broad
dish

doll, "barbiturate"
doll, "decent person"
honey

dollar
buck

dollars
a bill

doll-baby
honey

dollface
dish

dollop
broad

doll out
doll up

doll up, "dress one's best"

dolly
broad
dish
doll

dome
bean

domes
acid

dominoes
bennies

Dona Juanita
pot

done
pooped

done for
finished
kaput

done in
pooped

dong
cock

donicker
can

Don Juan
ladies' man
stud

donkey
mule

donkey's years
ages

donkeywork
scut work

donnybrook
donnybrook, "brawl"
free-for-all
hassle

do one's number
go into one's dance

doobie
joint
pot

doodad
gadget

doodle
cock
con
crap
cunt
gadget
goof off

doodly
zilch

doodly-squat
zilch

doo-doo
shit

doo-doo head
dope

doofunny
gadget

doohickey
gadget
zit

doomajigger
  gadget

doormat
  gofer
  lightweight
  patsy
  rug
  wimp

door pops
  crooked dice

do over
  con

doowhistle
  gadget

doozy
  humdinger

dopatorium
  dope den

dope
  the book
  butt
  dope, "narcotic"
  dope, "stupid person"
  great
  the poop
  pot

dope booster
  dealer

dope den, "marijuana
    venue"

doped up
  high

dope fiend
  junkie

dope gun
  works

dopehead
  junkie
  pothead

dope off
  goof off
  snooze

dope peddler
  dealer

doper
  junkie
  pothead

dope sheet
  the book

dope smoke
  hash
  pot

dopester
  junkie
  pothead

dope stick
  butt

dopey
  crazy
  ditsy
  dumb
  rocky

dopium
  big O

dopoe
  horse

do-re-mi
  dough

dorg
  pooch

do-righter
  straight

dork
  cock
  jerk

dorky
  dumb

dose
  dish

doss
  sack time
  snooze

doss house
  flophouse

dot
  acid

do tell
  so what

do the Dutch, "commit
    suicide"

dotty
  crazy

double
  double, "duplicate"
  moonlight

double-bagger
  scarecrow

double-barrel
  big-league

double bitchen
  great

double-clutcher
  asshole

double-clutching
  damn

doublecross
  con
  scam

double cross, "betrayal"

double-crosser
  con man

double deal
  double cross

double-distilled
  high-powered

double-dome
  egghead

double Dutch
  double-talk

double finn
  both hands

double-gaited
  AC-DC
  weird

double header
  joint

double in brass
  moonlight

double-O
  check out

double-quick
  on the double

double shuffle
  double cross
  razzle-dazzle
  scam
  snow

**double-talk, "unintelligible
  language"**

double-trouble
  bad news

double whammy
  whammy

double X
  double cross

doubloons
  dough

douche
  shoot up

douchebag
  scarecrow
  sleazebag

douchie
  patsy

dough, "money"

doughboy
  buck private
  grunt

dough-head
  dope

doughnut factory
  greasy spoon

doughpop
  clobber

do up
  blow grass
  clobber
  do
  a fix
  fix up
  shoot up

dove
  honey

dovey
  palsy-walsy

down
  buy
  cool
  deck
  depressed
  down, "depressed"
  great
  knock
  on the blink
  shoot up

down and out
  broke
  kaput

downer
  a bad scene
  bad trip
  doll

down for the count
  broke
  kaput
  out

down in the dumps
  down

down on one's luck
  out of luck

down the drain
  kaput

downtown
  horse

down trip
  a bad scene
  bad trip

drag
  bad trip
  blow grass
  butt
  cart
  clout
  drag, "boring person"
  high
  a smoke
  snort
  toke

drag one's ass
  goof off

drag down
  grab

drag one's feet
  goof off
  stall

dragged
  high

dragged out
  pooped

draggy
  dullsville

drag in
  show up

drag it
  goof off
  split

drag queen
  gay

dragster
  hot rod

dragsville
  dullsville

dragtail
  goof off

dram
  snort

drama
  soap opera

dramshop
  dive

drape ape
  kid

drapes
  threads

dratted
  damn

draw a bead
  zero in

draw a lot of water
  carry a lot of weight

draw a picture
  spell out

drawers
  undies

dream beads
  big O

dreamboat
  dish
  honey
  hunk

dreambox
  bean

dreamer
  junkie

dream girl
  dish

dream stick
  joint

dreamy
  great

dreck
  crap
  shit

dress down
  chew out

dress up
  doll up

dress-ups
  glad rags

dressy
  snappy

drifter
  bum

drifty
  high

drill
  shoot up

driller
  hit man

drink
  guzzle
  snort

drink one's beer
  shut up

drink Texas tea
  blow grass

drink to
  buy

drip
  drag
  jerk
  square
  wimp

dripper
  works

drippy
  corny
  square
  wimpish

drive
  a kick
  pizzazz

drivers
  bennies

drive the big bus
  barf

drive very fast
  floor it

droid
  square

drone
  wimp

drool
  corn
  have a hole in one's head
  jerk
  wimp

drooly
  great

drop
  blow
  deck
  fall
  fire
  knock out
  scrub
  shave
  shoot up
  snuff
  walk out on

drop a brick
  goof

drop a bundle
  take a beating

drop a dime
  squeal

drop a joint
  blow grass

drop one's bucket
  goof

drop case
  dope

drop dead
  fuck you

drop-dead list
  shit list

drop in
  show up

drop it
  knock off

drop kick
  dope

drop one's load
  come
  shit

drop on
  hang on

dropper
  cowboy
  goon
  hit man
  works

drop shot
  dope

drop the ball
  fuck up
  goof

drop the curtain
  wrap up

drop the dime
  squeal

drop the lug on
  bum
  put the bite on

drub
  clobber

druggie
  junkie

drugstore cowboy
  dude
  ladies' man

drum-beater
  flack

drunk
  have a load on
  lush
  on the sauce
  plastered

drunkard
  lush

dry booze
  dope

dry-gulch
  clobber
  snuff

dry up
  fluff
  shut up

the DTs
  the shakes

dub
  duffer
  fuck-up

ducat
  buck
  pasteboard

ducats
  dough

duck
  cookie
  guy
  pasteboard
  weasel

duck bumps
  goose bumps

duckbutt
  shorty

a duck egg
  zilch

duckfit
  blowup
  swivet

duckling
  honey

duck out
  break out
  split

duck out on
  walk out on

ducks
  honey

duck soup
  cinch
  easy as pie

duck-squeezer,
    "environmentalist"

ducky
  cool
  great
  honey

duct
  coke

dud
  crummy
  flop
  jerk
  letdown
  lightweight
  loser

dude
  dude, "dapper man"
  guy
  ladies' man

dude up
  doll up

duds
  threads

duff
  ass
  goof

duffer
  butterfingers
  duffer, "poor performer"
  guy
  old fart

dufus
  dope
  dumb

dugee
  horse

duke
  mitt
  sock
duke someone out
  knock out
dukes-up
  feisty
dukie
  pasteboard
dull
  dullsville
dull thud
  letdown
dull tool
  drag
  loser
dumb, "stupid"
dumbard
  dope
dumbbell
  dope
  dumb
dumb Dora
  ditz
  dope
dumbjohn
  patsy
  rookie
dumbo
  boner
  dope
dumdum
  crazy
  dope
  dumb
  jerk
dummy
  cock
  dope
  jerk

dummy dust
  angel dust
dummy up
  shut up
dump
  barf
  chuck
  clobber
  dive
  dump, "repulsive place"
  greasy spoon
  knock
  snuff
a dump
  a shit
dump all over
  knock
dump a load
  shit
dumpish
  down
dumpling
  honey
dump on
  bad-mouth
  knock
dumps
  the blues
dunderheaded
  dumb
dunnigan
  heist man
duplicate
  double
dust
  angel dust
  barrel
  break out
  coke
  dust bunny
  hassle

  sock
  split
dust bunnies
  house moss
dust bunny, "dust"
duster
  ass
dust kitty
  dust bunny
dust off
  clobber
dustup
  hassle
dusty butt
  shorty
dutch
  screw up
Dutchman
  kraut
Dutch rub, "torment"
dweeb
  grind
  jerk
  wimp
dwelling
  pad
dyke, "lesbian"
dyna
  gay
dynamite
  coke
  great
  high-powered
  horse
  pot
dynamite punch
  Sunday punch
dynamiter
  joint
dynamite stocks
  bennies

dyno
  horse

eager
  hungry

eager beaver
  **eager beaver, "active
    person"**
  grind

eagle-beak
  kike

eagle day, "pay day"

eagle-eye
  dick

eagle freak
  duck-squeezer

ear
  cauliflower ear
  snooze

earbanger
  brown-nose

ear-bender
  blabbermouth

earn one's wings
  go through the mill
  pay one's dues

earth
  angel dust

ease out
  split

ease up
  kick back

easing powder
  dope

Eastern European
  hunky

East Jesus
  jerk town

East Jesus State
  cow college

easy
  easy as pie
  laid-back

easy course
  gut course

easy digging
  cinch

easy-going
  laid-back

easy lay
  floozy

easy mark
  patsy
  softie

easy meat
  cinch

easy money
  gravy

easy task
  cinch

eat
  blow
  eat up
  scarf

eat cheese
  squeal

eat crow
  come down a peg

eat dirt, "be humiliated"

eater
  cocksucker

eatery
  greasy spoon

eat for breakfast
  clobber

eat high off the hog
  eat high on the hog

eat humble pie
  come down a peg

eatin' stuff
  dish

eat it
  blow
  eat dirt
  fuck you

eat like a horse
  pig out

eat out
  chew out

eats
  chow
  a feed

eat shit
  come down a peg
  eat dirt

eat up
  bite
  buy
  dig
  eat up, "accept readily"
  flip

eccentric
  flaky

eccentric person
  oddball

ecdysiast
  stripper

ech
  yuck

ecofreak
  duck-squeezer

edged
  pissed off
  plastered

edgy
  jittery

Edsel
  flop

the educated money
  the smart money

education
  flunk

eentsy-weentsy
  little bitty

eeyuck
  yuck

eff
  fuck

effective person
  hot shot

effing
  damn

effort
  a bitch
  bust one's ass
  flat-out
  flop
  in there

egg
  cookie
  egghead
  guy

eggsucker
  brown-nose

ego massage
  stroke

egotist
  grandstander

eightball
  jerk
  lightweight
  loser
  nigger

eighteen-carat
  honest-to-God

eighty-six
  chuck

eject
  bounce

elbow
  bag
  cop
  deck

elbow bender
  lush

elbow in
  butt in

electric chair
  the chair

electric Kool Aid
  acid

elegant
  great

elephant
  angel dust
  fatty

elevation
  big O

el foldo
  flop

Elk
  square

Elsie
  scarecrow

em
  M

emanations
  vibes

embalmed
  plastered

embrace
  clinch
  neck

emergency money
  case dough

emote
  ham

emphasize
  spotlight

the end of the line
  curtains

endowed
  hung

ends
  kicks

endsville
  great

endure
  hang tough
  take it

energetic
  full of piss and vinegar
  zingy

energy
  pizzazz

energy gun
  works

enforce
  clamp down

enforcer
  goon
  hit man

engine
  works

engine cylinder
  banger

English person
  limey

enjoy
  have a ball

entre nous
  on the QT

environmentalist
  duck-squeezer

equalizer
  rod

equipment
  basket

erase
  snuff

erection
  hard-on

escape
  break out

Ethel
 wimp

euchre
 con

euphemism
 blankety-blank

evade
 cop out

evasion
 weasel

even break
 square deal

event
 a ball

even the score
 get even

everything
 the whole shebang

every Tom Dick and Harry
 Joe Blow

every which way
 cockeyed
 fucked-up

evil
 great

exact
 on the nose

exactly
 smack

exaggerate
 blow up

examine
 check out

exceedingly
 like hell

excellence
 the McCoy

excellent
 great

excess baggage,
 "unnecessary person"

excessive talker
 blabbermouth

excited
 antsy
 pumped

excited sexually
 horny

exciting
 jazzed-up
 jazz up
 jazzy

exclamation
 I'll be damned
 Jeez
 jiggers
 no shit
 pow
 so what
 stick it
 way to go
 yuck

excrement
 shit

excuse me all to hell,
 "apology"

execs
 the brass

exhaust pipe
 asshole

exit
 croak

expecting
 knocked up

experience
 go through the mill
 pay one's dues

expert
 ace

expire
 fold

explain
 spell out

exploit
 plug into

expose secrets
 blow

extremely
 fucking

eye
 check out
 dick
 private eye
 the tube

the eye
 the once-over

eyeball
 check out

eyeful
 dish

eyeglasses
 specs

eye-opener
 bennies

eye-popper
 a hit

eyes
 peepers
 popeyed

eyewash
 bullshit
 flack
 soft soap

Eytie
 wop

fab
 great

fabby
 great

face
 chutzpa
 cookie

poker face
puss
whitey
face card
big shot
faced
plastered
face the music
bite the bullet
take it
factory
works
faddy
trendy
fade
fink
split
fade away
split
fag
butt
gay
a smoke
fagged out
pooped
faggot
gay
pot
scarecrow
fail
crash
flop
fold
failure
flop
loser
fair
on the level
fair and square
straight

fair dinkum
on the level
fair shake
square deal
fair-to-middling
bush
fairy
gay
fairy lady
dyke
fairy powder
dope
fake
phony
rig
wing it
works
fakealoo
works
fake it
bluff
wing it
fake off
goof off
fake out
a bad scene
con
snow
fakeroo
phony
fake up
rig
whomp up
fall, "be arrested"
fall about
break up
fall apart
blow one's top
fall down
show up

fall down on the job
flop
goof off
fall flat
flop
fuck up
fall for
bite
buy
eat up
fall guy
patsy
fall off the roof
have the rag on
fall on one's face
flop
fall out
break up
fall
show up
snooze
fall to
scarf
false
phony
false alarm
letdown
falsies, "false breasts"
the family jewels
balls
fan
fan, "devotee"
frisk
gab
shoot the breeze
fancy
great
fancy Dan
classy
dude

fancy footwork
razzle-dazzle

fancypants
dude
sissy

fancy rags
glad rags

fancy-schmancy
classy

fancy up
doll up

fangs
choppers

fanny
ass
cunt

fannybumper
mob scene

fantabulous
great

the fantods
the jitters

far gone
plastered

far in
great

farm
croak

farmer
dope

far out
cool
great
kinky
weird

far piece
a country mile

fart
cookie
fart, "flatulate"
guy

fart around
goof off
horse around

fashion plate
dude

fast burner
hot shot

fast chick
floozy

fasten on
hang on

fast footwork
razzle-dazzle

fast one
scam

fast shuffle
double cross
razzle-dazzle
scam
snow

fast-talk
bullshit
con
snow

fat
blubber
fatty
loaded

fat-ass
fatty

fatbrain
dope

fatbrained
dumb

fat cat
moneybags

fat chance
like hell

a fat chance, "no chance"

fat city, "ideal situation"

fat, dumb, and happy
in hog heaven

fate
that's the way the cookie
crumbles

fathead
dope
jerk

fatheaded
dumb

fat jay
joint

fatmouth
bullshit
gab
soft-soap

fatso
fatty

fatten up
have a field day

fatty, "fat person"

favorite
front runner

fay
gay
whitey

fear
freeze up

featherbed
goof off

feather-brained
dumb

feather merchant
goof-off

feather one's nest
make a killing
take care of numero uno

featherweight
lightweight
shorty
wimp

feature
  spotlight

Federal agent
  G-man

fed-up, "satiated"

feeb
  dope

Feeb
  G-man

feeblo
  dope
  junkie

feed
  chow
  dope
  dough

a feed, "meal"

feed and grain man
  dealer

feed bag
  bag
  deck

feed one's face
  scarf

feed the fish
  barf

feed the kitty
  kick in

feel, "caress"

a feel
  grab-ass

feel no pain
  have a load on
  plastered

feel one's oats
  full of piss and vinegar
  horse around

feel up
  feel
  grab-ass

feeped out
  pooped

feet
  tootsies

fegelah
  gay

feh
  yuck

feisty
  bullheaded
  feisty, "irascible"
  full of piss and vinegar

fella
  guy

Fella
  Jack

fellatio
  blow
  blow job

femme
  broad
  dyke
  gay

fennel
  pot

ferret
  oddball

ferry dust
  horse

fest
  wingding

fetcher
  dish

fiddle
  con
  doctor
  scam

fiddle around
  goof off

fiddle around with
  fool around with

fiddle-faddle
  bullshit

fiddlefart
  goof off

fiddler
  con man

Fiddler's Green
  fat city

fiddle with
  doctor
  fool around with

the fidgets
  the jitters

Fido
  pooch

fiend
  fan
  junkie

fiendish
  great

fierce
  great

fiesta
  wingding

fifty-fifty
  iffy

fig
  threads

a fig
  zilch

fight
  buck
  donnybrook
  rumble
  wingding

fighting
  deck
  free-for-all
  knock out

fighting mad
  pissed off

fig up
  doll up

figure, "make sense"

file
  fuck
  heist man

file 13
  the circular file

fille de joie
  hooker

filled in
  briefed

fill someone in
  fill someone in, "inform"
  spell out

filling station
  jerk town

fillmill
  gin mill

filly
  broad

filth
  mung

filthbag
  sleazebag

filthy
  dirty
  loaded

filthy lucre
  dough

filthy rich
  loaded

filthy with, "having much"

fin
  fin, "five dollars"
  wing

financial embarrassment
  the shorts

fine hammer
  dish

fine how-de-do
  snafu

fine kettle of fish
  bind

the finest
  the cops

fine-tune
  rejigger

finger
  bag
  cop
  deck
  fingerfuck
  peg
  snitch

finger someone
  squeal

a finger
  snort

the finger
  the bird

fingerfuck, "insert a finger
  into the vulva"

fingersmith
  heist man

finicky
  prissy

finiff
  fin

finish
  clobber
  fix someone
  knock out
  screw up

finished
  finished, "ruined"
  kaput

finish off
  clobber
  snuff

fink
  asshole
  fink, "traitor"
  scab
  snitch
  squeal

fink out
  back out

fire, "dismiss"

firearm
  heeled
  plug
  rod
  Tommy gun

fireball
  eager beaver
  hot shot

fired
  high

fire-eating
  feisty

fire on
  sock

fire-plug
  big O

fire stick
  rod

firetrap
  dive
  dump

fire up
  blow grass

firewater
  booze
  panther piss

fireworks
  flak
  hassle
  hoopla

the First Families
  the upper crust

first man
 top-kick

first off
 for openers

fish
 buck
 cookie
 floozy
 patsy
 rookie

fishball
 jerk
 sleazebag

the fish-eye
 the cold shoulder

fish or cut bait, "take action"

fishskin
 rubber

fish trap
 yap

fist
 mitt

fist-fuck
 jack off

fit
 works

fit to be tied
 pissed off

five
 mitt

five-and-dime
 piddly
 schlocky

five-by-five
 fatty

five dollars
 fin

five finger
 heist man

five fingers
 heist man

fiver
 fin
 mitt

fives
 bennies

five-spot
 fin

fix
 bind
 clobber
 kick ass
 rig
 snuff

a fix, "narcotics dose"
a fix, "situation"

the fix
 put-up job

fix someone, "punish"

fixer
 dealer
 shyster

fix someone's hash
 clobber
 fix someone

fix up
 fix up, "put in order"
 knock up
 rejigger

fizz
 dumb
 flop

fizzle
 flop
 fuck up
 go kerflooey

flab
 blubber

flabbergaster
 a hit

flack
 flack, "publicist"
 flack, "publicity"
 flak

flack out
 snooze

flag
 bust

flag it
 flunk

flak
 flack
 flak, "criticism"
 flak, "trouble"

flake
 angel dust
 bust
 coke
 dope
 flaky
 nut
 oddball

flake off
 bug
 split

flake out
 snooze

flaky, "eccentric"

flam
 scam

flamdoodle
 bullshit
 razzle-dazzle

flamer
 eager beaver
 gay

flaming
 gay

flap
 flak
 hoopla

flapdoodle
  bullshit
  corn
flapjaw
  blabbermouth
  gab
flapper
  mitt
  wing
flare-up
  blowup
  hassle
flash
  ace
  acid
  bag
  barf
  great
  high
  hot shot
  a kick
  piss
a flash
  a jiffy
flash one's hash
  barf
flash in the pan
  letdown
flash on
  dig
flash-sport
  dude
flashy
  glitzy
flat
  broke
  pasteboard
flat-ass
  broke
  honest-to-God
  stone

flatback
  hooker
flat blues
  acid
flat broke
  broke
flatfoot
  cop
  dick
flathead
  cop
  dope
flatheaded
  dumb
flat hoop
  square
flat on one's ass
  broke
flat-out
  flat-out, "unrestrainedly"
  lickety-split
flats
  acid
  crooked dice
flatten
  clobber
  deck
  knock out
flattened
  high
flatter
  stroke
flattery
  soft-soap
flat tire
  drag
  square
flatulate
  fart
fleabag
  flophouse

a flea in one's nose
  a bee in one's bonnet
flea powder
  dope
fleatrap
  flophouse
fleece
  con
fleecer
  con man
flesh
  cheesecake
flesh flick
  blue movie
flesh peddler
  hooker
flesh-presser
  glad-hander
flic
  cop
flick it in
  cop out
flier
  junkie
flimflam
  con
  scam
  snow
flimflam man
  con man
a fling
  a crack
fling woo
  neck
flip
  bad trip
  blow one's top
  cheeky
  crack up
  flip, "respond excitedly"
  freak out

go crazy
a kick
panic
smart-ass

flip one's lid
blow one's top
crack up
go crazy

flip out
bad trip
blow one's top
flip
freak out
go crazy

flipped
high

flipper
mitt
wing

the flip side, "opposite side"

flip the bird
give someone the finger

flit
gay

flivver
flop

float
goof off

floater
bum

floating
high

flong one's dong
jack off

flooey
on the blink
plastered

floor
barrel
deck

floored
kaput

floor it
barrel
floor it, "drive very fast"

floozy
floozy, "promiscuous woman"
hooker

flop
flop, "fail"
flop, "failure"
fuck up
snooze

flop joint
flophouse

Florida snow
coke

flossy
classy
glitzy
snappy

flower
gay
sissy
wimp

flub
boner
butterfingers
dope
fluff
goof
goof off

fluff
broad
fluff, "forget lines"
goof

fluffhead
ditz

fluffheaded
ditsy

fluff off
goof off

fluke
wing

flukum
flop

fluky
iffy

flummadiddle
bullshit

flummox
boner
flop
screw up
snafu

flummoxed
fucked-up
kaput

flunk, "fail in school"

flush
cut
flunk
loaded
shoot up

flusher
can

flush it
flunk

flute
cock
gay

fly
barrel
great
hack it
work

fly-bait
stiff

fly bull
cop

flying high
  high
  plastered

fly low
  barrel

fly off the handle
  blow one's top

fly right, "behave properly"

fly the coop
  break out
  split

fly the red flag
  have the rag on

flytrap
  yap

fog
  barrel

foggy
  rocky

fogy
  **fogy, "conservative
    person"**
  fogy, "old person"
  old fart

foil
  bag
  deck

fold
  cop out
  flop
  fold, "fail"
  fuck up
  wrap up

folding green
  dough

folding money
  dough

follower
  groupie

fonky
  cool

food
  chow
  a feed
  pig out

food for squirrels
  crazy
  nut

foo-foo dust
  coke

foofooraw
  donnybrook
  hoopla

fool around
  goof off
  horse around
  kid around
  sleep around

**fool around with, "tamper
  with"**

fool away
  blow

fooler
  long shot

fool-headed
  dumb

foolish powder
  coke
  horse

fool with
  fool around with

foon
  big O

foop
  gay

fooper
  gay

football
  bennies

foot it
  toddle

footsie
  palsy-walsy

footsies
  tootsies

footsie-wootsie
  palsy-walsy

foozle
  boner
  fogy
  fuck up
  goof
  snafu

foozler
  butterfingers
  fuck-up

for a fact
  for sure

for all one's worth
  flat-out

for certain
  for sure

for crying out loud
  Jeez

forecastle lawyer
  latrine lawyer

foreigner
  hunky

forever and amen
  for keeps

for free
  free gratis

for fun
  for kicks

forget it, "pardon"

forget lines
  fluff

for good
  for keeps

for goodness' sakes
  Jeez

for heaven's sakes
  Jeez

fork
  fuck
  heist man

for keeps, "permanently"

forkhander
  southpaw

for kicks, "for pleasure"

forking
  damn

fork it in
  pig out

fork out
  blow
  cough up
  kick in
  pick up the tab

form
  the book

for nothing
  free gratis

for openers, "as a
  beginning"

for Pete's sake
  Jeez

for pity's sakes
  Jeez

for real
  for sure
  honest-to-God

for starters
  for openers

for sure, "certainly"

for-sure
  honest-to-God

for the birds
  crummy

for the hell of it
  for kicks

for the love of Mike
  Jeez

forty ways to Sunday
  flat-out

forty winks
  a snooze

forwards
  bennies

fossil
  fogy
  old fart

foul
  dirty

foul ball
  jerk
  loser
  oddball

fouled-up
  fucked-up

foulup
  boner

foul up
  fuck up
  goof
  screw up
  snafu

found money
  gravy

four-flusher
  con man
  phony

the four hundred
  the upper crust

four-letter man
  asshole
  dope

four-O
  great

four-square
  square

four-star
  big-league

four-way hit
  acid

four-wheeler
  jalopy

fox
  con
  dish
  floozy

foxy
  high
  sexy

frabjous
  great

fracas
  free-for-all
  hassle

fracture
  break someone up
  wow

fractured
  high
  plastered

frag
  snuff

fraidy-cat
  chicken
  wimp

frail
  broad

frail job
  dish

frame
  bum rap
  frame, "incriminate
    falsely"
  stanza

frame-up
  bum rap

frantic
  great

frapping
  damn

frau
  broad
  old woman

fraud
  phony

frazzled
  high
  kaput
  pooped

freak
  fan
  flip
  freak out
  gay
  junkie
  nut
  oddball
  pothead

freaking
  damn

freak out
  bad trip
  crack up
  flip
  freak out, "experience a
    bad narcotics reaction"
  go crazy

freaky
  kinky

freebase
  coke

freebie
  Annie Oakley
  freebie, "something free of
    charge"
  free gratis

free-for-all, "brawl"

freeload
  bum

freeloader
  moocher

free lunch
  freebie

free ticket
  Annie Oakley
  blank check

freeze out
  cut
  give the cold shoulder

freeze up, "panic"

French
  blow
  fur pie

Frenchie
  rubber

French job
  blow job

French kiss, "kiss"

French letter
  rubber

French person
  Frog

French safe
  rubber

fresh
  cheeky
  chutzpa
  cool
  great

fresh up
  brush up

fretty
  jittery

fribble away
  blow

fried
  fucked-up
  high

  kaput
  plastered
  pooped

friend
  pal

friendly
  chummy
  palsy-walsy

friendship
  buddy up

frig
  ass
  con
  fingerfuck
  fuck
  a fuck

frigged
  screwed

frigging
  ass
  damn
  fucking
  scam

fright
  scarecrow

frighten
  scare the shit out of
  spook

frightened
  panic
  scared shitless

frisk, "search"

frisking powder
  coke

frit
  gay

fritter away
  blow

fritz
  screw up

Fritz
  kraut

fritzed
  on the blink

fritzer
  phony

frivol away
  blow
  horse around

'fro
  Afro

frobnitz
  gadget

frog-eater
  Frog

frogging
  damn

Froggy
  Frog

frogskin
  buck
  dough

frolic
  caper

from A to Z
  stone

from hunger
  crummy

from scratch, "from the beginning"

from the ground up
  flat-out
  from scratch

front
  shill

frontal
  straight

front name
  monicker

front office
  the brass

frontpage
  big-league

front runner, "probable winner"

froody
  great

frost
  flop
  letdown
  piss someone off

the frost
  the cold shoulder

frost someone's ass
  give someone a pain in the ass

frosted
  high

frosty
  high

froth
  brew

fruitcake
  gay
  nut
  oddball

fruitcakey
  crazy

fruit salad, "disabled person"

fruit wagon
  meat wagon

fruity
  crazy
  gay
  weird

fry
  crash

fry, "die in the electric chair"

fu
  pot

fubar
  fucked-up

fuck
  ass
  asshole
  con
  fuck, "copulate"
  fuck, "copulation"
  fuck, "maltreat"
  zilch

a fuck, "copulation"

fuck around
  fool around with
  goof off
  play games

fuck book, "pornographic book"

fucked
  screwed

fucked out
  pooped

fucked-up
  fucked-up, "chaotic"
  on the blink

fucker
  asshole
  gadget
  guy
  sucker

fuck film
  blue movie

fuckhead
  asshole
  jerk

fucking
  ass
  damn
  fucking, "conspicuous and complete"
  fucking, "extremely"
  scam
  yucky

a fucking
  the shaft

fucking ay
  bet your ass

fucking well told
  bet your ass

fuck off
  goof off
  jack off
  split

fuck over
  fuck

fuck up
  fuck
  fuck up, "blunder"
  goof
  screw up

fuck-up
  boner
  fuck-up, "bungler"
  snafu

fuck with
  doctor
  fool around with

fuck you
  **fuck you, "expression of
    strong defiance"**
  kiss my ass

fuck you and the horse you
    rode in on
  fuck you

fud
  fogy

fuddled
  rocky

fuddy-duddy
  fogy
  square

fudge
  cook up
  doctor

fudging one's undies
  panic
  scared shitless

fuel
  angel dust

full
  high

fullams
  crooked dice

full blast
  flat-out
  high
  lickety-split

full court press
  best shot

full fig
  glad rags

full moon
  bag
  deck

full-mooner
  nut

full of baloney
  full of shit

full of beans
  full of piss and vinegar
  full of shit

full steam
  lickety-split

full up
  fed-up

Fu Manchu
  pothead

fumble-fist
  butterfingers
  fuck-up

fumtu
  fucked-up

fun
  big O

horse around
  horseplay

fun and games
  kicks

funk
  the blues
  chicken out
  freeze up
  jerk
  panic
  spook

funk hole
  hideaway

funk out
  back out
  chicken out

funky
  cool
  great
  hunky
  kinky
  yucky

funny
  crazy
  flaky
  howl
  kinky
  weird

funny business
  dirty tricks
  monkey business

funny cigarette
  joint

funny farm
  booby hatch

funny stuff
  pot

fun-seeker
  playboy

furburger
  cunt

dish
  fur pie

furry
  creepy
  hairy

fuss
  hoopla
  sweat

fussy
  prissy

futy
  cunt
  fuck

futz
  con
  fuck
  a fuck
  old fart

futz around
  goof off

futz around with
  fool around with

futzed-up
  fucked-up

the fuzz
  the cops

fuzzled
  plastered

fuzznuts
  jerk

fuzz tub
  prowl car

fuzzy
  cinch
  cop
  high

fuzzy one
  doll

G
  grand
  works

gab
  chitchat
  gab, "speak"
  gab, "speech"
  shoot the breeze

gabber
  blabbermouth

gabble
  chitchat
  gab

gabby, "talkative"

gabfest
  schmooz

gadabout
  playboy

gadget, "device"

gadgetry, "device"

gadzooks
  Jeez

gaffer
  old fart

gag
  crack

ga-ga
  crazy
  ditsy

gage
  panther piss
  pot

gage butt
  joint

gag line
  punch line

Gainesville green
  pot

gal
  broad

gal Friday
  gofer

gall
  chutzpa

galley-west
  cockeyed
  fucked-up

galoot
  guy

gam
  schmooz

a gamble, "chance"

game
  gimpy
  racket

gammon
  razzle-dazzle

gammot
  horse

gams
  pins

gamy
  dirty

gander
  check out
  the once-over
  rubberneck

gang
  bag
  deck

gang bang, "copulation"

gangbusters
  a hit

ganger
  dope

gangster, "criminal"

ganja
  pot

ganze macher
  wheeler-dealer

garbage
  bullshit

crap
dope
pot

garbage down
scarf

garden variety
bush

gargle
guzzle
snort

gargle factory
dive
gin mill

gargoyle
scarecrow

gas
bullshit
chitchat
flop
gab
a hit
schmooz
shoot the breeze

a gas
a ball

gasbag
bigmouth
blabbermouth

Gas City
a ball

gas-guzzler
jalopy

gash
ass
bullshit
cunt
floozy
pot

gash hound
stud

gasket
works

gasman
bigmouth
flack

gasper
butt
joint
a smoke

gassed
high
plastered

gassed-up
jazzed-up

gasser
flop
a hit

gassy
gabby

gas up
jazz up

gat
rod

gate
shoot up
take

the gate
the axe

gatemouth
bigmouth
blabbermouth

gates
pot

gaudy
glitzy

gawk
rubberneck

gay, "homosexual"
gay, "homosexual male"

gay bird
playboy

gay-cat
dude

gay deceivers
falsies

gay dog
playboy

gazabo
guy

gazer
cop
dick

gazoo
ass
asshole

GB
doll

gear
great
pot
psych someone up

gearbox
dope

geared
high
pumped

geared up
high
pumped

gearhead
dope

gear someone up
psych someone up

gee
dough
grand
guy
Jeez
yucky

geech
scarecrow

geechee
nigger

gee-dee
damn

geed up
high

geek
jerk
lush
oddball
sleazebag

geepo
snitch

geets
dough

gee whiz
heist man
Jeez

geez
dope
shoot up

geezed
high

geezer
dope
fogy
guy
old fart
snort

gel
work

gelatin
acid

gelt
dough

gem
the McCoy

the gen
the poop
the straight dope

gendarme
cop

genitals
hung

gent
cookie
guy

George
Jeez

George smack
horse

German goiter
potbelly

German person
kraut

get
bug
dig
snuff

get a bang out of
dig
flip
get a kick out of

get one's act together
clean up one's act
get it together

get one's back up
blow one's top

get a kick out of
dig

get a line on
smoke out

get a little on the side
cheat

get a load of
check out

get along
get by
hit it off

get a move on
get the lead out

get a rise out of
piss someone off

get a wiggle on
get the lead out

get someone's back up
piss someone off

get behind
back
have a ball

get by, "perform minimally"

get cold feet
chicken out

get cracking
get the lead out

get down
blow grass
have a ball

get down on
bug

get down to cases
get down to brass tacks
lay it on the line
zero in

get even, "avenge"

get one's feet wet
take a crack at

get someone's goat
bug

get going
get the lead out
split

get one's hands on
grab

get hold of
grab

get one's hooks into
grab

get in one's hair
bug
give someone a pain in the ass

get into the act
  butt in

get in trouble
  knock up

get one's Irish up
  blow one's top

get it
  catch hell
  get it in the neck
  get me

get it all together
  get it together

get it in the neck
  get it in the neck, "be injured"
  take a beating

get it off
  come

get it off one's chest
  let it all hang out

get it off with
  fuck

get it on
  blow grass
  get the lead out
  have a ball

get it out of one's system
  let it all hang out

get it straight
  dig

get it together
  clean up one's act
  get it together, "organize life"

get one's jollies
  have a ball

get laid
  fuck

get lost
  fuck you

lay off
  split

get lucky, "enjoy luck"

get mad
  blow one's top

get me, "comprehend"

get moving
  split

get naked
  have a ball

get next to
  brown-nose

get off
  blow grass
  have a ball
  shoot up

get off someone's case
  get off someone's back

get off one's high horse
  come down a peg

get off on
  dig
  get a kick out of

get off the dime
  get the lead out
  split

get off the ground
  hack it
  work

get off with
  fuck

get on
  blow grass
  get by

get on board
  plug into

get on someone's case
  bug
  crowd

get on someone's list
  blow it with someone

get on someone's nerves
  bug

get on the ball
  clean up one's act
  get on the ball, "improve"

get on the bandwagon, "join a popular trend"

get on the stick
  get on the ball
  get the lead out

get out of here
  izzatso

get out of my hair
  lay off

get one's own back
  get even

get smart
  wise up

get some rack
  snooze

get sore
  blow one's top

get straight
  clean up one's act

get the air
  get the ax

get the business
  get it in the neck

get the drift
  dig
  get me

get the hang of
  dig

get the hell out
  split

get the idea
  dig

get the lead out of one's ass
  get the lead out

get the picture
  dig

get me
 wise up

get the sack
 get the ax

get through
 score

get to
 bug

get to first base
 work

get-together
 wingding

get to the bottom line
 get down to brass tacks

get tough with
 bulldoze

get under one's skin
 bug

get up
 brush up
 doll up
 threads

get-up-and-go
 pizzazz

get wise
 dig
 wise up

get with it
 clean up one's act
 dig
 get on the ball
 shoot up
 wise up

ghetto blaster
 ghetto box

ghost
 acid
 whitey

ghost turd
 dust bunny

ghow
 big O

GI
 buck private

gibble-gabble
 blabbermouth
 chitchat
 gab

giddy
 ditsy

giddyapper
 horse opera

giddybrain
 ditz

gidget
 gadget

gig
 asshole
 cunt
 scam
 wingding

a giggle
 a laugh

giggle smoke
 pot

giggy
 asshole
 cunt

gigmaree
 gadget

GI Joe
 buck private

gilhooley
 gadget

gills
 puss
 yap

gimbaljawed
 gabby

gimmick
 bag
 gadget
 gimmick, "device"
 works

gimmicks
 gadgetry
 works

gimpy, "limping"

gin
 coke
 donnybrook
 free-for-all

ginch
 ass
 broad
 cunt

ginchy
 great
 sexy

ginger
 guts
 pizzazz

gingerpeachy
 great

gingery
 zingy

ginhead
 lush

gink
 cookie
 guy
 jerk

gin mill
 dive
 gin mill, "bar"

ginned up
 plastered

ginzo
 hunky
 wop

girl
coke
gay
jail bait
girlie
broad
cheesecake
the GIs
the shits
gism
cum
pizzazz
git
split
give
stake someone to
give someone a bad time
bug
give a go
take a crack at
give a good talking to
chew out
give a look at
check out
give a miss, "avoid"
give someone a pain in the ass, "annoy"
give a piece of one's mind
chew out
give someone a ring, "telephone"
give something a shot, "try"
give someone a slap on the wrist, "punish mildly"
give a turn
spook
giveaway
freebie
give away
blow

give a whirl
take a crack at
give five, "shake hands"
give five to
sock
give good head
blow
give hail Columbia
chew out
give head
blow
give hell
chew out
kick ass
give someone his (or her) walking papers, "dismiss"
give in
fold
give it to
kick ass
sock
give it to someone in the neck
fix someone
give merry hell
chew out
kick ass
give out
croak
fold
fuck
go kerflooey
give some skin
give five
give the axe
fire
give the bum's rush
bounce
fire

give the business
chew out
clobber
rough up
snuff
give someone the business
con
fix someone
snow
give the cold shoulder, "snub"
give the devil
chew out
give the door
fire
give the finger
fuck
give someone the finger, "insult"
give the gate
fire
give the go-by
cut
give a miss
give the cold shoulder
give the nod to
go for
give the once-over
check out
give the shakes
spook
give the works
chew out
clobber
rough up
snuff
give up the ghost
croak
go kerflooey
give what-for
chew out

gizmo
  gadget
  guy
glad
  coke
glad-hander
  glad-hander, "insincere
      greeter"
  phony
glad rags, "best clothing"
glad stuff
  big O
  M
glamor girl
  dish
glamorous people
  the jet set
glamor puss
  dish
  hunk
glare
  stick out like a sore thumb
glass
  bennies
  works
glass arm, "vulnerable arm"
glass jaw, "vulnerable chin"
glazed
  high
  plastered
glim
  check out
glimmers
  peepers
glitch, "malfunction"
the glitterati
  the jet set
glitzy, "gaudy"
glob, "viscous mass"

globes
  tits
glom
  check out
  mitt
glommer
  mitt
glom on to
  grab
gloomy Gus,
      "melancholiac"
glop
  corn
  goo
  mung
gloppy
  corny
glory-grabber
  grandstander
glory hallelujah
  Jeez
gluey
  corny
glug
  snort
glutton
  pig
G-man, "Federal agent"
gnarly
  crummy
  great
gnatbrain
  dope
gnome
  bean counter
go
  come off
  hassle
a go
  a clip
  a crack

the go
  the OK
goad
  goose
the go-ahead
  the go-ahead, "permission"
  the OK
go all the way
  bust one's ass
  fuck
go along
  play ball
go along with
  buy
  get on the bandwagon
go ape
  blow one's top
  crack up
  go crazy
go ape over
  flip
  go crazy
go at
  chew out
  take a crack at
goat fuck
  snafu
goatish
  horny
go at it
  fuck
  hassle
gob
  glob
  swabby
  yap
go back to square one,
      "begin again"
go bananas
  crack up
  go crazy

go bananas over
flip

gobble
blow
pig out

gobble down
bite

gobbledygook
double-talk

gobbler
cocksucker
pig

gobble up
eat up
flip

go beddie-bye
snooze

go belly up
crash
croak
flop
fuck up
go broke
go kerflooey

go bonkers
go crazy

go broke
go broke, "become insolvent"
take a beating

gobs
bundle

go bust
go broke

the go-by
the cold shoulder

go crazy, "become insane"

godawful
crummy
damn
fucking
yucky

goddamn
damn

godfather
boss

godfer
kid

go down
come off
crash
go kerflooey

go down for the count
flop
take a beating

go downhill
go to hell

go down in flames
crash

go down on
blow

go down the drain
fuck up
go kerflooey
go to hell

God's gift to women
ladies' man

go easy
cool it

gofer, "subordinate"

go figure
that's the way the cookie crumbles

go fly a kite
fuck you
lay off

go for
bite
buy
dig
flip
get a kick out of

go for, "choose"
have a lech for

go-for
gofer

go for broke
bust one's ass
go for it

go for in a big way
have a lech for

go for it
bust one's ass
go for it, "risk all"

go fuck yourself
fuck you
kiss my ass

go-getter
eager beaver
hot shot

goggle
rubberneck

goggle-eye
panther piss

goggle-eyed
popeyed

goggles
specs

go-go
full of piss and vinegar
trendy
with it

a go-go
trendy

go great guns
ace
go over with a bang

go haywire
go crazy
go kerflooey

go hog wild
let oneself go

go home in a box
  croak

goies
  bennies

go into one's dance,
    "persuade"

go jump in the lake
  lay off

go kerflooey, "stop
    functioning"

gold
  coke
  dough
  pot

goldamn
  damn
  Jeez

Goldberg
  kike

gold braid
  the brass

goldbrick
  goof off

goldbricker
  goof-off

golden girl
  coke

goldern
  damn

goldfinger
  horse

gold leaf
  pot

gold leaf special
  joint

gold mine, "profit"

go like a bat out of hell
  barrel

golly
  Jeez

go-long
  Black Maria

goma
  big O
  M

go man go
  way to go

goms
  cop

gone
  cool
  great
  high
  plastered

goner
  goner, "doomed one"
  stiff

goney
  dope

gonga dust
  M

gonga smudge
  joint

gonged
  high
  plastered

goniff
  heist man

gonzo
  crazy
  nut

goo
  corn
  cum
  goo, "viscous fluid"

goober
  jerk
  joint
  oddball
  zit

good
  cool

good deal
  square deal
  way to go

good egg
  good guy

good gracious
  Jeez

good head
  blow job
  good guy

good Joe
  good guy

good-looker
  dish

good old boy
  cracker

goods
  dope
  score

the goods
  clout
  humdinger
  the McCoy
  the poop

good sport
  good guy

good time Charlie
  playboy

good-time man
  dealer

good way
  a country mile

good wife
  old woman

goody
  Christer
  goody-goody
  wimp

goody two-shoes
  goody-goody

goof
  blow grass
  boner
  dope
  fuck-up
  glitch
  goof, "blunder"
  jerk
  junkie
  nut
  oddball
  pothead

goof around
  goof off

goofball
  doll
  dope
  a fix
  nut
  oddball

goof butt
  joint
  pot

goofed
  high

goofer
  doll
  dope
  fuck-up

go off half-cocked, "act
    prematurely"

go off one's rocker
  crack up
  go crazy

go off the deep end
  blow one's top
  crack up

goof off, "avoid work"
goof off, "idle pleasure"
goof-off, "shirker"

goof-up
  boner
  butterfingers
  fuck-up
  goof
  screw up
  snafu

goofus
  dope
  flaky
  fuck-up
  gadget
  patsy

goofy
  crazy
  ditsy
  dope
  dumb
  flaky

goofy dust
  coke

goog
  black eye

googly-eyed
  popeyed

goo-goo
  crazy
  ditsy
  gook

gook
  crap
  goo
  gook, "Asian"

gooly butt
  joint

goombah
  gangster
  pal

goon
  angel dust
  goon, "ruffian"
  jerk

goon dust
  angel dust

go one on one with
  take on

gooney
  dope

goon squad, "ruffians"

goop
  dope
  goo

goopgobbler
  cocksucker

goophead
  zit

goopy
  corny

goose
  goose, "goad"
  jazz up

goose bumps, "gooseflesh"

goose-bumpy
  scared shitless

goosed-up
  jazzed-up

a goose egg
  zilch

gooseflesh
  goose bumps

goose it
  floor it

goose up
  jazz up

goosy, "touchy"

go out
  pass out

go out like a light
  pass out

go out of one's skull
  blow one's top

crack up
  go crazy

go out of one's way
  bust one's ass

go out on a limb
  stick one's neck out

go over
  bat around
  go over with a bang
  work
  wow

go over big
  wow

go overboard for
  flip

go over in a big way
  wow

go over like a lead balloon
  flop

go over the hill, "depart"

go over the wall
  break out

go over with a bang, "succeed"

goozlum
  goo

go peddle your papers
  lay off

go pfft
  flop

gopher
  gofer
  heist man

go places
  go over with a bang

go places and do things
  have a ball

go public, "reveal"

gorblimey
  Jeez

gorgeous
  great

gorilla
  bulldoze
  clobber
  cowboy
  goon
  hit man
  rough up

gork
  patsy

gorked
  high

gorm
  scarf

gormless
  dumb

go round and round
  hassle

go round the bend
  go crazy

gorp
  scarf

goshawful
  damn
  fucking

goshdarn
  damn
  Jeez

go soak your head
  fuck you
  lay off

go south
  crash
  flop
  heist
  split

the gospel
  the straight dope

gossip
  dirt

go straight
  fly right
  go straight, "reform"

gotcha
  bust

gotch-eyed
  popeyed

go the extra mile
  bust one's ass

go the limit
  bust one's ass
  fuck

go the whole hog
  bust one's ass

go through the mill
  go through the mill, "acquire practical experience"
  pay one's dues

got it
  get me

go to bat for
  back
  go to bat for, "defend"

go toe to toe
  hassle
  take on

go to hell
  come unglued
  fuck you
  go to hell, "deteriorate"

go to it
  fuck
  hassle

go to pieces
  come unglued
  crack up

go to pot
  come unglued
  go to hell

go to the dogs
  come unglued
  go to hell
go to the mat
  back
  hassle
go to the powder room
  check the plumbing
go to the wall
  bust one's ass
  take a beating
go to town
  barrel
  fuck
  go over with a bang
  have a ball
go to wrack and ruin
  go to hell
gouge
  con
gouger
  con man
  pothead
go under
  fuck up
  pass out
  take a beating
go up against
  buck
  take on
go up in someone's face
  chew out
go up in one's line
  fluff
go up in smoke
  go kerflooey
go up the spout
  fuck up
  go kerflooey
  go to hell

gourd
  bean
governor
  boss
gow
  big O
  cheesecake
  hot rod
  joint
gow crust
  big O
gowed
  high
gowed-up job
  hot rod
gowhead
  junkie
go with the flow
  keep one's cool
gow job
  hot rod
gowster
  junkie
  pothead
goynk
  big O
grab
  bust
  grab, "acquire"
grab-ass, "caressing"
grab-bag
  mish-mash
grabber
  gimmick
grabby, "attractive"
grabby, "greedy"
grab on
  neck
grad
  cool

gradehound
  grind
grads
  bennies
graft
  racket
gram
  bag
  deck
gramps
  old fart
grand, "thousand dollars"
Grand Central Station
  mob scene
grandly
  with flying colors
grand slam, "victory"
grandstander, "egotist"
grandstand it
  grandstand
grandstand player
  grandstander
grape parfait
  acid
grasp the nettle
  bite the bullet
grass
  pot
grassback
  floozy
grasshead
  pothead
graum
  sweat
gravel
  bug
  guts
gravy
  cinch

dough
  gravy, "bonus"

gravy train
  gold mine

gray
  whitey

gray-flannel
  square

gray matter
  smarts

graze
  scarf

grease
  big O
  clout
  snuff
  soft soap
  soft-soap

greaseball
  bean-eater
  grease monkey
  wop

grease down
  scarf

grease-gut
  bean-eater

greasehound
  grease monkey

grease job
  soft soap

grease monkey, "mechanic"

grease someone's palm, "bribe"

greaser
  bean-eater
  goon
  wop

greasy spoon, "restaurant"

the greatest
  great
  the most

greatest thing since sliced
  bread
  hot shot

the great one
  big shot

great Scott
  Jeez

greeby
  yucky

greedy
  grabby

greedy-guts
  pig

greefa
  pot

Greek
  bugger
  double-talk

Greek god
  hunk

green
  angel dust
  dough
  pothead

green around the gills, "nauseated"

green ashes
  big O

greenbacks
  dough

green dragon
  acid
  bennies
  doll

green folding
  dough

green griff
  pot

greenhorn
  greenhorn, "neophyte"
  rookie

greenie
  duck-squeezer

greenies
  bennies

the green light
  the go-ahead
  the OK

green Moroccan
  hash

green mud
  big O

green powder
  big O

green stuff
  dough

green swirls
  acid

green tea
  angel dust

green wedge
  acid

greeny
  greenhorn
  rookie

greta
  pot

grette
  butt

grief
  flak

griefer
  pothead

grifado
  high

grift
  scam

grifter
  bum
  con man
  heist man

grim
yucky

grin and bear it
hang tough
take it

grinch
gloomy Gus

grind
back-breaker
grind, "diligent student"
jerk

grinder
hero
jalopy
stripper

grinders
choppers

gripe
beef
bug
kvetch

griper
kvetch

grit
butt
guts
scarf

grits
chow

gritty
gutsy

groan
warble

groanbox
squeezebox

groceries
chow

grody
yucky

grog
booze
dope

grogged
plastered

groggery
gin mill

groggy
rocky

grog merchant
dealer

groid
nigger

grok
dig

grokking
on someone's
wavelength

grommet
kid
teenybopper

gronk out
go kerflooey

grooby
great

groove
bag
dig
have a ball
a kick

a groove
a ball
humdinger

groove on
dig
get a kick out of

groover
jerk

grooving
high
in the groove

groovy
cool
great
square
with it

grope
feel
grab-ass

gross
crummy
take
yucky

grouch
beef
kvetch

groucher
kvetch

grouchy
feisty

groudy
yucky

ground rations
ass

groupie
fan
groupie, "follower"

grouse
beef
kvetch

grouser
kvetch

growl
beef

growler
bitch box

grub
chow
a feed

grub-staker
angel

grub up
  grab
  scarf

grumbler
  kvetch

grumps
  the blues

grunch
  jerk
  mung

grunge
  fuck
  jerk
  mung

grungy
  crummy
  yucky

grunt
  gofer
  grind
  grunt, "infantry soldier"
  shit

the grunt
  the damage

grunt work
  scut work

guardhouse lawyer
  latrine lawyer

guck
  goo

guesser
  Blind Tom

guff
  bullshit
  chitchat
  gab
  sass

gug
  jerk

guilty
  catch redhanded

Guinea
  wop

gully-jumper
  hick

gully-low
  dirty

gulp down
  bite

gum
  big O
  gab

gumball
  party hat

gum-beater
  blabbermouth

gum-beating
  bullshit
  schmooz

gumbo
  goo

gumby
  jerk

gumfoot
  cop

gummed-up
  fucked-up

gummix up
  screw up

gummy
  corny

gump
  dope
  gay
  jerk

gumshoe
  cop
  dick

gum up
  fuck up
  screw up

gun
  heist man
  hit man
  works

gun down
  snuff

gunga
  dumb
  Jeez

gung ho
  antsy
  full of piss and vinegar

gunk
  goo

gunman
  hit man

gunner
  grandstander

gunny
  pot

gunpoke
  hit man

gunsel
  hit man

guru
  shrink

gushy
  corny

gussy up
  doll up

gut
  belly
  gut course
  potbelly

gut-buster
  back-breaker
  belly laugh
  belly-whopper

gut course, "easy course"

gutless
 chicken
 wimpish

gutless wonder
 wimp

guts
 chutzpa
 guts, "courage"
 guts, "viscera"
 innards

gutsy
 gutsy, "courageous"
 zingy

gutter
 shoot up

gut-thumper
 a hit

gutty
 cheeky
 gutsy

guy
 cookie
 gadget
 guy, "male person"

Guy
 Jack

guzzle
 binge
 guzzle, "drink"
 snort

guzzler
 lush

guzzle shop
 gin mill

guzzling
 on the sauce

gweebo
 grind
 jerk

gyp
 con

con man
 scam

gyp artist
 con man

gyppy tummy
 the shits

gyrene
 leatherneck

gyve
 joint

H
 horse

hack
 hack it
 whitey

a hack
 a crack

hack around
 goof off

hacked
 pissed off

hacker
 butterfingers
 duffer

hack it, "succeed"

had
 screwed

had it
 finished
 pooped

hag
 old bag
 scarecrow

hail Columbia
 Jeez

hair pie
 blow job
 cunt
 fur pie

hairsplitter
 cock

hairy
 creepy
 hairy, "difficult"
 horse
 yucky

hairy-chested
 he-man

the hairy eyeball
 the cold shoulder

half
 bag
 deck

half a mo
 a jiffy

half-assed
 crummy
 dumb
 half-assed, "careless"
 piddly

half-baked
 crazy
 crummy
 dumb
 half-assed

half bundle
 bag
 deck

half-cracked
 flaky

half in the bag
 plastered

half load
 bag
 deck

half-pint
 lightweight
 little bitty
 piddly
 shorty

halvah
 horse

halvahed
  high
ham, "overact"
ham-and-egger
  Joe Blow
ham-and-eggery
  greasy spoon
ham-fisted
  ham-handed
ham it up
  ham
hammer
  broad
  cock
  dish
  sock
hammer down
  flat-out
  lickety-split
hammerhead
  mule
hammer out
  whomp up
hand
  mitt
H and C
  coke
  horse
handcuffs
  bracelets
hand someone his (or her)
    head
  clobber
hand it to someone,
    "compliment"
handkerchief-head
  fink
handle
  feel
  monicker
  take

handle the reins
  boss
hando
  great
hand out
  stake someone to
hand over
  kick in
hand over fist
  like hell
handshake
  give five
handshaker
  glad-hander
  phony
hang
  goof off
hang around
  goof off
  sit tight
hang around with
  hang out with
hang in
  hang tough
hang it easy
  cool it
hang it up
  knock off
hang loose
  cool it
hang on
  hang on, "accuse"
  hang tough
  sit tight
hang one on
  clobber
hangout
  pad
hang out
  goof off
  stick out like a sore thumb

hang out with, "associate
    with"
hang together
  figure
hang tough
  hang tough, "endure"
  take it
hang up
  shut up
hanky-panky
  grab-ass
  monkey business
  razzle-dazzle
  scam
happen
  come off
happies
  kicks
happy dust
  dope
happy
  plastered
  tickled
harass
  roust
hard
  great
  horny
  tough
hard-assed
  tough
hardball
  big-league
  the big leagues
hard-boiled egg
  bad man
  goon
hard case
  goon
hard cash
  dough

hard coin
  bundle

hard-hat
  redneck

hardhead
  mule
  nigger
  whitey

hardheaded
  bullheaded

hard job
  back-breaker

hard John
  G-man

hard-legs
  dude

hard-luck story
  tear-jerker

hardnose
  mule
  tough

hardnosed
  bullheaded
  feisty
  tough

hard nut to crack
  mule

hard-on, "erection"

a hard-on
  hot pants

hard put
  out of luck

hard row to hoe
  back-breaker

hard stuff
  booze
  M

hard up
  horny
  out of luck

hardware
  rod

har-har
  break up

harness bull
  cop

harp
  Mick

harpoon
  works

Harry
  horse

harum-scarum
  rootin'-tootin'

hash
  bat around
  dope
  great
  hash, "hashish"

hashery
  greasy spoon

hashhead
  junkie

hashhouse
  greasy spoon

hashish
  hash

hash mark, "service stripe"

hash over
  bat around

hash session
  schmooz

hash stripe
  hash mark

hash up
  screw up

hassle
  bug
  hassle, "conflict"
  roust

hasty job
  a lick and a promise

hat
  lid

hatchet-face
  scarecrow

a hatchet job
  the axe

hatchet man
  hit man

hate
  hate someone's guts

hatrack
  beanpole

hatty
  stuck-up

haul
  score
  take

haul ass
  barrel
  split

hauler
  hot rod

haul in
  bust

haul it
  split

haul over the coals
  chew out

haul the mail
  barrel

have
  con

have someone
  fuck

have a bag on
  have a load on

have a ball, "enjoy"

have a bellyful
  fed-up

have a bird
  blow one's top

have a bug up one's ass
  have a hair up one's ass

have a case on
  have a lech for

have a catfit
  blow one's top

have a chip on one's
    shoulder
  have a hair up one's ass

have a conniption fit
  blow one's top
  make a scene

have a crack at
  give something a shot
  take a crack at

have a crush on
  have a lech for

have a few marbles missing
  have a hole in one's head

have a field day, "succeed"

have a fit
  blow one's top
  make a scene

have a gander at
  check out

have a go at
  give something a shot
  take a crack at

**have a hair up one's ass,
    "be touchy"**

have a hard-on for
  hate someone's guts
  have a lech for
  have hot pants

**have a hole in one's head,
    "be stupid"**

have a lech for, "crave"

have a load on, "be drunk"

have a lock on
  have something cinched

have a looksee
  check out

have an attitude
  beef

have a party
  fuck

have a screw loose
  have a hole in one's head

have a shit fit
  blow one's top
  make a scene

have a short fuse
  have a hair up one's ass

have a shot at
  give something a shot
  take a crack at

have a tantrum
  make a scene

have a thing for
  have a lech for

have balls, "be courageous"

have bang to rights
  catch redhanded

**have someone by the balls,
    "have a decisive
    advantage"**

have by the short hairs
  have someone by the balls

have clout
  carry a lot of weight

have cold
  catch redhanded

have dead to rights
  catch redhanded

have egg in one's beer
  eat high on the hog

have eyes for
  have a lech for

have for breakfast
  clobber

have guts
  have balls

have hacked
  have something cinched

have one's head up one's
    ass
  have a hole in one's head

have hot pants, "lust for"

have it all over
  beat

have it bad for
  have a lech for

**have it both ways, "have
    with certainty"**

have it down pat
  dig

have it good
  eat high on the hog

have it in for
  hate someone's guts

have it made
  eat high on the hog
  have something cinched

have it pegged
  dig

have kittens
  blow one's top

have knocked
  have something cinched

have someone's lunch
  clobber

have made
  have something cinched

have no use for
  hate someone's guts

have someone on
kid
snow

have over a barrel
have someone by the balls

have someone pegged
have someone's number

have rocks in one's head
have a hole in one's head

have taped
have something cinched

have someone taped
have someone's number

have the curse
have the rag on

have the drop on
have someone by the balls

have the hots
have a lech for
have hot pants

have the last word
boss

have the nerve
have balls

have the rag on,
"menstruate"

have one's ticket punched
pay one's dues

have wired
have something cinched

have your cake and eat it
have it both ways

Hawaiian sunshine
acid

hawkshaw
dick

hay
chicken feed
pot

hay butt
joint

hay-eater
whitey

hayhead
pothead

haymaker
sock
Sunday punch

hayseed
hick

haywire
cockeyed
crazy
flaky
full of shit
on the blink

haze
acid
rough up

Hazel
horse

H-cap
horse

head
bean
blow job
can
cookie
dish
fur pie
high
junkie
a kick
pothead
yap

headache
bad news
drag
jerk

headcase
nut

head cheese
boss

head job
blow job

head kit
works

headlights
tits

headline
spotlight

one's head off
flat-out
one's head off, "mightily"
like hell

head out
split

head over heels
flat-out

headpiece
bean

headshrinker
shrink

head up
boss

heap
jalopy

heaped
high

heart
ticker

heartbreaker
ladies' man

hear the birdies sing
pass out

hearts
bennies

hearts and flowers
corn

heart-stopper
a hit

heartthrob
 honey

heart-to-heart
 schmooz

heat
 flak
 rod
 stanza

the heat
 the cops

heater
 rod

heat merchant
 kvetch

heave
 barf

the heave-ho
 the axe

heaven and hell
 angel dust

heaven dust
 coke

heavenly
 great

heavens to Betsy
 Jeez

heavy
 bad man
 big-league
 big shot
 bruiser
 cool
 goon
 great
 hairy
 heavy, "important"

heavy breathing
 ass

heavycake
 stud

heavy coin
 bundle

heavy hash
 hash

heavy man
 goon

heavy money
 bundle

heavy sledding
 back-breaker

heavyweight
 ace
 big-league
 big shot
 bruiser
 fatty
 heavy

Hebe
 kike

hedge one's bets
 play it safe

the heebie-jeebies
 the jitters
 the shakes

heel
 asshole
 shill

heeled
 heeled, "armed"
 loaded

heeler
 asshole

heesh
 dope
 hash

hefty
 big-league
 hairy
 heavy
 high-powered

heifer
 broad

heinie
 ass
 asshole

Heinie
 kraut

heist
 heist, "robbery"
 heist, "steal"
 hike

heist man, "thief"

hell
 barrel
 a bitch
 hell around
 Jeez

hellacious
 great

**hell around, "pursue
 pleasure"**

hell-bender
 binge

hell-bent
 lickety-split

**hell breaks loose, "things
 deteriorate"**

hell dust
 M

heller
 eager beaver

hellhole
 dive
 dump

a hell of a, "remarkable"

hell of a mess
 bind
 snafu

hell of a note
 bind
 a bitch

hell on wheels
  a bitch

hell's bells
  Jeez

hell to pay
  bind

a helluva
  a hell of a

the hell you say
  izzatso

helter-skelter
  fucked-up

he-man
  he-man, "aggressively masculine"
  he-man, "masculine male"
  hunk

hem and haw
  stall
  weasel

hemorrhage
  blowup

hemp
  pot

hen
  broad

hen-pecked
  pussy-whipped

Henry
  horse

hep
  cool
  trendy
  with it

hepcat
  dude

hepped
  with it

hepped on
  into

hepped up
  antsy

her
  coke

herbs
  pot

Herkimer Jerkimer
  hick
  jerk

herms
  angel dust

hero
  hero, "sandwich"
  horse

heroin
  horse

hero sandwich
  hero

Hershey bar
  nigger

heterosexual
  straight

het up
  antsy
  pissed off

hex
  whammy

hey
  Jeez
  way to go

hick, "rural person"

hickdom
  the boondocks

hickey
  gadget
  zit

hickory
  billy club

hicksville
  corny
  dullsville

hidden element
  catch

hide
  broad
  hide out
  park

hideaway, "hiding place"

hideout
  hideaway
  pad

hide out, "hide"

higgledy-piggledy
  fucked-up

high
  high, "intoxicated"
  high, "intoxication"
  plastered

high and mighty
  snooty

highball
  barrel
  split

highbrow
  egghead

high-class
  classy
  great

higher-up
  big shot

highfalutin
  classy
  snooty

highflag
  ride the arm

high-geared
  high-powered

high-grade
  classy

high-hat
  classy
  cut

give the cold shoulder
  snooty
  stuck-up
  swell
  the upper crust
highjack
  heist
high-jinks
  horseplay
highlight
  spotlight
high muckety-muck
  big shot
highpockets
  beanpole
high-power
  big-league
high-powered
  heavy
  high-powered, "powerful"
high-pressure
  lean on someone
  talk someone into
high-rent
  classy
  great
hightail it
  barrel
  break out
  split
high-toned
  classy
high-up
  big shot
high, wide, and handsome
  with flying colors
hijacker
  heist man
hijo
  Jeez

hike
hike, "increase" (v and n)
  split
  toddle
hilarity
  a howl
hillbilly
  cracker
  hick
a hill of beans
  zilch
him
  horse
himself
  big shot
  boss
hincty
  snooty
  stuck-up
  whitey
hind end
  ass
hind legs
  pins
hindside
  ass
hinge
  the once-over
hip
  cool
  snappy
  with it
the hip gee
  the smart money
hipped
  with it
hipper-dipper
  great
hippo
  fatty

hips
  curtains
hired gun
  hit man
hired help
  gofer
his highness
  boss
his nibs
  big shot
  boss
hit
  blow grass
  a crack
  a fix
  go over with a bang
  high
  a kick
  put the bite on
  score
  shoot up
  snuff
a hit, "success"
hit below the belt
  play dirty
hitch
  bit
  catch
  glitch
  hitchhike
hitch a ride
  hitchhike
hitchy
  antsy
  jittery
hitfest
  donnybrook
hit for six
  go over with a bang
hit it
  ace
  go over with a bang

hit it big
  clean up

hit it off
  buddy up
  hit it off, "get along"

hit man, "assassin"

hit on
  proposition
  rough up
  sock

hit-or-miss
  half-assed

hit out
  split

hit pay dirt
  go over with a bang
  hack it

hits
  crooked dice

hit spike
  works

hitter
  hit man

hit the bottle
  guzzle

hit the bricks
  split
  walk

hit the canvas
  pass out

hit the ceiling
  blow one's top

hit the hay
  blow grass
  snooze

hit the jackpot
  come on strong
  go over with a bang
  make a killing

hit the mark
  hack it

hit the road
  split

hit the sack
  snooze

hit the sauce
  guzzle

hit the sidewalk
  toddle

hit the skids
  go kerflooey
  go to hell

hit the trail
  split

hitting on all six
  cool

hit town
  show up

hit up
  bum
  put the bite on
  shoot up

hit someone where he (or
    she) lives
  clobber
  sock

hizzoner
  Blind Tom

ho
  hooker

hoagie
  hero

hoakie
  jerk

hobble
  bind

hobo
  bum

hock
  bug

hockey
  bullshit

  cum
  shit

hocus
  coke
  horse
  M

hocus-pocus
  monkey business

hod
  nigger

ho-dad
  bigmouth
  jerk
  phony
  smart-ass
  wimp

ho-daddy
  bigmouth

hoedown
  donnybrook
  hassle
  wingding

hog
  angel dust
  bike
  cock
  hash
  junkie
  pig
  pimpmobile
  pot
  scarecrow

the hog
  angel dust

hoggish
  grabby

hoggy
  grabby

hog heaven
  fat city

hog it
  pig out

hogleg
  rod
hogwash
  bullshit
ho-hum
  dullsville
hoist
  heist
hoity-toity
  classy
  snooty
hoka toka
  blow grass
hoke
  bullshit
  flack
  scam
hoked-up
  phony
hoke up
  cook up
hokey
  phony
hokey-pokey
  bullshit
  flack
  monkey business
  razzle-dazzle
  scam
hokum
  bullshit
  flack
  razzle-dazzle
hokus
  dope
holder
  dealer
hold someone's feet to the
  fire, "punish"
hold one's horses
  cool it
  sit tight

holding
  dirty
  loaded
hold it
  cool it
  sit tight
hold off
  stall
hold out
  hang tough
  sit tight
hold the phone
  sit tight
hold the whip hand
  have someone by the balls
hold together
  figure
hold up
  figure
  heist
holdup man
  heist man
hold water
  figure
hole
  ass
  asshole
  banger
  bind
  cooler
  cunt
  dive
  dump
the hole
  the slammer
hole up
  hide out
hole-up
  hideaway
holier-than-thou
  Christer
  goody-goody

holler
  beef
  squeal
holler quits
  fold
holly-golly
  bullshit
  flak
Holmes
  pal
holy cats
  Jeez
holy cow
  Jeez
Holy Joe
  Bible-banger
  Christer
holy mackerel
  Jeez
holy Moses
  Jeez
holy smokes
  Jeez
holy terror
  eager beaver
  kid
hombre
  guy
Hombre
  Jack
home and dry
  in
homeboy
  gay
  pal
home free
  in
home in
  zero in
home run
  homer

homo
  gay
homosexual
  gay
homosexuality
  come out
hon
  honey
honcho
  big shot
  boss
  the brass
hondo
  fan
honest
  straight
honest-to-God, "authentic"
honest-to-God, "truly"
the honest-to-God truth
  the straight dope
honest-to-goodness
  honest-to-God
honey
  broad
  dish
  doll
  honey, "beloved person"
  humdinger
honey oil
  hash
honeypie
  honey
honeypot
  cunt
honey up
  brown-nose
  soft-soap
Hong Kong dog
  the shits
honk
  barrel

feel
honk, "sound the horn"
honked up
  antsy
honker
  schnozz
honky
  whitey
honky-tonk
  dive
honyocker
  hick
hooch
  ass
  booze
  pot
hooched up
  plastered
hoochery
  gin mill
hooch-hound
  lush
hood
  cowboy
  goon
hoodang
  wingding
hoodlum
  cowboy
  goon
hooey
  bullshit
  izzatso
hoof it
  split
  toddle
hoofs
  tootsies
hoo-ha
  donnybrook
  hoopla

Jeez
  so what
  wingding
hoohaw
  big shot
hook
  con
  gimmick
  grab
  heist
  horse
  hustle
  mitt
  snort
the hook
  the axe
hooked, "addicted"
hooker
  hooker, "prostitute"
  snort
hook in
  talk someone into
hook it
  split
hooknose
  kike
hook up with
  hang out with
hooky
  grabby
hooley
  binge
hooligan
  goon
a hoop and a holler
  a jiffy
hooperdooper
  humdinger
hoopla
  flack

flak
hoopla, "commotion"

hoopy
jalopy

the hoosegow
the slammer

hoosier
hick

a hoot
a howl
a laugh
zilch

hootchie-cootchie
ass

a hoot in hell
zilch

hootmalalie
gadget

hoover
blow

hop
big O
bullshit

hopfest
beer bust

hop gun
works

hophead
junkie
pothead

hop it
split

hop on the bandwagon
get on the bandwagon

hopped up
antsy
full of piss and vinegar
high
jazzed-up

hopped-up job
hot rod

hopping mad
pissed off

hoppy
gimpy

hopster
junkie

hop to it
get the lead out

hop up
jazz up
shoot up

horizontal bop
a fuck

horked
antsy

horn
cock
hard-on
schnozz
snort

hornblowing
flack

horndog
stud

horn in
butt in

horniness
hot pants

hornswoggle
con
snow

horny, "excited sexually"

horny bastard
stud

horror
scarecrow

horror film
chiller

the horrors
the shakes

horse
fuck
goof off
grand
horse, "heroin"

horse and wagon
works

horse around
goof off
horse around, "be boisterous"

horsed
high

horsefeathers
bullshit

horseheads
bennies

horselaugh
belly laugh

the horselaugh, "laugh"

horse opry
horse opera

horseplay, "fun"

horse race
a gamble

horse radish
horse

horses
crooked dice

horse's ass
asshole
jerk

horseshit
bullshit
chickenshit

hose
cock
con
fuck

hose job
blow job

hoser
  con man

hosing
  scam
  the shaft

hospital
  bone factory

hoss it
  toddle

hot
  antsy
  dirty
  great
  horny
  hot, "performing well"
  hot, "popular"
  pissed off

a hot
  a feed

hot air
  bullshit
  chitchat
  flack

hot-air artist
  bigmouth
  blabbermouth

hot and bothered
  jittery
  pissed off

hot and cold
  coke
  horse

hot as a three-dollar pistol
  horny

hotbox
  cunt

hot diggety
  hot damn

hot dish
  dish

hot dog
  grandstand
  grandstander
  hot damn
  hot shot

hot dogger
  hot shot

hot-eyed
  antsy

hot favorite
  front runner

hotfoot
  barrel

hot grease
  bad news

hot horse
  front runner

hot iron
  hot rod

hot jay
  pot

hot notion
  brain wave

hot number
  dish
  hot shot

hot pants, "sexual desire"

hot patootie
  dish

hot poo
  hot damn
  humdinger

hot rock
  hot shot

hot rocks
  hot pants

hot rod, "car"

the hots
  hot pants

hot seat
  the chair

hot shit
  hot damn
  hot shot
  humdinger

hotshot
  ace
  big shot
  dude
  eager beaver
  ladies' man

hot shot, "effective person"

hot sketch
  dish

hot spit
  hot damn
  humdinger

hot spot
  bind

hot squat
  the chair

hot stick
  joint

hot stuff
  ace
  dope
  hot shot
  humdinger
  score

hotsy-totsy
  cool
  great

hot tip
  tip

hot to trot
  antsy
  horny

hot under the collar
  pissed off

hot water
  bad news
  bind
hot ziggety
  hot damn
hound
  asshole
  bug
  pooch
hound dog
  ladies' man
  stud
house ape
  kid
house-cleaning,
      "reorganization"
house dick
  dick
house moss
  dust bunny
house nigger
  fink
house of ill repute
  whorehouse
how about that
  Jeez
how-de-do
  bind
  a fix
  flak
  hoopla
how goes it
  how's tricks
howl
  beef
a howl
  a howl, "hilarity"
  a laugh
howler
  boner

how's that?
  come again
how's things
  how's tricks
hubba-hubba
  on the double
hubby, "husband"
huckleberry
  guy
  jerk
huffy
  feisty
  pissed off
hug
  clinch
  heist
hugger-mugger
  fucked-up
huggy-huggy
  palsy-walsy
hulk
  bruiser
hully-gully
  bullshit
human dynamo
  eager beaver
humbug
  phony
  snow
humdinger, "remarkable
      person or thing"
hummer
  dope
  humdinger
hummer hustler
  eager beaver
humongous
  monster
hump
  ass
  barrel

  cart
  fuck
  a fuck
  get the lead out
hump one's chops
  shoot the breeze
humpery
  ass
hump the hound
  goof off
hump the sage
  blow grass
humpy
  sexy
Hun
  kraut
hung, "having impressive
      male genitals"
hung like a bull
  hung
hungry, "ambitious"
hung up
  hooked
  square
hunk
  ass
  bag
  deck
  he-man
  hunk, "attractive man"
hunker down
  take it
hunk of change
  dough
hunky
  built
  cool
  he-man
  horny
  hunky, "attractive"
  hunky, "foreigner"
  sexy

hunky-dory
  cool

hurrah's nest
  bad news
  snafu

hurry
  get the lead out

hurtburger
  flop

hurting
  antsy

husband
  hubby

hush-hush
  on the QT

hustle
  con
  get the lead out
  heist
  hustle, "prostitute oneself"
  pizzazz
  scam
  snow

hustler
  con man
  hot shot

hustle up
  get the lead out

hutch
  pad

hyena
  asshole

hype
  con
  dealer
  a fix
  flack
  scam
  shoot up
  snow

hype artist
  flack

hyped-up
  antsy
  phony

hyper
  antsy
  flack
  great
  jittery

hype stick
  works

hype up
  cook up
  jazz up

ice
  clinch
  clobber
  coke
  cool
  cut
  great
  snuff

the ice
  the cold shoulder

ice bag
  pot

iceberg
  cold fish

icebox
  cooler
  the slammer

ice cream
  dope

ice cream man
  dealer

iced
  in the bag

ice maiden
  cold fish

iceman
  heist man
  hit man

ice out
  cut

ice pack
  pot

icky
  corny
  square
  yucky

idea
  brain wave

ideal situation
  fat city

identify
  peg

idiot box
  the tube

iffy, "uncertain"

iffy proposition
  a gamble

iggle
  talk someone into

ignorance
  not know shit from Shinola

ignorant stripe
  hash mark

Ike
  kike

I kid you not
  honest-to-God
  no fooling

ill
  off one's feed

I'll be
  I'll be damned

I'll be damned if
  like hell

I'll drink to that
  bet your ass

illegal saloon
  blind pig

ill-regarded
  on someone's shit list
I'll tell the world
  bet your ass
illuminated
  plastered
I'm all right Jack
  fuck you
imitation
  act
immediately
  on the double
immense
  great
I'm not just whistling Dixie
  no fooling
imp
  kid
impaired
  plastered
impassive
  poker face
important
  big deal
  big-league
  heavy
important money
  bundle
important person
  big shot
importune
  put the bite on
improve
  get on the ball
improvise
  wing it
impudence
  sass
  smart-ass
impudent person
  smart-ass

in
  high
  hot
in, "successful"
  trendy
in a bad way
  plastered
in a big way
  like hell
in a bind
  out of luck
in a box
  out of luck
in a bubble
  hot
in a corner
  up the creek
in a dither
  antsy
in a flutter
  antsy
in a fog, "confused"
in a funk
  down
  scared shitless
in a haze
  in a fog
in a holding pattern
  on hold
in a hole
  out of luck
  up the creek
in a huff
  pissed off
in a jam
  out of luck
  up the creek
in a lather
  antsy
  pissed off

in a mess
  out of luck
  up the creek
in a muddle
  in a fog
in-and-out
  ass
in a pickle
  out of luck
  up the creek
in a pig's ass
  izzatso
  like hell
in a pinch
  up the creek
  when the chips are down
in a pucker
  jittery
  pissed off
in a session
  high
in a state
  antsy
  jittery
in a stew
  jittery
  pissed off
in a sweat
  antsy
  jittery
  pissed off
in a tight spot
  out of luck
in a tizzy
  antsy
  jittery
  pissed off
in a tough spot
  up the creek
in a walk
  with flying colors

in a zone
high
hot
in a fog

in bad shape
out of luck

in-betweens
bennies

in one's birthday suit
bare-ass

in business
hooked

incapacity
out of one's depth

in cement
carved in stone

incense
pot

incentive
coke

in clover
in hog heaven

in cold storage
on hold

increase
hike

in one's cups
plastered

in deep trouble
out of luck
up the creek

Indian hemp
pot

Indian rope
hash

the Indian sign
whammy

indifference
one couldn't care less
not give a damn
so what

in Dutch
out of luck
up the creek

ineffective
cut no ice

inescapably
dead to rights

infantry soldier
grunt

in fat city
in hog heaven

inferior
crummy
schlocky

inferior liquor
panther piss

inferior position
play second fiddle

inferior things
crap

inflated
jumped-up

influence
carry a lot of weight

info
the poop

inform
fill someone in

information
the poop
tip
wise me up

informed
briefed

informer
snitch

in front
up front

in good shape
cool

ingratiation
play up to

in great shape
cool

the in group, "clique"

inhalation
snort
toke

inhale
scarf

in high gear
lickety-split

in hog heaven, "contented"

in hot water
out of luck

injury
get it in the neck

injustice
bum rap

in kilter
cool

inky-dink
nigger

inky-dinky
little bitty

in like Flynn
in

in mothballs
on hold

innards
chutzpa
guts
innards, "viscera"

inning
chapter

innocent
clean

in nothing flat
on the double

in orbit
  high

in-out
  ass

in overdrive
  lickety-split

in over one's head
  out of one's depth
  up the creek

in pig heaven
  in hog heaven

in place, "available"

inquiry
  what's up

insane
  crazy
  go crazy

insane person
  nut

inside
  in stir

insiders
  the in group

insides
  innards

insincere greeting
  glad-hander

insolvent
  go broke

in spades
  flat-out
  like hell
  with flying colors

inspection
  the once-over

instant Zen
  acid

instinctively
  by ear

in stir, "imprisoned"

insult
  fink
  give someone the finger
  kiss my ass
  knock
  the bird

intelligence
  smarts

intense
  great

intestinal fortitude
  guts

in the altogether
  bare-ass

in the bag
  cinched
  in the bag, "certain"
  kaput
  plastered

in the buff
  bare-ass

in the catbird seat
  in the driver's seat

in the chips
  loaded

in the clear
  clean

in the clutch
  when the chips are down

in the crunch
  when the chips are down

in the deep freeze
  on hold

in the doldrums
  down

in the dough
  loaded

in the driver's seat, "having authority"

in the dumper
  kaput

in the dumps
  down

in the family way
  knocked up

in the groove
  in the groove, "performing well"
  with it

in the hopper
  in the pipeline

in the icebox
  on hold

in the money
  loaded

in the pipeline, "imminent"

in the pocket
  high
  in the groove

in the raw
  bare-ass

in there pitching
  in there

in the soup
  out of luck
  up the creek

in the works
  in the pipeline

in the worst way
  like hell

intimidate
  bulldoze

intimidation
  lean on someone

into, "absorbed in"

into it
  with it

in town
  cool

in transit
  high

in trouble
up the creek

intrude
butt in

IOU
tab

irascible
feisty

irie
great

Irish person
Mick

iron
bike
jalopy
rod

iron man
buck

iron out
snuff
work out

irritate
bug

irritation
Jeez

ishkabibble
one couldn't care less

iso
cooler

Italian person
wop

itchy
antsy
horny
jittery

item
cookie

it's a new ball game, "the situation has changed"

it's nothing
forget it

itsy-bitsy
little bitty

it takes two to tango, "this matter entails cooperation"

ivories
choppers

ivory-dome
dope
egghead

izzatso, "expression of disbelief"

J
joint

jab
bust
a fix
knock
shoot up
sock

jabber
gab
junkie
works

jabberer
blabbermouth

jabberjack
bullshit

jaboney
goon
greenhorn

jack
dough
shoot up

Jack, "Mister"

jack around
fool around with
goof off

jack someone around
kid

jackass
dope
jerk

jacked-up
high
jumped-up

jackie
gay

jackleg
con man
scab

jack off, "masturbate"

jack-off
jerk

jack off the spike
shoot up

jackroll
heist

jack up
chew out
clobber
hike
jazz up
roust
shoot up

jag
binge
jerk

jagged
high

jag-off
jerk

jahooby
pot

jail
cooler
the slammer

jail bait, "young girl"

jailbird
con

jailhouse lawyer
  latrine lawyer
jake
  cop
jakes
  can
jalopy, "car"
jam
  bennies
  bind
  coke
  cunt
  fuck
  have a ball
  roust
Jamaican
  pot
jamboree
  wingding
jam Cecil
  bennies
jammed up
  up the creek
jammies
  rod
jamming
  in the groove
jammy
  great
jamoke
  guy
jane
  broad
  can
Jane Doe
  Jane
jang
  cock
jape
  kid around

jarhead
  dope
  leatherneck
  nigger
jarrer
  a hit
jasper
  cookie
  guy
  hick
jaw
  chitchat
  gab
  schmooz
  shoot the breeze
  talk someone into
jawbone
  on the cuff
  talk someone into
jawfest
  schmooz
jay
  hick
  joint
  patsy
  pot
jaybird
  hick
jay smoke
  joint
jazz
  ass
  bullshit
  clout
  dirt
  fuck
  a fuck
  jazz up
  pizzazz
jazz-bo
  dude

jazzed
  jazzed-up
  pumped
jazz up
  goose
  jazz up, "make more
    exciting"
jazzy
  glitzy
  jazzy, "exciting"
JC water-walkers
  sneakers
jeasly
  piddly
the jeebies
  the jitters
jeegee
  horse
Jeepers Creepers
  Jeez
jeff
  square
  whitey
Jefferson airplane
  roach clip
jelly
  cinch
  cunt
  gravy
jellybean
  bennies
  dope
  rookie
jelly-belly
  fatty
  potbelly
jellyfish
  chicken
  wimp
jelly-roll
  ass

cunt
  stud
jenny
  broad
jerk
  asshole
  drag
  jerk, "tedious person"
  wimp
jerk someone around
  bug
  kid
jerk someone's chain
  bug
  con
  kid
  snow
jerk off
  goof off
  jack off
  shoot up
jerk someone off
  kid
jerk-off
  hick
  jerk
jerk town, "small town"
jerkwater
  piddly
jerkwater town
  jerk town
Jerry
  kraut
Jersey green
  pot
Jesus H. Christ
  Jeez
jet fuel
  angel dust
the jet set, "glamorous people"

Jew canoe
  Caddy
jewelry
  basket
Jewish person
  kike
jibber-jabber
  double-talk
  gab
a jif
  a jiffy
jig
  nigger
jigaboo
  nigger
jigger
  cock
  gadget
  screw up
  snort
jiggers, "exclamation of warning"
jiggerypokery
  bullshit
  dirty tricks
jiggins
  dope
  patsy
jiggle
  cheesecake
jig-jig
  ass
jillionaire
  moneybags
jillionth
  umpty-umpth
jim-dandy
  great
  humdinger
jim-jam
  jazz up

the jimjams
  the jitters
  the shakes
jimjick
  gadget
jimmied-up
  on the blink
jimmy in
  butt in
jimmy up
  screw up
jingle
  buzz
jingleberries
  balls
jinglebrains
  ditz
jingo
  pot
jinx
  whammy
jism
  clout
  cum
  goo
jit
  nigger
jitney
  jalopy
the jitters, "nervousness"
jittery, "nervous"
jive
  bullshit
  chitchat
  flack
  joint
  kid
  kid around
  line
  pot
  razzle-dazzle

jive and juke
  have a ball

jive-ass
  bullshit

jive dojee
  horse

jive session
  schmooz

jivey
  with it

jizz
  cum

joan
  knock

job
  blow job
  broad
  caper
  cookie
  heist
  jalopy

jobber
  dealer

jobbie
  cookie

Job's antidote
  works

jock
  cock
  disc jockey
  jock, "athlete"

jocker
  gay

jockey
  play games

jockstrap
  jock

Joe
  buck private
  guy

Jack
Joe Blow

Joe College, "college man"

Joe Millerism
  chestnut

Joe Yale
  Joe College
  white shoe

john
  can

John
  cock
  Joe Blow
  rookie
  straight
  sugar daddy

John Barleycorn
  booze

John Bull
  limey

John Doe
  Joe Blow

John Dogface
  buck private

John Farmer
  hick

John Law
  cop

John Ls
  long johns

johnny
  can

Johnny
  cock
  guy
  Joe Blow

Johnny-come-lately
  greenhorn
  rookie

Johnny Trots
  the shits

John Q Citizen
  Joe Blow

John Roscoe
  rod

johnson
  cock
  pot

Johnson and Johnson
  works

joint
  bag
  butt
  cock
  dive
  dump
  joint, "marijuana
    cigarette"
  the slammer
  works

join up with
  hang out with

joke
  crack
  kid
  kid around

joker
  catch
  cookie
  guy
  jerk

jollies
  kicks

jollification
  wingding

jolly beans
  bennies

jolt
  bit
  clobber
  clout
  high
  joint

a kick
shoot up
snort
Sunday punch

jolted
  high

jolter
  a hit

joltheaded
  dumb

jones
  cock
  horse

josh
  kid
  kid around

joskin
  hick

joy dust
  coke
  horse
  M

joy house
  whorehouse

joyjuice
  booze

joy knob
  cock

joy pellet
  bennies
  doll

joy pop
  a fix

joy powder
  coke
  horse

joy prick
  a fix

joy smoke
  pot

joy stick
  cock

J smoke
  joint
  pot

juane
  pot

Judas priest
  Jeez

jug
  bag
  deck
  the slammer

juggins
  dope
  patsy

juggle
  doctor

juggler
  dealer

juggle with
  doctor

jughead
  dope

jugheaded
  dumb

jugs
  tits

juice
  angel dust
  booze
  clout
  cum
  guzzle

juiced
  plastered

juice dealer
  loan shark

juiced-up job
  hot rod

juicehead
  lush

juice-joint
  dive

juice up
  goose
  jazz up

juicy
  dirty

juicy morsel
  dirt

ju ju
  pot

juke
  play hooky

juke house
  whorehouse

jumbo
  bruiser
  fatty
  monster

jump
  fry
  fuck
  heist
  hike
  kick ass

jump all over
  chew out
  fix someone
  kick ass

jump someone's bones
  fuck

jump down someone's
    throat
  chew out

jumped-up, "inflated"

jumping Jehosaphat
  Jeez

jump on
  chew out

the jumps
  the jitters
  the shakes
jump salty
  blow one's top
jump up
  hike
  jazz up
jumpy
  jittery
jungle bunny
  nigger
junk
  chuck
  crap
  crummy
  schlocky
junked up
  high
junker
  dealer
  jalopy
  junkie
junk-heap
  jalopy
junkie
  fan
  junkie, "addict"
junk peddler
  dealer
junky
  crummy
  schlocky
just for the hell of it
  for kicks
K
  angel dust
  grand
kafooster
  bullshit

kaif
  pot
kale
  dough
kanjac
  pot
Kaps
  angel dust
kaput
  finished
  kaput, "ruined"
karma
  vibes
kayo
  clobber
  knock out
  Sunday punch
kayoed
  kaput
kayo shot
  Sunday punch
kazoo
  ass
  asshole
  can
K-blast
  angel dust
kee
  bag
  deck
keef
  pot
keek
  a fix
keel over
  fuck up
keen
  antsy
  great
keep cool
  keep one's cool

keeper of mistress
  sugar daddy
keep hands off
  stick to one's knitting
keep one's mouth shut
  shut up
keep one's nose clean
  fly right
keep on trucking
  hang tough
keep posted
  fill someone in
keep one's shirt on
  cool it
  keep one's cool
  sit tight
keep one's trap shut
  shut up
keep your nose out of this
  lay off
keg
  bag
  deck
kegger
  beer bust
keg party
  beer bust
keister
  ass
  asshole
kelsey
  hooker
kelt
  whitey
keltch
  whitey
Ken
  square
kenkoy
  horse

Kentucky blue
  pot
kerboom
  pow
kerflooey
  on the blink
kerflummoxed
  fucked-up
a kettle of fish
  a fix
key
  bag
  great
  Joe College
  white shoe
keyed up
  antsy
  high
khazer
  pig
khazeray
  crap
ki
  bag
kibitz
  butt in
kibitzer, "meddler"
kibosh
  screw up
kick
  bag
  beef
  bobtail
  clout
  fire
  goof off
  high
  humdinger
  pizzazz
  snort
a kick, "pleasure"

kick apart
  spell out
kick around
  bat around
  goof off
kick ass, "punish"
kick-ass
  clout
  pizzazz
  tough
kick back, "relax"
kicked out
  finished
kicker
  catch
  punch line
kick in
  cough up
  croak
  kick in, "contribute"
kick in the ass
  pick-me-up
kick off
  croak
kick out
  bounce
kick out the jams
  have a ball
  let oneself go
kick over
  heist
kick over the traces
  let oneself go
kicks, "pleasure"
kicks, "shoes"
kickshaw
  gadget
kick stick
  joint
kick the bucket
  croak

kick the gong around
  shoot up
kick the shit out of
  clobber
kick the tires
  check out
kick-up
  donnybrook
  wingding
kick up a fuss
  beef
  make a scene
kick up a storm
  beef
  make a scene
kick up one's heels
  have a ball
  horse around
kicky
  great
kid
  kid, "child"
  kid, "deceive"
  kid, "joke"
  kid around
  snow
kid oneself
  buy
kiddo
  kid
kid stuff
  cinch
kike, "Jewish person"
kill
  break someone up
  go over with a bang
  nix
  scrub
  snuff
  wow
killer
  back-breaker

great
humdinger
joint

a killer
 a bitch
 a laugh

killer-diller
 humdinger

killer stick
 joint

killerweed
 angel dust

killjoy
 gloomy Gus

killout
 humdinger

kingfish
 boss

King Kong
 doll
 panther piss

kingpin
 boss

king-size
 monster

king's ransom
 bundle

kink
 glitch
 jerk

kinky
 flaky
 gay
 kinky, "sexually deviant"
 weird

kip
 pad
 sack time
 snooze

kipe
 heist

kishkes
 belly
 guts
 innards

kiss
 French kiss
 neck
 snort

kiss ass
 brown-nose

kisser
 puss
 yap

kiss goodbye
 chuck

kiss my ass
 fuck you
 kiss my ass, "expression of defiance"

kiss off
 the axe
 cut
 fire
 walk out on

kissy-huggy
 palsy-walsy

kit
 works

the kit and caboodle
 the whole shebang

kitchen
 belly

kite
 bag
 deck
 hike

kitten
 dust bunny

Kitty
 Caddy

klooch
 broad

klutz
 butterfingers
 dope
 jerk

klutzy
 dumb
 ham-handed

knee-bender
 Bible-banger

knee deep
 up to one's ass

knee-high
 little bitty

knee-slapper
 belly laugh
 a howl

knife in the arm
 a fix

knob
 bean
 cock

knob job
 blow job

knock
 bad-mouth
 bust
 knock, "criticize harshly"
 knock, "disparage"
 sock

the knock
 the damage

knock around
 bat around
 goof off
 hell around

knock back
 guzzle

knock someone back
 set someone back

knock someone's block off
  clobber
  sock

knock cold
  knock out

knock dead
  break someone up

knock down
  deck
  grab
  shave

knock-down-drag-out
  donnybrook
  flat-out
  free-for-all
  hassle
  rootin'-tootin'

knocked
  cinched

knocked out
  high
  plastered
  pooped

knocked up, "pregnant"

knockers
  tits

knock for a loop
  clobber

knock someone for a loop
  wow

knock someone into the
    middle of next week
  clobber

knock it off
  shut up

knock someone's lights out
  clobber
  knock out
  wow

knock off
  clobber
  fuck

guzzle
heist
kick back
knock off, "cease work"
scrub
snuff

knock someone off his (or
    her) perch
  take someone down a peg

knockout
  dish
  great
  humdinger

knock out
  clobber
  **knock out, "make
    unconscious"**
  rustle up

knock oneself out
  bust one's ass

knock someone out
  wow

knockout drops
  Mickey Finn

knockover
  heist
  rumble

knocks
  kicks

knock someone's socks off
  go over with a bang
  wow

knock stiff
  knock out

knock the daylights out
    of
  clobber
  knock out

knock them dead
  go over with a bang
  wow

knock something together
  knock something out

knock up, "impregnate"

knothead
  dope

knot the score
  get even

know a thing or two
  know one's onions

know from nothing
  not know shit from Shinola

know-how
  smarts

know-it-all
  smart-ass

**know one's onions, "be
    competent"**

know what makes someone
    tick
  have someone's number

knucker
  heist man

knuckle
  bean

knuckle down
  bust one's ass

knuckle-dragger
  goon

knucklehead
  dope

knuckleheaded
  dumb

knuckle sandwich
  sock

knuckle under
  fold

knucksman
  heist man

K O
  knock out

Kona gold
pot

kook
nut
oddball

kooky
crazy
ditsy

Kools
angel dust

kopecks
dough

kosher
honest-to-God
square
straight

kraut, "German person"

kvetch
beef
kvetch, "complainer"

ky
bag

L
acid

label
monicker

labonza
belly
potbelly

lack-brained
dumb

lack of money
the shorts

lackwitted
dumb

lacy
gay

lad
guy

la-de-da
classy

dude
snooty

ladies' man,
"womanizer"

lady
broad

the Lady
coke

Lady H
horse

lady-killer
dude
ladies' man

lady of the evening
hooker

Lady Snow
coke

Lady White
coke
dope

a laff
a howl

a laff riot
a howl

lag
bit

lagger
con

laid-back, "relaxed"

laid out
hunky
kaput
plastered

laid, relaid, and
parlayed
screwed

lajara
cop

lam
break out

sock
split

lamb
honey
patsy

lambaste
blast
clobber
knock
tan

lamby-pie
honey

lame
dumb
jerk
square

lamebrain
dope

lamebrained
dumb

lame duck
straight

lampoon
spoof

lamps
peepers

land
catch redhanded
grab

land on
chew out

land one
sock

landslide
grand slam

landsman
pal

lap up
bite
buy
guzzle

lard-ass
fatty
goof-off

lardhead
dope

large
big-league
heavy
hot
monster

large charge
a kick

large number
umpty-umpth

large order
back-breaker

large quantity
scads

lark
kid around

larrup
sock
tan

lassie
broad

last roundup
curtains

latch on
dig

latch on to
grab

the latest
dirt

lather
blowup
clobber
sock
swivet
tan

lathered
pissed off
plastered

Latino
bean-eater

latrine
can

latrine lawyer, "contentious person"

L A turnabouts
bennies

laugh
belly laugh
break up
the horselaugh
a howl
a laugh

laugh and scratch
shoot up

laughing academy
booby hatch

laughing grass
pot

laughing soup
booze

launching pad
shooting gallery

laundry list, "agenda"

lav
can

the law
cop

lawyer
shyster

lay
ass
fuck
a fuck

layabout
goof-off

lay a fart
fart

lay an egg
flop
fuck up

lay back
kick back

lay doggo
hide out

lay down
cough up

lay down on the job
goof off

lay down the law
chew out

lay down one's tools
knock off

lay flat
deck

lay in the aisles
break someone up

lay into
blast
chew out

lay it on
bullshit

lay it on the line
get down to brass tacks
lay it on the line, "speak directly"

lay it on thick
blow off
soft-soap

lay it on with a trowel
bullshit
soft-soap

lay low
break someone up
hide out

lay off
knock off
lay off, "exclamation of warning"

lay on
fill someone in

lay one
fart

lay one on
sock

layout
dive
pad
works

lay out
blow
clobber
deck
knock out
snuff
spell out

lay oneself out
bust one's ass

lay out cold
knock out

lay out in lavender
deck
knock out

lay pipe
fuck

lay the make
proposition

lay them in the aisles
go over with a
bang
wow

lay tube
fuck

lay up
kick back

laze around
goof off

lazybones
goof-off

LBJ
acid

lead balloon
flop

leader
boss

leaders
the brass

lead-pipe cinch
cinch

lead-pipe course
gut course

lead with one's chin
stick one's neck out

the leaf
coke

leak
piss
squeal

lean and mean
hungry

lean green
dough

leaning forward in the
saddle
pumped

lean on
bulldoze
crowd
roust

lean on someone,
"intimidate"

leapers
bennies

leaping and stinking
high

the leaping heebies
the jitters

leaping lizards
Jeez

leap on the bandwagon
get on the bandwagon

the leather
sock

leather dew
dope

leatherneck, "Marine"

leathers
kicks

leave in the lurch
walk out on

leave it be
stick to one's knitting

leave out in the cold
walk out on

leaves
pot

Leb
hash

Lebanese
hash

a lech
hot pants

lech after
have hot pants

lefty
pinko
southpaw

leg
broad

leg art
cheesecake

legbiter
kid

legit
honest-to-God
straight

leg it
toddle

legitimate
  straight

a leg-pull
  a put-on

legs
  pins

lemkee
  big O

lemon
  crap
  dope
  flop
  jalopy
  letdown
  loser
  lude

lemonade
  dope

leno
  joint

leper grass
  pot

ler
  hooker

lesbian
  dyke

less than no time
  a jiffy

let a fart
  fart

let someone breathe
  get off someone's back

letdown, "disappointment"

let 'er rip
  let oneself go

let fly
  peg

let fly at
  blast
  plug

let oneself go, "be
  uninhibited"

let one's hair down
  lay it on the line
  let oneself go
  let it all hang out

let have it
  blast
  chew out

let someone have it
  clobber
  fix someone
  kick ass
  sock

let her rip
  barrel

let in on
  fill someone in

let it all hang out
  blow
  lay it on the line
  let oneself go
  **let it all hang out, "speak
    candidly"**

let loose
  have a ball
  let oneself go

let loose at
  blast
  plug

let's have it again
  come again

let sleeping dogs lie
  stick to one's knitting

let's see the color of your
  money
  put up or shut up

lettuce
  dough

let someone turn in the
  wind
  **hold someone's feet to the
    fire**

let well enough alone
  stick to one's knitting

let wind
  fart

level
  get down to brass tacks
  lay it on the line
  let it all hang out
  on the level

lez
  dyke

liberal
  pinko

license to print money
  gold mine

lick
  beat
  blow
  clobber
  a crack
  smidgen
  sock

**a lick and a promise, "hasty
  job"**

lick ass
  brown-nose

lickety-split
  flat-out
  lickety-split, "rapidly"

lick to a frazzle
  clobber

lid
  bag
  deck
  lid, "hat"

lid poppers
  bennies

lie on one's oars
  goof off
lift
  heist
  heist man
  a kick
lifter
  heist man
light
  doll
  split
  with it
light artillery
  works
light-fingered
  sticky-fingered
light-footed
  gay
light into
  blast
  chew out
  kick ass
lightning
  bennies
  panther piss
lightning hash
  hash
lightning smoke
  big O
light on his feet
  gay
light out
  split
lights
  party hat
lights out
  curtains
light up
  blow grass
light upstairs
  dumb

lightweight
  gofer
  lightweight, "trivial person"
like
  back
  hit it off
like a bat out of hell
  lickety-split
like all get-out
  like hell
like falling off a log
  easy as pie
like fun
  izzatso
  like hell
like hell, "exceedingly"
like hell, "never"
like shit through a tin horn
  flat-out
like shooting fish in a barrel
  easy as pie
like sixty
  lickety-split
  like hell
like stealing candy from a baby
  easy as pie
lily
  humdinger
  sissy
  wimp
lily-livered
  chicken
  wimpish
lily white
  clean
lime-juicer
  limey

limp-dick
  lightweight
  wimp
limp dishrag
  wimp
limping
  gimpy
limp-wrist
  gay
line
  a fix
  line, "try at persuasion"
  racket
  shoot up
line dog
  grunt
line one's nest
  take care of numero uno
line of chatter
  line
line of country
  bag
  racket
line of hooey
  line
line out
  warble
line one's pockets
  clean up
liner
  junkie
line shot
  a fix
line up with
  hang out with
lip
  gab
  sass
  shyster
lip mover
  dope

lip proppers
bennies

lippy
cheeky
gabby

lipstick on a dipstick
blow job

lip the dripper
shoot up

Lipton's punk
pot

liquidate
clobber
snuff

liquor
booze

liquored up
plastered

list
laundry list

lit
plastered

little bit
little bitty
smidgen

little boy in the boat
clit

little devil
kid

little drink of water
shorty

little guy
gadget

little Mickey
Mickey Finn

little money
chicken feed

little old me
yours truly

little pisher
kid

little shaver
kid

little shot
gofer
lightweight

little squirt
shorty

little woman
old woman

lit up
plastered

lit up like a Christmas tree
plastered

live high on the hog
eat high on the hog

live it up
have a ball

live wire
eager beaver

livid
pissed off

living doll
doll

living picture
double

lizzie
jalopy

lizzy
wimp

load
bag
deck

loaded
high
loaded, "wealthy"
plastered

loaded with
filthy with
lousy with

loadie
lush

a load of
the once-over

load of dirt
dirt

load of wind
blabbermouth

loan shark, "usurer"

loaves
ass

lobo
cowboy
goon

lobster
butterfingers

local yokel
hick

lock
cinch

locked
high

lock horns
hassle

lock, stock, and
barrel
stone
the whole shebang

the lockup
the slammer

loco
crazy

loco weed
pot

locus
dope

log
joint

loid
heist

lollapalooza
humdinger

lollygag
  goof off
  neck

lollypop
  honey

long
  bag
  deck

long chalk
  a country mile

long drink of water
  beanpole

long green
  dough

longhair
  egghead

long-handle underwear
  long johns

long shot, "unlikely winner"

long time
  ages

long time no see
  how's tricks

longwinded
  gabby

loo
  can

loogan
  dope
  goon

look
  check out
  the once-over

look-alike
  double

look alive
  get the lead out

looker
  dish

look-in
  bite

looking good
  way to go

looksee
  the once-over

loony
  crazy
  nut

loony bin
  booby hatch

loony-tune
  crazy
  nut

looped
  plastered

loopy
  crazy
  ditsy
  flaky

loose
  cool
  loaded

loosen up
  let oneself go

looseygoosey
  cool

loot
  dough
  score
  take

lop
  jerk

lopper-jawed
  cockeyed

the lord and
    master
  hubby

Lord Fauntleroy
  sissy

lords of creation
  the brass
  moneybags

Lordy
  Jeez

lose consciousness
  pass out

lose one's cool
  blow one's top

lose one's gourd
  go crazy

lose intentionally
  take a dive

lose-lose situation
  catch-22

lose one's marbles
  crack up

lose out
  fuck up

loser
  con
  flop
  lightweight
  loser, "failure"
  wimp

lose one's shirt
  go broke

lose sleep
  sweat

lose one's wig
  blow one's top

Lothario
  ladies' man

loud
  glitzy

loudmouth
  bigmouth
  blabbermouth
  blow off

loud-talk
  blow off

lounge
  night spot

lounge lizard
  ladies' man

louse
  asshole

loused-up
  on the blink

louse up
  goof
  screw up

lousy
  crummy
  loaded

lousy deal
  bum rap
  the shaft

lousy rich
  loaded

lousy with, "abundant in"

love
  honey

love handles
  spare tire

love juice
  cum

lovely
  dish

lovely magic
  angel dust

love-muscle
  cock

lover
  honey
  pothead

lover-boy
  ladies' man
  stud

Love Saves
  acid

love up
  grab-ass
  neck

love weed
  pot

lovey
  honey

lovey-dovey
  grab-ass
  palsy-walsy

low
  bad trip

low-down
  crummy
  down

the lowdown
  dirt
  the poop
  the straight dope

lower the boom
  fix someone
  kick ass
  sock

low-fullams
  crooked dice

low-level Munchkin
  gofer

low-life
  bum

low man on the totem pole
  gofer

low-rent
  bush
  crummy
  floozy
  schlocky

lozies
  pot

LSD
  acid

L7
  square

lubber
  butterfingers

lubricated
  plastered

luck out
  get lucky

lucre
  dough

Lucy in the sky with
    diamonds
  acid

lude, "methaqualone"

luded out
  high

luer
  works

lug
  cart

lulu
  dish
  humdinger

lummox
  butterfingers
  dope
  jerk

lump
  dope

lumpish
  dumb

lump it
  eat dirt

lunch box
  dope

lunch hook
  mitt

lunch up
  have a field day

lunchy
crazy
dumb

lung
banger

lungs
tits

lunker
jalopy

lunkhead
dope
jerk

lunkheaded
dumb

luscious
sexy

lush, "drunkard"

lushed up
plastered

lusher
lush
pothead

lush roller
heist man

luxo
classy

M
M, "morphine"
pot

Mac
Jack

mach
pot

macher
big shot
wheeler-dealer

machinery
works

macho
he-man
hunk

macho it out
hang tough

Mach Picchu
pot

mack, "procurer"

mackman
mack

mad
pissed off
piss-off

made of money
loaded

mad money
case dough

Mafioso
gangster

Maggie
pot

maggot
butt
whitey

magic dust
angel dust

magoo
big shot

mahogany juice
big O

mahoska
dope

maiden
bug

mainline
a fix
shoot up

mainliner
junkie

main man
pal

main squeeze
boss

maison joie
whorehouse

major-league
big-league

the major leagues
the big leagues

make
check out
dig
fuck
heist
peg
shit

a make
ass

make a big stink
blow up

make a break for it
break out

make a bundle
clean up
make a killing

make a buy
score

make a circuit clout
homer

make a circus play
grandstand

make a deal
cut a deal

make a federal case
blow up

make a full-court press
bust one's ass

make a funny
kid

make a fuss
beef

make a go of it
hack it

make a grandstand play
  grandstand

make a hash of
  screw up

make a how-de-do
  make a scene

make a killing
  clean up
  make a killing, "profit"

make a meet
  score

make a mess
  goof
  screw up

make a mint
  clean up

make a move on
  proposition

make an ascension
  fluff

make a pass
  proposition

make a patsy of
  con

make a pig of oneself
  pig out

make a pinch
  bust

make a pit stop
  piss

make a scene, "cause a
  disturbance"

make a stab
  take a crack at

make a stink
  beef
  make a scene

make big money
  clean up

make book
  bet one's ass

make someone's hair curl
  scare the shit out of

make hash of
  clobber

make it
  fuck
  go over with a bang
  hack it
  work

make it big
  go over with a bang

make it hot for
  chew out
  fix someone
  kick ass

make it snappy
  get the lead out

make mincemeat of
  clobber

make no bones
  lay it on the line

make no never-mind
  cut no ice

make official
  clinch

make out
  get by
  neck

make-out artist
  ladies' man
  stud

make out like a bandit
  come on strong
  go over with a bang
  hack it

make out with
  fuck

make someone say
  uncle
  clobber

make oneself scarce
  break out
  split

make sense
  figure

make short work of
  clobber

makes no never mind
  forget it

make someone sore
  piss someone off

make the cut
  hack it

make the fur fly
  hassle

make the grade
  hack it

make the man
  score

make the riffle
  hack it

make the scene
  show up

make tracks
  barrel
  split

make up to
  play up to

make waves
  make a scene

make whoopee
  have a ball

malarkey
  bullshit

male
  he-man

male genitals
  basket

male person
  guy

malfunction
 glitch

maltreat
 fuck

maltreated
 screwed

mama
 broad

mama's boy
 sissy
 wimp

mamber
 blood

man
 dyke
 hubby
 Jeez
 sugar daddy

Man
 Jack

the Man
 boss
 cop
 the cops
 whitey

man-about-town
 playboy

manage
 boss
 get by

man alive
 Jeez

man Friday
 gofer

mangoes
 tits

mangy
 crummy

mangy with
 lousy with

manhandle
 bulldoze
 rough up

Manhattan eel
 rubber

Manhattan white
 pot

man-hole
 cunt

man in the boat
 clit

man in the front office
 boss

manipulate
 play games

man-jack
 guy

man mountain
 bruiser

the man of the house
 hubby

man on the street
 Joe Blow

man's best friend
 pooch

man's man
 he-man

man upstairs
 boss

man with a paper ass
 lightweight

map
 puss

maracas
 tits

marble city
 boneyard

marble-dome
 dope

marble orchard
 boneyard

march
 toddle

mare
 broad

maricon
 gay

marijuana
 pot

marijuana cigarette
 joint

marijuana stub-holder
 roach clip

marijuana user
 pothead

marijuana venue
 dope den

Marine
 leatherneck

mark
 patsy
 squeal

marker
 tab

marmalade
 bullshit

Marmon
 M

marshmallow
 whitey

marvy
 great

Mary
 dyke
 gay
 pot

Mary Jane
 pot

Mary Owsley
 acid

masculine
he-man

mash
proposition

mashed
plastered

masher
ladies' man
stud

mask
puss

massacre
clobber

massage
clobber
rough up

massage someone's ego
stroke

massage parlor
whorehouse

mastermind
boss

masturbate
jack off

mat
broad
old woman

match
bag
deck

matsakaw
horse

Maui
pot

maul
clobber

mavin
ace

maxed
high

max out
ace

mayate
nigger

mayo
coke
horse

mazuma
dough

the McCoy
honest-to-God
horse
humdinger
the McCoy, "excellence"

meal
a feed

meal ticket
angel

mean
feisty
great
hairy

mean bean
ace

mean green
angel dust
dough

meanie
bad man

measly
crummy
piddly

meat
ass
bag
basket
cock
cunt

the meat and potatoes
the bottom line

meat-axe
clobber

meatball
dope
jerk

meathead
dope

meatheaded
dumb

meathook
mitt

meathound
stud

meat wagon, "ambulance"

meatware
innards

mechanic
card sharp
grease monkey

meddler
kibitzer

medic
sawbones

mediocre
bush

mediocrity
the bush leagues

med mojo
coke

megabucks
bundle

megg
pot

the megillah
the whole shebang

melancholy
down
gloomy Gus

melee
free-for-all

mell of a hess
bind
snafu

mellow
 cool
 laid-back
 pal
 plastered
 with it

mellow out
 goof off
 kick back

melonhead
 dope

melons
 tits

meltdown
 crash

melted out
 broke

Melvin
 jerk

member
 cock

memory hole
 the circular file

me, myself, and I
 yours truly

mensch
 he-man
 the McCoy

menstruate
 have the rag on

mental
 crazy

mental hospital
 booby hatch

mental job
 nut

mentally
 upstairs

mentally numb person
 zombie

merchandise
 dope
 horse

the merry ha-ha
 the horselaugh

mesca
 pot

Mescin
 bean-eater

meshugah
 crazy

meshugana
 nut

mess
 bind
 can of worms
 mish-mash
 scarecrow
 sleazebag
 snafu

mess around
 goof off
 play games

mess around with
 fool around with

messed-up
 fucked-up

mess someone over
 fuck

mess up
 clobber
 rough up
 screw up

mess with
 doctor
 fool around with

messy
 fucked-up
 half-assed
 yucky

methaqualone
 lude

meth head
 junkie

Mex
 pot

Mexican standoff
 standoff

mezonny
 dough

mezz
 great
 joint

MF
 asshole

Mick, "Irish person"

mickey
 Mickey Finn

Mickey
 Mick

Mickey Finn, "chloral
   hydrate"

Mickey Mouse
 chickenshit
 corn
 crap
 crummy
 dope
 gadgetry
 piddly
 schlocky
 snafu

Mickey Mouse around
 goof off

Mickey Mouse course
 gut course

Mickey Mouse ears
 party hat

microdots
 acid

microgram
 bag

middle
  belly

middle-age spread
  potbelly
  spare tire

middle leg
  cock

the middle of nowhere
  the boondocks

midget
  shorty

midnight oil
  big O

miff
  bug
  give someone a pain in the ass
  piss someone off
  piss-off

miffed
  pissed off

miggle
  joint

mightily
  one's head off

mighty
  fucking
  great

mighty Joe Young
  doll

mighty mezz
  joint
  pot

mighty Quinn
  acid

mildly impaired
  plastered

military
  bobtail
  buck private
  go over the hill

grunt
  hash mark
  latrine lawyer
  leatherneck
  swabby
  top-kick

military discharge
  bobtail

milk
  con

milk-livered
  chicken
  wimpish

milk the cash cow
  clean up

milktoast
  wimp

milk wagon
  Black Maria

the mill
  the slammer

milligram
  bag

Milquetoast
  chicken
  wimp

Milwaukee goiter
  potbelly

mince
  jerk

mince pies
  peepers

mind detergent
  acid

mind-fucker
  bad news
  a bad scene

mind one's own business
  stick to one's knitting

ming
  joint

mink
  dish

the minor leagues
  the bush leagues

mint
  bundle

mintweed
  angel dust

miscue
  boner

miser
  tightwad

misfire
  letdown

misfortune
  a bad scene
  a bitch

mish-mash
  can of worms
  mish-mash, "mixture"

miss
  broad

Miss Emma
  M

misses
  crooked dice

missie
  broad

missing some marbles
  dumb

missionary
  dealer

missis
  broad

Miss Morph
  M

miss the boat
  blow it with someone
  fuck up

missumis
  old woman

mist
  angel dust

mistaken
  full of shit

mister
  guy

Mister
  Jack

the mister
  hubby

Mister Bad Guy
  bad man

Mister Big
  boss

Mister Moneybags
  moneybags

Mister Tom
  fink

Mister Whiskers
  Uncle Sam

mite
  mitt, "hand"
  smidgen

mitt-glommer
  glad-hander

mitts
  bracelets

mix it up
  hassle

mixture
  mish-mash

mix-up
  free-for-all
  hassle
  snafu

MJ
  pot

mo
  gay

M O
  pot

a mo
  a jiffy

moan
  beef

moaner
  kvetch

mob scene, "crowd"

mobster
  button man
  gangster

moby
  monster

mockie
  kike

mocus
  fucked-up

mod
  snappy
  with it

modams
  pot

Model-T
  schlocky

modoc
  dope

mohasky
  high
  pot

mohoska
  clout
  pizzazz

mojo
  dope
  pot

moke
  moocher

molasses
  big O

moll
  broad

moll-buzzer
  heist man

momma
  broad
  sucker

mommix
  screw up

mommixed-up
  fucked-up

momzer
  asshole
  moocher

mon
  dough

Monday morning
    quarterback
  bigmouth

money
  angel
  a bill
  blow
  broke
  buck
  bundle
  case dough
  chicken feed
  cough up
  the damage
  dough
  fin
  freebie
  free gratis
  go broke
  grand
  gravy
  grease someone's palm
  kick in
  loaded
  make a killing
  moneybags
  paperhanger
  pick up the tab
  sawbuck
  set someone back

the shorts
tab
take
tightwad

moneybags, "wealthy
person"

money punch
Sunday punch

monicker, "name"

monkey
guy
patsy

monkey around
fool around with
goof off

monkey business
dirty tricks
monkey business,
"deception"

monkey cocaine
coke

monkeydoodle
bullshit

monkey drill
works

monkey dust
angel dust

monkeyshines
horseplay

monkey talk
double-talk

monkey with
fool around with

monkey-wrench in the
works
glitch

monster, "large"

Montezuma's revenge
the shits

a month of Sundays
ages

moo
dough

moocah
M
pot

mooch
bum
dope
heist
moocher
patsy

mooch around
goof off

moocher
bum
moocher, "parasite"

moolah
dough

moon
bag
deck
panther piss

mooning

moonlight, "work at a
second job"

moonshine
bullshit
flack
panther piss

moose
bruiser

moose milk
panther piss

mooter
joint
pot

mope
dope

mopey
down

mop up
wrap up

mop up the floor with
clobber

mopus
dough

morphine
M

morsel
dish

mortal lock
cinch

mosey along
split
toddle

mosquito
coke

mossback
fogy

the most
great
humdinger
the most, "superior one"

the mostest
great
the most

mother
asshole
damn
dealer
gadget
sucker

motherfucker
asshole
gadget
sucker

motherfucking
damn

motorcycle
bike

motor-mouth
  blabbermouth

motor-mouthed
  gabby

mouldy
  crummy

mountain dew
  panther piss

mouse
  black eye
  broad
  feel

mousy
  chicken
  wimpish

mouth
  yap

mouthbreather
  dope

mouth off
  blow off
  bullshit
  gab
  shoot the breeze

mouth on someone
  squeal

mouthpiece
  shyster

move
  heist

move someone back
  set someone back

movies
  horse opera

mow down
  break someone up
  clobber
  wow

moxie
  chutzpa
  clout

  guts
  pizzazz
  smarts

mox nix aus
  one couldn't care
    less
  forget it

Mr Charley
  whitey

Mr Morpheus
  M

Mr Nice Guy
  doll
  good guy

Mr Twenty-six
  works

mu
  pot

mucho dinero
  bundle

muck
  big shot
  goo
  mung

muck about
  fool around with
  goof off

mucked-up
  fucked-up

mucker
  asshole

mucket
  gadget

muckety-mucks
  the brass

muck up
  goof
  screw up

muck-up
  boner

muck with
  fool around with

mucky-muck
  big shot

mud
  hash
  pot

muddled
  plastered

muddlehead
  ditz

muddle-headed
  dumb

muddle through
  get by

mudhole
  jerk town

mud lark
  kid

muff
  beaver
  boner
  cunt
  fuck up
  rug
  screw up

muff-diver
  cunt-lapper

muffer
  butterfingers
  duffer

muffins
  tits

mug
  guy
  heist
  mug shot
  patsy
  puss
  yap

mugger
 goon
 heist man

muggle
 joint

muggled
 high

mugglehead
 pothead

muggles
 joint

mug shot, "photograph"

muhfuh
 asshole

mule
 mule, "obstinate person"
 panther piss

mulish
 bullheaded

mullethead
 dope

mulletheaded
 dumb

mulligan
 Mick

mulligrubs
 the blues

mumbo-jumbo
 bullshit
 double-talk

Munchkin
 kid

munch out
 scarf

mung
 goo
 mung, "filth"
 screw up

munsh
 big O

murder
 bad news
 clobber
 wow

murder weed
 pot

murphy
 con
 scam

muscle
 clout
 a fix
 goon
 horse

musclehead
 dope

muscle in
 butt in

muscle man
 goon

mush
 bullshit
 corn
 puss
 yap

mush-head
 dope

mushheaded
 dumb

mushy
 corny

muss
 snafu

mussed-up
 fucked-up

musta
 pot

mutt
 dope
 jerk
 pooch

muttonhead
 dope

muttonheaded
 dumb

muzzle
 schnozz

muzzler
 cop

muzzy
 rocky

my ass
 like hell

my eye
 like hell

my God
 Jeez

my lonesome
 yours truly

My Man
 Jack

nab
 bust
 cop
 grab
 heist

nabber
 heist man

nabob
 big shot

nada
 zilch

nail
 bust
 catch redhanded
 dig
 fuck
 grab
 joint
 peg
 sock
 works

nail down
  clinch
  peg
  spell out

nailed down
  cinched

nail it
  barrel
  floor it

nail someone to the wall
  hold someone's feet to the
    fire

naked
  bare-ass

name
  monicker

the name of the game
  the bottom line

one's name is mud
  kaput

nancy
  gay
  sissy

narc
  cop
  dick

narco
  cop
  junkie

narcotic injection
  shoot up

narcotics
  acid
  angel dust
  bad trip
  bag
  bennies
  big O
  blow grass
  coke
  dealer
  deck

dirty
do
doll
dope
dope den
a fix
freak out
hash
high
hooked
horse
joint
junkie
lude
M
pot
pothead
roach clip
score
shooting gallery
shoot up
snort
toke
works

narcotics apparatus
  works

narcotics dose
  a fix

narcotics experience
  freak out

narcotics-free
  clean
  straight

narcotics intoxication
  high

narcotics possession
  dirty

narcotics quantity
  bag
  deck

narcotics seller
  dealer

narcotics use
  do

narcotics venue
  shooting gallery

nark
  kibitzer
  shill
  snitch
  squeal

narkied
  hooked

narrow down on
  zero in

narrow-gauge
  bush
  piddly

narrow squeak
  cliffhanger

nasty
  great
  yucky

nasty bits
  basket

nasty crack
  knock

natch
  bet your ass

natter
  chitchat
  gab
  shoot the breeze

natural
  cinch

natural-born
  honest-to-God

naughty
  dirty

nauseated
  green around the gills

Navy
  butt

neanderthal
  redneck

near thing
  cliffhanger

neat
  cool
  great

neaten up
  fix up

neb
  wimp

nebbie
  doll

nebbish
  jerk
  lightweight
  warm body
  wimp

the necessary
  dough

neck, "kiss"

needle
  bug
  works

needle candy
  dope

needle park
  shooting gallery

negative
  nix
  nope

nelly
  gay

nemmie
  doll

neophyte
  greenhorn
  rookie

Nepalese hash
  hash

nerd
  grind
  jerk

nerdmobile
  pimpmobile

nerts
  crazy

nerve
  chutzpa
  guts

nervous
  cool
  jittery

nervous Nellie
  wimp

nervousness
  the jitters

nervy
  cheeky
  gutsy

nest egg
  case dough

net
  grab

never looking back
  with flying colors

never-was
  loser

new kid on the block
  greenhorn

new magic
  angel dust

new situation
  it's a new ball game

New York white
  pot

NG
  kaput
  schlocky

nice girl
  floozy

nice going
  way to go

nice hunk of change
  bundle

Nice Nelly
  Christer
  goody-goody

nick
  bust
  heist

nickel bag
  bag
  deck

nickels and dimes
  chicken feed

nickel-squeezer
  tightwad

nifty
  great

nifty number
  dish

nigger, "black person"

nigger rich
  loaded

nightclub
  night spot

nightingale
  snitch

night spot, "nightclub"

nightstick
  billy club

nimby
  doll

nincompoop
  dope

nine days' wonder
  letdown

nine-to-fiver
  square

ninny
  ditz
  dope

nip
  heist
  snort

nippers
  bracelets

nit
  zilch

nitery
  night spot

nit-pick, "quibble"

nitro
  great

the nitty-gritty
  the bottom line

nitwit
  dope

nitwitted
  dumb

nix
  nix, "reject"
  nope
  zilch

nix out
  split

no-account
  crummy
  schlocky

nob
  swell

no bargain
  lightweight
  scarecrow

no big deal
  forget it

noble weed
  pot

nobody
  lightweight
  wimp

nobody home
  crazy

nobody to write home
    about
  lightweight

the nobs
  the upper crust

no bull
  honest-to-God

no buts about it
  for sure
  honest-to-God

no chance
  a fat chance

no cinch
  hairy

nocks
  dope

no-count
  schlocky

the nod
  the go-ahead
  the OK

noddy
  dope
  high
  in a fog

no dice
  nope

no end
  as shit

**no fooling, "expression of
    honesty"**

noggin
  bean

no go
  nope

no-good
  crummy
  schlocky

no great shakes
  lightweight

nohow
  like hell

no ifs, ands, or buts
  for sure
  honest-to-God

noise
  gab

noise tool
  rod

no jive
  no shit

no kidding
  honest-to-God
  no shit

no-neck
  redneck

nonentity
  lightweight

nonfunctioning
  on the blink

nonsense
  bullshit

nonstarter
  lightweight
  loser

nonunion worker
  scab

noodle
  bean
  dope
  goof off

noodlehead
  dope

noogie
  Dutch rub

nooky
ass
cunt

nope, "negation"

no picnic
a bitch
hairy

noplaceville
jerk town

no prize package
lightweight
scarecrow

no problem
forget it

no sale
nope

nose
coke
schnozz
snitch

the nosebag
chow

nose burner
joint

nose candy
coke
dope

nose in
butt in

nose-picker
hick

nose powder
coke

nosh
cheat

no shit
honest-to-God
izzatso

no shit, "expression of
credulity"

no sirree
nope

no slouch
ace
hot shot

no snap
hairy

no soap
nope

no spring chicken
old bag

no sweat
easy as pie
forget it

Nosy Parker
kibitzer

not all there
crazy
dumb

not a pot to piss in
the shorts

not a prayer
a fat chance

not bat an eye
keep one's cool

not be born yesterday
know one's onions

not be seen dead with
hate someone's guts

not blink an eye
keep one's cool

not blow a gasket
cool it
keep one's cool

not bottle it up
let it all hang out

not buy
nix

notch
ass
cunt

notcherie
whorehouse

notch girl
hooker

not cricket
dirty

not cut the mustard
fuck up

no tea party
a bitch

not get one's balls in an
uproar
cool it
keep one's cool

not get to first base
fuck up

not give a shit
not give a damn

not give someone the time
of day
hate someone's guts

not hack it
fuck up

not have a clue
have a hole in one's head

not have brains enough to
come in out of the rain
have a hole in one's head

nothing
wimp
zilch

nothing doing
nope

nothing to write home
about
lightweight

not hold one's breath
sit tight

no time at all
a jiffy

not know one's ass from
    one's elbow
  have a hole in one's head
  not know shit from Shinola

not let out a peep
  shut up

not lose one's cool
  keep one's cool

not make a diff of
    bitterence
  cut no ice

not make the grade
  fuck up

not meddle
  stick to one's knitting

not much of a bargain
  lightweight

not on your life
  nope

not play games
  play hardball

not play with a full deck
  have a hole in one's head

not right bright
  dumb

not say boo
  shut up

not sign off on
  nix

not tightly wrapped
  crazy

not too shabby
  great

not turn a hair
  keep one's cool

not up to snuff
  off one's feed

not worth a plugged nickel
  not worth a damn

no two ways about it
  for sure

nougat
  dope

no way
  like hell
  nope

no-win situation
  catch-22

nozzle
  schnozz

nudge
  bug
  nudnik

nuggets
  bennies
  dough

nuke
  clobber

nuked
  kaput

numb
  dumb

number
  act
  cookie
  joint
  a put-on
  racket
  scam

number cruncher
  bean counter

numbered out
  high

number one
  boss

numbers
  the book

number thirteen
  M

number three
  coke

number two
  shit

numbnuts
  jerk

numbskull
  dope

numbskulled
  dumb

numero uno
  boss

nut
  bean
  fan
  nut, "insane person"
  oddball

nutcase
  nut

nut college
  booby hatch

nut-cruncher
  ball-buster

nut doctor
  shrink

nut house
  booby hatch

nuts
  balls
  crazy

the nuts
  great
  humdinger

nutty
  crazy
  flaky

nut up
  go crazy

nympho
  floozy

O
  bag
  big O
  deck

Oakley
  Annie Oakley

oater
  horse opera

Oaxacan
  pot

obfuscated
  plastered

obscene
  dirty

obsession
  a bee in one's bonnet

obstinate
  bullheaded

obstinate person
  mule

occupation
  grease monkey
  racket
  sawbones
  shrink
  shyster

oddball
  kinky
  oddball, "eccentric
    person"
  weird

odd man out
  excess baggage

odds and ends
  mish-mash

odds-on favorite
  front runner

odds splitter
  crooked dice

odd stick
  oddball

of a sort
  bush

ofay
  whitey

off
  crazy
  fuck
  on the blink
  snuff

off artist
  heist man

offbeat
  kinky

off one's bird
  crazy

off-color
  dirty

off one's feed
  green around the gills
  off one's feed, "ill"

off one's head
  crazy

office worker
  desk jockey

off the cob
  corny

off the habit
  clean

off the record
  on the QT

off the top
  up front

off the wall
  crazy
  kinky
  weird

off-tone
  dirty

of sorts
  bush

O G
  honest-to-God

oglers
  peepers

Ohio bag
  bag
  deck

oil
  bullshit
  hash
  horse
  soft soap

oil bags
  ass

oiled
  plastered

oiler
  bean-eater
  pothead

oil someone's palm
  grease someone's palm

oink
  cop

OK
  buy
  cool
  get me
  OK, "affirmation"

the OK
  the go-ahead
  the OK, "permission"

okey-dokey
  cool
  OK

Okie
  cracker
  hick

the old army game
  scam

old bat
  old bag

old-boy network
  the in group
old fart, "old man"
old-fashioned music
  corn
old geezer
  old fart
the old heave-ho
  the axe
oldie
  chestnut
old lady
  old woman
old Madge
  coke
old maid
  goody-goody
old man
  boss
  old fart
  sugar daddy
the old man
  hubby
Old Man Trouble
  bad news
old person
  fogy
old Siwash
  cow college
old slave
  coke
Old Smoky
  the chair
old smoothie
  smoothie
old softie
  softie
Old Sparky
  the chair

oldster
  fogy
  old fart
old Steve
  horse
old ticker
  ticker
old-timer
  fogy
  old fart
old woman
  old bag
  old woman, "wife"
on
  high
  hooked
on a roll
  hot
on a tear
  pissed off
once-over
  check out
the once-over, "inspection"
a once-over lightly
  a lick and a promise
on cloud nine
  high
on deck
  in place
the one
  hash
on one's ear
  broke
one-arm joint
  greasy spoon
one bitch of a
  a hell of a
one could care less
  one couldn't care less

on edge
  jittery
one-eyed monster
  the tube
one for the book
  a hit
one hell of a
  a hell of a
one-horse
  bush
one-horse town
  jerk town
one hundred dollars
  a bill
one-liner
  crack
one of the boys
  Joe Blow
one-on-one
  hassle
oner
  humdinger
  the most
one red cent
  zilch
oneself
  yours truly
one-spot
  ace
  buck
one-stoplight town
  jerk town
the one that wrote the book
  ace
one thin dime
  zilch
one-toke weed
  pot
one too many
  excess baggage

one-way guy
  doll
  good guy

one-way hit
  acid

on one's game
  hot

on someone's get-lost list
  on someone's shit list

on hold, "postponed"

on ice
  cinched
  on hold

onion
  bean

on one's last legs
  pooped

on line
  in place

on tap
  in place

on the arm
  free gratis
  on the cuff

on the back burner
  on hold

on the ball
  on the ball, "alert"
  with it

on the beam
  great
  in the groove
  with it

on the bean
  on the nose

on the blink,
      "nonfunctioning"

on the bottle
  on the sauce

on the bum
  on the blink

on the button
  on the nose

on the cob
  corny

on the cuff
  free gratis
  on the cuff, "borrowed"

on the dot
  on the nose

on the double
  lickety-split
  on the double,
      "immediately"

on the finger
  on the cuff

on the fire
  in the pipeline

on the fritz
  on the blink

on the gow
  high

on the gravy train
  loaded

on the hill
  knocked up

on the hog
  broke

on the hook
  out of luck

on the horse
  hooked

on the hot seat
  out of luck
  up the creek

on the house
  free gratis

on the juice
  on the sauce

on the legit
  on the level
  straight

on the level
  fly right
  honest-to-God
  on the level, "fair"
  straight

on the make
  hungry

on the mojo
  hooked

on the money
  on the nose

on the monkey wagon
  hooked

on the needle
  hooked

on the nod
  high

on the nose, "exact"

on the pipe
  hooked

on the QT, "secretly"

on the rims
  broke

on the rocks
  broke
  kaput

on the ropes
  out of luck

on the same wavelength
  on someone's wavelength

on the sauce, "drinking
      liquor"

on the shelf
  on hold

on the shikker
  on the sauce
  plastered

on the skids
  kaput

on the spot
  in there
  out of luck
  up the creek

on the square
  straight

on the stick
  on the ball

on the stuff
  high
  hooked

on the up-and-up
  fly right
  honest-to-God
  straight

on tick
  on the cuff

onto
  have someone's number

on top of it
  in there

on top of the world
  in hog heaven

on one's uppers
  broke

ooch
  scrunch

oof
  clout
  pizzazz

oofless
  broke
  dullsville

oofus
  dope
  dough

oofy
  loaded

oogah
  honk

ook
  jerk
  wimp

ookus
  dough

oomph
  clout
  pizzazz

oomph girl
  dish

oonch
  scrunch

oops
  barf

ooze
  toddle

op
  dick
  private eye

Op
  big O

open-and-shut
  cinched

open one's face
  open one's yap

open up
  let it all hang out

open up on
  plug

open one's yap, "speak"

operator
  eager beaver
  ladies' man
  wheeler-dealer

opium
  big O

opportunity
  a fat chance

opposite side
  the flip side

optics
  peepers

orange crush
  cop

orange cryst
  angel dust

orange cubes
  acid

orange peaches
  bennies

ordinary guy
  Joe Blow

Oreo
  fink

organized
  plastered

organized life
  get it together

orgasm
  come

ork
  barf

ornery
  feisty

oroy
  horse

oryide
  lush

oscar
  rod

ossifer
  cop

ossified
  dumb
  high
  plastered

ostentatious car
  pimpmobile

ostracize
blackball

the other side of the coin
the flip side

ouch
Jeez

ounce man
dealer

our betters
the brass

out
cool
high
out, "unconscious"

outasight
great

the outback
the boondocks

outclassed
out of one's depth

out cold
out

outer
acid

outfit
works

out-front
straight

out in left field
fucked-up

out in the cold
finished

out like a light
out

out of business
kaput

out of circulation
in stir

out of commission
on the blink

out of one's depth
out of one's depth,
   "incapable"
out of luck
up the creek

out of one's gourd
crazy

out of it
finished
high
out
rocky

out of one's league
out of one's depth

out of luck
kaput
out of luck, "unfortunate"

out of sight
great

out of one's skull
crazy

out of sorts
green around the gills

out of the box
kaput

out of the woods
in

out of this world
great

out of town
in stir

out of whack
on the blink

out on a limb
up the creek

out on one's ass
finished
kaput

out on one's ear
finished

out on one's feet
pooped
rocky

outpoint
beat

out the window
kaput

out to lunch
crazy

outz
jerk

oven
cooler

overact
ham

overdosed
high

overeat
pig out

over one's head
out of one's depth

overtaken
plastered

Owsley
acid

O Z
bag
deck

pachuco
bean-eater

pack
carry
cart
horse

package
bundle
dish

packed up
high
on the blink

packet
  bundle

pack fudge
  bugger

pack heat
  carry

pack in
  knock off
  wrap up

packing heat
  heeled

pack it in
  knock off

pack it up
  shut up

pack some mud
  bugger

pack the mail
  barrel

pack up
  go kerflooey
  knock off
  wrap up

pad
  pad, "dwelling"
  toddle

paddle
  tan

paddlefoot
  grunt

paddlewhack
  tan

pad down
  frisk
  snooze

pad duty
  sack time

paddy
  cop
  Mick
  whitey

paddy wagon
  Black Maria

pad out
  snooze

paesan
  pal

pain
  jerk
  nudnik

painful rubbing
  Dutch rub

pain in the ass
  bad news
  a bad scene
  drag
  jerk
  nudnik

painted into a corner
  up the creek

paint remover
  panther piss

paint the town red
  have a ball
  paint the town red,
    "carouse"

pair
  tits

paisano
  pal

Pakistani hash
  hash

pal
  Jack
  pal, "friend"

palaver
  gab
  schmooz
  shoot the breeze

paled
  pooped

paleface
  whitey

palm oil
  dough

palooka
  lightweight

palsy-walsy
  chummy
  pal
  palsy-walsy, "friendly"

pal together
  buddy up

pal up with
  hang out with

pan
  bad-mouth
  knock
  puss

Panama gold
  pot

pancake turner
  disc jockey

panhandle, "beg"

panhandler
  moocher

panic
  break someone up
  panic, "become
    frightened"

a panic
  a howl

panjandrum
  big shot

pan juice
  big O

pan out
  go over with a bang
  pay off

pansified
  wimpish

pansy
  gay
  sissy
panther sweat
  panther piss
pantry
  belly
pantywaist
  sissy
  wimp
paper
  Annie Oakley
  bag
  deck
paper-assed
  wimpish
paper-pusher
  paperhanger
paper tiger
  bigmouth
paperweight
  desk jockey
pappy
  old fart
paradise
  coke
parallel parking
  a fuck
paralyzing tension
  choke up
parasite
  moocher
pardner
  pal
pardon
  forget it
pardon me for living
  excuse me all to hell
park
  neck
  park, "place"

park it in the bleachers
  homer
parlor pink
  pinko
part cheeks
  bugger
part that goes over the
    fence last
  ass
party
  ass
  cookie
  fuck
  a fuck
  have a ball
  wingding
party hat, "lights"
party-pooper
  gloomy Gus
pass
  proposition
passed out
  high
passers
  crooked dice
pass out
  croak
  pass out, "lose
    consciousness"
pass up
  give a miss
paste
  clobber
  sock
pasteboard, "playing card"
pasteboard, "ticket of
    admission"
pasteboard shark
  card sharp
pasted
  hooked

paste on
  hang on
pasty
  green around the gills
patch out
  split
pate
  bean
pato
  gay
pat oneself on the back
  blow off
pat someone on the back
  hand it to someone
patootie
  ass
  dish
patron
  angel
  rabbi
patsy, "victim"
patter
  gab
  shoot the breeze
patty
  whitey
patyo de gayina
  pot
Paul Pry
  kibitzer
paunch
  potbelly
paw
  feel
  mitt
pay
  cough up
pay a bill
  pick up the tab
pay day
  eagle day

pay one's dues
  go through the mill
  pay one's dues, "acquire
    practical experience"
payoff
  pay dirt
  punch line
pay off
  fire
  pay off, "yield profit"
the payoff
  the bottom line
  curtains
payoff punch
  Sunday punch
pay the freight
  pick up the tab
pay the piper
  bite the bullet
PCP
  angel dust
p'd
  pissed off
PDQ
  on the double
peabrain
  dope
peabrained
  dumb
peace
  acid
  angel dust
peach
  dish
  humdinger
  squeal
peachy
  great
peahead
  dope

peaheaded
  dumb
peaked
  green around the gills
  off one's feed
peanut
  doll
  lightweight
  little bitty
  piddly
  shorty
peanut-brained
  dumb
peanuts
  chicken feed
pearl-diver, "dishwasher"
pearlies
  choppers
pea shooter
  rod
peck
  cracker
  whitey
pecker
  cock
peckerhead
  asshole
  jerk
peckerwood
  cracker
  whitey
peddle ass
  hustle
peddler
  dealer
pee
  piss
a pee
  a piss
peed
  pissed off

peek
  the once-over
peekers
  peepers
peeler
  cop
  stripper
peel out
  split
peenie
  cock
pee someone off
  piss someone off
peep
  the once-over
  open one's yap
pee one's pants
  break up
pee-pee
  piss
peeper
  private eye
peepers
  peepers, "eyes"
  shades
peeps
  peepers
peet
  pete
peeve
  bug
  **give someone a pain in the
    ass**
peeved off
  pissed off
peewee
  little bitty
  piddly
  shorty
peg
  peg, "identify"

peg, "throw"
plug
snort

peg out
croak
fuck up
go kerflooey

pegs
pins

pekoe
big O

the pen
the slammer

pencil pusher
desk jockey

penis
cock

penniless
broke

penny ante
piddly

penny-pincher
tightwad

penny pool
piddly

pennyweighter
heist man

pen-pusher
desk jockey

pen yen
big O

peola
nigger

peon
gofer

people upstairs
the brass

pep
pizzazz

pep-em-ups
bennies

pepped-up
jazzed-up

pepper
pizzazz

pepper-belly
bean-eater

pepper-upper
pick-me-up

pep pills
bennies

peppy
full of piss and vinegar
jazzy
zingy

pep up
jazz up

percentage
bite
pay dirt

perch
neck

percolate
toddle

Percy
sissy
wimp

a per-each
a clip

perforate
plug

perform
fuck

performance record
the book

performing well
hot
in the groove

perform minimally
get by

perform spectacularly
grandstand

perico
coke

perishing
antsy

perker-upper
pick-me-up

perk up
goose

perky
zingy

permanently
for keeps

permission
the go-ahead
the OK

perplex
can of worms

persnickety
prissy

person
ace
ass
asshole
bad man
baldie
ball-buster
bean counter
bean-eater
beanpole
bigmouth
big shot
bitch
blood
boss
the brass
brick-top
broad
brown-nose
bruiser
bum
butterfingers

button man
camel-jammer
Chink
cold fish
con
con man
cookie
cracker
cunt-lapper
desk jockey
disc jockey
dish
ditz
doll
dope
drag
duck-squeezer
dude
duffer
dyke
eager beaver
egghead
excess baggage
fan
fink
flack
floozy
fogy
Frog
front runner
gangster
gay
glad-hander
gloomy Gus
G-man
gofer
goner
good guy
goody-goody
goof-off
gook
goon
greenhorn
grind
groupie
grunt

guy
heist man
he-man
hick
hit man
honey
hooker
hot shot
hubby
humdinger
hunk
hunky
Jack
jail bait
Jane
jerk
Joe Blow
Joe College
kibitzer
kid
kike
kraut
kvetch
ladies' man
latrine lawyer
leatherneck
lightweight
limey
loan shark
loser
Mick
monicker
mule
nigger
nudnik
nut
oddball
old bag
old fart
old woman
pal
patsy
phony
pig
pinko
playboy

pothead
private eye
pro
redneck
scab
scalper
scarecrow
shill
shorty
shrink
shyster
sissy
sleazebag
smar

persons
  the in group
  the jet set

persuade
  talk someone into

persuader
  goon
  rod

persuasion
  go into one's dance
  line

pesky
  damn

peso
  buck

pesos
  dough

pet
  broad
  feel
  honey
  neck

pete-box
  pete

pete-man
  heist man

peter
  cock

Mickey Finn
 pete

peter-eater
 cocksucker

Peter Funk
 shill

peter man
 heist man

peter out
 fold
 fuck up

Peter Pan
 angel dust

petrified
 plastered

petty spirit
 chickenshit

pfft
 flop
 kaput

phenom
 a hit
 humdinger

phew
 yuck

Philadelphia
 Philly

philander
 cheat

Philly, "Philadelphia"

phiz
 puss

phonies
 crooked dice

phonograph record
 platter

phony
 glad-hander
 phony, "false"
 phony, "false one"

phony baloney
 bullshit
 phony

phony rap
 bum rap

photo finish
 standoff

photograph
 mug shot

phutz
 con
 fuck
 a fuck

phutzing
 ass

physician
 sawbones

physique
 build

Piccadilly commando
 hooker

piccolo player
 cocksucker

pick 'em up and lay 'em
 down
 get the lead out

picker-upper
 pick-me-up

pickin's
 score

pickle
 bind
 screw up

pickled
 plastered

picklepuss
 kvetch
 scarecrow

pick-me-up, "stimulant"

pick nits
 nit-pick

pick on
 bug

pickup
 bust

pick up
 blow grass
 bust
 check out
 hike
 score

pick up on
 dig

pick up the check
 pick up the tab

picky
 prissy

a picnic
 a ball
 cinch

piddle
 piss

a piddle
 a piss

piddle around
 goof off

piddle away
 blow

piddling
 bush
 little bitty

piddly
 little bitty
 piddly, "trivial"

pie
 cinch
 gravy

piece
 ass
 bit

bite
broad
coke
deck
floozy
a fuck
horse
M
piece, "share"
rod

piece of ass
ass
floozy
a fuck

piece of butt
ass

piece of cake
cinch

piece of cash
bundle

piece of change
dough

piece of cheese
cookie

piece of crap
crap

piece of jack
dough

piece of shit
asshole
bullshit
crap

piece of tail
ass
floozy
a fuck

piece of the racket
piece

piece of trade
hooker

piece pillow
bag

piece up
divvy

pie-eyed
plastered

pie-faced
dumb

piety
Christer

pie wagon
Black Maria

the pif
the poop
the straight dope

piffle
bullshit

pig
cop
floozy
pig, "glutton"

pigeon
patsy
shill
snitch

pigeonhole
peg

pigfucker
asshole

piggish
grabby

piggy
grabby

pighead
mule

pigheaded
bullheaded

pig heaven
fat city

pig iron
panther piss

pig killer
angel dust

pig-meat
loser

pig out, "overeat"

pigs
crooked dice

pig sweat
panther piss

piker
goof-off
tightwad

piki
big O

pile into
blast
chew out

pile it up
bullshit

pile of shit
bullshit

piles
bundle

pile up
rack up
total

pile up some Zs
snooze

pill
doll
drag
jerk

pillhead
junkie

pillow
deck

pill-peddler
sawbones

pill pillow
big O

pill-popper
 junkie

pill-pusher
 sawbones

pimp
 knock

pimp dust
 coke

pimple
 bean
 zit

pimpmobile, "ostentatious
 car"

pimp stick
 butt

pin
 check out
 joint
 peg

pincers
 peepers

pinch
 bind
 bust
 heist

pinch a loaf
 shit

pinchpenny
 tightwad

pin down
 peg
 zero in

pin someone's ears back
 chew out

pinga
 cock

ping in the wing
 a fix

pin gun
 works

pinhead
 dope
 jerk
 junkie

pinheaded
 dumb

pinjabber
 junkie

pink
 gay
 pinko
 whitey

pinked
 plastered

pinko, "liberal"

pink Owsley
 acid

pink-slip
 fire

the pink slip
 the axe

pink swirl
 acid

pinner
 joint

pin on
 hang on

pinpoint
 zero in

pins, "legs"

pin shot
 a fix

pinto bean
 bean-eater

pint-size
 little bitty
 piddly

pinup
 cheesecake

pin-up
 dish
 hunk

pious person
 Christer

pip
 humdinger
 zit

the pip
 the blues

pipe
 check out
 cinch
 open one's yap
 shoot up
 warble

pipe course
 gut course

pipe down
 shut up

pipe up
 open one's yap

pipperoo
 humdinger

pippy-poo
 piddly

pip-squeak
 lightweight
 shorty

pisher
 kid

piss
 beef
 crummy
 piss, "urinate"
 piss, "urine"
 piss someone off

a piss, "urination"

piss and vinegar
 pizzazz

pissant
  asshole
  lightweight
  piddly
piss away
  blow
piss-cutter
  ace
  eager beaver
  hot shot
  humdinger
pissed
  pissed off
  plastered
pisser
  ace
  back-breaker
  eager beaver
  hot shot
  humdinger
pisshead
  asshole
pissing contest
  hassle
pissing on ice
  in hog heaven
piss off
  split
piss someone off, "anger
      someone"
piss-off, "anger"
piss one's pants
  break up
piss on ice
  eat high on the hog
piss on you
  fuck you
piss or get off the pot
  fish or cut bait

piss-poor
  broke
  crummy
piss-ugly, "ugly"
piss up a storm
  beef
  make a scene
pissy
  crummy
  piddly
pissy-ass
  bush
  piddly
pistol
  ace
  eager beaver
  hot shot
  humdinger
pistol Pete
  stud
pit
  cunt
  shoot up
pitch
  bugger
  flack
  gimmick
  line
  proposition
pitch in
  pig out
  scarf
pitch into
  blast
  chew out
  kick ass
pitch woo
  neck
the pits
  the pits, "wretched place"
  yucky

pix
  gay
pixies
  bennies
pixilated
  crazy
  flaky
pizzazz
  clout
  pizzazz, "energy"
place
  dive
  park
places
  the boondocks
  night spot
plack shit
  big O
plain Jane
  Jane
plain vanilla
  vanilla
plank
  fuck
plank down
  cough up
plant
  shill
plant one on
  sock
plaster
  buck
  tail
plastered, "drunk"
plaster saint
  Christer
plastic
  phony
  square
plastic person
  zombie

plate
  dude
  platter
play
  hack it
  play ball
  work
play along
  play ball
play around
  cheat
  goof off
  sleep around
play ball,
    "cooperate"
play bouncy-bouncy
  fuck
playboy
  ladies' man
  playboy, "pleasure-
    seeker"
play dirty pool
  play dirty
play down
  soft-pedal
played out
  kaput
  pooped
player
  mack
play footsie
  buddy up
play for a sucker
  con
  snow
play for keeps
  play hardball
play for time
  stall
play games, "manipulate"

play grab-ass
  feel
play hardball, "be serious"
play hell with
  screw up
play hide-the-weenie
  fuck
play hooky, "be absent"
playing card
  pasteboard
play in Peoria
  work
play it by ear
  wing it
play it close to the chest
  pussyfoot
play it cool
  cool it
play it safe, "avoid risk"
play kissie-kissie
  neck
play kissie with
  play up to
play lickey-face
  neck
play merry hell with
  screw up
play musical beds
  sleep around
  swing
play possum
  hide out
play rough
  play hardball
play safe
  play it safe
play second fiddle, "occupy
    an inferior position"
play slap and tickle
  feel

play smacky lips
  neck
play stinky-pink
  fingerfuck
play the dozens on
  con
play the game
  play ball
play the skin flute
  blow
play tonsil hockey
  neck
play to the gallery
  grandstand
play up
  spotlight
play up to
  brown-nose
  play up to, "ingratiate"
play with oneself
  jack off
pleased as Punch
  tickled
pleaser
  floozy
pleasure
  for kicks
  get a kick out of
  have a ball
  hell around
  a kick
  kicks
pleasure-seeker
  playboy
pleiku pink
  pot
plingstem
  panhandle
plonk
  jerk
  smack

plonked
 plastered
plow
 fuck
plow into
 blast
 chew out
plow jockey
 hick
pluck
 con
 fuck
 heist
plug
 phony
 plug, "progress steadily"
 plug, "recommendation"
 plug, "shoot"
plug along
 plug
plug for
 back
plugged
 phony
plugged in
 with it
a plugged nickel
 zilch
plugger
 hit man
plugging
 flack
plug into, "exploit"
plugola
 plug
plug-ugly
 cowboy
 goon
plum
 fucking
 stone

plumb
 fucking
 stone
plumber
 screw up
plumb tuckered
 pooped
plummy
 great
plump
 smack
plump for
 go for
plumpie
 fatty
plunk
 buck
 plug
 smack
plunk down
 cough up
plush
 classy
plute
 moneybags
pocket one's pride
 eat dirt
pocket-size
 little bitty
pod
 pot
p o'd
 pissed off
pod person
 dope
 oddball
 zombie
podunk
 jerk town
the pogey
 the slammer

poggie
 rookie
pogo pogo
 coke
pogue
 gay
 jerk
 rookie
point
 works
pointed head
 dope
 egghead
pointer
 tip
point the finger at someone
  for
 hang on
pointy-headed
 dumb
poison
 bad news
 coke
 horse
poke
 blow grass
 dough
 fuck
 a fuck
 goose
 sock
poke one's nose into
 butt in
poker
 cock
poker face, "impassive face"
the pokey
 the slammer
poky
 little bitty
 piddly

pole
  cock

poler
  grind

police
  billy club
  Black Maria
  bracelets
  bust
  cop
  the cops
  dick
  frisk
  mug shot
  party hat
  prowl car
  rabbi
  roust
  rumble
  snitch
  tin

police badge
  tin

police car
  prowl car

police officer
  cop

police up
  fix up

police van
  Black Maria

polish apples
  brown-nose

polish off
  clobber
  scarf
  snuff
  wrap up

polish up
  brush up

polluted
  high
  plastered

pom-pom
  ass

ponce
  mack

pong
  Chink

pony up
  cough up
  kick in

poo
  Jeez
  shit
  zilch

pooch, "dog"

pooched-out belly
  potbelly

poodle-faker
  ladies' man

poof
  gay

pooh-bah
  big shot
  boss

poontang
  ass
  cunt

poo out
  fold

poop
  ass
  clout
  dope
  jerk
  pizzazz
  shit
  zilch

a poop
  a shit

the poop, "information"

poop chute
  asshole

pooped out
  pooped

pooped up
  briefed

poophole
  asshole

poopied
  plastered

poo-poo
  asshole
  shit

poop out
  fold
  fuck up
  go kerflooey

poop someone up
  spell out

poopsy
  honey

poopsy-woopsy
  honey

poop up
  fill someone in

poor boy
  hero

poor fish
  Joe Blow
  lightweight

poorish
  off one's feed

the poor man's
  bush

poor-mouth
  bad-mouth
  knock

poor performer
  duffer

poor slob
  jerk
  lightweight
  loser

poot
  crap
  jerk
  shit
poot around
  goof off
poot-butt
  jerk
  kid
  young squirt
poove
  gay
pop
  ass
  a fix
  fuck
  shoot up
  sock
a pop
  a clip
pop at
  plug
pop someone's cherry, "end someone's virginity"
pop one's cookies
  come
pop one's cork
  blow one's top
popeyed
  cockeyed
  popeyed, "having protruding eyes"
pop for
  pick up the tab
popo
  ass
popoff
  bigmouth
pop off
  blow off
  bullshit
  croak

gab
  shoot the breeze
  split
pop off at the mouth
  blow off
poppa
  sugar daddy
popper
  rod
poppet
  dish
poppied
  high
poppy
  big O
poppycock
  bullshit
poppy-headed
  hooked
poppy rain
  big O
poppy train
  big O
popskull
  panther piss
popular
  hot
popular trend
  get on the bandwagon
pop up
  show up
porch
  potbelly
pork
  cock
  fuck
pork out
  pig out
porky
  fatty

porno
  porn
pornographic book
  fuck book
pornographic film
  blue movie
pornography
  fuck book
  porn
porthole
  asshole
portsider
  southpaw
posh
  classy
post
  fill someone in
postponed
  on hold
pot
  can
  dope
  dope den
  plug
  pot, "marijuana"
  potbelly
  sock
potato
  bean
  buck
potatoes
  dough
potatohead
  dope
potato patch
  fruit salad
potbelly, "paunch"
potchkie around with
  fool around with
potent
  great

potgut
  potbelly

pothead
  junkie
  pothead, "marijuana user"

pothouse
  dive

pot lush
  pothead

pot out
  blow grass
  go kerflooey

potsy
  tin

potted
  high
  plastered

pottle-dripped
  high

potty
  can
  crazy
  ditsy

pound
  fuck

the pound
  the slammer

poundcake
  dish

pound one's ear
  snooze

pound one's meat
  jack off

pound the pavement
  toddle

pour down the drain
  blow

pour it on
  barrel
  come on strong
  get the lead out

pour on the coal
  barrel
  get the lead out

pow
  clout
  pizzazz
  pow, "sound of a blow"
  sock

powder
  break out
  clobber
  coke
  hash
  horse
  pot
  split

powdered joy
  dope

power
  the brass
  clout

power a homer
  homer

powerful
  high-powered

power hit
  blow grass

powerhouse
  ace
  eager beaver

powerhouse punch
  Sunday punch

powers that be
  the brass

powie
  pow

pow-wow
  schmooz

pox
  big O

PR
  flack
  pot

practical experience
  go through the mill

practice
  brush up

prairie dew
  panther piss

praise
  stroke

prank
  doll up

prat
  ass

prat-prowl
  frisk

prattle
  gab

pray to the porcelain god
  barf

precious
  honey

precise statement
  spell out

predicament
  bind

preference
  bag

preggers
  knocked up

pregnant
  knocked up
  knock up

prematurity
  go off half-cocked

preparation
  in the pipeline

prepped
  briefed

press
crowd

press the bricks
toddle

press the flesh
give five

pressure
crowd
lean on someone
talk someone into

prestigious
classy

pretentious talker
bigmouth

pretty boy
goon

pretty ear
cauliflower ear

pretty kettle of fish
snafu

pretty penny
bundle

pretty pickle
bind

pretty radical
great

pretty scary
cool

prick
asshole
cock
works

prick someone's balloon
take someone down a peg

prickly
goosy

prick-teaser
cock-teaser

prim
prissy

primed
briefed

prime the pump
score

primo
great

primp
doll up

prince
doll
good guy

prink
doll up

prison
in stir
stir-crazy

prison sentence
ace
bit
both hands

prissy, "prim"

prittle-prattle
chitchat

private eye
dick
private eye, "detective"

privates
basket

Private Slipinshits
buck private

pro
hooker
pro, "professional"
rubber

probable winner
front runner

proboscis
schnozz

procurer
mack

prod
a fix

produce
knock something out
rustle up

professional
pro

profile
grandstand

profit
clean up
gold mine
make a killing
pay dirt

prog
chow

progress steadily
plug

prole
working stiff

promiscuity
swing

promiscuous woman
floozy

promise to pay
tab

promo
flack

promote
rustle up

prong
cock
fuck

prong-on
hard-on

pronto
on the double

prop
a fix

proper behavior
fly right

418

prophet of doom and gloom
  gloomy Gus

proposition, "invite to sex"

props
  falsies

prosper
  eat high on the hog

pross
  hooker

prostitute
  hooker
  hustle

prostitution
  hooker
  whorehouse

prosty
  hooker

protruding eyes
  popeyed

the provinces
  the boondocks

prowl
  frisk

prowl car, "police car"

prune
  patsy

prunish
  prissy

prut
  mung

pseudo
  phony

psyched
  antsy
  pumped

psychiatrist
  shrink

psycho
  crazy
  nut
  weird

psych someone up, "arouse"

PT
  cock-teaser

pub
  flack

pubcrawl
  paint the town red

pubes
  beaver

public address system
  bitch box

publicity
  flack

publicity person
  flack

pucker
  flak
  piss-off
  swivet

pucker-assed
  chicken

pud
  cock
  jerk

puddinghead
  dope

puddingheaded
  dumb

puddle jumper
  jalopy

pudgy-wudgy
  fatty

puff
  big O
  flack
  plug
  a smoke
  toke

puffed
  knocked up

puffed up
  jumped-up
  stuck-up

puffery
  flack

puff job
  plug

puffy
  angel dust

pug
  goon

puke
  barf

pukey
  yucky

pulborn
  horse

pull
  blow grass
  clout
  a smoke
  snort
  toke

pull a boner
  goof

pull a fast one
  con
  snow

pull an el foldo
  flop
  fold

pull someone's chain
  con
  snow

pull down
  grab

puller
  junkie
  pothead

pull one's freight
  split

pull funny business
  play dirty

pull in
  bust
  show up

pull in one's horns
  come down a peg
  cool it

pull it off
  hack it

pull one's leg
  snow

pull someone's leg
  kid

pull no punches
  lay it on the line

pull oneself off
  jack off

pull out
  split

pull out all the stops
  let oneself go

pull one's pud
  jack off

pull one's punches
  cool it
  soft-pedal

pull something funny
  play dirty

pull someone's string
  con
  snow

pull the wool over
    someone's eyes
  con
  snow

pull up one's socks
  clean up one's act

fly right
  get on the ball

pull your head out
  wise up

pulverize
  clobber

pummel
  rough up

pump
  fuck
  ticker

pump bilge
  piss

pumped
  knocked up
  pumped, "excited"

pumped up
  jazzed up
  phony
  pumped

pumper
  ticker

pumpkin
  bean

pumpkinhead
  dope

pumpkinheaded
  dumb

pumpkin roller
  hick

pump ship
  piss

pump up
  blow up
  jazz up

pump someone up
  psych someone up

punch
  clout
  a kick
  pizzazz

punch line
  sock
  Sunday punch

punchboard
  floozy

punch-drunk
  pooped
  punch-drunk, "dazed"

punched-up
  jazzed-up
  zingy

punch in
  show up

punch line, "funny
    statement"

punch out
  split

punch-out
  hassle

punch someone out
  clobber

punch up
  jazz up

punchy
  jazzy
  punch-drunk
  rocky
  zingy

puncture
  plug

pundit
  ace

punish
  fix someone
  hold someone's feet to the
    fire
  kick ass
  rough up

punish mildly
  give someone a slap on the
    wrist

punk
  asshole
  bugger
  crummy
  gay
  green around the gills
  jerk
  kid
  lightweight
  off one's feed
  schlocky
  young squirt

punk kid
  kid
  young squirt

punk out
  cop out

Punta Rojas
  pot

pup
  kid
  pooch
  young squirt

puppies
  tootsies

puppy
  gadget
  kid
  pooch
  wimp

pure
  horse

pure love
  acid

purp
  pooch

purple haze
  acid

purple heart
  bennies
  doll

purring like a kitten
  high

pus-bag
  sleazebag

pus-gut
  fatty
  potbelly

push
  bug
  clout
  crowd
  dealer
  floozy
  go for
  pizzazz
  plug
  snuff

pushbox
  squeezebox

push someone's button
  bug

pushed out of shape
  pissed off

pusher
  dealer
  paperhanger

push for
  go for

push off
  snuff

pushover
  cinch
  floozy
  patsy
  softie
  wimp

push-push
  ass

push the panic
    button
  panic

push up daisies
  croak

puss, "face"

pussy
  ass
  broad
  cunt

pussycat
  broad
  doll
  wimp

pussyfoot
  pussyfoot, "be careful"
  stall

pussy-whipped,
    "hen-pecked"

pustle-gut
  fatty
  potbelly

put
  fuck

puta
  floozy
  hooker

put a bun in the oven
  knock up

put a move on
  proposition

putana
  hooker

put one's ass on the line
  stick one's neck out

put a tuck in someone's tail
  take someone down a peg

put away
  clinch
  clobber
  scarf
  snuff

put someone away
  wow

put someone back
  set someone back

put one's back into it
  bust one's ass

put balls on
  jazz up

put one's cards on the table
  lay it on the line

put down
  knock

put down for
  peg

put one's feet up
  kick back

put one's foot in one's
    mouth
  goof

put hair on
  jazz up

put in an appearance
  show up

put in order
  fix up

put in plain English
  spell out

put in stitches
  break someone up

put in the bag
  clinch

put in the box
  wrap up

put in the can
  clinch

put in the picture
  briefed
  fill someone in

put someone in the picture
  spell out

put in the shade
  beat

put in words of one syllable
  spell out

put it across
  hack it

put it away
  scarf

put it in one's ear
  stick it

put it in your ear
  fuck you

put it on the line
  lay it on the line

put it over
  hack it

put it over on
  snow

put it to someone
  fuck

put it to the wood
  barrel

put me in the picture
  wise me up

put one's money on
  back

put someone's nose out of
    joint
  **give someone a pain in the
    ass**
  piss someone off
  **take someone down a
    peg**

puton
  phony

a **put-on,** "deception"

put someone on
  kid
  snow

put on airs
  put on the ritz

put on one's best bib and
    tucker
  doll up

put one over
  snow

put one toe in first
  run it up the flagpole

put on frills
  put on the ritz

put on ice
  clinch
  snuff

put on one's Sunday clothes
  doll up

put on swank
  put on the ritz

put on the crap list
  blackball

put on the ditch list
  blackball

put on the dog
  doll up
  put on the ritz

put on the feed bag
  scarf

put on the floor
  knock out

put on the frost
  cut
  give the cold shoulder

put on the gloves
  hassle

put on the high hat
  cut
  put on the ritz

put on the rack
  chew out

put on the ritz, "display
    wealth"

put on the shit list
  blackball

put out
fuck
kick in

put out like a light
knock out

putrid
crummy
yucky

put the arm on
bum
bust
put the bite on

put the blocks to
clobber
fuck
lean on someone

put the chill on
cut

put the claw on
bust
put the bite on
squeal

put the collar on
bust

put the eye on
check out

put the fear of God into
chew out
scare the shit out of

put the finger on someone
squeal

put the freeze on
cut
give the cold shoulder

put the gakk on
chew out

put the grab on
heist

put the hammer down
barrel
floor it

put the heat on
crowd
lean on someone

put the kibosh on
nix
screw up

put the lid on
wrap up

put the lug on
bum
put the bite on

put the make on
proposition

put them in the aisles
go over with a bang

put the moves on
proposition

put the pedal to the metal
barrel
floor it

put the screws to
crowd

put the shit on
knock

put the skids to
bounce
chuck
clobber
take someone down a peg

put the sleeve on
bust
put the bite on

put the slug on
sock

put the squeeze on
crowd
lean on someone

put the touch on
bum
put the bite on

put the wood to
kick ass

put through the wringer
chew out

put together
cook up

put one's two cent's worth
in
butt in
open one's yap

putty arm
glass arm

putty-head
dope

put up
rig

put up a squawk
beef

put-up job, "dishonest
prearrangement"

put someone wise
fill someone in

put your money where your
mouth is
put up or shut up

putz
asshole
cock
wimp

putz around
goof off

putz around with
fool around with

quack
lude
phony

quad
lude

the quad
the slammer

quail
 broad
 dish

Quakertown
 Philly

the quality
 the upper crust

quarrel
 hassle

quarter bag
 bag
 deck

quarter moon
 hash

quarter ounce
 bag

quas
 lude

queen
 gay

queer
 crazy
 flaky
 gay
 kinky
 phony
 screw up
 weird

queer duck
 oddball

queer in the head
 crazy

queer it with someone
 blow it with someone

quibble
 nit-pick

quick and dirty
 greasy spoon

quick one
 quickie

quick on the trigger
 goosy

quick-over
 the once-over

quick push
 floozy

quick sex
 quickie

quick shuffle
 razzle-dazzle

quickstep
 on the double

the quickstep
 the shits

quiff
 floozy
 hooker

quill
 works

quim
 ass
 cunt

quit cold
 walk out on

quit fucking the dog
 get the lead out

the quivers
 the jitters

R A
 piss-off

rabbi, "patron"

rabbit
 split

rabbit's foot
 security blanket

rabbity
 chicken
 wimpish

racehorse
 bug
 coke

racked
 cinched
 in the bag

racket
 flak
 hoopla
 racket, "occupation"
 scam

rack out
 chew out
 snooze

rack time
 sack time
 a snooze

rack up
 rack up, "achieve"
 total

racy
 dirty

rad
 great

radiclib
 pinko

radio
 ghetto box

radio performer
 disc jockey

rafts
 bundle

rag
 pasteboard

rag and a bone and a hank
  of hair
 broad

rag-bag
 mish-mash

rag-chewing
 gab
 schmooz

rage
 blowup

the rage
hot

Raggedy Ann
acid

raggedy-pants
crummy

raghead
camel-jammer

rag out
doll up

rags
threads

ragweed
pot

raid
rumble

rail it
goof off

railroad
bulldoze

railroad weed
pot

raincoat
rubber

raise a ruckus
beef
have a ball
make a scene

raise a welt
shoot up

raise Cain
beef
make a scene

raise someone's dander
piss someone off

raise hell
have a ball
make a scene
paint the town red

raise hell with
chew out

raise the dickens with
chew out

raise the roof
beef
have a ball
make a scene

rake it in
clean up

rake-off
bite

rake over the coals
chew out

rake up
grab

rake up one side and down
the other
chew out

rally
wingding

ralph up
barf

ram-bam thank you ma'am
quickie

ramble
split

ramble-scramble
fucked-up

rambunctious
full of piss and vinegar
rootin'-tootin'

ram it
fuck you
kiss my ass
stick it

rammy
horny

rampageous
rootin'-tootin'

ramrod
cock

ramshackle
beat-up

randan
binge

randy
horny

rane
coke

ranged
antsy

Rangoon
pot

rank
the big leagues
bug
crummy

rank-out
knock

ranky dank
square

rap
bad-mouth
gab
knock
schmooz
shoot the breeze

a rap
zilch

rap club
whorehouse

rapemobile
pimpmobile

rap someone's knuckles
give someone a slap on the
wrist

rapping
gab
schmooz

rap session
schmooz

rap with
  hang on

rare back
  bust one's ass

rarin' to go
  antsy
  full of piss and vinegar
  pumped

raspberry
  the bird

rassle up
  rustle up

rat
  asshole
  bad man
  scab
  snitch
  squeal

rat around
  goof off

rat-ass
  crummy

ratboy
  hit man

ratchet-mouth
  blabbermouth

rat-fink
  asshole

rat-fuck
  asshole
  cool
  goof off
  have a ball
  kinky

rathole
  dive
  dump
  stash

rat on
  squeal

rat out
  back out
  cop out

rat poison
  horse

rats
  Jeez

a rat's ass
  zilch

rat's nest
  snafu

ratter
  snitch

rattle
  gab

rattlebrain
  ditz

rattlebrained
  ditsy

rattle someone's cage
  bug

rattle cages
  make a scene

rattle someone's chain
  con
  snow

rattletongue
  blabbermouth

rattling
  great

ratty
  beat-up
  crummy
  yucky

raunch
  fuck
  porn

raunchy
  crummy
  dirty
  yucky

rave about
  flip

rave-up
  wingding

raving beauty
  dish

raving mad
  pissed off

raw
  dirty
  tough

raw deal
  bum rap

a raw deal
  the shaft

raw recruit
  rookie

razoo
  the bird

razor
  divvy

razz
  knock

the razz
  the bird

razzle-dazzle, "deception"

razzmatazz
  corn
  razzle-dazzle
  scam

reach back
  bust one's ass

read
  dig

read someone
  have someone's
    number

readiness
  in the pipeline

readjust
rejigger

read someone like a book
have someone's number

read me
get me

read my lips
fuck you
get me

read the riot act
chew out
clamp down
kick ass

the ready
dough

ready to drop
pooped

the real George
humdinger

real guy
the McCoy

really into it
with it

really-truly
honest-to-God

the real McCoy
the McCoy

real money
bundle

ream
bugger
chew out
con
fuck

reamer
cock

reaming
scam

ream out
chew out

rear
ass

recap
rehash

receipts
take

recommendation
plug

red
doll
horse
pot

red ass
the blues

red-assed
pissed off

red-carpet
classy

a red cent
zilch

red chicken
horse

Red Cross
M

Red Devil
doll

redeye
panther piss

red gunyon
pot

redhanded
dead to rights

red-head
brick-top

red-hot
antsy

red Lebanese
hash

red-light
hustle

redneck
cracker
hick
redneck, "bigoted person"

red-necked
pissed off

red oil
hash

red rock
horse

red up
fix up

reefer
dope
joint
junkie
pot
pothead

reefer hound
pothead

reeling
plastered

ref
Blind Tom

reform
go straight

register
shoot up

regular
fucking
great
honest-to-God

regular guy
good guy

rehash, "review"

rehaul
rejigger

reject
dope
nix

rejigger, "readjust"

relax
kick back

relaxed
laid-back

religionist
Bible-banger

reltney
cock

remain in place
sit tight

remarkable
a hell of a

remarkable person or thing
humdinger

remote regions
the boondocks

renege
back out

reorganization
house-cleaning

repeat
come again

repeaters
crooked dice

reprimand
catch hell
chew out

repulsive place
dump

respond excitedly
flip

restaurant
greasy spoon

rest one's jaw
shut up

retard
dope

retool
rejigger

return the compliment
get even

Reuben
hick

revamp
rejigger

reveal
go public

revenge
get even

review
brush up
rehash

rev up
jazz up

revved-up
jazzed-up

RF
asshole
bum rap

RF session
schmooz

rhubarb
donnybrook
flak
free-for-all
hassle

the rhubarbs
the boondocks

rhythms
bennies

rib
broad
bug
knock

ribs
chow

rib-tickler
crack
a howl

rice-belly
Chink

Richard Roe
Joe Blow

ricky-tick
corn
corny

ride
ass
bug
fuck
a fuck
gut course
jalopy
knock

ride it out
hang tough

ride old Sparky
fry

ride shank's mare
toddle

ride shotgun for
go to bat for

ride the arm, "collect unmetered taxi fare"

riding the witch's broom
hooked

riff
act
joint

a riffle
a crack

rig
rig, "prearrange dishonestly"
works

rigged fight
put-up job

right
  get me
  OK

righteous
  great

righteous bush
  pot

righteous dealer
  dealer

righteous egg
  good guy

right guy
  good guy

right-handed
  straight

right in there
  in there

righto
  OK

right on
  bet your ass
  OK
  on the nose
  way to go

the right stuff
  the McCoy

right there
  in there
  with it

right you are
  OK

rigmatick
  can of worms

rig-out
  threads

rig up
  doll up
  whomp up

rile
  bug
  piss someone off

riled up
  pissed off

ring
  buzz

ring-a-ding
  razzle-dazzle

ring someone's bell
  wow

ring-ding
  dope

ringding-do
  can of worms

ring down the curtain
  wrap up

ringer
  double

ring in
  show up

ring off
  shut up

ringtail
  asshole
  jerk

ringtailed snorter
  humdinger

ring the bell
  come on strong
  hack it

rinky-dink
  corny
  crap
  crummy
  piddly

riot
  donnybrook
  free-for-all
  a hit

a riot
  a howl
  a laugh

rip
  bad-mouth
  binge
  a crack
  knock

rip-ass
  barrel

ripe
  dirty
  plastered

rip into
  blast
  chew out

ripoff
  heist
  scam

rip off
  con
  heist
  split

rip on
  knock

ripped
  high
  plastered

rippers
  bennies

ripping
  great

a ripple
  a crack

riproaring
  rootin'-tootin'

riproaring drunk
  plastered

ripsnorter
  a hit
  humdinger

risk
  stick one's neck out

risk all
  go for it

risky business
  a gamble

ritz
  swank

ritz it
  put on the ritz

ritz up
  doll up

ritzy
  classy
  great

rivets
  dough

roach
  butt
  joint

roach bender
  pothead

roach holder
  roach clip

road dog
  pal

road dope
  bennies

roaring drunk
  plastered

roast
  bad-mouth
  blast
  chew out
  fry
  knock

robbery
  caper
  heist

rock
  buck
  coke

horse
  sock

rock and sock
  sock

rock 'em–sock 'em
  rootin'-tootin'

rocket
  pot

rocket fuel
  angel dust

rockhead
  dope

rocks
  balls

rock the boat
  make a scene

rocky
  green around the gills
  plastered
  rocky, "dazed"

rod
  cock
  hit man
  hot rod
  rod, "firearm"

rod boy
  hit man

rodded
  heeled

rodman
  hit man

Roger
  OK

rolf
  barf

roll
  ass
  con
  fuck
  a fuck
  heist

roller
  heist man

rollers
  crooked dice

roll in
  show up
  snooze

rolling in
  up to one's ass

rolling in it
  loaded

roll in the hay
  ass
  a fuck

roll over
  clobber

rolls
  ass

Romeo
  ladies' man

romp over
  clobber

the roof caves in
  hell breaks loose

rook
  con
  rookie

rooker
  con man

rookie
  greenhorn
  rookie, "neophyte"

rooking
  scam

room
  night spot

rooming house
  flophouse

roost
  pad

rooster
  stud

rooster brand
  big O

root
  butt
  cock
  joint

rooter
  fan

root for
  back

rootin'-tootin', "boisterous"

root tonic
  big O

rooty
  horny

rooty-toot
  corn

rope in
  con
  snow

roscoe
  rod

rosebud
  asshole

rose garden
  fruit salad

roses
  bennies

rosewood
  billy club

rosy
  cool
  plastered

rot
  bullshit
  suck

rotchy
  yucky

rotgut
  panther piss

rotten
  crummy
  yucky

rotten deal
  bum rap
  the shaft

rotten egg
  asshole
  bad man

rotter
  asshole

rough
  dirty
  hairy

rough-and-tumble
  rootin'-tootin'

rough as a cob
  hairy

rough-ass
  tough

rough customer
  goon

roughneck
  goon

rough stuff
  dirty tricks
  porn

rough up
  clobber
  rough up, "pummel"

round brown
  asshole

roundheels
  floozy

roundhouse
  sock

round the bend
  crazy

round up
  grab

rouser
  a hit

roust
  bug
  bulldoze
  bust
  roust, "harass"
  rumble

routine
  act
  line

Rover
  pooch

row
  donnybrook
  free-for-all
  hassle

row-de-dow
  donnybrook

rowdy-dowdy
  rootin'-tootin'

rowing with one oar in the
    water
  crazy

a row of pins
  zilch

royal
  great

royal blues
  acid

royal fucking
  bum rap
  the shaft

rub
  feel
  snuff

rubber
  hit man
  rubber, "condom"
  rubberneck

rubber boots
  rubber
rubber heel
  cop
  dick
rubberneck, "stare"
rubber room
  booby hatch
rubbish
  bullshit
rube
  greenhorn
  hick
rub off
  jack off
rub out
  clobber
  snuff
rub parlor
  whorehouse
rub one the wrong way
  **give someone a pain in the
    ass**
ruckus
  donnybrook
  flak
  free-for-all
  hassle
  hoopla
  wingding
ruction
  donnybrook
  free-for-all
  hassle
ruddy
  damn
rude
  cheeky
ruffian
  goon
  goon squad

rug, "wig"
rug ape
  kid
rugged
  hairy
ruined
  finished
  kaput
rule the roost
  boss
rum
  booze
rumbag
  lush
rumble
  donnybrook
  free-for-all
  heist
  rumble, "fight"
  rumble, "raid"
rum customer
  oddball
rum-dum
  crazy
  dope
  dumb
rumhound
  lush
rummage
  crap
rummed up
  plastered
rummy
  dumb
  lush
rum one
  oddball
rump
  ass

rumpot
  lush
rumpus
  donnybrook
  flak
  free-for-all
  hassle
  hoopla
  wingding
run
  boss
run after
  play up to
run a number
  snow
run a number on
  clobber
  con
runaround
  scam
run circles around
  beat
run down
  bad-mouth
  knock
  spell out
run in
  bust
run-in
  free-for-all
  hassle
run into the ground
  blow up
run it by again
  come again
run it up the flagpole and
    see if anybody salutes
  run it up the flagpole
running amok
  high

run off at the
    mouth
  blow off
  bullshit
  gab
  shoot the breeze
run-of-the-mill
  bush
run on empty
  flop
run out
  break out
run out of gas
  fold
run out on
  walk out on
run ragged
  pooped
the runs
  the shits
runt
  shorty
runty
  little bitty
  piddly
run wide open
  barrel
rupture oneself
  bust one's ass
rural person
  hick
rush
  high
  a kick
rustle
  heist
  rustle up
rustle one's bustle
  get the lead out

rustler
  heist man
rustle up, "produce"
rusty-dusty
  ass
rutabaga
  buck
s
  pot
sack
  bag
  clobber
  deck
  fire
  sack time
the sack
  the axe
sack artist
  goof-off
sack drill
  sack time
  a snooze
sack out
  snooze
sack time
  sack time, "sleep"
  a snooze
sad
  crummy
sad apple
  jerk
  lightweight
  loser
  wimp
Sadie Thompson
  hooker
sad sack
  lightweight
  loser
  wimp

safe
  rubber
safecracker
  heist man
safety
  play it safe
  rubber
  works
sagebrusher
  horse opera
sail into
  blast
  chew out
sailor
  swabby
sakes alive
  Jeez
saleslady
  hooker
saloon
  gin mill
salt
  horse
salt and pepper
  pot
salty
  dirty
  feisty
salve
  dough
  soft soap
sam
  cop
sam how
  big O
sandbag
  bulldoze
  clobber
Sandoz
  acid

sandwich
 hero

san lo
 big O

San Quentin quail
 jail bait

Santa Claus
 sugar daddy

Santa Maria gold
 pot

sao
 asshole

sap
 dope
 jerk

sapfu
 snafu

saphead
 dope
 jerk

sapheaded
 dumb

sapperoo
 dope

sappo
 dope

sappy
 corny
 crazy
 dumb

sardine can
 mob scene

sashay
 toddle

sass, "impudence"

sassy
 cheeky
 smart-ass

satch
 blabbermouth

satch cotton
 works

satchel
 rig

satchelmouth
 bigmouth
 blabbermouth

satchelmouthed
 gabby

satiated
 fed-up

satisfactory
 cool

sativa
 pot

saturated
 plastered

Saturday night special
 rod

sauce
 sass

the sauce
 booze

sauced
 plastered

sausage
 cock
 dope
 pot

save your breath
 shut up

savvy
 dig
 get me
 smarts

saw
 sawbuck

sawbones, "physician"

sawbuck
 both hands
 sawbuck, "ten dollars"

sawed-off runt
 shorty

saw logs
 snooze

say amen to
 buy

says which
 come again
 izzatso

says who
 izzatso

say uncle
 fold

scab, "nonunion worker"

scads
 bundle
 scads, "large quantity"

scaffle
 angel dust

scag
 horse
 jerk

scale down
 shave

scalp
 clobber

scalper, "ticket seller"

scam
 con
 racket
 scam, "swindle"

the scam
 the straight dope

scammer
 con man

scanky
 crummy

scar
 horse

scarecrow, "ugly person"

scared stiff
  scared shitless

scaredy-cat
  chicken
  wimp

scare shitless
  scare the shit out of
  spook

scare stiff
  scare the shit out of
  spook

scare up
  grab
  rustle up

scarf
  chow
  chuck
  heist
  scarf, "eat"

scarf out
  pig out

scarf up
  scarf

scarper
  break out
  split

scary
  creepy

scat
  barrel
  horse

scatter
  hideaway

scatterbrain
  ditz

scatterbrained
  ditsy

scatty
  crazy
  ditsy

scene
  bag

schizo
  crazy

schiz out
  go crazy

schlechts
  horse

schlemazel
  lightweight

schlemiel
  dope
  jerk
  loser
  wimp

schlep
  butterfingers
  cart
  dope
  jerk

schlepper
  jerk
  nudnik

schleppy
  dumb
  ham-handed

schlock
  crap
  crummy
  horse

schlocky
  crummy
  schlocky, "inferior"

schloomp
  butterfingers
  dope
  goof off

schloomp around
  goof off

schmack
  horse

schmaltz
  corn

schmaltzy
  corny

schmear
  clobber
  soft-soap

the schmear
  the whole shebang

schmeck
  horse

schmegeggy
  bullshit
  dope

schmendrick
  dope
  loser
  wimp

schmo
  dope
  guy
  jerk
  loser
  wimp

schmooz
  schmooz, "conversation"
  shoot the breeze

schmuck
  asshole
  cock

schneider
  clobber

schnockered
  plastered

schnook
  jerk
  loser
  patsy

schnorrer
  moocher

schnozzola
  schnozz

schtoonk
 jerk

schvartze
 nigger

scissorbill
 scab

scoff
 chow
 heist
 scarf

sconce
 bean

scooch
 scrunch

scoop
 heist
 the poop
 snort

the scoop
 the poop

scoot
 barrel
 buck
 split

scope on
 check out

scope out
 check out

scorch
 barrel
 blast

score
 bite
 fuck
 hack it
 heist
 pay dirt
 score, "buy narcotics"
 score, "loot"
 take

the score
 the bottom line
 the damage

score with
 fuck

Scotch
 chintzy

Scotsman
 tightwad

scott
 horse

scout
 guy

scrag
 clobber
 fuck
 scarecrow
 snuff

scram
 break out
 split

scramble-brained
 dumb

scrap
 chuck
 free-for-all
 hassle
 scrub

scrape by
 get by

scrape up
 grab
 rustle up

scrap-heap
 chuck

scrap iron
 panther piss

scrappy
 feisty

scratch
 dough
 scrub

scratch someone's back
 soft-soap

scratch house
 flophouse

scraunch
 clobber

a scream
 a howl
 a laugh

the screaming meemies
 the jitters
 the shakes

screech
 panther piss

screw
 ass
 con
 cop
 fuck
 a fuck
 split

screw around
 goof off

screw around with
 fool around with

screwball
 crazy
 nut
 oddball

screwed over
 screwed

screwed-up
 fucked-up

screwing
 ass

a screwing
 the shaft

screw-loose
  glitch
  nut
  oddball
screw off
  goof off
  jack off
screw-off
  goof-off
screw over
  fuck
screw the pooch
  goof off
screw up
  fuck up
  goof
  screw up, "spoil"
screw-up
  boner
  fuck-up
  snafu
screw with
  fool around with
screwy
  cockeyed
  crazy
  flaky
  fucked-up
  plastered
screw you
  fuck you
  kiss my ass
scrimmage
  free-for-all
scrip
  buck
scrog
  fuck
scronched
  plastered

scrooch
  scrunch
Scrooge
  tightwad
scrounge
  bum
  rustle up
scrounger
  moocher
scrounge up
  bum
  rustle up
scroungy
  yucky
scrub
  bush
  duffer
  gofer
  scrub
scrub the slate clean
  go back to square one
scruff
  get by
scruff along
  get by
scruffy
  crummy
scrump
  fuck
scrumptious
  great
scrunch up
  scrunch
scrunge
  mung
scud
  scut work
scuffle
  free-for-all
  get by

scuffle along
  get by
scum
  asshole
  cum
  sleazebag
scumbag
  asshole
  rubber
  sleazebag
scum of the earth
  asshole
scumsucker
  asshole
  cocksucker
  sleazebag
scumsucking
  yucky
scunge
  mung
scurve
  asshole
  sleazebag
scut
  scut work
  sleazebag
scuttle
  nigger
scuttlebutt
  dirt
  the poop
scut work, "tedious work"
scuzz
  asshole
  mung
  scarecrow
scuzzbag
  asshole
  sleazebag
scuzzy
  yucky

seagoing bellhop
  leatherneck

sea lawyer
  latrine lawyer

sealing wax
  big O
  hash

search
  frisk

seat
  ass

seat-man
  shill

a sec
  a jiffy

second fiddle
  gofer

second job
  moonlight

second-rater
  duffer

second-story man
  heist man

second-stringer
  gofer
  lightweight

secret
  on the QT

secret associate
  shill

section eight
  nut

secure
  knock off

security blanket, "source of
    emotional security"

see a man about a dog
  check the plumbing

seed
  butt

seedy
  beat-up
  green around the gills

seeing pink elephants
  plastered

see red
  blow one's top

see Steve
  snort

see where one is coming
    from
  dig

seguro que
  bet your ass

self-interest
  take care of numero uno

self-starter
  eager beaver

sell
  con
  scam
  talk someone into

sell a bill of goods
  con
  snow

sell down the river
  fuck

sell on
  talk someone into

sell out
  fuck
  squeal

sell-out
  double cross

semen
  cum

seminude
  cheesecake

semolia
  dope

send
  blow grass
  wow

send away with a flea in his
    (or her) ear
  take someone down a peg

send it home
  shoot up

send to hell in a handbasket
  screw up

send to kingdom come
  snuff

send to the showers
  fire

send up
  blow grass
  spoof

send west
  snuff

sensaysh
  a hit

sent
  high

sentimental
  corny

sentimentality
  corn
  tear-jerker

sent to the showers
  finished

sergeant
  top-kick

serious
  great

serious money
  bundle

seriousness
  get down to brass tacks
  no fooling
  play hardball

service stripe
  hash mark

sesky
  sexy

sess
  pot

session
  stanza

set
  a fix
  schmooz
  works

set someone back, "cost"

set in concrete
  carved in stone

set in one's ways
  bullheaded

set of threads
  threads

set of wheels
  hot rod
  jalopy

set on one's ass
  high

set over
  snuff

set sail
  split

set the world on fire
  come on strong

settle
  snuff

settle accounts
  get even

settle someone's hash
  clobber
  fix someone
  kick ass
  snuff
  take someone down a peg

settle the score
  get even

set-to
  free-for-all
  hassle

set to rights
  fix up

setup
  cinch
  gut course
  pad
  patsy
  put-up job

set up
  frame
  rig

severe
  tough

sewed up
  cinched

sewer
  shoot up

sew up
  clinch
  wrap up

sex
  AC-DC
  ass
  balls
  basket
  beaver
  blow
  blow job
  bugger
  cheat
  cherry
  clit
  cock
  cocksucker
  cock-teaser
  come
  come out
  cruise

cum
cunt
cunt-lapper
dyke
feel
fingerfuck
floozy
French kiss
fuck
fur pie
gang bang
gay
grab-ass
hard-on
have hot pants
hooker
horny
hot pants
hung
jack off
jail bait
kinky
neck
pop someone's cherry
porn
proposition
quickie
rubber
sexy
sleep around
straight
stud
swing
whorehouse

sex act
  a fuck

sex job
  dish
  floozy

sex pot
  dish
  hunk

sexual arouser
  cock-teaser

sexual desire
  hot pants

sexually attractive
  sexy

sexually promiscuous male
  stud

sexual promiscuity
  sleep around

sexual search
  cruise

sex wagon
  pimpmobile

sexy
  great
  horny
  sexy, "sexually attractive"

shabby
  dirty

shackup
  floozy

shack up
  swing

shade
  nigger

shades, "sunglasses"

shadow
  nigger
  tail

shady
  dumb

shady business
  dirty tricks

shaft
  fuck

the shaft
  bum rap
  the shaft, "unfair treatment"

shafted
  screwed

shag
  bug
  fuck
  a fuck
  great
  split
  toddle

shag ass
  split

shagger
  tail

shake
  cop out
  frisk

a shake
  a jiffy

shake a leg
  get the lead out

shakedown
  scam

shake down
  bum
  con
  frisk
  put the bite on

shake hands on
  buy

shake it
  get the lead out

the shakes
  the jitters
  the shakes, "delirium tremens"

shake the money tree
  clean up

shake-up
  house-cleaning

shaky
  green around the gills

shallow-brained
  dumb

shamus
  cop
  snitch

shank it
  toddle

shanks
  pins

shape
  build

shape up
  clean up one's act

share
  bite
  piece

shark
  card sharp
  con man

sharp
  card sharp
  con man
  cool
  great
  with it
  works

sharpen up
  brush up

sharper
  con man

sharpie
  card sharp
  con man
  dude

sharpster
  card sharp

shat on
  screwed

shatting on one's uppers
  broke

shave, "decrease"

shaved
  plastered

shaver
guy

shebang
dive

the shebang
the whole shebang

shee-it
Jeez

sheen
jalopy

sheeny
kike

sheep-dip
panther piss

sheesh
hash
Jeez

sheets
angel dust

sheik
dude
ladies' man

shekels
dough

shell
cough up

shellac
clobber
panther piss

shell game
scam

shell out
blow
cough up
kick in
pick up the tab

shemale
broad

shemozzle
donnybrook
flak

hoopla
split

shenanigans
horseplay

Sherlock
dick

she-she
broad

shiever
snitch

shikker
lush
plastered

shill
billy club
flack
shill, "secret associate"

shiller
shill

shim
square

shindig
wingding

shindy
binge
donnybrook
free-for-all
hassle
hoopla
wingding

shine
cop out
cut
panther piss

shiner
black eye

shine up
brush up

shine up to
brown-nose
play up to

shirker
goof-off

shirty
feisty
pissed off

shishi
hash

shit
asshole
bullshit
crap
dope
horse
Jeez
pot
shit, "defecate"
shit, "excrement"
zilch

a shit, "defecation"

shit a brick
blow one's top
make a scene

shitass
asshole
jerk

shit bricks
blow one's top

shit bullets
panic

shitcan
can
chuck

shit-can
scrub

the shit end of the stick
the shaft

shitface
asshole

shitfaced
plastered

shit-for-brains
dope

441

shit for the birds
  bullshit
  chickenshit
shit green
  panic
shithead
  asshole
shitheaded
  dumb
shitheel
  asshole
the shit hits the fan
  hell breaks loose
shithole
  dump
shithook
  asshole
shithouse
  can
  dump
shit in high cotton
  eat high on the hog
shit in your hat
  fuck you
shitkicker
  hick
shitkickers
  boondockers
shit-kicking
  tough
shit list, "undesired
  persons"
shit-list
  blackball
shit on
  screwed
shit on wheels
  hot damn
  hot shot
shit on you
  fuck you

shit or get off the pot
  fish or cut bait
shit out of luck
  kaput
  out of luck
shit one's pants
  panic
the shits, "diarrhea"
shitstick
  asshole
shitstorm
  snafu
shitsure
  bet your ass
  for sure
shitter
  asshole
  can
shitting one's pants
  scared shitless
shitty
  crummy
  yucky
the shitty end of the stick
  the shaft
shitwork
  scut work
shivery
  creepy
shlong
  cock
shoe
  cop
  white shoe
shoe polish
  panther piss
shoes
  boondockers
  kicks
  sneakers

shoo-in
  cinch
shook up
  jittery
shoot
  blow
  come
  Jeez
  plug
  shoot up
shoot someone a line
  soft-soap
shoot one's cookies
  barf
shoot down
  clobber
  screw up
shoot from the hip
  go off half-cocked
shoot gravy
  shoot up
shooting gallery, "narcotics
  venue"
shooting iron
  rod
the shooting match
  the whole shebang
shoot oneself in the foot
  cut one's own throat
shoot one's load
  come
shoot one's lunch
  barf
shoot off one's mouth
  blow off
  gab
shoot on
  knock
shoot the breeze, "chat"
shoot the bull
  blow off

gab
shoot the breeze

shoot the crap
blow off
shoot the breeze

shoot the works
bust one's ass
go for it

shoot up, "inject
narcotics"

shoot one's wad
come
go for it

shopping bag lady
bum

shopping list
laundry list

short
bag
broke
deck
jalopy
snort

short arm
cock

the short end of the stick
the shaft

short heist
heist

short order
a fix

short person
shorty

short piece
bag
deck

the shorts, "lack of
money"

short time
a jiffy

short-witted
dumb

shorty, "short person"

shot
bag
big shot
a fix
kaput
knock
on the blink
plastered
pooped
snort
sock

a shot
a clip
a crack

shot down
finished

shot down in flames
kaput
out of luck

shot in the arm
pick-me-up

shot up
high

shout
stick out like a sore thumb

shouter
broad

shout up
spotlight

shove it
fuck you
kiss my ass
stick it

shovelhead
dope

shoveling the black stuff
hooked

shovel it in
pig out

shovel the shit
bullshit

shove off
split

show
show up

show a leg
get the lead out

showboat
grandstand
grandstander

shower cap
rubber

showoff
grandstander

show off
grandstand

show the gate
fire

show up
beat
blow
show up, "arrive"

shpilkes
the jitters

shriek
horse

shrimp
jerk
shorty

shrink, "psychiatrist"

shrinker
shrink

shtarker
goon

shtick
act

shtoonk
asshole

shtup
  ass
  fuck
shuck
  bluff
  bullshit
  chuck
  con
  goof off
  kid
  kid around
  wing it
shuffle
  toddle
shuffle along
  split
shuffler
  con man
shush your mouth
  shut up
shut down
  crash
shuteye
  sack time
  a snooze
shut one's face
  shut up
shut out
  clobber
shut up, "command to stop
    talking"
shut up, "stop talking"
shut up shop
  knock off
shuzit
  pot
shvantz
  cock
shylock
  loan shark

shyster
  asshole
  con man
  shyster, "lawyer"
sick
  crazy
  weird
  yucky
sick as a dog
  green around the gills
sickie
  nut
  oddball
sick in the head
  crazy
sicko
  crazy
  nut
  oddball
  weird
  yucky
sick of
  fed-up
sickroom
  weird
sicksicksick
  crazy
  weird
  yucky
sick up
  barf
sidekick
  pal
side-splitter
  belly laugh
  a howl
sidestep
  weasel
sidetrack
  bust
sidewalk susie
  hooker

sidewheeler
  southpaw
sidewinder
  goon
sight
  scarecrow
sign in
  show up
sign off
  shut up
sign off on
  buy
sigoggling
  cockeyed
silk
  whitey
silk-stocking
  classy
Silly Billy
  ditz
simmer
  blow one's top
simmer down
  cool it
simoleons
  buck
  dough
simon-pure
  honest-to-God
simp
  dope
  jerk
simple as ABC
  easy as pie
since Hector was a pup
  ages
sing
  open one's yap
  squeal
  warble

sing another tune
  come down a peg

singer
  snitch

singing
  high

singing the blues
  down

single
  buck

single out
  zero in

sing out
  open one's yap
  squeal

sink
  clobber
  screw up

sinsemilla
  pot

sip
  blow grass

sis
  broad
  sissy

sissified
  chicken
  wimpish

sissy
  broad
  chicken
  gay
  sissy, "effeminate male"

sissy-pants
  sissy

sister
  blood
  broad
  M

sit in the catbird seat
  eat high on the hog

sit on one's hands
  goof off

sit pretty
  eat high on the hog

sit still for
  buy

sit tight
  hide out
  sit tight, "remain in place"
  sit tight, "wait"

sitting duck
  patsy

sitting pretty
  eat high on the hog
  in the driver's seat

situation
  a fix

Siwash
  cow college

six feet up a bull's ass
  loaded

sixgun
  rod

six of one and half a dozen
    of the other
  standoff

sixteenth
  bag

six ways to Sunday
  cockeyed
  flat-out

size up
  check out

sizzle
  blow one's top
  fry

SK
  hick

skag
  butt

jerk
  scarecrow

skank
  hooker
  scarecrow

skanky
  yucky

skate
  goof off
  split

skedaddle
  break out
  split

skeezer
  broad
  hooker

skell
  bum

skewgee
  cockeyed
  fucked-up
  half-assed

skid
  horse

skiddoo
  split

Skid Row bum
  bum

skillet
  nigger

skimble-skamble
  fucked-up

skin
  beat
  buck
  cheesecake
  clobber
  con
  rubber

skin alive
  blast
  clobber

fix someone
kick ass

skin along
barrel

skinch
smidgen

skin-diver
cocksucker

skin flick
blue movie

skinflint
chintzy

skin flute
cock

skin game
scam

skinhead
baldie

skin lesion
zit

skinner
con man

skinning
scam

the skinny
the poop
the straight dope

skinny down
shave

skin out
break out
split

skin pop
a fix
shoot up

skins
dough

skin-search
frisk

skint
broke

skin through
get by

skip
break out
cut
give a miss
split

skip out on
walk out on

skipper
boss

Skipper
Jack

skirt
broad

skirt-chaser
ladies' man
stud

ski-trip
a fix

skivvies
undies

skoofus
joint

skookum
great

skosh
smidgen

skullduggery
dirty tricks
monkey business

skunk
asshole
beat
clobber
scarecrow

skunk out of
con

skygodlin
cockeyed

sky out
split

sky rockets
bennies

sky rug
rug

sky up
split

sky-west
fucked-up

slab
buck

slack
goof off

slacker
goof-off

slag
bad-mouth
horse
knock

slam
bad-mouth
do
knock
sock

the slam
the slammer

slam-bang
half-assed
rootin'-tootin'

the slammer, "jail"

slanging match
hassle

slant
the once-over

slant-eye
gook

slant-eyes
Chink

slap
  knock
  smack

slap and tickle
  grab-ass

slap-bang
  smack

slapdash
  half-assed

slap five
  give five

slap-happy
  punch-drunk

slap in the face
  knock

slap on
  on the nose

slash
  broad
  dish

slash-and-gash film
  chiller

slasher
  chiller
  kid

slaughter them
  go over with a bang

slay
  break someone up
  clobber
  wow

sleaze
  bum
  crap
  sleazebag

sleazeball
  asshole
  sleazebag
  yucky

sleazy
  dirty
  yucky

sled
  bike

sleep
  coke
  sack time
  sleep around, "be sexually
    promiscuous"
  snooze
  a snooze

sleep around
  swing

sleeper
  doll
  horse
  long shot

sleep with someone
  fuck

Sleepy Town
  Philly

sleighrider
  junkie

sleighriding
  high

sleuthhound
  dick

slewed
  plastered

slice
  bite
  piece

slice-and-dice film
  chiller

slice of the melon
  piece

slick
  great

slick chick
  dish

slicker
  con
  con man
  dude
  smoothie
  snow

slicker game
  scam

slick up
  doll up

slide
  split

slim
  butt

slimeball
  sleazebag

sling the bull
  blow off
  bullshit

slinky
  sexy

slip
  kick in

slip someone
  stake someone to

slip a cog
  crack up
  goof

slip one's cable
  croak

slipper
  clean up one's act
  go straight

slip the info
  fill someone in

slip one's trolley
  go crazy

slip-up
  boner
  glitch

slit
  cunt
slob
  butterfingers
  fuck-up
  jerk
  lightweight
  loser
  sleazebag
slonchwise
  cockeyed
slop
  corn
slop chute
  asshole
slope
  gook
  split
slope-out
  cinch
sloppy
  corny
  fucked-up
  half-assed
sloppy Joe's
  greasy spoon
sloshed
  plastered
slot
  cunt
slow coach
  dope
sludge
  goo
sludgeball
  sleazebag
sluff
  goof off
sluff course
  gut course

slug
  clobber
  snort
  sock
a slug
  a clip
slug down
  guzzle
slugfest
  donnybrook
slugged
  plastered
slug it out
  hassle
slug-nutty
  punch-drunk
slurp
  blow
  guzzle
  snort
slurpy
  great
slush
  corn
slushy
  corny
slut's wool
  dust bunny
slutty
  sexy
smack
  horse
  pow
  smack, "exactly"
  sock
a smack
  a clip
  a crack
smack dab
  smack

smacker
  buck
smackhead
  junkie
smacko
  pow
smack up
  total
small
  little bitty
small amount
  smidgen
small beer
  chicken feed
  chickenshit
small-beer
  bush
  piddly
small change
  chicken feed
  chickenshit
  piddly
small potatoes
  chicken feed
  chickenshit
  lightweight
small-time
  bush
  piddly
the small time
  the bush leagues
small-timer
  lightweight
small town
  jerk town
smart aleck
  smart-ass
smart-alecky
  cheeky
  smart-ass

smart-ass
  cheeky
  smart-ass, "impudent"
  smart-ass, "impudent
    person"
smarten
  fill someone in
smarten up
  brush up
  fill someone in
  wise up
  the smart money, "wise
    prediction"
smart piece
  a country mile
smarts, "intelligence"
the smart set
  the upper crust
a smart spell
  ages
smarty
  smart-ass
smartypants
  smart-ass
smash
  crash
  hash
  a hit
  sock
smashed
  high
  plastered
smashing
  great
smash mouth
  neck
smashup
  crash
smash up
  total

smear
  beat
  clobber
  sock
the smear
  the whole shebang
smeck
  horse
smecker
  junkie
smell
  suck
smeller
  schnozz
smitch
  smidgen
smoke
  barrel
  blow one's top
  bullshit
  butt
  clobber
  dope
  nigger
  plug
  pot
  a smoke, "act of smoking"
smoke and joke
  goof off
smoke and mirrors
  razzle-dazzle
smoke marijuana
  blow grass
smoke out, "discover"
Smokey the Bear
  cop
the smoky seat
  the chair
smolder
  blow one's top

smooch
  heist
  neck
smooth
  great
smoothie
  dude
  hunk
  ladies' man
  smoothie, "sophisticated
    person"
smother
  clobber
smuck
  con
  fuck
snaffle
  heist
snafu
  boner
  fucked-up
  on the blink
  screw up
  snafu, "confusion"
snag
  catch
  grab
snake
  floozy
  scarecrow
snakebit
  kaput
snake-bitten
  kaput
snake poison
  panther piss
snap
  cinch
  clout
  go crazy
  pizzazz

snap one's cookies
barf

snap it up
get the lead out

snapper
dish
punch line

snappers
choppers

snappy
full of piss and vinegar
snappy, "stylish"
zingy

snap to it
get the lead out

snarf
jerk

snarky
feisty

snarl up
screw up

snatch
broad
cunt
heist

snatch defeat from the jaws
of victory
cut one's own throat

snazz
swank

snazz up
doll up

snazzy
classy
great
snappy

sneaks
sneakers

sniff
snort

sniff out
smoke out

sniffy
snooty

snifter
snort

snipe
butt

snit
swivet

snitch
heist
snitch, "informer"
squeal

snitzy
classy

snobbish
snooty

snooker
con
snow

snooks
honey

snookums
honey

snoop
kibitzer

snoot
cut
give the cold shoulder
schnozz

snooty, "snobbish"

snooze, "sleep"

a snooze, "sleep"

snop
pot

snorbs
tits

snorf
scarf

snort
coke
snort, "drink"
snort, "inhalation"

snorter
a hit
humdinger

snotnose
kid
rookie
young squirt

snottiness
chutzpa

snotty
cheeky
snooty

snout
schnozz

snow
coke
horse
snow, "deceive"

snowball
bulldoze
coke

a snowball's chance in hell
a fat chance

snowbird
junkie

snowed
high

snowed under
up to one's ass

snow flakes
coke

snow job
line
scam
snow

snowmobile
snort

snozzle
 schnozz
 snort

snozzled
 plastered

the snozzlewobblies
 the shakes

snub
 the cold shoulder
 cut
 give the cold shoulder

snubby
 rod

snuff
 buck
 clobber
 snuff, "kill"

snuff film
 chiller

snuff out
 clobber
 snuff

snuffy
 plastered

snug
 rod

snuggy
 dish

snurge
 goof off

soak
 binge
 lush
 sock

soaked
 plastered

so-and-so
 asshole
 blankety-blank

soap
 lude

soap opera
 soft soap

S O B
 asshole

sob story
 tear-jerker

sob stuff
 corn
 tear-jerker

social club
 blind pig

social prestige
 classy

sock
 blast
 clobber
 clout
 knock
 sock, "punch" (*v* and *n*)

sock away
 stash

sockeroo
 a hit
 humdinger

sock it to
 blast
 fix someone

sock line
 punch line

socko
 great
 pow

sodbuster
 hick

sodomize
 bugger

sod you
 fuck you
 kiss my ass

soft
 dumb
 easy as pie

soft-ass
 wimpish

softball
 bush
 doll
 piddly

softie, "compliant person"

soft in the head
 dumb

soft-pedal, "de-emphasize"

soft soap
 soft soap, "flattery"
 stroke

soft-soap, "flatter"

soft touch
 softie

softy
 sissy

sol
 cooler

S O L
 kaput
 out of luck

solar plexus
 belly

soldier
 buck private
 button man
 gangster
 goof off

sole
 hash

solid
 great
 honest-to-God
 with it

some
 a hell of a

some skin
  mitt

something
  humdinger

something else
  great
  a hit
  humdinger
  the most

something fierce
  flat-out
  like hell

something in the sock
  case dough

something on the ball
  smarts

something screwy
  glitch

something to write home
      about
  a hit
  humdinger

song
  line

song and dance
  flack
  line

son lo tar
  big O

son of a bee
  guy

son of a bitch
  asshole
  back-breaker
  a bitch
  guy

son of a gun
  guy

son of one
  hash

sophisticated person
  smoothie

soppy
  corny

sore
  pissed off

sorehead
  kvetch

soreheaded
  feisty

sorry
  half-assed

a sort of a
  bush

sort out
  fix up
  spell out
  work out

so-so
  bush

so's your old man
  fuck you

sot
  lush

soul brother
  blood

soul kiss
  French kiss

soul sister
  blood

sound
  the bird
  bug

sound off
  gab
  shoot the breeze

sound the horn
  honk

soupbone
  wing

souped-up
  jazzed-up

souped-up job
  hot rod

soupy
  corny

sourpuss
  kvetch
  scarecrow

souse
  guzzle
  lush

soused
  plastered

Southerner
  cracker

south of the border
  kaput
  schlocky

southpaw, "left-handed
      person"

south side
  ass

so what else is new
  so what
  **that's the way the cookie
      crumbles**

sozzled
  plastered

space bandit
  flack

space cadet
  junkie
  nut
  oddball

spaced
  high
  in a fog

spaced out
  crazy

  in a fog

space-out
  nut
  oddball

spacey
  high
  in a fog

spade
  nigger

spaghetti
  wop

spang
  smack

Spanish athlete
  bigmouth

spank
  tan

spanking
  great

spar
  hassle

spare tire
  potbelly
  spare tire, "fat waist"

sparkle plenties
  bennies

spark plug
  eager beaver

spastic
  dope
  dumb
  oddball

spat
  hassle

spazz
  dope
  dumb
  oddball

spazzy
  dumb
  weird

speak
  open one's yap

speakeasy
  blind pig

speak for itself
  stick out like a sore thumb

speak nonsense
  bullshit

spear-carrier
  gofer

specimen
  cookie

speck bum
  bum

speckled birds
  bennies

specs, "eyeglasses"

speed
  barrel
  bennies
  lickety-split

speedball
  coke
  junkie

spell out, "explain"

spend extravagantly
  blow

spicy
  dirty

spiel
  flack
  gab
  line

spieler
  blabbermouth

spiff
  swank

spiffed
  plastered

spiff up
  doll up

spiffy
  classy
  great

spike
  scrub
  works

spiked
  high

spike up
  shoot up

spill
  blow
  lay it on the line

spill one's guts
  blow
  lay it on the line
  let it all hang out
  squeal

spill the beans
  squeal

spinach
  bullshit
  crap

spin one's wheels
  goof off

spit
  zilch

spit and image
  double

spitball
  knock

spit it out
  let it all hang out

spit tacks
  blow one's top
  make a scene

spitting image
  double
spiv
  moocher
spizzerinctum
  guts
  pizzazz
splash
  bennies
  high
  shoot up
splashy
  glitzy
splice the main brace
  guzzle
splint
  joint
split
  bite
  break out
  split, "depart"
split a gut
  break up
  bust one's ass
split hairs
  nit-pick
split some buns
  bugger
split the scene
  split
splivins
  bennies
splurgy
  glitzy
spoil
  screw up
  snuff
spoiling
  antsy
spondulics
  dough

sponge
  lush
  moocher
spoof
  kid
  snow
  spoof, "lampoon"
a spoof
  a put-on
spook
  nigger
  oddball
  scare the shit out of
  spook, "frighten"
spooked
  scared shitless
spoon
  bag
  deck
  neck
  works
spoony
  ditz
sport
  bingle
  Blind Tom
  bug
  chapter
  dude
  guy
  Jack
  ladies' man
  playboy
  stanza
sporting house
  whorehouse
sporting proposition
  a gamble
sports
  homer
  jock
sports official
  Blind Tom

spot
  bind
  bit
  dive
  snort
  zero in
spot someone
  stake someone to
spot as
  peg
spotlight
  spotlight, "emphasize"
  zero in
spouter
  blabbermouth
spout off
  blow off
  gab
spread
  a feed
  fuck
spread oneself
  bust one's ass
spread it on thick
  bullshit
  soft-soap
spree
  binge
springbutt
  eager beaver
spring for
  pick up the tab
sprout
  kid
sproutsy
  flaky
sprout wings
  clean up one's act
spruce up
  doll up

sprung
  high
  plastered
spudge around
  get on the ball
  get the lead out
spunk
  clout
  come
  cum
  guts
  pizzazz
spunky
  gutsy
spurt
  come
squab
  broad
square
  on the level
  smack
  square, "conformist"
  square, "conformistic"
  straight
square accounts
  get even
square apple
  straight
square deal, "fair
    treatment"
square dealer
  good guy
squarehead
  kraut
square John
  good guy
  Joe Blow
square joint
  butt
square one
  it's a new ball game

square peg
  excess baggage
square shooter
  good guy
squaresville
  square
squat
  pad
  shit
  zilch
a squat
  a shit
squat hot
  fry
squaw
  broad
  old woman
squawk
  beef
  snitch
  squeal
squawk box
  bitch box
squeak by
  get by
squeaker
  cliffhanger
  snitch
squeak through
  get by
squeaky clean
  clean
  square
squeal
  snitch
  squeal, "tattle"
squeal like a stuck
    pig
  beef

squeeze
  scrunch
squeezebox, "accordion"
squiffed
  plastered
squiffy-eyed
  plastered
squint
  the once-over
squirrel
  acid
  banger
  cunt
  nut
  oddball
  stash
squirrel away
  stash
squirrel-food
  nut
squirrely
  crazy
  flaky
squirt
  guy
  jerk
  kid
  shorty
  young squirt
  zilch
squish
  softie
squishy
  corny
a stab
  a crack
stabber
  works
stack
  joint
  rig

455

stack asses
  kick ass

stacked
  built

stack some Zs
  snooze

stack the cards
  play dirty
  rig

stack up
  figure
  rack up
  total

stage a walkout
  walk

staggerer
  a hit

stake
  case dough

staker
  angel

stake someone to, "give"

stall around
  goof off
  stall

stallion
  dish
  stud

stand
  set someone back

stand someone
  stake someone to

stand behind
  back
  go to bat for

stand for it
  take it

stand one's ground
  sit tight

standoff, "deadlock"

standoffish
  snooty

standout
  a hit

stand pat
  sit tight

stand still for
  buy
  eat up
  play ball

stand the gaff
  hang tough
  take it

stand-up
  gutsy

stand up and be counted
  take it

stand up and take it
  bite the bullet

stand up for
  go to bat for

stand up to
  take on

stanza
  chapter
  **stanza, "division of a
    game"**

star
  ace

starch
  clout
  pizzazz

starchy
  full of piss and vinegar

star dust
  angel dust

stare
  rubberneck

stare one in the face
  stick out like a sore thumb

star-fucker
  groupie

starker
  goon

starkers
  bare-ass

start from scratch
  go back to square one

stash
  bag
  park
  stash, "conceal"

stash away
  stash

state
  swivet

state of the art
  with it

the state pen
  the slammer

static
  flak

stats
  the book

stay loose
  cool it

stay put
  sit tight

stay the course
  take it

steal
  heist

steam
  blow one's top
  clout
  piss someone off
  pizzazz

steamed
  horny
  pissed off

steamed up
  antsy
  pissed off

steamroller
  bulldoze
  clobber

steamy
  dirty
  sexy

steer
  tip

steerer
  shill

stem
  works

stems
  pins

stemwinder
  eager beaver
  humdinger

stemwinding
  high-powered

stencil
  joint

step on one's dick
  fuck up
  goof

step on it
  barrel
  fuck up
  get the lead out

step on the gas
  barrel

step out on someone
  cheat

stepped-up job
  hot rod

step up
  hike

stern
  ass

Stetson
  lid

stew
  binge
  blow one's top
  blowup
  flak
  lush
  piss-off
  snafu
  sweat
  swivet

stewbum
  bum
  lush

stewed
  plastered

stick
  beanpole
  con
  fogy
  hang tough
  jerk
  joint
  shill

stick country
  the boondocks

stick for
  bum

stick in the mud
  fogy

stick in there
  hang tough

stick it
  fuck you
  kiss my ass
  stick it, "expression of defiance"

stick it out
  hang tough
  take it

stick it to
  fix someone

hold someone's feet to the
  fire

stick man
  cop

stick one's neck out, "risk"

stick one's nose into
  butt in

stick of tea
  joint

stick out a mile
  stick out like a sore thumb

sticks
  pins

the sticks
  the boondocks

stick to one's guns
  sit tight

stick to one's knitting, "not meddle"

stick to your knitting
  lay off

stickum
  goo

stickup
  heist

stick up for
  back
  go to bat for

stickup man
  heist man

stick with it
  take it

sticky
  corny
  hairy

sticky-fingered, "thievish"

sticky wicket
  bad news
  bind

stiff
  bum
  bust
  con
  flop
  fuck
  guy
  jerk
  phony
  plastered
  rough up
  stiff, "corpse"
  working stiff
stiff-arm
  rough up
stiffen
  knock out
stiffneck
  mule
stiffnecked
  bullheaded
stiff one
  hard-on
stimulant
  pick-me-up
sting
  con
  heist
  scam
stinger
  catch
  con man
stingy
  chintzy
stink
  beef
  flak
  suck
stinker
  asshole
stinking
  crummy

damn
  loaded
  plastered
  yucky
stinking drunk
  plastered
stinking rich
  loaded
stinking with
  filthy with
stink-list
  blackball
stinko
  crummy
  plastered
stink to high heaven
  suck
stinkweed
  pot
the stir
  the slammer
stir around
  get on the ball
stir bird
  con
stir-bugs
  stir-crazy
stir one's stumps
  get the lead out
a stitch
  a howl
  a laugh
stitched
  plastered
stoked
  tickled
stoke up
  scarf
stoking
  great

stomach
  belly
  potbelly
stomach Steinway
  squeezebox
stomp
  clobber
  rough up
stompass
  tough
stompers
  boondockers
stone
  fucking
  honest-to-God
  stone, "totally"
stone broke
  broke
stoned
  high
  plastered
stone fox
  dish
stoner
  junkie
stonies
  hot pants
stony
  broke
stooge
  brown-nose
  gofer
  shill
stooge around
  stall
stool
  snitch
  squeal
stop functioning
  go kerflooey

stop talking
 shut up

stop the show
 go over with a bang

storch
 guy
 patsy

Storch
 Joe Blow

storm
 barrel

the story
 the bottom line

stow it
 fuck you
 knock off
 shut up
 stick it

STP
 bennies

strafe
 kick ass

straight
 butt
 high
 honest-to-God
 square
 straight, "heterosexual"
 straight, "heterosexual male"
 straight, "honest"
 straight, "legitimate"
 straight, "narcotics-free"

straight-arrow
 square
 straight

the straight dope, "truth"

straighten out
 blow grass
 fly right

straighten someone out
 spell out

straighten up
 fly right

straighten up and fly right
 clean up one's act
 fly right

straight face
 poker face

straight from the shoulder
 straight

the straight scoop
 the straight dope

straight-shooting
 straight

straight talk
 the straight dope

strange
 weird

strangioso
 kinky
 weird

strap
 jock

strapped
 broke
 heeled

straw
 pot

strawberry fields
 acid

streak
 barrel

street job
 hot rod

stretch
 bit

stretch one's luck
 stick one's neck out

stretch some jeans
 bugger

stretch the rules
 play dirty

strictly between us
 on the QT

strike
 sock
 walk

strike oil
 go over with a bang
 hack it

strike out
 fuck up

striker
 eager beaver

string along
 snow

string along with
 buy

string bean
 beanpole

string with
 hang out with

stripper, "strip-tease dancer"

strip-search
 frisk

strip-tease dancer
 stripper

strive
 bust one's ass

stroke
 jack off
 stroke, "flatter"
 stroke, "flattery"

stroke book
 fuck book

stroker
 hot rod

strong-arm
 bulldoze
 goon
 rough up

strong-arm man
 goon

strong-arm squad
 goon squad

strongbox
 pete

stronger than pig-shit
 high-powered

struggle
 wingding

strugglebuggy
 jalopy

strung out
 high
 hooked

stubborn as an ox
 bullheaded

stuck on oneself
 stuck-up

stuck-up
 snooty
 stuck-up, "conceited"

stud
 dude
 guy
 ladies' man
 stud, "sexually
   promiscuous male"

student
 grind
 junkie

studhammer
 ladies' man
 stud

Studley
 hunky

stuff
 ass
 booze
 broad
 coke
 cunt

dope
fuck
guts
pot

stuff oneself
 pig out

the stuff
 clout
 dough
 humdinger
 smarts

stuffed
 fed-up

stuffings
 innards

stuff it
 fuck you
 kiss my ass
 stick it

stuffy
 pissed off
 square

stuka
 bennies

stumblebum
 bum

stumbler
 doll

stump for
 go to bat for

stump it
 toddle

stump-jumper
 hick

stump liquor
 panther piss

stumps
 pins

stunner
 dish

a hit
 humdinger

stunning
 great

stupe
 dope

stupid
 dumb
 have a hole in one's head

stupid person
 dope

stupper
 doll

style
 grandstand

stylish
 snappy

stylishness
 swank

stymied
 up the creek

sub
 hero

submachine gun
 Tommy gun

submarine sandwich
 hero

subordinate
 gofer

succeed
 go over with a bang
 hack it
 work

success
 a hit

successful
 have a field day
 in

suck
 blow
 blow job

brown-nose
 clout
 snort
 suck, "be disgusting"
suck air
 panic
suck around
 brown-nose
 goof off
suck eggs
 suck
sucker
 con
 guy
 jerk
 patsy
 snow
 sucker, "thing"
suckered
 screwed
sucker game
 scam
sucker-punch
 blind-side
suck face
 neck
suck hind tit
 play second fiddle
suck-in
 scam
sucking canal water
 up the creek
suck it up
 bust one's ass
 clean up one's act
suck off
 blow
suck-off
 brown-nose
 yucky

suck rope
 suck
suck up to
 brown-nose
 play up to
suck wind
 fuck up
suction
 blow job
 clout
suds
 brew
sudser
 soap opera
suds scenario
 soap opera
suedehead
 baldie
suffering cats
 Jeez
sugar
 acid
 coke
 dough
 honey
 horse
 M
sugar-bun
 honey
sugar cube
 acid
sugar daddy
 angel
 sugar daddy, "keeper of
  mistress"
sugar stick
 cock
sugar tit
 security blanket
suicide
 do the Dutch

suit
 pro
sultry
 sexy
sumbitch
 asshole
 back-breaker
 guy
Sunday best
 glad rags
Sunday punch, "hard blow"
sunglasses
 shades
sunk
 kaput
 out of luck
sunshades
 shades
sunshine
 acid
sunshine girl
 grind
super
 great
super blow
 coke
super-duper
 great
supergopher
 good guy
super grass
 angel dust
a supergroove
 a ball
superior
 the most
super Kools
 angel dust
super soaper
 lude

support
  back

support one's claims
  put up or shut up

supremo
  pot

sure
  bet your ass
  for sure
  have it both ways

sure as shootin'
  for sure

sure bet
  cinch

sure enough
  honest-to-God
  OK

sure shot
  cinch

sure success
  have something cinched

sure thing
  cinch
  for sure
  honest-to-God
  OK

surfeit
  up to one's ass
  up to here

surfer
  angel dust

surpass
  beat

surprise
  I'll be damned

surveillance
  tail

susfu
  fucked-up

suspense
  cliffhanger

suss out
  dig
  smoke out

swabby, "sailor"

swack
  sock

swacked
  plastered

swag
  pay dirt
  score

swallow
  bite
  buy
  eat up
  snort

swallow the apple
  choke up
  freeze up

swallow whole
  bite

swallow with a glass of
      water
  clobber

swamp
  clobber

swank
  classy
  swank, "stylishness"

swank it
  doll up
  put on the ritz

swank up
  doll up

swanky
  classy

swap spit
  neck

swat
  sock

sweat
  blow one's top
  blowup
  sweat, "worry"

sweat bullets
  panic

sweat hog
  floozy
  scarecrow

sweep
  beat
  grand slam

sweet
  great

sweet baby
  broad

sweeten someone up
  soft-soap

sweet Fanny Adams
  zilch

sweetheart
  broad
  doll
  honey
  humdinger
  the McCoy

sweetie-pie
  honey

sweet Jesus
  M

sweet Mary
  pot

sweet momma
  broad

sweet Morpheus
  M

sweet patootie
  broad
  dish
  honey

sweet talk
  bullshit
  soft soap
  stroke
sweet thing
  broad
swell
  dude
  great
  swell, "aristocrat"
swelled up
  stuck-up
swell-elegant
  great
swellheaded
  stuck-up
the swells
  the upper crust
swift
  dumb
swig
  guzzle
  snort
swill
  guzzle
swim
  work
swimming in
  up to one's ass
swindle
  con
  scam
swindler
  con man
swing
  fuck
  sleep around
  swing, "be promiscuous"
swinge
  tan

swinger
  floozy
swingin'
  square
swinging both ways
  AC-DC
swing man
  dealer
swipe
  heist
  knock
  panther piss
  sock
swish
  classy
  gay
Swiss purple
  acid
switched on
  high
  with it
switch on
  goose
swivet, "angry fit"
swizzled
  plastered
swoop
  barrel
swozzled
  plastered
sycophant
  brown-nose
syrup
  horse
T
  pot
T A
  cheesecake
tab
  a fix
  M

pasteboard
peg
tab, "acknowledgment of debt"
the tab
  the damage
table finisher
  pig
table grade
  dish
tabs
  acid
  bennies
tackhead
  dope
tacky
  bush
  crummy
  schlocky
  yucky
taco
  bean-eater
tad
  smidgen
tag
  monicker
  sock
tail
  ass
  broad
  tail, "surveiller"
one's tail is dragging
  pooped
tailormade
  butt
tail peddler
  hooker
take
  buy
  clobber
  con
  pay dirt

score
take, "receipts"

take a back seat
  play second fiddle

take a bath
  fuck up
  go broke
  take a beating

take a bow
  way to go

take a brace
  clean up one's act

take a break
  kick back
  knock off

take a breather
  kick back

take a bye
  give a miss

take a chill spill
  cool it

take a crack at
  give something a shot
  plug
  take a crack at, "try"

take a crap
  shit

take action
  fish or cut bait

take a D
  do the Dutch

take a dekko at
  check out

take a dig at
  bad-mouth
  knock

take a dive
  flop
  take a dive, "lose
    intentionally"

take a douche
  split

take a dump
  shit

take a fall
  fall

take a flyer
  stick one's neck out

take a flying fuck
  fuck you

take a gander
  rubberneck

take a gander at
  check out

take a hike
  split

take a hinge at
  check out

take a leak
  piss

take a lick at
  give something a shot
  take a crack at

take a load off
  kick back

take a pop at
  plug

take a potshot at
  knock
  plug

take a powder
  break out
  split

take a power nap
  snooze

take a rain check
  give a miss

take a reading
  check out

take a riffle at
  give something a shot

take a run at
  take on

take a runout powder
  break out
  split

take a scunner at
  hate someone's guts

take a shit
  shit

take a shot at
  give something a shot

take a squint at
  check out

take a swipe at
  bad-mouth
  knock

take a walk
  lay off
  walk
  walk out on

take a whack at
  give something a shot

take a whizz
  piss

take care of
  fix someone
  snuff

take care of business
  ace

take care of number one
  take care of numero uno

take-charge guy
  eager beaver

take down a notch
  take someone down a peg

take downtown
  clobber

take fire
  work

take five
  kick back
  knock off

take for a ride
  snow
  snuff

take someone for a ride
  con

take forty winks
  snooze

take French leave
  go over the hill

take heat
  take it

take in
  snow

take into camp
  clobber

take it
  bite the bullet
  eat dirt
  hang tough
  take it, "endure"

take it all
  beat

take it easy
  cool it
  kick back
  pussyfoot

take it in the ear
  fuck you

take it on the chin
  hang tough
  take a beating
  take it

take it on the lam
  break out
  split

take it out of someone's
    hide
  tan

take it standing up
  take it

take it to the street
  go public

take one's medicine
  bite the bullet
  take it

taken
  screwed

taken to the cleaners
  screwed

takeoff
  act

take off
  heist
  shoot up
  snuff
  split
  work

take off one's hat to
  hand it to someone

take off one's high hat
  come down a peg

take on
  buck
  roust
  take on, "challenge"

take one step at a time
  pussyfoot

takeout
  bite

take out
  clobber
  snuff

take shit
  eat dirt

take one's stand
  sit tight

take ten
  kick back
  knock off

take the bait
  bite

take the cake
  beat

take the gas
  fuck up

take the heat off
  cool it

take the pipe
  choke up
  freeze up
  fuck up

take the rap
  bite the bullet
  take it

take the starch out of
  take someone down a peg

take the strop to
  tan

take the wind out of
    someone's sails
  take someone down a peg

take time out
  kick back

take to the cleaners
  clobber

take to the woodshed
  tan

tale of woe
  beef
  tear-jerker

talk
  bat around
  bigmouth
  blabbermouth
  bullshit
  chitchat
  dirt
  double-talk
  gab
  gabby
  get down to brass tacks

open one's yap
  sass
  schmooz
  shoot the breeze
  shut up
  squeal

talkative
  gabby

talk big
  blow off
  bullshit

talk someone's ear off
  gab

talkfest
  schmooz

talk someone into,
    "persuade"

talk is cheap
  put up or shut up

talk straight from the
    shoulder
  lay it on the line

talk-talk
  gab

talk through one's hat
  bullshit

talk to the big white phone
  barf

talk-trap
  yap

talk turkey
  get down to brass tacks
  lay it on the line

talk up a storm
  gab

talky
  gabby

talky-talk
  gab

tall
  high

tall person
  beanpole

the tall timbers
  the boondocks

tambourine man
  dealer

tamper
  doctor

tamper with
  fool around with

tan
  sock
  tan, "spank"

T and A
  cheesecake

tangle
  hassle

tangle-foot
  panther piss

tangle-footed
  plastered

tan someone's hide
  tan

tank
  flop
  guzzle
  rig
  take a dive

the tank
  the slammer

tanked
  plastered

tank job
  put-up job

tank town
  jerk town

tank up
  guzzle

tanky
  plastered

tantrum
  blowup

tap
  broke
  put the bite on
  shoot up

Tap City
  broke

tap dance
  cop out
  pussyfoot
  stall
  weasel

taped
  cinched
  in the bag

tap out
  flop
  go broke
  go kerflooey
  take a beating

tapped
  broke

tapped out
  broke
  kaput
  pooped

taps
  curtains

tard
  dope

tarfu
  fucked-up

the tariff
  the damage

tart
  broad

tart up
  doll up

taste
  bite
  blow grass

a fix
  piece

tater
  bingle

tater trap
  yap

tats
  crooked dice

tattle
  blow
  squeal

tatty
  bush
  crummy
  schlocky

tawny
  great

taxi fare
  ride the arm

TCB
  ace

t'd off
  pissed off

tea
  joint
  pot

tea'd up
  high

teahead
  pothead

team up
  buddy up

team up with
  hang out with

tea party
  cinch

tear
  barrel
  binge
  paint the town red

tear around
  hell around

tearing mad
  pissed off

tearing up the pea patch
  full of piss and vinegar

tear into
  blast
  chew out

tear-jerker, "sentimental
  story"

tear off a piece
  fuck

tear off a strip
  chew out

tear up the peapatch
  make a scene

teary
  corny

tease
  cock-teaser

tea-stick
  joint

tec
  dick

techie
  tech

tedious person
  jerk

tedious work
  scut work

tee'd off
  pissed off

teen
  teenybopper

teenager
  teenybopper

teentsy
  little bitty

teenybopper, "teenager"

tee someone off
  piss someone off

tee off on
  chew out

teeth
  choppers

teetotally
  stone

telephone
  give someone a ring

telephone call
  buzz

television
  the tube

tell all
  blow

tell a thing or two
  chew out

tell it like it is
  lay it on the line
  let it all hang out

tell it to the Marines
  izzatso

tell off
  chew out

tell tales out of school
  squeal

tell where to get off
  take someone down a peg

telly
  the tube

temple bells
  hash

ten
  dish

tenderfoot
  greenhorn
  rookie

ten dollars
  sawbuck

tenner
  both hands
  sawbuck

Tennessee blue
  pot

tennies
  sneakers

tens
  bag

tense up
  choke up

ten-spot
  both hands
  sawbuck

ten yards
  grand

teo
  pothead

terrific
  great

terrifying
  creepy

testicles
  balls

test the water
  run it up the flagpole

tetched
  crazy

tetchy
  crazy
  feisty
  goosy

Texas tea
  pot

Thai weed
  pot

that'll do it
  way to go

that's life
  that's the way the cookie
    crumbles

that's my boy
  way to go

that's the way the ball
    bounces
  that's the way the cookie
    crumbles

that way
  knocked up

there
  high
  with it

there's no way
  like hell

there you go
  that's the way the cookie
    crumbles

they are a dime a dozen
  the woods are full of
    something

thick
  dumb
  palsy-walsy

thickbrain
  dope

thickskull
  dope

thickskulled
  dumb

thief
  heist man

thievish
  sticky-fingered

thin
  broke

a thin dime
  zilch

thing
  bag
  joint
  sucker

a thing
  a bee in one's bonnet

the thing
  hot

thingamajig
  gadget

things come unstuck
  hell breaks loose

thin in the upper crust
  dumb

thinker
  egghead

thin-skinned
  goosy

third leg
  cock

third rail
  panther piss

third-rater
  lightweight

third-stringer
  gofer

third wheel
  excess baggage

thirteen
  joint

those in the know
  the in group

thou
  grand

thousand dollars
  grand

thrashing
  great

threads, "clothing"

three bricks shy of a load
  dumb

three-letter man
  gay

three sheets to the wind
  plastered
thrill
  high
thriller
  joint
thrill pill
  doll
throat
  grind
throne
  can
throw
  peg
a throw
  a clip
throw
  take a dive
throw a bird
  give someone the finger
throw a curve
  snow
throw someone a curve
  con
throw a fit
  blow one's top
throw a fuck into
  fuck
throw a hyper
  blow one's top
throw a pass
  proposition
throw a scare into
  scare the shit out of
throw away
  blow
  chuck
throw bouquets at
  hand it to someone

throw curves
  snow
throw in the towel
  cop out
  fold
throw in with
  buy
  hang out with
throw leather
  hassle
throw out on one's ear
  bounce
throw over
  walk out on
throw overboard
  walk out on
throw something together
  knock something out
throw the book at
  clamp down
  kick ass
throw the bull
  blow off
  bullshit
  gab
throw the hooks into
    someone
  con
thrusters
  bennies
thumb
  hitchhike
  joint
thumb down
  blackball
  nix
thumbs up
  the go-ahead
  the OK

thump
  hassle
  sock
thumping
  great
  high-powered
thunderbox radio
  ghetto box
Thunder weed
  pot
thwack
  sock
a tick
  a jiffy
ticked off
  pissed off
ticker, "heart"
the ticket
  great
ticket of admission
  pasteboard
ticket seller
  scalper
tickety-boo
  great
tickled pink
  tickled
tick someone off
  piss someone off
tickytacky
  crummy
tiddly
  plastered
tidy sum
  bundle
tie
  works
tie a can to
  fire

tied up
  in the bag
tie into
  blast
  plug into
tie off
  shoot up
tie one on
  clobber
tie one's shoes
  clean up one's act
  fly right
  get on the ball
  wise up
tie up
  shoot up
  wrap up
tiff
  hassle
tiger sweat
  panther piss
tight
  broke
  chintzy
tight as a drum
  chintzy
tight as a tick
  plastered
tight as Kelsey's nuts
  chintzy
tighten one's wig
  blow grass
the tights
  the shorts
tight spot
  bind
tightwad, "miser"
till one can taste it
  up to here
till hell freezes over
  for keeps

till one is blue in the face
  flat-out
till the cows come home
  for keeps
time
  ages
  bit
  a jiffy
time in
  show up
timidity
  chicken out
tin
  bag
  chicken feed
  deck
  dough
  tin, "police badge"
tin-can
  blackball
tingle
  high
tinhorn
  bush
  crummy
  lightweight
  piddly
tinik
  horse
tinkle
  buzz
  piss
a tinkle
  a piss
tinpot
  piddly
  schlocky
tin star
  private eye
tipoff
  tip

tipover
  rumble
tip over
  heist
tipster
  snitch
tipsy
  plastered
tip the elbow
  guzzle
tiptoe
  pussyfoot
tip-top
  great
tired
  pooped
tit art
  cheesecake
titivate
  doll up
tits
  great
  tits, "breasts"
tits and ass
  cheesecake
titties
  tits
tittle-tattle
  chitchat
  dirt
tizzy
  blowup
  flak
  swivet
TL
  brown-nose
T-man
  pothead
TNT
  horse

toad skin
  buck

toady
  brown-nose

to a fare-thee-well
  flat-out

toast
  cool
  fry
  great
  kaput

tobacco
  a smoke

to beat the band
  flat-out
  lickety-split
  like hell

toddle, "walk"

toddle off
  split

toddler
  kid

to-do
  flak
  hoopla

toe the mark
  clean up one's act
  fly right

toff
  swell

together
  cool

tog out
  doll up

togs
  threads

to hell and gone
  flat-out

toilet
  can
  check the plumbing

piss
  a piss
  shit
  a shit
  the shits

toke
  blow grass
  butt
  toke, "inhalation"

toker
  pothead

toke up
  blow grass

tokus
  ass

tokus-licker
  brown-nose

Tom
  fink

tomato
  broad
  dish

tomcat
  ladies' man

tom-cat
  stud

tom-cat around
  hell around

tomfool
  crazy

Tommy gun, "submachine gun"

tommyrot
  bullshit

tongue
  shyster

tongue job
  blow job

tongue-wag
  schmooz

tongue-wagger
  blabbermouth

tongue-wagging
  gab

too big for one's britches
  stuck-up

tooie
  doll

tool
  barrel
  cock
  grind
  patsy

toole
  doll

toolie
  tech

tool in
  show up

tools
  works

too much
  great
  the most

toot
  binge
  coke
  honk
  a kick
  snort

tootie fruity
  sissy
  wimp

tootonium
  coke

toot one's own horn
  blow off

tootsie
  broad
  honey

Tootsie Roll
  horse

tootsie-wootsies
  tootsies

toot sweet
  on the double

top
  top-kick

top brass
  the brass

top dog
  boss

top-drawer
  classy
  great

top-hat
  snooty

top-kick, "sergeant"

top-notch
  great

topple
  clobber

the tops
  great
  humdinger
  the McCoy
  the most

top sawyer
  boss

top sergeant
  dyke
  top-kick

top-shelf
  classy

topsider
  big shot
  boss

top story
  bean

torch
  joint

torch up
  blow grass

torment
  Dutch rub

torn up
  high

torpedo
  hero
  hit man
  joint

torqued
  pissed off

tosh
  bullshit

to spare
  up to here

toss
  frisk
  standoff

a toss
  a clip

toss around
  bat around

toss one's cookies
  barf

toss in the towel
  fold

toss off
  guzzle
  jack off

toss out
  fire

toss overboard
  chuck

toss up
  walk out on

toss-up
  standoff

tot
  snort

total, "wreck"

totaled
  high
  kaput

total loss
  loser

totally
  stone

totally bitchen
  great

tote
  blow grass
  cart

to the max
  as shit
  flat-out
  like hell

touch
  bum
  caper
  put the bite on

touch-and-go
  iffy

touch up
  bum
  put the bite on

touchy
  goosy
  have a hair up one's ass

tough
  goon
  great
  hairy
  tough, "severe"

tough break
  tough shit

tough grind
  back-breaker

tough guy
  goon

tough it out
  hang tough
  take it

tough luck
  tough shit

tough noogies
  tough shit

tough shit
  bad news
  one couldn't care less
  **tough shit, "expression of
    bad luck"**

tough spot
  bind

tough stuff
  bad news

tough titty
  tough shit

tout
  flack

town
  jerk town

town bike
  floozy

town pump
  floozy

track record
  the book

trade
  ass
  cruise

trade punches
  hassle

tragic magic
  horse

train
  gang bang

train with
  hang out with

traipse
  toddle

traitor
  fink

tramp
  floozy

tranqued
  high

trans
  jalopy

transport
  cart

transportation
  jalopy

trap
  night spot
  yap

trappings
  threads

trash
  bullshit
  clobber
  knock
  total

trashy
  crummy
  schlocky

travel
  floor it

travel agent
  acid
  dealer

tree-hugger
  duck-squeezer

trendy
  snappy
  trendy, "au courant"
  with it

trick
  bit

caper
  fuck
  squeal

trick out
  doll up
  fuck

tricky
  hairy

trigger
  blow grass
  hit man

trigger man
  hit man

trim
  ass
  clobber
  con
  cunt

trip
  clobber
  fall
  high

tripe
  bullshit
  crap

tripes
  guts
  innards

triple whammy
  whammy

tripped out
  high

trips
  acid

trip up
  goof

trite story
  chestnut

trivial
  piddly

trivial person
  lightweight

troll
  cruise
  dope

trot
  split

the trots
  the shits

trotters
  pins
  tootsies

trouble
  bad news
  bind
  flak
  make a scene
  up the creek

trouble and strife
  old woman

trouble-shoot
  rejigger

trounce
  clobber

truck
  crap
  split

truck along
  split

truck drivers
  bennies
  doll

truly
  honest-to-God

trumpet
  schnozz

trun
  peg

truth
  the straight dope

try
  give something a shot
  take a crack at

a try
  a crack

try out
  run it up the flagpole

TS
  tough shit

tsuris
  bad news

tub
  fatty
  jalopy

tube
  floozy
  joint

the tube, "television"

tube it
  flunk

Tubesville
  kaput

tub of lard
  fatty

tubular
  great

tuck
  chow

tuck away
  scarf

tuckered out
  pooped

tuck in
  scarf

tuck one's tail
  come down a peg

tuifu
  snafu

tum
  belly

tumble
  fall

tumble for
  buy

tumble to
  dig

tummy
  belly

tum-tum
  belly

tuna
  cunt

tuna wagon
  jalopy

tuned
  plastered

tuned in
  on someone's wavelength

tunnel
  hide out

turd
  asshole
  shit

turf
  bag

turista
  the shits

turkey
  blow grass
  coke
  dope
  flop
  jerk
  loser
  wimp

turkey-shit
  chickenshit

turkey-shoot
  cinch

turnabouts
  bennies

turn chicken
  chicken out

turn down cold
  nix

turned off
  clean
  fed-up

turned on
  cool
  flip
  high
  horny
  with it

turn in
  snooze

turn-off
  gloomy Gus

turn off someone's water
  take someone down a peg

turn on
  blow grass
  goose

turn someone on
  wow

turn on the afterburners
  barrel

turn on the heat
  come on strong

turnout
  threads

turn out
  bounce

turn purple
  blow one's top

turn the cold shoulder
  cut
  give the cold shoulder

turn the trick
  hack it

turn thumbs down
  blackball
  nix

turn tricks
  hustle

turn up
  show up

turn up one's nose
  give the cold shoulder

turn up one's toes
  croak

turn yellow
  chicken out

tush
  ass

tusker
  scarecrow

tusks
  choppers

tussle
  free-for-all

twat
  ass
  cunt

tweenager
  teenybopper

twenty-five
  acid

twerp
  jerk

twiddle-twaddle
  bullshit

twig
  dig

twimble
  dope

twink
  oddball

a twink
  a jiffy

a twinkling
  a jiffy

twist
  broad
  joint

twist someone's arm
  lean on someone
  talk someone into

twisted
  high

twister
  binge
  pothead

twisty
  sexy

twit
  jerk

two-bagger
  scarecrow

two-bit
  bush
  crummy
  piddly
  schlocky

two-by-four
  little bitty
  piddly

two-fisted
  he-man

two hoops and a holler
  a jiffy

two hoots in hell
  zilch

two shakes of a lamb's tail
  a jiffy

two-time
  cheat
  double cross

two-timer
  con man

two-way hit
  acid

two whoops in hell
  zilch

typewriter
  Tommy gun

U
  collitch

U B B
  bet your ass

ugh
  yuck

ugly
  piss-ugly

ugly customer
  cowboy
  goon

ugly person
  scarecrow

uh uh
  nope

ump
  Blind Tom

umph
  clout

umptieth
  umpty-umpth

unadorned
  vanilla

uncertain
  iffy

unchangeable
  carved in stone

uncle
  cop
  M

Uncle Sugar
  Uncle Sam

Uncle Tom
  fink

unconscious
  knock out
  out

uncool
  square

undercover man
  dick

under one's hat
  on the QT

underpinnings
  pins

under the gun
  up the creek

under the influence
  plastered

under the table
  plastered

under the weather
  green around the gills
  off one's feed

underwear
  long johns
  undies

under wraps
  on the QT

undesired persons
  shit list

undies, "underwear"

unethical practice
  play dirty

unfair treatment
  the shaft

unfortunate
  out of luck

ungodly
  crummy

unhep
  square

unholy mess
  bind
  snafu

unidentified person
  what's-his-name

unidentified things
  glob
  goo
  Mickey Finn
  mish-mash
  mung
  sucker
  umpty-umpth

uninhibited
  let oneself go

unintelligible language
  double-talk

unkink
  kick back

unkjay
  crap
  junkie

unlax
  kick back

unlikely winner
  long shot

unload
  chuck
  let it all hang out

unmentionables
  undies

unnecessary person
  excess baggage

unreal
  great

unrestrainedly
  flat-out

untogether
  fucked-up

unwind
  kick back

up
  high

hike
a kick

up against it
hooked
out of luck
up the creek

up against the wall
fuck you

up-and-up
honest-to-God
straight

upchuck
barf

up front
straight

up front, "in advance"

up gefucked
fucked-up

uphills
crooked dice

upmarket
classy

upper
a kick

the upper crust,
  "aristocracy"

upper-cruster
swell

upper-crusty
classy

uppers
bennies

upper story
bean

uppity
snooty
stuck-up

ups
bennies

upscale
classy
great

up shit creek
up the creek

upstage
give the cold shoulder

upstairs, "mentally"

up stakes
split

up the creek, "in trouble"

up the kazoo
up to here

up the river
in stir

up the spout
kaput

up the wall
crazy

uptick
hike

uptight
jittery

up to one's ass, "surfeited"

up-to-datey
trendy

up to here
fed-up
up to one's ass
up to here, "surfeited"

up to here with
filthy with

up to scratch
cool

up to snuff
cool

up to the ears
plastered

up to the eyeballs
filthy with
plastered
up to here

up to the gills
plastered

up to the mark
cool

uptown
coke

up yours
fuck you
kiss my ass

urinate
piss

urination
a piss

urp
barf

use
do

use one's bean
wise up

useless reward
win the porcelain hairnet

use smoke and mirrors
snow

US Government
Uncle Sam

usurer
loan shark

utility infielder
gofer

vagrant
bum

vamoose
break out
split

vamp
bluff

clobber
  wing it

vamp till ready
  wing it

vanilla
  straight
  vanilla, "unadorned"
  whitey

varmint
  bad man

varnish remover
  panther piss

varoom
  barrel

varsity
  collitch

va-va-voom
  sexy

veg
  goof off

vegetable
  dope

vegetable garden
  fruit salad

veg out
  goof off

vehicle
  banger
  bike

vein shooter
  junkie

velvet
  gravy
  pay dirt

the veritable cack
  the straight dope

verse
  stanza

vert
  oddball

very
  as shit

vestpocket
  little bitty

vet
  check out
  jalopy

vetting
  the once-over

vials
  acid

vibrations
  vibes

vic
  con
  patsy

vicious
  great

victim
  patsy

victory
  grand slam

video
  the tube

viewpoint
  where one is at

villain
  bad man

vinegar-puss
  scarecrow

vines
  threads

VIP
  big shot

viper
  dealer

viper weed
  pot

virgin
  cherry

virginity
  pop someone's cherry

virtuous person
  goody-goody

viscera
  guts
  innards

viscous fluid
  goo

visit
  schmooz

vittles
  chow

vomit
  barf

vomity
  yucky

vonce
  joint

voomy
  sexy

vote for
  go for

vroom
  barrel

vulnerable arm
  glass arm

vulnerable chin
  glass jaw

vulva
  cunt

wacko
  crazy
  flaky
  oddball
  weird

wacky
  crazy
  flaky
  weird

wacky weed
  pot

wad
  bundle

wade into
  blast
  chew out

waffle
  clobber
  cop out
  stall
  weasel

wafflestompers
  boondockers

wagering
  crooked dice
  make a killing

wag the tongue
  gab
  shoot the breeze

Wahegan
  pot

wail
  warble

wailing
  great

wait
  sit tight

wake-ups
  bennies

walk
  toddle
  **walk, "discontinue
    something"**
  walk, "strike"

walkaway
  cinch

walkboy
  pal

walk cool
  kick back

walk heavy
  carry a lot of weight

one's walking papers
  the axe

walk on eggs
  pussyfoot

walk out
  walk

walk out on, "abandon"

walkover
  cinch

walk the straight and
    narrow
  go straight

wall banger
  lude

wallop
  clobber
  clout
  a kick
  sock

walloping
  monster

wall-to-wall
  stone

walrus
  fatty

waltz
  chapter
  cinch
  stanza
  toddle

waltz off
  split

waltz out on
  walk out on

walyo
  guy
  wop

wamper-jawed
  cockeyed

wampum
  dough

wang
  cock

wank off
  jack off

want list
  laundry list

warble
  open one's yap
  warble, "sing"

warm body, "any person"

warm someone's ear
  gab

warmed-over cabbage
  chestnut

warm fuzzies
  stroke

warm man
  moneybags

warm someone's seat
  tan

warning
  jiggers
  lay off

warp out
  split

warts and all
  the straight dope

wash
  figure
  standoff

washed up
  kaput

washout
  flop

wash out
  flop
  go broke
  scrub

washtub weeper
  soap opera

wash-up
  crash

waste
  blow grass
  clobber
  snuff
  total

wastebasket
  the circular file

wasted
  broke
  high
  kaput

watering hole
  dive
  gin mill

watermelonhead
  dope

wax
  blowup
  clobber
  swivet

waxed
  plastered

waxy
  pissed off

way out
  cool
  great
  high
  weird

way to go, "congratulation"

way to hell and gone
  a country mile

wazoo
  ass
  asshole

weak
  wimpish

weak in the head
  dumb

weak-kneed
  chicken

weakling
  wimp

weak sister
  chicken
  sissy
  wimp

wealth
  bundle

wealthy
  loaded

wealthy person
  moneybags

weapons
  carry
  rod

wearing her apron high
  knocked up

wear the pants
  boss

weary Willy
  bum

weasel
  snitch
  squeal
  weasel, "evade"

weasel out
  back out
  cop out

web-foot
  duck-squeezer

wedding bells
  acid

wedges
  acid

wee bit
  smidgen

weed
  butt
  joint
  pot

weedhead
  junkie
  pothead

weeds
  threads

ween
  grind

weenchy
  little bitty

weenie
  cock
  grind
  jerk

weentsy
  little bitty

weeper
  tear-jerker

weewaw
  cockeyed

wee-wee
  piss

weigh in
  butt in
  show up

weigh in with
  kick in

weinie
  cock

weird
  cool
  crazy
  flaky
  great
  kinky
  weird, "strange"

weirded out
  high

weirdo
  nut
  oddball
  sleazebag
welcome to the club
  that's the way the cookie
    crumbles
well-built
  built
well-endowed
  hung
well-heeled
  loaded
well-hung
  hung
well-upholstered
  built
welsh
  back out
wench
  broad
West Coast turnabouts
  bennies
wet blanket
  drag
  gloomy Gus
wet-nose
  rookie
wetware
  bean
wet one's whistle
  guzzle
whack
  bite
  pow
  sock
a whack
  a clip
  a crack
whacking
  monster

whack off
  jack off
whack wack
  angel dust
whale
  ace
  blast
  bruiser
  clobber
  fatty
  tan
whale into
  blast
wham
  pow
  sock
wham-bam thank you
    ma'am
  quickie
whambang
  monster
  pow
whammo
  pow
whammy, "curse"
whang
  sock
whatchamacallit
  gadget
what cooks
  what's up
what do you say
  what's up
what do you want from me
  one couldn't care less
what else is new
  so what
what gives
  what's up

what goes around comes
    around
  that's the way the cookie
    crumbles
what it takes
  clout
  smarts
what say
  what's up
what's cooking
  what's up
what's happening
  what's up
what's-his-face
  what's-his-name
whatsit
  gadget
what's the good word
  what's up
what turns you on
  kicks
wheat
  pot
wheel
  big shot
wheeler-dealer, "busy
    person"
wheels
  jalopy
  pins
when push comes to shove
  when the chips are down
when the eagle shits
  eagle day
where one's head is at
  where one is at
where one is coming from
  where one is at
where it's at
  the straight dope

where the rubber meets the
    road
the bottom line

where the sun doesn't shine
asshole

wherewithal
dough

whiff
coke
fuck up
snort

whip out
give five
whomp up

whip-out
dough

whipped
high
kaput
pussy-whipped

whipsaw
clobber

whip the dog
goof off

whistle-blower
snitch

whistle stop
jerk town

whistle tooter
Blind Tom

white
coke

whitebread
square

white buck
white shoe

white death
coke
M

white horse
coke

white knuckle
cliffhanger

white-knuckled
scared shitless

white lady
coke

white lightning
acid
panther piss

white linen
M

white meat
whitey

white merchandise
M

white mosquito
coke

white mule
panther piss

white nurse
horse
M

white Owsley's
acid

white paste
coke

white person
whitey

white powder
coke
M

whites
bennies

white Sandoz
acid

white shoe
Joe College
white shoe, "college
    student"

white silk
M

white stuff
coke
horse
M

white tape
coke
M

white tornado
coke

white trash
cracker

whitewash
clobber

whitey, "white person"

whiz
ace
hot shot
humdinger

whiz-bitch
back-breaker

whiz kid
ace
hot shot

whizz
piss

the whole ball of wax
the whole shebang

the whole enchilada
the whole shebang

the whole hog
flat-out

the whole kit and caboodle
the whole shebang

the whole megillah
the whole shebang

the whole nine yards
flat-out
the whole shebang

the whole schmear
the whole shebang

the whole shooting match
  the whole shebang

the whole show
  the whole shebang

the whole story
  the straight dope

the whole works
  the whole shebang

whomp
  clobber
  sock

whomp up
  cook up
  knock something out
  rustle up
  whomp up, "devise"

a whoop
  zilch

whoopdedoo
  wingding

whooper-dooper
  binge

whoop it up
  have a ball
  hell around

whoopla
  flack

whoops
  barf
  boner

whoozis
  gadget
  what's-his-name

whop
  clobber
  sock

a whop
  a crack

whopper-jawed
  cockeyed

whopping
  monster

whore
  floozy

whore around
  hell around

whorehouse, "brothel"

who you kidding
  izzatso

whup
  clobber

Wichita
  double cross

wicked
  great
  hairy

wide open
  flat-out
  lickety-split

wide place in the road
  jerk town

widget
  gadget

wienie
  cock

wife
  old woman

wig
  dig
  flip
  great
  rug

wigged out
  high
  weird

wiggle out
  back out

wiggy
  cool
  great

high
weird

wig out
  crack up
  flip
  go crazy

wild
  antsy
  cool
  great

wild-ass
  crazy

wild cat
  panther piss

wild weed
  pot

the willies
  the jitters

wimp
  chicken
  jerk
  wimp, "weakling"

wimpish, "weak"

wimpy
  wimpish

the wim-wams
  the jitters

win a few lose a few
  that's the way the cookie
    crumbles

windbag
  bigmouth
  blabbermouth

windbox
  squeezebox

wind down
  kick back

windjammer
  bigmouth
  blabbermouth

windows
  specs

wind up
  wrap up

windy
  gabby

wing
  bluff
  wing, "arm"
  wingding
  wing it

wingding
  binge
  swivet
  wingding, "party"

winging
  in the groove

wing it
  bluff
  wing it, "improvise"

wings
  coke
  M

wing-wang
  asshole

wingy
  high

wink
  a snooze

a wink
  a jiffy

winkie
  asshole

winkle out
  smoke out

winks
  sack time

winner
  a hit
  hot shot

humdinger
  long shot

wino
  bum
  lush

win one's wings
  go through the mill

win out
  hack it

winter rat
  jalopy

winter underwear
  long johns

win the fur-lined bathtub
  win the porcelain hairnet

wipe someone's ass
  brown-nose

wiped
  plastered

wiped out
  broke
  high
  kaput
  plastered

wipe one's nose
  fly right
  go straight

wipe out
  clobber
  fix someone
  fuck up
  screw up
  snuff
  total

wipe-out
  grand slam
  loser

wipe the slate clean
  go back to square one

wipe up the floor with
  clobber

wire
  heist man

wired
  antsy
  cinched
  high
  in the bag
  jittery

wired into
  into

wired job
  put-up job

wired up
  cinched
  in the bag

wire-puller
  wheeler-dealer

wise
  smart-ass
  with it

wise-ass
  cheeky
  smart-ass

wisecrack
  crack
  kid

wise guy
  smart-ass

wise-guy
  cheeky

wise me up, "request for information"

the wise money
  the smart money

wisenheimer
  smart-ass

wise prediction
  the smart money

wise to
  have someone's number

wise up
fill someone in
wise up, "become aware"

wish list
laundry list

witch
bitch
broad
coke
horse
M
scarecrow

witch Hazel
horse

with a bang
with flying colors

with a smoking gun
dead to rights

with bells on
with flying colors

with one's hand in the till
dead to rights

with it
dig
on the ball
trendy
with it, "cognizant"

with knobs on
with flying colors

without a pot to piss in
broke

without a red cent
broke

without a sou
broke

without a stitch
bare-ass

without brain one
dumb

without mussing a hair
with flying colors

without one dollar to rub
against another
broke

with one's pants down
dead to rights

with rocks in the head
dumb

with the goods
dead to rights

wiz
ace
hot shot

wobble weed
angel dust

wolf
angel dust
ladies' man
stud

woman
broad
dish
Jane

womanizer
ladies' man
stud

wombat
nut
oddball

Wonder Bread
square

wonk
grind
jerk

wonky
cockeyed
green around the gills

wood
cracker
whitey

woodchuck
cracker

woodenhead
dope

woodenheaded
dumb

wooden-stake
scrub

woodhead
dope

woodhick
hick

the woods are full of
something, "something
is plentiful"

woof
blow off
bullshit
gab

woofer
blabbermouth

wool
broad

woolhat
cracker

woolies
long johns

woozy
plastered
rocky

wop, "Italian person"

woppitzer
kibitzer

word
bet your ass
the poop

the word
the poop

word-slinger
blabbermouth

work
goof off

moonlight
work, "succeed"

work both sides of the
    street
have it both ways

worked up
antsy

worker
scab
working stiff

working girl
hooker

working stiff, "worker"

work into the ground
blow up

work on
lean on someone

work
back-breaker

work out
fuck
work
work out, "repair"

work over
clobber
rough up

works
basket
cock
works, "narcotics
    apparatus"

the works
best shot
the whole shebang

work up
cook up

world-beater
hot shot

world-class
great

worm
angel dust
asshole
jerk

worm-food
stiff

worm out
back out
cop out

wormy
yucky

worn to a frazzle
pooped

worried stiff
jittery

worry
sweat

the worser half
hubby

worthless
not worth a damn

wow
break someone up
humdinger
wow, "delight extremely"

wowser
humdinger

wow them
go over with a bang

wrangle
hassle

wrap up
clinch
wrap up, "complete"

wreck
clobber
fix someone
jalopy
total

wrecked
high

wren
broad

wretched place
the pits

wrinkle
glitch

wristlets
bracelets

wrongarmer
southpaw

wrong number
bad man

wrong 'un
bad man

wussy
wimp

wuzzup
what's up

X-double-minus
crummy

X-rated
dirty

XX
double cross

yackety-yack
bullshit
chitchat
gab
shoot the breeze

yack it up
gab

yahoo
dope

yakoo
whitey

Yale
works

yammer
beef
gab

yang
 cock

yank
 fuck
 roust

yank someone's chain
 bug
 kid

yantsy
 antsy
 jittery

yap
 beef
 bullshit
 dope
 gab
 hick
 jerk
 patsy
 yap, "mouth"

yapper
 blabbermouth

yapping
 gab

yappy
 gabby

yard
 a bill
 cheat
 cock

yardbird
 con
 rookie

yard bull
 cop

yard rat
 kid

yatata
 gab

yawner
 chestnut

yawny
 dullsville

yaw-ways
 cockeyed

yeah
 bet your ass
 OK

yecch
 yuck

yecchy
 yucky

yegg
 cowboy
 goon
 heist man

ye gods
 Jeez

yell bloody murder
 beef

yell blue murder
 beef

yell one's head off
 beef

yellow
 chicken

yellow fever
 acid

yellow jacket
 doll

yellow sunshine
 acid

yellow ticket
 bobtail

yen chee
 big O

yen chiang
 big O

yen pock
 big O

yenta
 blabbermouth
 kibitzer

yentz
 con
 fuck

yentzed
 screwed

yentzer
 con man

yep
 bet your ass
 OK

yerba
 pot

yesca
 pot

yes indeedy
 OK

yes man
 brown-nose

yes sirree
 OK

Yid
 kike

yield profit
 pay off

yikes
 Jeez

ying-yang
 asshole
 cock

yip
 gab

yipe
 Jeez

yodel
 warble

yoke
 heist

yokel
  hick

yokeldom
  the boondocks

yoker
  heist man

yold
  patsy

you ain't just whistling
    Dixie
  bet your ass

you betcha
  bet your ass
  OK

you better believe it
  bet your ass
  honest-to-God

you can't win them all
  **that's the way the cookie
    crumbles**

you-know-what
  blankety-blank
  gadget

you know what you can do
    with it
  fuck you
  kiss my ass

you name it
  the whole shebang

youngblood
  blood

young girl
  jail bait

young male
  young squirt

young punk
  kid
  young squirt

young Turk
  eager beaver

young 'un
  kid

your basic
  vanilla

you're damn tootin'
  bet your ass

you're full of hops
  izzatso

you're full of shit
  izzatso

you're telling me
  bet your ass

your Uncle Dudley
  yours truly

you said a mouthful
  bet your ass

you wouldn't shit me
  izzatso
  no shit
  so what

yowzah
  OK

yo-yo
  dope
  jerk

yuck, "expression of
    disgust"

yucky
  crummy
  yucky, "disgusting"

yuk
  break up

a yuk
  a howl

yummy
  great

yup
  OK

z
  deck

Z
  snooze

Zacatecas purple
  pot

zap
  clobber
  pizzazz
  plug
  pow
  snuff

zappy
  full of piss and vinegar
  jazzy
  zingy

zazzed-up
  jazzed-up

zazz up
  jazz up

zazzy
  classy
  glitzy
  jazzy

zebra
  Blind Tom

Zee
  snooze

Zelda
  square

Zen
  acid

zerk
  dope

zerking
  ditsy
  flaky
  weird

zero
  zilch

zero cool
 cool
 great
zero in, "single out"
zetz
 sock
zhlub
 jerk
 sleazebag
zig
 nigger
zigaboo
 nigger
zig-zig
 ass
zilch
 Joe Blow
 zilch, "nothing"
 zit
zillionth
 umpty-umpth
zing
 barrel
 high
 a kick
 knock
 pizzazz
 snuff
zing along
 barrel
zinger
 punch line
zingy
 full of piss and vinegar
 jazzy
 zingy, "energetic"

zip
 barrel
 gook
 pizzazz
 zilch
zip gun
 rod
zip one's lip
 shut up
zipped
 high
zippo
 pizzazz
 zilch
zippy
 full of piss and vinegar
 jazzy
 zingy
zip top
 kike
zit, "skin lesion"
zizz
 pizzazz
 snooze
 a snooze
zod
 jerk
 oddball
zoid
 square
zol
 joint
zombie
 dope
 oddball

zombie buzz
 angel dust
zone
 junkie
 oddball
zoned out
 high
zoner
 junkie
 oddball
zonk
 clobber
 pass out
zonked
 high
 plastered
zooey
 yucky
zoom
 angel dust
 barrel
 pot
zoom buggy
 jalopy
zot
 zilch
zowie
 pizzazz
 pow
Zs
 sack time
zuch
 snitch
zup
 what's up